New Trends in
Conceptual Representation:
Challenges to Piaget's Theory?

The Jean Piaget Symposium Series
Available from LEA

SIGEL, I. E., BRODZINSKY, D. M., & GOLINKOFF, R. M. (Eds.) • New Directions in Piagetian Theory and Practice

OVERTON, W. F. (Ed.) • Relationships Between Social and Cognitive Development

LIBEN, L. S. (Ed.) • Piaget and the Foundations of Knowledge

SCHOLNICK, E. K. (Ed.) • New Trends in Conceptual Representation: Challenges to Piaget's Theory?

New Trends in Conceptual Representation: Challenges to Piaget's Theory?

Edited by
Ellin Kofsky Scholnick
The University of Maryland, College Park

LAWRENCE ERLBAUM ASSOCIATES, PUBLISHERS
1983   Hillsdale, New Jersey   London

Lawrence Erlbaum Associates, Inc., Publishers
365 Broadway
Hillsdale, New Jersey 07642

Library of Congress Cataloging in Publication Data
Main entry under title:

New trends in conceptual representation.

Bibliography: p.
Includes index.
1. Cognition in children. 2. Cognition. 3. Piaget,
Jean, 1896–   . I. Scholnick, Ellin Kofsky.
BF723.C5N48   1983   155.4′13   83-1431
ISBN 0-89859-260-7

Printed in the United States of America
10 9 8 7 6 5 4 3 2 1

To Jean Piaget who provided a framework for appreciating my son, Matthew, and to Matthew who provided a framework for appreciating Piaget.

List of Contributors

Sharon Lee Armstrong, Wesleyan College

Harry Beilin, Graduate School and University Center, CUNY

Rodney R. Cocking, National Institute of Education, Washington, D.C.

Leslie B. Cohen, The University of Texas at Austin

Richard De Lisi, Rutgers, The State University of New Jersey

Henry Gleitman, The University of Pennsylvania

Lila R. Gleitman, The University of Pennsylvania

Ellen M. Markman, Stanford University

Edith D. Neimark, Douglass College, Rutgers, The State University of NJ

Katherine Nelson, Graduate School and University Center, CUNY

Eleanor Rosch, The University of California at Berkeley

Ellin Kofsky Scholnick, The University of Maryland, College Park

Irving E. Sigel, Educational Testing Service

Barbara A. Younger, The University of Texas at Austin

Contents

Preface

This is a challenging time for students of cognitive development. In the late 1950s, there was *one* major theory of cognitive development, Jean Piaget's. No other theory of mental life was as detailed in its descriptions of diverse aspects of cognition, so rich in its provision of experimental tasks for studying children, and so integrative in its approach to explaining the hows, whys, and whens of development. However, as Piaget's research program gained wide currency, there were many empirical and theoretical challenges to it. First Piaget's constructivism occupies a middle ground between the reliance on socialization practices and reliance on innate constraints as explanations for the pace, direction, and ultimate outcome of cognitive growth. It is simple to argue that all behavior is learned and that its final shape is determined by the vagaries of different learning conditions. Empirical demonstrations of the acquisition of factual knowledge are not hard to obtain. It is similarly easy to claim all behavior is preformed, merely needing to be released under appropriate circumstances. Again there is enough uniformity in the sequence of development of physical characteristics and some cognitive skills and enough species differences to support that view. However, it is very difficult to insist the environment only has an impact when filtered through the person's schemes and to demonstrate that those schemes undergo systematic changes in ways not constrained from the beginning. There is a necessary sequence and yet the subject constructs that necessity. Secondly, Piaget's theory occupies a middle ground between two levels of explanation of psychological function. One looks at observable data and the other at idealized abstract formal behavior. Again it is comparatively easy to analyze what is needed to solve a particular task. It is much harder to specify the underlying principles that unite diverse tasks, although that analysis is made easier by conceding that people may not always act upon intuited rules. The most vulnerable viewpoint is an attempt to link fragmented behaviors with reflective, integrated abstract appreciation of rules. The theorist must describe how and when the child goes from mastering behavior to constructing and applying increasingly abstract rules. There must be explanations of the failures in translating performance into competence and vice versa. Finally, Piaget has tried to integrate three theoretical perspectives, a model of biological equilibrium, of constructive evolution, and of mathematical logic. In some cases he has borrowed the models from other realms in which consensus on theory is lacking. Consequently, Piaget has been challenged frequently.

In the mid-1970s, cognitive science, an alternative model of cognitive development, began to emerge with alternative explanations of cognitive growth. It, too, took a middle ground. The model posits innate hardware for processing experience but a growing knowledge base induced by experience that is capable of producing more efficient and generalizable processing procedures. The model approached the issue of levels of generality by incorporating contextual constraints upon thinking. Strategies were always qualified by knowledge of the specific contexts where strategies were applicable and those contexts could differ in generality. Cognitive science drew upon different models, such as the computer and different forms of conceptual representation such as scripts, schemata, and prototypes. The models were drawn from perceptual and semantic analyses rather than logical ones. The dilemma for the student of cognitive development was to decide what this new model explained that the old one did not, and what realms of explanation were lost in adopting the new model. Were there any additional assumptions bought when adopting the new model?

Piaget's death in September of 1980 was a third cause of the crisis. The major source of creative use and development of the theory was Piaget and the Genevans around him. Our view of Piaget's theory had become fossilized. He was the major extender of the theory of new domains. His last decade was spent fundamentally reorganizing the theory to incorporate more precise explanations of the nature of cognitive change, and the growth of cognition from fragmented, practical actions to self-aware cognitive systems. He simultaneously de-emphasized logico-mathematical elements, but many psychologists were unaware of these changes. Hence the major reviser of Piaget's theories, and the most sensitive registrant of contradictions of the theory with data and of theoretical notions with one another was gone.

What better way to commemorate his life's work than by examining the challenges to it in a delimited but fundamental realm, the nature of representation. After all, Piaget claimed that the resolution of contradiction fosters the development of changes within the individual and within scientific theory. We can apply that model to a discussion of the contents of this symposium. When Piaget discusses cognitive growth, he asserts that it begins with contradictions, phenomena not easily assimilated into extant cognitive schemes. Two kinds of phenomena are discussed in this book. Cohen and Younger describe infant discrimination of equivalence and prototype classifications prior to the active construction of nonfigural classes and demonstration of class logic. The second phenomenon in evidence for other kinds of conceptual organization such as prototypes (Rosch), scripts (Nelson), and collections (Markman). These phenomena are dealt with by several strategies that dismiss the existence of the conceptual alternative (e.g. Gleitman), suggest the alternative is an outgrowth or predecessor of logical classes (e.g. Neimark, De Lisi, and Scholnick), allow for a proliferation of concepts (e.g. Rosch), or claim that while each kind of concept exists as a discrete entity, some fundamental process such as abstraction or decontextualization links the different conceptual forms (e.g. Cocking).

However, many of these solutions to the challenge are not entirely satisfactory because the issues are broader than just when concepts emerge and what form they take. There are some deeper points of disagreement that require a broader analysis. Beilin and Sigel provide an analysis of the historical roots and core assumptions of the cognitive science versus the Piagetian position. Beilin examines functionalist and structuralist theories while Sigel focuses on the differing definitions of a concept. Each author suggests that Piaget and his challengers provide different, incomplete perspectives on the same issues which need to be incorporated into a model of cognitive development.

You may not agree with any of the attempts to recognize the challenges of competing views and synthesize them. But at least the interchange of divergent assumptions makes explicit the nature of the challenges and some methods for their resolution that might lead to a future broader and more precise theory of representation.

My thanks go to the Jean Piaget Society for sponsoring the debate and to the contributors who made it so vibrant.

Ellin Kofsky Scholnick
University of Maryland

New Trends in
Conceptual Representation:
Challenges to Piaget's Theory?

WHERE IS THE CHALLENGE?

1

The New Functionalism and Piaget's Program

Harry Beilin
City University of New York Graduate School and University Center

The comparison of any current development journal with one from even 5 years past shows a striking contrast. For about 15 to 20 years the field was dominated by a structuralist orientation, principally through Piaget's theory; not so today. In this essay, I examine the alternative to the structuralist point of view that increasingly contends with Piaget's theory as the dominant explanatory model for cognitive development. Beyond detailing the nature of this orientation, I suggest that the new functionalism, or neofunctionalism as I refer to this metatheoretical orientation, will in due course suffer the same fate as older functionalism, losing its credibility as an explanatory model and its utility as a method for conducting research, if the virtues of a structuralist analysis are ignored.

In the historic shifts that occurred from the "early," to the "middle," and now to the "new" functionalism to be described, the most important issue was over the nature and acceptability of "mental events" in accounts of psychological functioning. Functionalism has always distrusted theoretical terms denoting processes or structures far removed from observable behavior. Despite a continuing distrust for "inferred entity" terms of a "global" and highly abstract nature, the most significant change in the new functionalism is the willingness to entertain the possible reality of mental acts. In accepting the reality of inferred mental entities, despite the restrictive canons of behaviorism, the new functionalism has come much closer to the practices of contemporary structuralism. The latter rarely hesitates to posit organized relations or structures in mind that stand in a causal relation to behavior, even if the character of these events is inferred from contexts other than controlled experiments.

In parallel to the new functionalists, the modern structuralist is a very different kind of psychologist from such early structuralists as Titchener, whose structuralism was associated with the analysis of consciousness into the elements of sensation and who offered in turn a description of the laws (usually associational) of their composition. Modern structuralists are distinguished from the older both by differences in method and by a greater emphasis on the logically or systematically organized nature of cognition.

In a sense, the early distinction between structure and function paralleled the distinction between anatomy (as the study of biological forms) and physiology (as the study of biological function). Although the analogy is to some extent still true, the meanings of structure and function terms become much more complex, as the rest of this chapter details. Nevertheless, the deep philosophical divisions that characterized the debates between early structuralists and functionalists define the agenda for the change of scene in the present, as one metatheoretical program replaces the other.

The new functionalism, which presently engages the attention of many if not most developmental psychologists, is new because it differs significantly from the functionalism of James, Dewey, Angell, and Woodworth. Yet it bears more than a slight resemblance to that point of view, which managed to survive in psychology despite the overwhelming recent influence of structuralism with which Piaget himself is identified (Piaget, 1970). It is ironic, however, that no less an authority than Edwin Boring, both in 1929 and 1950, classified Piaget among the functionalists in his well-known history of experimental psychology (Boring, 1950). Then again, as indicated, the definitions of functionalism and structuralism in the days of the early practitioners differed from the definitions of today. I would like to develop the nature of the change in functionalism here and examine the status of Piaget's research program in light of the new functionalism.

EARLY FUNCTIONALISM

To discern the nature of the new functionalism adequately requires a delineation of earlier functionalisms. Modern functionalism emerged as a reaction to the theoretical assumptions of the earliest of the experimental psychologists, such as Titchener.[1] In fact it was Titchener who labeled the movement functionalism to contrast it with his self-styled structuralism. The program of the elementalists like Titchener was to structurally analyze, inventory, and classify the basic elements of consciousness, which were thought to be the basic or elemental sensations. This program was given impetus by Titchener and Mach's conception of sensation as the starting point for psychology and physics (Brunswik,

---

[1]Woodworth's (1948) brief account of the functionalist movement identifies even earlier beginnings in the armchair psychology of a prior period, starting from about 1830.

1952). This early "structuralism" emphasized: (1) the (usually introspective) analysis of conscious processes into elements (sensations); (2) the determination of the manner and laws of connection (association) of those elements (Boring, 1950). Although some early practitioners believed that mind is a process, the structuralists sought nonetheless to reduce that process to its elements. James, on the other hand, through his highly influential "stream of consciousness" metaphor emphasized the process as the primary datum. He asserted further that consciousness contains knowledge and not sense data and that man is what he is capable of doing (Boring, 1950). In this manner the notion of function was made explicit by James. It was not the function, however, of the "act psychologists" (like Brentano),[2] but the function of the Darwinian evolutionists.

This evolutionist influence was to become a central thesis in functionalism. According to Boring (1950) it manifested itself in the tenet that: "Mind has a use and it can be observed in use [p. 515]." James, however, thought of consciousness as if it were an organ with a function, and it was not until two developmentalists (G. Stanley Hall and James Mark Baldwin) came on the scene that Darwinian evolutionism had its major impact. This impact reflected itself in Hall's "genetic psychology" and Baldwin's "mental development" (Wozniak, 1981). Baldwin was also the critical figure in a famous controversy with Titchener over the role of the reflex arc in psychology, a controversy that John Dewey attempted to mediate. Titchener in turn mounted an attack (or counterattack) on Dewey, which was leveled against functionalism itself. Baldwin and Dewey argued that activity should not be conceived as originating in a stimulus from a central process that eventuated in a response but rather that activity entailed a complete cycle, the "reflex circuit" for Dewey and the "circular reaction" for Baldwin,[3] in which the relation of the response to the succeeding stimulus was as important as its relation to the preceding stimulus (Hilgard, 1956). According to Boring (1950), the argument between Baldwin and Titchener was essentially over whether psychology should study "human nature" and therefore individual differences, which was Baldwin's position, or whether it should be concerned with the "generalized mind," which was the view championed by Titchener. The former was to represent the functionalist position, the latter the structuralist, even to the present.

The Darwinian evolutionist flavor of functionalism was most evident in the

---

[2]Heidbreder (1933): "act psychology, a psychology which maintains that psychic processes are essentially acts which refer to and are directed toward contents. This conception is in striking contrast with the Wundtian view that the psychic processes themselves are contents [p. 98]." In general, the distinction that was being developed was between function as process and function as growing, developing activity in an evolutionary sense, both of which were to be distinguished from the idea of a fixed entity (mind) capable of analysis that characterizes the structuralism of Titchener.

[3]Baldwin's "circular reaction" was used later by Piaget in characterizing the sensorimotor period.

document that all commentators agree defined the early functionalist position, the 1906 American Psychological Association presidential address of James Rowland Angell (1908). In this paper Angell discussed three aspects of the functionalist "movement" (as Heidbreder, 1933, referred to it). First, functionalism is concerned with operations, whereas structuralism is concerned with contents. In contrast to the analysis of consciousness into its elements, the functionalist's task is to discover *how* a mental process operates, *what* it accomplishes, and under *what conditions* it appears (Heidbreder, 1933). One recalls in this the Jamesian criticism of "moments of consciousness," of sensation, and of ideas as persisting entities. Only mental functions were said to persist. Just as the same physiological function might be performed by different structures, so the same mental function might be performed by ideas greatly different in their contexts. Thus, functionalism was said to be a cause–effect psychology concerned with mental operations in context (Hilgard, 1956).

Second, functionalism as a movement was interested in the utility of mental processes. Mental activity was not to be studied by itself, but rather as part of the totality of biological activity and as part of organic evolution. Functions and structures are what they are because they enable the organism to survive through facilitating adaptation to the environment. Functionalism thus deals with the problem of mind as it mediates between the environment and the needs of the organism. Consciousness, in general, was said to serve in "selective accommodation" inasmuch as it accompanies "selective varation of response to stimulation." Particular processes, such as perceiving, willing, and feeling, were all said to show some form of selective accommodation (Heidbreder, 1933). In essence, consciousness serves to help the organism resolve conflicts that arise when habits no longer suffice. Hilgard (1956) believed this general position made legitimate applied psychologies, such as educational and industrial psychology and mental hygiene, for the normally experimentally oriented psychologists who had either been trained in Wundt's laboratory or were influenced by it.

Third, Angell addressed the mind–body problem that psychology inherited from philosophy, a problem with which psychologists of that day were very much concerned. The functionalist's solution was to assume an interaction between the physical and the psychological, doing away with a dualism that held the physical and mental to be different orders of events (Heidbreder, 1933). If there was an implied dualism in the study of the physiological substantiation of mental events that functionalists sought, it was a purely "practical" one (as in psychosomatic medicine). The only position that the functionalist was inclined to reject on this score was the view of consciousness as an epiphenomenon of neural activity (Hilgard, 1956).

For Angell, the three characteristics of functionalism—the stress on operations, the utility of mental function, and mind–body interaction–converged on what he (see Watson, 1979) considered to be the fundamental problem of the functionalist: "One of determining just how mind participates in accommodating reactions [p. 249]."

Behaviorism and Functionalism

Chicago (Angell's) functionalism did not satisfy all of its adherents, and James B. Watson, a student of Angell's, was one. In a 1913 paper that defined the "behaviorism" that was to become the dominant movement in American psychology for almost four decades, Watson rejected both functionalism and introspectionism, principally the latter (Herrnstein & Boring, 1965). Nevertheless, Watson's behaviorism was an outgrowth of functionalism's philosophic position in its concern with the organism's adaptation to its environment compared to which introspectionism's analysis of consciousness into its elements seemed unimportant, uninteresting, and irrelevant (Herrnstein & Boring, 1965). In one move Watson (see Herrnstein & Boring, 1965) offered a solution to: "the problem of how to interpret the objective data of behavior in terms of the subjective contents of the mind [p. 507]." Watson accomplished this, according to Herrnstein and Boring, in truly functionalist fashion by holding that the objective data themselves constituted the total data of psychology, as Loeb had already done in America and as Sechenov and Pavlov had done in Russian physiology. Watson in effect became a new kind of functionalist, bringing to it not only the evolutionary concepts of modern biology, which the functionalists had already accomplished, but also the objectivity of its methods. As Watson (see Herrnstein & Boring, 1965) wrote: "I feel that behaviorism is the only consistent and logical functionalism. In it one avoids both the Scylla of parallelism [between consciousness and behavior] and the Charybdis of interaction. . . . I believe one can write a psychology . . . and . . . never use the terms consciousness, mental states, mind, content, introspectively verifiable, imagery and the like [p. 513]."

In his 1913 paper Watson (see Herrnstein & Boring, 1965) attacked functionalists as merely substituting the terms "function" and "process" for structural terms and thereby assuming they had solved the problem of understanding behavior: "The terms sensation, perception, affection, emotion, volition are used as much by the functionalist as by the structuralist. The use of the word 'process' . . . after each . . . serves to remove the corpse of 'content' and leave 'functionalism' in its stead. Surely if those concepts are elusive when looked at from a content standpoint, they are still more deceptive when viewed from the angle of function [p. 513]." We return to this criticism later, for it applies to the present generation of functionalists as it did in Watson's time.

For Heidbreder (1933), the conditions that insured success for functionalism did the same for Watson's behaviorism: "Practically, behaviorism did what functionalists did, and did it more dramatically. It cut the Gordian knot, which functionalism had merely loosened to give psychology a wider tether [p. 239]." It freed psychology from the constraints of a psychology of consciousness and introspectionism. In doing so, however, it introduced its own considerable restraints. In making the subject matter of psychology behavior (i.e., movements in space and time) rather than mental function, psychological processes of any sort, or conscious contents, behaviorism introduced a repression that only the later reaction to it reversed. Instead of functionalism's open attitude to all methods, behaviorism limited itself to "objective methods" of observation with or without instruments, testing, even verbal reports if treated as behavior, and above all, conditioning techniques.[4]

Watson's behaviorism shared with functionalism a rejection of science based on consciousness alone, and with functionalism it fostered the attitude of viewing psychological processes as part of an adaptive response to the environment. In its attempt, however, to solve the mind–body problem by rejecting certain types of data, it insured that its account would be incomplete and even unintelligible (Heidbreder, 1933).[5]

MIDDLE FUNCTIONALISM

Although Watson's behaviorism dominated American psychology for many decades, a truer functionalist view was kept alive in the dynamic psychology of Robert S. Woodworth at Columbia. Despite Woodworth's acceptance of the essential stimulus–response (S–R) model of behavior common at the time, his views of it were more akin to those of Dewey and Baldwin than those of Watson. Like Dewey he saw the S–R reaction as an event that could not be isolated from the events that preceded or followed it. In accord with other functionalists, he believed that the subject matter of a "dynamic" psychology was both consciousness and behavior. As a consequence, he took the important step of introducing the "organism" into S–R psychology, transforming it into S–O–R. His position toward introspectionism was largely agnostic. He accepted introspection as a legitimate method but rejected it as the sole method for psychology. For him the central question for psychology was: "How does it work?" The problem of defining mechanisms in causal sequences, as well as the stress he placed on understanding drives and the motivations of behavior, marked his functionalism, At the same time, he along with other learning experimenters of the era transformed an earlier association. Whereas the earlier associationists (e.g., Ebbinghaus) started with effects and tried to infer causes, the newer associationists

---

[4]Watson's intellectual history, of course, is more complex, as is the relation of behaviorism to both functionalism and the early structuralism. Some details of that history are detailed and interpreted by Kendler (1979).

[5]In current philosophy of psychology a lively debate on "functionalism" is presently in progress (see, e.g., Block, 1980). The discussion centers largely on the mind–body problem, but because that discussion relates only tangentially to the thesis of this chapter it is not detailed.

started with "known causes" or conditions and observed their effects (Wood-worth, 1948).

In many ways Woodworth represents the prototypic functionalist. Heldbreder (1933) writes: "Taking as his starting-point the concrete, he has pledged himself to get as complete an account as possible of the workings of those processes in terms of cause and effect—not to stand through thick and thin for consciousness as opposed to mechanism, or for any other hypothesis that is off the main line of his inquiry [pp. 325–326]." It was Woodworth's type of functionalism, which for convenience sake can be called middle functionalism, that coexisted with behaviorism during the period of its ascendancy, behaviorism's consolidation in the Hull–Spence logical positivist theory of behavior, and its subsequent decline.

The character of functionalism changed in subtle ways both as a consequence of behaviorism and as a reaction to it. Although functionalism appeared as a differentiable entity early in the history of psychology, it has been difficult to articulate clearly what it represented, particularly in the era following Angell's declaration. As Hilgard (1956) wrote: "Because contemporary functionalism is so loosely articulated, a point of view without acknowledged leadership and with few loyal and self-conscious adherents, it defies precise exposition [p. 333]." Hilgard, nevertheless, tried to communicate its flavor rather than define its principles. He said of the functionalism current in the 1940s and 1950s:

1. *It is tolerant, but critical.* What he implied was that functionalism is eclectic, borrowing freely from other traditions particularly in its vocabulary and its methods. It was tolerant, for example, of introspection, objective observation, case studies, and mental tests. Its eclecticism extended across the boundary between the pure and the applied as well.

2. *It is relativistic.* In accepting the multiple origin of psychological activity, functionalism tends toward defined relations and avoids the quest for "constants" (as Carr put it) or for psychological "laws" expressed without reference to all influential variables.

3. *Continuities are preferred to discontinuities or typologies.* Functionalism seeks continuities in function. Even in cases where qualitative differences appear, the functionalist seeks intermediate cases. This continuity of function leads to what McGeoch identified as a "dimensional principle" in which two classes of variation are distinguished: situational dimensions (which refer principally to task differences) and process differences (which occur in rote learning as distinct from problem solving). For a considerable period psychological experimentation and exploration was based on a quest for the dimensional characteristics of behavior and development.

Within the developmental context functionalism's preference is clearly for continuity theories rather than stage theories. During this era stagelike theories (e.g., Gesell & Ilg, 1949), although enormously popular with the applied professions and the public, were on the periphery of interest to "scientifically oriented'' psychologists even though the content of Gesell's analysis and description of child behavior and development was very functional.

4. *The method of choice is experimental.* As Hilgard (1956) put it: "In its modern form, functionalism is dedicated to the experimental method. The issues toward which the functionalist is so tolerant become a part of his science only when they are translated into experimental form [p. 335]." This restriction does not appear to hold for contemporary functionalism, which on methodological issues has again become very tolerant.

5. *There is a bias toward association theory and environmentalism.* The functionalism of the 1940s and 1950s on the surface appears to be theoretically neutral, but its biases are clearly toward associationism. Although one might be tempted by its methodological eclecticism and its attention to a diversity of subject matters to believe that functionalism is a simple methodological ecumenism, its philosophic commitments when pressed are shown to be closer to the tenets of traditional empiricism than to alternative philosophies and, within empiricism, to be drawn to associationist doctrine and an emphasis on the environmental control of behavior.

Drawing on typical research of the era, Hilgard showed how functionalists provided an experimental analysis of the learning process in respect to motivation, rate of learning, transfer of training, and retention. Hilgard pointed to the three salient characteristics of the functionalism of the 1940s and 1950s—its empiricism, its lack of a unified integrated system, and the fact that its laws were quantitative and descriptively close to the data. Hilgard (1956) commented that the price paid for stating issues so they could be readily tested results in a collection of many 'laws' without hierarchical structure. "Dimensional analysis puts data in order for exposition and for verification, but in itself does not connect the data into an economical scientific system. Such a system has to be logically structured as well as empirically sound [p. 364]." This criticism of middle functionalism can be applied with about equal justification to much of contemporary functionalism.

Hilgard saw in the 1950s that functionalism's eclecticism could encompass a variety of newer developments by virtue of their philosophic compatibility. He saw the growing "operationism" as compatible with functionalism, and a natural extension of the heritage of James and Dewey, and by implication, as less compatible with logical positivism, which was by then well in place with the behavioristic theories of Hull and Spence. Hull–Spence theory moved behaviorism far from the course charted for it by Watson, for one reason by not limiting it to associationist process; Tolman was to move it even further (Kendler, 1979). Operationalism, however, did not take hold and in fact was swept aside in the flood of the cognitivism and structuralism to come. Further, Hilgard saw the introduction of mathematical models in the newer mathematical psychology as functional models, in the mathematical sense of function. In addition, Hilgard saw functionalism encompassing the functional analysis of Skinner (essentially dimensional analysis), as well as the probabilistic functionalism of Brunswik. He also saw the trend toward miniature systems as congenial to functionalism even if these entailed the test of special theories because: "it is sometimes necessary to accept provisional (heuristic) interpretations that permit you to move ahead with the analysis [Hilgard, 1956, p. 366]." One senses in this the considerable reluctance of the functionalist to admit theories (particularly, "grand theories") based on an extensive set of hypothetical constructs.

Hilgard (1956) himself was apparently well disposed to functionalism because of its "willingness to accept new dimensions as they were discovered." He could see, however, that functionalism did not satisfy the desire for "a neat system with a few postulates and interchangeable constants that would enable one to move logically from one part of the system to another [p. 479]." But he said prophetically that it was possible to seek systematic elegance within the tolerance of a functionalist position. Inasmuch as such elegant systems worked well in the physical sciences, they should work well for psychology.

In the 1950s it was already evident that a reaction to behaviorism was taking hold. Functionalism itself was part of that reaction, but the more revolutionary changes were embodied in the cognitive response to behaviorism. Cognitivism was the product of a confluence of influences. At first, its principal source was Gestalt theory, which at the time influenced studies in learning as with Tolman's molar behaviorism, in social and personality psychology through Lewin and Asch's influence, in perception through Koffka, Köhler, and Wertheimer, in problem solving through Wertheimer and Köhler, and in developmental psychology through Heinz Werner. The postwar reports of Piaget's research had a powerful influence as well, particularly in developmental psychology, and late in the 1950s there came into psychology other influences that completed the revolution: Chomsky's generative transformational grammar together with cybernetics, information theories, and the associated computer models. By the mid-1960s the cognitive revolution was in full swing, and the retreat of behaviorism was complete except for the continuing, if diminished, influence of Skinner and the operant conditioning model. The cognitive revolution, in an oversimplified way, can be characterized by the greater willingness to infer the psychological reality of mental processes and structures from a wide variety of sources and with a wide variety of methods.

What was seen and labeled as a neobehaviorist accommodation to the cognitive revolution, evident at first in the mediationist theories of Osgood and the Kendlers, which had origins in Hull–Spence theory, was in fact the first signs of the new functionalism. This, I claim, was on the basis of Osgood and the Kendlers' attitude toward mental constructs. Their positing of mediational (mainly verbal) variables came very close to the conceptual constructs of cognitivists, although H. Kendler (1979) maintains considerable skepticism of so-called black-box theories whose constructs are not tied to experimental variation and control.

Throughout the cognitivist and structuralist era that followed, functionalism was a latent force, gradually undergoing a metamorphisis and ready to emerge, as it has in the past few years, with a powerful thrust against the structuralist theories that dominated many areas of psychology in the later 1950s, '60s, and '70s. What emerged is the new functionalism, revitalized first by its encounter with behaviorism and then by its struggle with cognitivism.

THE NEW FUNCTIONALISM

The current form of functionalism has not gone unrecognized. Zimmerman and Whitehurst (1979) note two changes in particular. First, most current functionalist theories of human behavior have introduced a variety of constructs hitherto unacceptable even in functionalist discourse (e.g., plans, feelings of self-efficacy, etc.). They have been made acceptable, according to Zimmerman and Whitehurst, by being related to specifiable measurement operations, but the reasons for their acceptability are probably more complex.[6] Next is the recognition that "some of the important stimulation variables in a functional analysis of human behavior may be private [1979, p. 3]," that is, not publicly observable as is demanded by methodological behaviorism. In radical behaviorism (identified with Skinner), "private" events (e.g., expectations, choices, beliefs,etc.) are admissible, but they become part of the phenomena to be explained and are not part of the explanation. Thus, for Skinner, reports of one's inner world are clues to conditions affecting the individual's behavior, which can become part of the prediction of behavior but not part of the control of behavior, inasmuch as phenomenological events are not directly manipulable. The contemporary functionalist, on the other hand, is willing to admit such events as part of the explanation of behavior.

The problem for the functionalist in admitting such constructs and losing the possibility of direct public verifiability is in not knowing with certainty that "private stimulation" and related constructs are a psychological reality and not mere fictional accounts offered by the theorist. It is the seeming "fictional" character of structuralist explanations that distinguishes them from what neo-functionalists are willing to admit in their use of cognitive constructs. Thus, Zimmerman and Whitehurst (1979) conclude: "Functional explanations based

---

[6]Chomsky's (1959) attack on Skinner's behaviorism, for example, no doubt had a profound effect on attitudes toward positivism and made many psychologists more sympathetic to structuralist and cognitivist claims.

on real events as opposed to fictional constructions have a primary role to play in the prediction and particularly the control of human behavior [p. 3]."[7]

If there is any place for logico-mathematical and related explanations, according to Zimmerman and Whitehurst (1979), it is to serve "in understanding the abstract pattern of response systems [p. 3]." As in earlier functionalisms, logico-mathematical formulations serve a descriptive function in relating and characterizing the abstract properties of a behavioral system. They may serve even further as a basis for predicting broad classes of behavior across individuals, for example as an extrapolation of behavior. Inasmuch as one is not capable of treating such abstract variables independently in having them under the investigator's control, one is blocked, according to functionalists, from a causal explanation and thus logico-mathematical explanations "have no utility in the control of behavior [p. 3]." Logico-mathematical explanations are useful, then, but in ways that differ from true functional explanations.

On this basis Zimmerman and Whitehurst (1979) reason: "There is nothing incompatible among functional, neuro-physiological-structural and logico-mathematical-structural explanations. There is no way an accurate functional explanation can violate the principles of a structural explanation or vice versa [p. 2]." We return to this point again because it has important consequences. To Zimmerman and Whitehurst, then, the newer functionalism is characterized by the introduction of inferred mental constructs, the acceptability of private events, and the use of abstract levels of description.

Contemporary functional theories are classified by Zimmerman and Whitehurst (1979) in three groups: (1) radical behaviorism, which owes its origins to Skinner and Kantor; (2) cognitive behaviorism, which is an interactionist viewpoint that treats cognitive "mediators" as both entities to be explained and entities that explain and is best exemplified in Bandura's (1977) social learning theory and most particularly in his ideas concerning "expectations of personal efficacy that determine whether coping behavior will be initiated [p. 191]." The reason these constructs as well as those of plans, rules, images, and covert verbal responses are acceptable to functionalists according to Zimmerman and Whitehurst (1979) is that they are "relatively simple, discrete, stimulus-bound behav-

---

[7]"Fictional construction" is a positivist euphemism for "mentalism." Wartofsky (1971) in a pointed argument observes that there is much needless discussion in psychology (and philosophy) over "mentalism" in psychological explanation. The term is used pejoratively by behaviorists when what is proposed is no more than "theoretical imaginativeness." If the term is equivalent simply to cognitivist, Wartofsky (1971) says: "So what? . . . to permit the perversities of an old-fashioned and ill-advised behaviorist reductionism to dictate that all who refuse to be held within its injunctions are hereafter to be labeled 'mentalists' is simply to substitute one perversity for another [p. 140]." Further, to be "'squarely among the mentalists in that those mechanisms and processes are inferred entities created to observed behavior' . . . is no more than being 'squarely among the scientists who create theories to explain the way the world is' [p. 141]."

iors that are for the most part direct products of experience that happen to have become covert in the course of experience. Those covert phenomenon are not considered to be behavior per se but separate processes [p. 12].'' Such covert behaviors are often treated just like overt behavior except for their lack of public observability; (3) operational information processing, which refers to a functional variant of the information-processing approach. Zimmerman and Whitehurst have difficulty in categorizing informational processing as either structuralist or functionalist. They conclude by placing it in both traditions and maintaining that the structural-functional relation is not a dichotomy but a continuum. Their reason for treating information processing as structural is that its processing follows a structured path determined only by its own content. This limited concept of structural theory differs, for example, from the somewhat richer definition offered by Gardner (1981): ''Structuralism is an attempt to discern the arrangements of elements underlying a given domain isolated by an analyst. The structuralist notes variation in the arrangements; he then attempts to relate the variations by specifying rules whereby one can be transformed to another [p. 170].'' As is shown later, Gardner's definition is even less demanding than Piaget's. Further, Zimmerman and Whitehurst state that there is little interplay between the external environment and cognitive processing once information has entered the system. The process that occurs between input and output is a function of a preprogrammed structure. Hence, information-processing systems based on a computer analogy (in the Newell & Simon tradition) are distinguished from those simply influenced by that tradition, with the former being structural and the latter functional. However, the distinction in these terms is questionable inasmuch as the latter theories do not differ from the former in their assumptions, and some information-processing theories combine the features of both approaches (e.g., the incorporation of procedural semantics into a computer-driven information-processing system, see Anderson, Kline, & Beasley, 1980). Yet, there is no question that one of the principal contributions to the new functionalism has come from information-processing theories, and the nature of such theories as representative of the new functionalism requires closer examination because of the manner in which it treats both structure and function.

Information Processing and the New Functionalism

In developmental psychology, information-processing theory has increasingly become the framework for research in memory, problem solving, mathematical and scientific reasoning, and more. The approach, to date, has rarely been applied to social cognition or to social personality development or affectivity.

Its rise in significance in developmental psychology in the past 5 years coincides with the retreat from Piagetian structuralism and the more general turn in psychology to functionalism, particularly with the decline in influence of generative transformational theory in psycholinguistics and comparable turns from structuralism in anthropology, sociology, and the philosophy of science. In other words, we are very much in the middle of a general shift from the way scientific problems have been conceptualized, investigated, and explained in the recent past.

The information-processing approach evolved from revolutionary developments in the 1930s, '40s, and '50s in cybernetics (Norbert Weiner), game theory (von Neumann), communications, and information theory (Shannon) that gave rise to the computer and a variety of other advances in electronic technologies. Psychology was affected most directly at first in mathematical learning theory, decision theory, and information theory, all three of which have in one way or another been superseded by information-processing models based for the most part on the operations of the computer as a model for the characterization of intelligence and cognition (Miller, Galanter, & Pribram, 1960). The information-processing approach has been successful to date, according to Siegler (in press), because of:

1. Its conception of humans as symbol manipulators.
2. Its utilization of a variety of formalisms for characterizing cognition and cognitive processing. There are three sets of such formalisms: (1) precise computer languages such as production systems; (2) "tangible" representations such as flow diagrams and decision trees that represent the temporal course of processing; (3) general notions such as plans, schemata, scripts, and frames that provide ways in which knowledge may be organized. Siegler holds that these formalisms strike a happy balance among precision, flexibility, and intuitive appropriateness for characterizing human cognitive activity.
3. Its arsenal of powerful analytic procedures such as chronometric methods, protocol analyses, rule assessment methods, and eye movement analyses. In the use of these methods patterns within subject data are of greater importance than how often subjects are correct.

Information processing also addresses issues of longstanding interest to psychology such as modes of representation, serial or parallel processing, the difference between knowing how and knowing that, and so on. Siegler also observes that inherent in the information-processing approach is the expectation that many aspects of human information processing do not undergo change with age, that is, adults and children are the same with respect to sensory registers, short-term memory, long-term memory, and so forth.

Symbolic Representation.   Adoption of the "symbol" as the basic unit of analysis in information processing (Newell, 1980; Newell & Simon, 1972) represents a radical departure from behaviorism, although not so radical when viewed from the perspective of a broader based functionalism. A symbol in an information-processing system is defined by "patterns." According to Simon (1979b):

"A pattern is some kind of arrangement of a substate associated with processes for creating and copying such arrangements, and for discriminating among them . . . a symbol is simply a pattern that can be discriminated by an information processing system [p. 70]." Information-processing theories based on the processing of symbols, however, introduce constraints on the system. They are more restricted than theories that ostensibly range over a wide display of representations. Not all cognitive theories characterize information as symbolically represented, however. It is not necessarily so, for example, when representation is in the form of images or sensorimotor representations.

Research on mental imagery, particularly by Shepard and his colleagues (Cooper & Shepard, 1973; Shepard & Metzler, 1971), has done much to show the limitations of the computer model in accounting for the data of mental rotation experiments. Although Shepard has proposed that mental imagery and mental rotation are best accounted for by an analogue model, in which an isomorphic mapping of the representation to the thing represented is implied, he has not gone unchallenged by those who argue for computer-based propositional representation, which would be one form of symbolic representation (Pylyshyn, 1978). Whether or not differences between the propositional and analogue or imagery models can be adjudicated solely by experimental evidence (Anderson, 1978), it is evident that noncomputer-based information-processing models of psychological processes may in fact describe some psychological processes in a more satisfying and adequate fashion than propositional or other computer-compatible models. It shows that the ostensive virtue of a symbol-based processing system carries with it the potential for imposing constraints on understanding the nature of psychological processes.

In sum, the need for symbolic representation introduces a constraint on processing. If information must be represented symbolically to be simulated by a computer, it means that sensori-motor representation, for example, requires a symbolic form for representation. Although this is clearly possible, a price must be paid in limiting the information that can be processed by such a symbol requirement because it is doubtful that motoric and kinesthetic information embodied in physical action can be represented adequately in a symbolic code (Pribram, 1977). To the extent that there is any truth to the cliché that a picture is worth a thousand words, the same would be true for pictorial representation. At the same time, it cannot be denied that the symbol is capable of representing vast amounts of certain kinds of information very economically.

Although contemporary information-processing theories emphasize the processing aspects of cognition and the functions inherent in cognition, they nevertheless represent a change from earlier functionalist theories in their shift to treating symbolic processes as acceptable psychological entities. In a significant departure from behaviorism, in particular, mentalisms become acceptable—or so it would appear.

The claim that information-processing theories characterize humans as symbol processors suggests that these theories not only characterize cognitive processes but they are cognitive theories as well. In this vein one has to make a distinction between cognitive$_1$ theories, which detail the nature of cognitive functions, and cognitive$_2$ theories, which are cognitive because their explanations are cognitive, that is, they are based on the assumption that mental entities of an abstract nature account for (i.e., are in a causal relation to) cognitive behaviors and functions. In cognitive$_1$ theories the hypothesized causal agents are not hypothesized abstract mental entities, but S–R associations or other elements of behaviorist and functionalist hypotheses. If one asks whether information-processing theories and models are cognitive$_1$ or cognitive$_2$ theories, the answer is not difficult to come by. First, the primary assumption in most information-processing theories is that the fundamental processes upon which processing is based are associational. Simon (1979b), for example, asserts that the "text of LTM [long-term memory] is an associative structure—a system of nodes interconnected by numerous links [p. 42]." These associations provide the network that organizes elements in memory.

Intimations of behaviorism are also evident in Simon's characterization of "production systems" that are so central to a number of present-day information-processing systems (e.g., those of Anderson, 1976; Klahr, 1980). A production system is composed of two parts: a condition and an action. Whenever the (C) condition of a production is satisfied, the (A) action of that production is executed (i.e., C→A, analogous to the manner of an S→R relation). Simon (1979b) writes: "The reader will not mislead himself badly if he equated the arrow in a production with a special kind of S–R structure [p. 342]." In sum, information-processing theories are based on a conception of symbol processing, organized by a system of associations and associational processes that are distinguished from cognitive theories, in which the causal agents defining behavior are abstract mental entities.

Information Processing and Structural Formalisms.   Formal systems and devices are probably the most salient characteristic of information-processing models, for example, the flow diagrams that reflect the assumption of serial processing, the production systems that map a computer language form to the analysis of task solutions, as well as list and branching list structures that represent the organization of information in memory. These formalisms serve in information processing as do all formal languages: to provide a vehicle for description, explanation, and codification of data and concepts. But, just as algebra is both a formal language and a mathematical theory, so production systems are a formalization and entail a set of theoretical assumptions (Siegler's, in press, opinion to the contrary notwithstanding). These formalisms are a means of mapping information and concepts onto a form that can be processed by a computer in a manner analogous to FORTRAN or other computer languages. As Newell (1972) points out, however, production systems are not as theoretically neutral as most computer languages, although it is arguable whether any computer language can be completely neutral theoretically. As already indicated, production systems on the model of C(condition)→A(action) are based on a theory of associations in Simon's view. A formalization that entails such an assumption is far from neutral. Consequently, the use of production systems to display or test Piaget's theory is not likely to succeed, at least from a Piagetian perspective, because of the incompatibility of the specific assumptions of both theories. Nor is the reduction of Piagetian ideas to an information-processing theory likely to succeed without a significant change in the theory's assumptions, which is of course what Klahr and Siegler (Klahr, 1980; Klahr & Wallace, 1976; Siegler, 1978) attempt in their reduction of Piagetian notions to information-processing theory.

The use of formalisms, however, is fully in keeping with the objectives and practices of functionalism. Neither abstractness, symbolic obscurity, nor logical difficulty disqualify a formalism from application or use within a scientific theory whether structural or functional. The structure of formalisms, however, does not endow the entities to which they are applied with the properties of the formalisms themselves. In other words, employing highly structured formal systems (either mathematical or logical) in theories does not in and of itself make them structuralist theories. If it were so, most scientific theories would by their use of mathematical equations and formulas become structural. Rather, a psychological theory may be said to be structural if its constructs, which are purported to be in a causal relation to behavior, are related to one another by logical or formal relations. The nature of formal languages used to describe or represent these relations is a different matter.

In describing his own structuralism Piaget (1970) proposes more explicit criteria for defining the properties of a structuralist theory:

> As a first approximation, we may say that a structure is a system of transformations. Inasmuch as it is a system and not a mere collection of elements and their properties, these transformations involve laws: the structure is preserved or enriched by the interplay of its transformation laws, which never yield results external to the system nor employ elements that are external to it. In short, the notion of structure is composed of three key ideas: the idea of wholeness, the idea of transformation, and the idea of self-regulation [p. 5].

Wholeness implies properties over and above those conferred by the distinctive features of the elements that constitute the whole. Thus, the integers of the number system do not exist except as parts of a system of relations. Information-processing systems are proposed as systems of component processes, with each component in turn composed of further elements. Is a list or branching list structure within a processing system a structure in the sense defined by Piaget? In other words, are the logical procedures or natural processes by which the system as a whole is formed primary or are they merely another set of constituents of the system? In a structuralist theory, the logical or natural laws of composition are its central defining property and not merely an adjunct to the fact that a totality or a system emerged from sets of elements. A set of such structure-defining laws is lacking in information-processing systems. Information-processing list structures and semantic structures serve more like the systems of associations in behaviorism, more like Hull's family-habit hierarchy, than the logical formalisms of structural theories like those of Piaget, Chomsky, or Levi-Strauss. Information-processing structures are designed in accordance with their own intentions to be bottom-up systems of organization. Thus, Simon (1979b) writes:

> Information processing psychology has sometimes been referred to as "the new mental chemistry." The atoms of this mental chemistry are symbols, which are combinable into larger and more complex associative structures called lists and list structures. The fundamental "reactions" of the mental chemistry employ elementary information processes that operate upon symbols and symbol structures: copying symbols, storing symbols, retrieving symbols, inputting and outputting symbols, and comparing symbols. Symbol structures are stored in memories, often classified as short term and long term memories [pp. 63–64].

This statement is reminiscent of the characterizations of the classic English associationist philosophers as the "mental chemists" of the 18th and 19th centuries in the way they treated complex ideas built up from sensations (Reitman, 1965). Thus, information processing attempts to characterize, describe, and explain cognitive mechanisms utilizing formalisms built on a theory of associations that lacks the completeness of a coherent system of logic to tie the system together. The lack of wholeness is noted by Newell (1973) in a particularly candid analysis of information-processing research. He stated that each experimental effort resulted in a unique model for that task. What was lacking was the glue to put all the efforts together. As Newell (1973) put it: "Our task in psychology is first to discover that structure which is fixed and invariant so that we can theoretically infer the method [used to perform the task] . . . without such a framework within which to work, the generation of new methods, hence new explanations, for old phenomena, will go on *ad nauseum*. There will be no discipline for it, as there is none now [p. 296]." Without such a coherent theory, an endless number of models is possible for any given task. Newell's own solution to the control problem was to propose the concept of productions or production systems, but it would not be amiss to say that information-processing theory, even at this date, is a collection of models lacking a coherent theory of the logical or natural processes by which cognitive structures as wholistic entities are formed.

Piaget's second criterion, that a cognitive structure must be accompanied by transformations to account for both the structuring process and the structured products of the process, appears to be most closely approximated in information processing by the notion of directed associations within a production system. The meaning implicit in the idea of directed associations is not clearly delineated in the information-processing literature. But as an association, whether directed or not, it does not appear to approximate an account of how invariants across processed domains, comparable to the grouping structures of Piaget, came into being, nor does it account for generativity in a processing system, comparable to transformation rules in Chomsky's grammar.

For all its emphasis on processing in a time frame, information-processing theories lack an explanation for how cognitive structures come into being and how structures are transformed into other structures. Thus, despite its attempts to be dynamic, the theory is static in the absence of a set of transformation rules for the creation of structure. It must be granted, however, that this deficiency has been noted and that some efforts at making systems account for developmental change have been attempted (e.g., Klahr & Wallace, 1976), but the means for achieving this are based on traditional assumptions, which are identified again later.

Finally, the self-regulating property for structures that entails self-maintenance, stability, and closure of the system of structures is missing from the mechanistic conception that defines information processing. Despite the information-processing model's origins in cybernetic theory and the significant embrace of feedback loops into the system, these only enter into particular procedures such as those in problem solving or directed search in memory.

Taken together, information processing does not fit the criteria for a structuralist theory, at least as defined by Piaget and exemplified by a number of contemporary theories. The reason for emphasizing this is that some observers (e.g., Resnick, personal communication; Zimmerman & Whitehurst, 1979) consider information-processing theory to be a sign not of a new functionalism but of a new structuralism. I wish to argue instead that these theories are not intended to account for cognitive processes and structures in the way structuralist theories do (i.e., in the way of cognitive$_2$ rather than cognitive$_1$ theories). Instead, their method is twofold. One is to work from the bottom-up, that is, to start with data in the form of, for example, problem-solving protocols and provide a detailed description and codification of these data in a computer-derived formal language according to a model that can account for the data. The computer is then available to test the model or alternative models for their fit to the data. The second approach is to start top-down, expressing an existing theory in a form that makes it operationally testable. Experiments or other forms of observation are then devised that permit comparing the predictions of the theory with the empirical facts. The constraint imposed upon a theory (viz., that it must be transposable to a computer-processing language) restricts some theories as candidates for test in an information-processing framework. Information processors are generally contemptuous of such theories, describing them as vague and imprecise. This does not mean that the theories are in principle untestable; they are only untestable in terms of a computer-driven information-processing procedure. In turn, the most likely candidates for test in a computer-based procedure are theories that are themselves models, generalizations, or lawlike statements close to the form of data languages. For this reason alone, much of information processing pertains to the direct modeling of experimental and observational data and accounts for the many different models of discrete problem solving and reasoning that Newell (1973) decried.

Since Newell's injunction, attempts have been made to create more encompassing information-processing models such as the Anderson (1976) ACT model, which is based in part on a combination of propositional network representation of declarative knowledge with a production system model of procedural knowledge. The latter development suggests that quite abstract theories of a logical type are possible within the information-processing framework. In fact deriving such models is the stated goal of information processing, as it is for all scientific theories, in order that the theory apply to the largest possible class of cases. But that is not what appears to have resulted, at least in developmental research of the past 15 years of so. The resulting state of affairs may be the consequence of Simon's (1972) view, that the process of arriving at explanations for behavior is the work of induction (the bottom-up tactic) and not deduction, despite the recognition that it is not possible to go directly from "facts" to a theory. Whether information-processing theory has been inhibited by this orientation to theory and model development is not evident, but something is clearly impeding progress in the development of information-processing models of development.

What is it that information-processing theories aim to explain then? Their avowed intent is to account for behavior and, as already suggested, not in structuralist terms. The alternative is in a functionalist account. But the distinction is not so clear-cut, at least insofar as information-processing theorists characterize their own views. For Newell (1972), who directly addresses the distinction between structure and function, what is structure and what is function depends, within a time perspective, on what is fixed and what is changing. As what is structure in one context may be seen as process in another context and vice versa, he suggests that the simplest tactic is to consider the state of the system at any point as its structure and whatever changes that state as process. This interpretation differs from that of the structuralists, who view structures as enduring forms that are ostensibly represented in the brain or nervous system in some way. Because the state of a developing system at any point in time is still part of a performing system, the momentary structure is partly processlike and partly structurelike. In a computer, structure consists of various material parts whose activation constitutes performance. The material parts are in the program and in the data the program acts on. Structure, in turn, in a computer-modeled information system is represented by the knowledge necessary for processing and the general and specific task processing programs. Knowledge is more structurelike, whereas the programs are more processlike. The dual roles of structure and function are evident when the system is in fact not performing. There is a processlike object that plays the role of structure, which also serves as the source for process when the time for performance comes. Thus, (Newell, 1972) what is structure and function depends on time and the dynamic properties of the processing system. What is acting is process, what is acted upon (i.e., object) is structure, and "structure" and "process" serve only "a general umbrella-like function" [p. 139]. Newell goes on to specify four types of functional process that enter into a developmental information-processing system: induction (from no knowledge to knowledge), assembly (constructing a program out of component primitive operations), compilation (obtaining a program specific to a task from a general one), and adaptation (analogical program→specific program).

In essence, then, the structural elements in the system are subordinated to a functional description with the aim of explaining behavior. For Simon (1972), achieving the goal of explaining behavior in information-processing terms is accomplished by: "a description of an organization of simple information processes that (a) is consistent with what we know of the physiology of the nervous system, (b) is consistent with what we know of behavior in tasks other than the ones under consideration, (c) is sufficient to produce the behavior that is under consideration, and (d) is relatively definite and concrete [pp. 18–19]." The last two criteria are particularly cogent for characterizing information processing models. In the first instance [(c)], if an information processing model can be shown to be sufficient to (i.e., simulate) the behavior by a computer program, it serves as an adequate explanation of the behavior. At the same time it must be definite and concrete in specifying a set of operations.

Earlier functionalisms also aimed at specificity, as did behaviorism as well, but none attempted to meet a sufficiency criterion (c) inasmuch as earlier functionalisms did not set as a goal the simulation of behavior by way of a model. This approach is designated by Simon (1972) as "explanation by synthesis," that is, "synthesizing a process capable of humanoid behaviors." The closest earlier approaches came to a sufficiency criterion was with mathematical models that employed curve-fitting devices in the attempt to model experimental outcomes and, possibly, with the trial-and-error models of the early learning theorists. More generally, the attempt at explanation was achieved by physiological or psychophysical reduction or by meeting the logical empiricist criterion for causal explanation by showing that varying a stimulus (independent) variable had an effect upon a response (dependent) variable, when as many potentially affecting affecting variables as possible were held constant.

Environmentalism. Another feature of information-processing theories, at least of the kind exemplified by Simon (1972), is interest in the environment of "the rational man" whose behavior is simulated. According to Simon (1972): "Any adaptive system must take on, as well as it can, the shape of its environment; hence a careful examination of the environment [which many simply be the task environment faced by the subject] may tell us a great deal about the adaptive system [p. 20]." In this vein Simon models his views on those of his Brunswikian forerunners in psychology, that is, on the functionalists of the past. Information-processing models rarely, however, go beyond an analysis of the specific task faced by the subject so that the environmentalism of present-day information processes is considerably restricted, and discussion of the environment is largely academic.[8]

In sum, information-processing theories share with other functionalist approaches a stress on function and process, a concern for precision and concrete detail, an assessment of the (task) environment, for the most part reliance on associations and a modified S–R model, and a conception of processing as a form of adaptation. To this extent they are very much like middle functionalism. However, they add new characteristics to the functionalist position: explanation by synthesis (through computer simulation models of behavior) and the conception of humans as processors of symbols.

Information–Processing-Inspired Theories

In addition to computer-based information-processing theories, there is an even larger group that could be said to be directly influenced by information-processing models. These latter theories are often subsumed under information-processing models because of common goals and methods, but it would be more correct to identify their commonality as sharing a functionalist rather than an information-processing perspective. Thus, classifying the work of Bruner, Rosch, Trabasso, Brainerd, Paris, Gelman, Markman, Flavell, Nelson and the neo-Piagetians, Pascual-Leone, Case, and many others into a single category is legitimate if it is based on a common functionalism. What characterizes the work of this group is first and foremost the stress on process, function, and procedural knowledge. Even where there is a willingness to talk of structure, it is in a functionalist context that ordinarily lacks generalized structures for the entire system, as is also true for information-processing theories as such. Although a number of terms suggesting structure are used by this group, they are used in characteristically functionalist ways.

Schemata. Structures such as schemata, the organizational entities that Piaget and Barlett made popular, are conceived of by functionalists as dynam-

---

[8]Other functionalists like Bruner and Vygotsky place much greater stress on the role of the environment through the effects of society and culture on individual development and behavior, although Bruner's (1980) most recently expressed position is that there is a biological basis for culture. Vygotsky's (1962, 1978) work has been the inspiration for a number of neofunctionalists. The attraction of that work at least in part is the stress he placed on the cultural context of development, particularly in respect to tool and symbol use.

ically organized representations. To some, such schemata are aspects of a system engaged in the process of organizing knowledge under the control of a program of procedures that embody a set of functions and operations (Bobrow & Norman, 1975). Although such schemata may be conceived of as spatially or temporally organized (e.g., scene and event schemata), they are data-driven, environmentally contingent, and their functional aspects are stressed. There is often the accompanying claim that these systems appear early in development, and thus children and adults share a common processing mechanism (Mandler, 1978). This conception of schemata differs considerably from the schemata and scheme constructs in Piaget's theory, in which the constructs are given a much more logical and theoretical interpretation.

Rules.   Schemata are not the only structure-like constructs that find a place in contemporary functionalism. The "rule" is another, exemplified in its use by Siegler (in press). For Siegler (1978), a rule has two meanings or uses. First, it is a means of summarizing data, as in a mathematical equation, a sentence, a production system, or other formalism. Rules in this sense, Siegler holds, are merely "representations"—that is, characterizations of what is induced by the experimenter. They are in the experimenter's head. In the other sense, rules correspond to the way in which the data of observation were generated—that is, a theory of how the data came to be. An example of the latter presumably is Rule I of the balance scale problem, part of which holds that if one side on the scale goes down it has more weight (Siegler, 1978).

The functional role of a rule system is more evident in the description by Fowler (1980) of the relation of rules to concepts: "Concepts pull things together in a mental construction of a phenomenon, but more useful . . . is the concept of *rule*, which shifts emphasis to the dynamic, process aspect of cognition. A rule may be seen as the operational, defining (criterial) aspect of a concept, specifying the actions required for demonstrating the characteristics of a concept [p. 173]." Fowler (1980) continues: "Cognitive rules involve the internal representation of actions for recognizing characteristics and processes defining concepts, in a manner similar to Piaget's action-based theory of cognitive development. . . . Concepts define the cognitive structure representing phenomena and rules define the generic operations necessary to identify and make use of the structure [p. 173]." Thus, rules become another vehicle for the representation of the dynamic processslike characteristics of a cognitive system.

Scripts.   According to Siegler (in press), scripts are structurelike entities that attempt: "to capture knowledge of a higher order than would ordinarily be depicted in production systems or semantic networks." Schank and Abelson (1977) took the idea that scripts are predetermined sequences of actions that define a situation and from it developed a schema model of event knowledge. Scripts include knowledge of likely actions, probable actors, and props (the theater metaphors are obvious) that allows the participant observer to anticipate, predict, and recount a sequence of events for particular "plays" in particular "plays" in particular contexts. Nelson (1978), who adopted the model for studies of children's event knowledge, details three representational levels: the event representation, the script, and the event structure. The event, as in a verbal report or script of an event, is said to be organized in a manner analogous, if not isomorphic, to the underlying (mental) schematic event representation, which may or may not reflect the (real-world) event structure. The event structure is the organization of the event or events in the real world, as with the events that occur in a restaurant, a birthday party, and so on. Further, as Nelson writes in this volume: "The child's initial mental representations are in the form of scripts for familiar events involving social interaction and communication. . . . It is a generalized representation of an activity that has occurred more than once, rather than a collection of experiences." Here again, event representations and scripts have dynamic representations as processes and functional relations, as is the case with schemata, rules, and other structurelike forms, which in contemporary functionalism serve to embody a conception of functional relations and processes and procedures for actions. They are offered as a counterpart to an organization of knowledge of the world as categorically and hierarchically organized knowledge.

Strategies.   Other organizational notions, such as strategies, convey rather directly the idea of a functional and procedural organization that is more obviously associated with functionalist theories (e.g., Bruner, Goodnow, & Austin, 1956).

Skills.   Another feature of contemporary functionalism, evident both in information-processing theories and those theories inspired by them, is emphasis on skills and skill development. It motivates a growing body of research on knowledge and processing differences between experts and novices (Larkin *et al.,* 1980; Simon & Simon, 1978) and is evident in the studies of Gelman on the principles underlying counting skills (Gelman & Gallistel, 1978), the studies of Gibson on reading skills (Gibson, Osser, Schiff, & Smith, 1963), those of Simon and Simon (1978) on spelling skills, Bereiter and Scardemalia (1980) on writing skills, Groen on arithmetic skills (Groen & Parkman, 1972), and others. Skills may be thought of as a description of the ability to perform a task with varying degrees of competence; the term itself conveys this notion. In this sense the processes that enter into a skill or the attributes of a skill are emphasized. In the functionalist tradition this sense of the term is usually interpreted in terms of procedural knowledge or rules for performance or a combination of knowledge and procedures. The skill concept is also employed as an alternative to structuralist explanations of competence. In this sense skills characterize abilities acquired as a function of experience, built up ordinarily through trial-and-error learning (with feedback) by associational processes that account for the progressive elaboration of complex systems of performance. Gagné's (1968) conception of Piagetian conservation operations as skills is an example of this trend. More than one theory of cognitive development in the functionalist tradition is based on progressions in skill organization (e.g., Fischer, 1980; Gagné, 1968).

Decomposition of Cognitive Processes.   Analysis by synthesis, the method of information processing, is in practice a method of decomposition. It is related conceptually to elementalism, which has a long history in psychology, and is identified in particular with the empiricist (and behaviorist) traditions. In this, the basic unit of analysis is taken to be the smallest meaningful psychological entity. In contemporary functionalism there is also a tendency to identify such units, but they appear at more than one level of analysis. The "node" of a semantic or propositional network is one, with the "link" an associative relation that becomes the basis of a functional unit. The "symbol" is another, more general, conceptual unit. In addition to defining a set of conceptual units, the functionalist is interested in the decomposition of functional systems to their components such as memory, representations, and so forth. Explanations of cognitive development rooted in this orientation focus on how these component systems function in respect to performance at particular ages. Deficits and differences in performance are attributed in turn to functional deficiencies. An example of this is Trabasso's (1975) attribution of the appearance of transitive inference in Piaget's experiments at the age of about 7, not to structural factors described by Piaget, but to deficits in the memory capacities of younger children. The alternative process he proposes is a linear ordering function already instantiated in the young child. However, Trabasso leaves open the question of the origin of this function, including the possibility that it is wired into the system as a species capacity. But the differences between results obtained by Piagetians and functionalists in these transitive inference experiments are considerable and suggest that they are tapping different capacities, in one case structural, in the other functional.[9]

Comparably, Siegler (1976) attributes developmental differences in the performance of Piagetian tasks to difficulties in encoding by younger children. Siegler (1976) is very critical of such constructs as stages, critical periods, readiness, and other as mere labels that are no more than place holders for an adequate explanation and, in turn, offers an account of age differences in conceptual learning in terms of an encoding hypothesis, which is said "to explain a good part of the developmental change in responsiveness to experience [p. 519]." But, then, in another context Siegler (in press) has to admit that his model does not show how encoding occurs. Thus, one set of functional constructs is substituted for another, not because of explanatory adequacy based on a test of

---

[9]Cf. Perner, Steiner, and Straehelin (1981); Russell (1981).

truth values, but ostensibly because it is part of a preferred functional explanation.

Although other examples exist for how a decompositional approach is characteristic of the functionalist position, these should suffice to indicate the research and epistemological strategy. They reflect the desire to reduce complex processing to the most elemental units or components of a processing system. Whereas the attempt is to keep explanation as close to the data as possible, present-day functionalists have been so influenced by the nature of the system they attempt to explain, cognition itself, that they are forced to introduce explanatory constructs (e.g., encoding and linear ordering function) that entail explanatory difficulties equal to those of structuralist theories.

Functional Parallels to Structural Description. As already suggested, in a number of functionalist theories, skills, schemata, rules, functions, and processes appear as substitutes for the organizational units of structuralist theories. A further example of functional equivalents for structural constructs is to be found in Gelman's research on number (Gelman & Gallistel, 1978). The logicist characterization of number by Peano, Frege, Russell and others, was transformed by Piaget into a logic of classes and a logic of relations that are realized in the natural numbers as coordinated groupings of one-to-one correspondence relations, class relations, and order relations. These, in turn, appear in a functionalist account of counting principles by Gelman and Gallistel (1978) as a one–one correspondence principle, an order irrelevance principle, a cardinal principle, and so on. Thus, a logically structured set of interrelations is transformed into a loosely related set of functional principles held together in the context of a counting skill.

Rosch (1978), in turn, in her analysis of the nature of concepts transforms a classical structuralist description of concepts to a more functional characterization. In Rosch's earliest conception of conceptual thinking, categorizations of real-world entities and properties are said to be highly determined, not as in traditional theories by the observer's ''arbitrary'' constructions of their relations, but rather by the correlational structures of the real world. The basic level of concepts reflects this correlation or perceived world structure, but the characterization of basic level attributes is, at least in principle, equivalent to the intentional properties of classically defined concepts. Further, the properties of prototypes of each level of categorization, which most highly typify the properties of the correlational structures of real-world relations, parallel in principle the classically defined extensional properties of concepts of more convenient accounts. Rosch's theory, despite its functional focus, has been influenced further by developments in the logic of fuzzy sets that formalized longstanding observations concerning the imprecise boundaries between categories. Her theory retains other elements of classical concept theory in its vertical/horizontal organization, the former based on an inclusiveness metric, the latter on similarities and differences, with equivalences based on Wittgensteinian family resemblances.

One may, without undue distortion, consider the basis of family resemblance as a form of intentional definition with a functional emphasis. In general, Rosch's theory is probabilistic rather than deterministic, with the basic level categories formalized in terms of cue validity, which is conceived as an associational and probabilistic construct. Rosch (1978) characterizes her theory as a structural theory; in part, this is true in its vertical/horizontal organization and the like. However, in its attempt to explain the sociocultural context in which prototypes occur, in the associationist and probabilistic nature of its basic constructs (e.g., cue validity), and in its utilitarian emphasis on perceived and linguistically defined attribute structures that mirror world structures, it falls squarely into the functionalist tradition. The theory at first appears as a radical departure from classical definitions of concepts in terms of intensional and extensional properties, but it is in essence a recast functionalist interpretation of these same distinctions. Rosch emphasizes that her theory is not a theory of development, although it is evident from Piaget's (1962) earlier reference to the prototype notion that it can have a place in a developmental theory whether functionalist, structuralist, or both.

In sum, the fact that parallels between functional and structural descriptions of psychological phenomena can be identified, as we have attempted to do, is not meant to belittle the functionalist achievement when it results in an advance in understanding of cognitive activity, as is the case with each of the investigators cited. But as Watson pointed out long ago, when constructs from one theoretical convention are merely transferred to another, it adds nothing to our understanding and may in fact detract from it. In the end, it is evident that functionalist metatheoretical limitations parallel the limitations of structuralist metatheory. Whereas structural theory puts less stress on the processing characteristics of psychological systems and the context of performance, functionalist accounts neglect the commonalities and interdependencies inherent in analogous processes and procedures.

Inferences of Internal States.   One of the consequences of the behaviorist influence on functionalism was a reluctance to admit inferred cognitive states and processes into one's theory on the grounds that these constructs represented epiphenomena, mere "labels," metaphysical constructions, and the like. With the methodological advances of recent structuralist theories and for other reasons as well, there has been a greater willingness to entertain a score of constructs that vanished from psychologists' concerns for at least four decades. With the new functionalism, these constructs have been welcomed into functionalist theories. Not only that, contemporary functionalists have introduced a host of hypothetical entities of their own. To the processes of imagery, consciousness, and mental representations that Watson banished from psychology have been added short-term and long-term memory stores, executive functions, propositional networks, levels of processing, problem spaces, schemata, and so on, all inferred entities whose ontological status or psychological reality have to be inferred from the observation of behavior and performance. Neofunctionalists tend to keep their constructs as close to observable behavior as possible, consistent with the earlier functionalist distinction between hypothetical constructs and intervening variables, the latter being generally more acceptable to functionalists in that they are closer to the data of observation. The distinction between hypothetical constructs and intervening variables has been difficult to maintain, however, in present-day functionalism. The blurring of the distinction between what is or is not acceptable in a functionalist theory is due to the greater acceptability of hypothetical constructs into psychological theorizing (e.g., propositional networks, etc.), although many, but not all, functionalists still eschew those that entail extensive logical structures of the type employed by Piaget.

In sum, I suggest that the new functionalism, like structuralism, is a metatheory, a system of beliefs, a point of view, and a method of research rather than a coherent theory. As a metatheoretical orientation it is impervious to test. Its general validity cannot be attested to, only its utility as a research method or as a guide to theory building, and only theories *within* the tradition are open to truth value tests. The same is true for structuralism as a general orientation, in distinction to particular theories like Piaget's. Thus, the question is not whether the views of the various researchers in this tradition are correct, for example, in the way they address issues relative to Piaget's views. In most cases, functionalist and structuralist theories assert different things. To delineate functional relations, comparable to the manner in which Piaget delineates structure, reflects on the fact that attention has been directed to different aspects of the same or related problems. Only in the attempt to confront one structural explanation with another or one functional explanation with another is a test of validity possible. Thus, traditional means of theory comparision according to criteria of parsimony, scope of application, and so on, cannot be applied when one is comparing structure, like that of a wing, with the function of flying.

These metatheories, which others have characterized as "world views," are in our interpretation not incompatible with one another, as Overton and Reese (1973), for example, might hold. Instead, because they focus on different aspects of the functioning system they are complementary rather than incompatible, and, as I suggest, the only adequate theory of behavior and development is one that integrates both functional and structural descriptions into a single theory. How can it be done? Part of the answer lies in Piaget's own formulations.

Piaget and the New Functionalism

In developmental psychology, the new functionalists have been particularly critical of Piaget's theory on a number of grounds, although they respect it on others. The feature they approve of most is the cleverness of the tasks he and his associates have used to expose the nature of the child's thought. A surprising number of studies conducted by contemporary functionalists take these tasks as their reference point, interpret them differently, redefine the concepts they address, and restructure the means of assessing them.

Piaget is criticized for his "clinical" research methods, for the "vagueness" of his concepts (e.g., those of assimilation and accommodation), for his mode of explanation proposing as he does a system of logical structures as causal agents, for his discontinuity theory of development based on generalized stage structures, for his purported underestimation of the young child's competencies, for both underestimating and overestimating the cognitive competencies of the adult, and for neglecting the influence of social and cultural contexts on performance. In the main, the dissatisfaction with Piaget's theory is with its structuralism and his neglect of processes and functions in development.

There are a number of ironies in these criticisms, least of which is the reference to Piaget's underestimation of the young child's knowledge, when it was Piaget who brought the world's attention to the fact that cognitive development begins with birth, and it was he who detailed the nature of that development in the early years. Another is the general lack of appreciation of the functional elements in Piaget's theory and Piaget's own attitudes toward structuralism. His position (Piaget, 1970) is very succinctly put: "Structuralism is a method, . . . whose doctrinal consequences have been quite various. Because it is a method, its applicability is limited; . . . it admits the legitimacy of . . . other methods. Far from ousting genetic or functionalist studies, it rather implements them by giving them the benefit of its very powerful instruments of analysis [p. 143]."

As a method, structuralism is a search for structures, structures that cannot be located in observable relations, in behavior as such. A structure is a "form" or system of invariants within a set of transformations considered independently of the transformations themselves. It is this type of notion that has been most bothersome to functionalists, namely, abstract entities treated independently of the elements that constitute them. Yet, at the same time it is clear that modern-day functionalists introduce comparable constructs into their theories, as is the case with propositional and semantic networks in information-processing theories and the various structurelike constructs such as schemata and scripts of related theories. What, then, is the difference between information-processing usage and Piaget's? One essential difference is that Piaget sees these structures as constructed out of the organism's own activity, whereas in information-processing theories the "structures" are simply described, and interest in them is principally in how the system performs and how the model of such a system accords with predictions of the behavior it purports to model. Or alternatively, the assumption is that the "structures" or "principles" are natively given and the nature of development is either that of differentiation and/or association.

Construction for Piaget also entails a functional system, but the relation between structure and function is an intimate one. To biologists an intimate and necessary relation between structure and function is generally accepted. In cognitive psychology there are many, as Piaget (1970) notes, who think of structures as excluding all functionalism. In Piaget's own theory (1970) the functional essence is in assimilation:

> Assimilation is the process whereby a function once exercised, presses toward repetition, and in reproducing its own activity produces a schema into which the objects propitious to its exercise, whether familiar (recognitory assimilation) or new (generalizing assimilation), become incorporated. So assimilation, the process of activity common to all life, is the source of that continual relating, setting up correspondences, establishing functional connections, and so on, which characterizes the early stages of development, and it is assimilation, again, which finally gives rise to those general schemata we call structures . . . assimilation is the functional aspect of structure-formation, intervening in each particular case of constructive activity, but sooner or later leading to the mutual assimilation of structures to one another, and so establishing even more intricate inter-structural connections [pp. 71–72].

Functionalists consider this concept of assimilation vague, yet they do not hesitate to refer to "learning" and employ it to cover an almost equal range of activities with equal "vagueness." The usual explanation for this is that learning can be operationalized in a way assimilation cannot. However, an experiment in which 3–year–olds are contrasted with 6–year–olds in their ability to acquire a particular concept, such as conservation (the assimilationist argument is that the younger will not, whereas the "learning" theorist has to assume they both will, although to different degrees), can serve equally well as an operational criterion for assimilation (and the lack of it) as a pre–post-training experiment does for "learning."

Piaget (1971) refers to *function* in two senses. First is in the sense of a mathematical function [e.g., $y = f(x)$], which is that of the symbolic representation of an operation that carries out a set of transformations. The other sense is that of a biological function, which implies the existence of a system of self-supporting structures and embraces activities that keep it self-sustaining. Both the mathematical and biological senses contain the idea of variation and determining activities. Cognitive functions are more nearly related to biological functions, although mathematical functions may be applied with justification to abstract representations of both cognitive and biological functions. Function and operation are closely related and practically synonymous in use. However, people tend to speak of operations when they put emphasis on subject actions and function when they think of the relations between variables. Piaget applies function to an organized group of structures together with their functioning. That is, functioning refers to the activation or activity of a structure.

Piaget frankly admits that the distinction between structure and function is imprecise, but he insists that the distinction is necessary in that the same "organ" may change its function (in the case where cognitive structures of one stage function differently at the next stage and when the structures of the earlier stage become substructures of the later stage) and, further, that the same function may be carried out by a great number of different "organs" (as in the case of actions, e.g., "pushing" or "pulling," which are carried out by different anatomical structures in different ways).

Piaget considers the relation between structure and function in two ways. First, he (Piaget, 1971) maintains that functional analysis is necessary to the delineation of structures: "Functional analysis represents the essential framework which must be set up before any structural analysis. . . . In our problem . . . there can be no question of investigating structural isomorphisms until we have examined the functional correspondences which alone can endow them with an acceptable meaning [p. 145]." Thus, in any analysis, an understanding of function must precede that of structure. But second, once a functional analysis is carried out, it is necessary to an understanding of the phenomenon in question to proceed to a structural analysis. An analysis of functions without an understanding of their interrelations endows them with only partial meaning. In this context Piaget (1970) wonders, for example, why Bruner's "strategies" must remain isolated instead of becoming integrated into systems. Gholson's (1980) research on problem-solving strategies shows how such integrated systems of strategies are in fact demonstrable.

Piaget's longstanding claims to being as interested in function as in structure probably account in part for Boring's (1929, 1950) early characterization of Piaget as a functionalist. It probably also reflects the nature of Piaget's early work on cognitive development, which manifested less of the structuralist emphasis gained in the 1940s and 1950s. His early work shows more of the influence of Claparade, Janet, and J. M. Baldwin, all functionalists. Although the later structural emphasis in the theory shows more of the influence of mathematicians and logicians, the biological influence of function has persisted in his theory particularly in the mechanisms of equilibration. Notwithstanding this continuing interest, in recent years the Genevan group has clearly felt the pressure of the rising functionalism and has increased its emphasis on the functional aspects of the theory. As a consequence, one sees in recent work the extensive research on the development of semilogical thought in the 2 to 7 year period (the "logic" of functions) (Piaget, Grize, Szeminska, & Bang, 1977). Out of this effort, too, developed Piaget's excursion into a new direction in the study of correspondences, established by processes of comparison that in a functional and structural analysis yield, in typical Piagetian fashion, hypotheses concerning the construction of morphisms and category structures. In addition, there is the work of Inhelder and her colleagues on strategies in the process of concept acquisition (Inhelder, Sinclair, & Bovet, 1974) and the very explicit expansion of the theory to account for procedural knowledge (Inhelder & Piaget, 1980). Also evident in the Genevan group are the more functional orientations of Cellerier (1972) on information processing, Mounoud (Mounoud & Hauert, 1982) in his research on infancy, and Karmiloff-Smith (1979) on language.

Thus, functionalism has been a constant and consistent presence in Piaget's theory, but it differs from the new functionalism in ways that suggests future difficulty for the new functionalists. For one, as our analysis has shown, the new functionalism is still, for many of its adherents, in the tradition of classical empiricism, wedded to associationism. For all its implications of activity and functioning, it remains for most of the new functionalists a relatively passive-organism theory as Neisser (1978) argues. Increasingly, there is greater reliance on the idea of natively given competencies, which is new to functionalism, although a nondevelopmentalist continuity orientation is not new. Despite attempts to introduce "self-modifying" processes into information-processing theory, there is still reliance on concept-formation principles based on equivalence classes or identity to account for "redundancy reduction" and the extraction of higher order rules (Klahr, 1980; Klahr & Wallace, 1976), the difficulties of which have been pointed out by Flavell (1970). Klahr also introduces a "time line" notion reminiscent of Tanner's "time tally mechanisms" (1970), which fits better into the self-regulating mechanisms Piaget discusses than the information-processing theory offered. Since the days when Piaget's theory was criticized for failing to account for transitions in stage development (Kessen, 1962), no one among the new functionalists has been able to account for transitions in any alternative characterization, except to solve the problem by doing away with stages, which is probably a futile effort, as recent reversals among some leading functionalists suggest (in particular, Flavell, 1981). If nothing else, the stage concept still appears to be a useful heuristic device to account for observed developmental changes, even if stages cannot be validated on empirical grounds alone (Beilin, 1971).

The decompositional approach to functional analysis is a powerful research tool for what it displays of the nature of functional entities but, without corresponding constructive methods that build or search for the interrelations among functions (i.e., that search for functional correspondences and structural isomorphisms), the new functionalism will proliferate strategies and functions for each task studied until the enterprise sinks from its own weight, as Hilgard saw with an earlier functionalism. Some information processors recognize the problem, but their solutions are of the same type as created the problem—they remain within the same set of assumptions, or they simply hold off facing the problems with promissory notes.

Information-processing systems, even though they go by that name, are not systems that integrate the totality of their functions. "Control" processes control only parts of the system, and in development they clearly do not impel the systems forward. They lack the "open system" properties of a biological system, which cognitive development more nearly approximates than the mechanisms of the physical systems embodied in the workings of the computer. Information-processing theorists realize the problems faced by the need to model living systems, and their response is that their models are inherently neutral and devoid of theoretical bias. Yet, the lack of success they experience in modeling developmental systems should make one pause. For as long as they fail to model the properties of a constructive self-regulating system of schemes with abstract properties that progressively integrate the results of the child's experience into existing structures, they will continue to rediscover radical empiricism and nativism.

There is no question that the new functionalism has made great strides over older functionalisms. It has done so by taking advantage of advances in technology and theory drawn from areas both within and outside of psychology. It has also made advances through an increasing approximation to and adoption of features from cognitive theory, but clearly it is trapped by self-imposed constraints, particularly the unwillingness to conceive of schemes with properties that exceed those of their components. It is as though they will not accept the possibility that salt (sodium chloride) can have chemical and physical properties different from those of sodium and chlorine. Thus, to functionalists the chemistry of cognitive theories, as we have described them, is alchemy. On the other hand, until recently, the structural biochemists of cognition have shied away from functionalist approaches for fear that universals in behavior would be lost sight of. Like structuralism, however, functionalism has potent analytic instruments at its disposal. For developmental psychology, then, the solution is not exclusively in either tradition. Instead, developmental psychology would do well to take advantage of the virtues of both functionalist and structuralist methods in the service of providing an integrated view of the developing organism.

In recent years, efforts in this direction have been made, including those of the Genevans themselves. In particular, the efforts of Pascual-Leone (1976) and Case (1974) stand out. However, in their attempts to enlist the vigor of the functionalist method, they have vitiated the power of the structuralist method. Neither "working memories," "varying M-power," nor successively empowered "executive strategies" sufficiently capture the heuristic force of a Piagetian constructive system.

In addition, the efforts of Gholson and myself (1978) to integrate hypothesis testing theory and the problem-solving strategies it reveals with a Piagetian constructivism offer evidence that a theoretical model that takes advantage of both traditions is possible. Other efforts at integrating functional and structural analyses are evident in a variety of quarters, such as the work of Dienes and Jeeves (1965) on mathematical reasoning, Dean (1979) on imagery, and Liben (1974) on memory, to name just a few examples, as well as my own work on the strategies and structures evident in the young child's knowledge of congruence in transformational geometry (Beilin, 1971; Beilin & Klein, 1981a,b). Neither the structuralism of the recent past nor the new functionalism of the present can succeed by themselves in offering proper insight into cognitive development. Only a theory forged from a synthesis of the two traditions offers that possibility.

SUMMARY AND CONCLUSIONS

Functionalism has been marked by three periods in its history. The early functionalists, following the lead of James, Dewey, and Angell, set the framework for all later developments by emphasizing the processes of development, which defined one type of function, and by adopting the Darwinian conception of adaptation, which defined a second type of function. The latter utilitarian emphasis led these functionalists to a concern with the environmental context for behavior and development and also influenced an interest in applied problems. The mind–body problem, which the early functionalists inherited from philosophy and at first concerned the nature of mind and the role of consciousness, continues to this day in the concern with the nature of hypothetical entities of mind.

The initial phase in functionalism ended with the rise of behaviorism, which even for Watson extended aspects of the functionalist program. A second era in functionalist metatheory resulted from the impact of behaviorism, with which it did not contrast too sharply. Postbehaviorist functionalism was seen as a tolerant program in its acceptance of introspection, objective observation, and a variety of other methods, although its preference was for experimentation. Its tolerance extended to accepting the multiple origins of psychological activity instead of seeking "constants," or what would now be identified as universals. Continuities were preferred to discontinuities, and so stage theories were approached unsympathetically. Fundamental to middle functionalism, as with the earlier phase, was a bias toward associationism, elementalism, and environmentalism. One of the limitations of functionalism seen by Watson was a tendency to take structural concepts and relabel them as functional; Hilgard next saw functionalism as a loose set of theoretical notions with no logical unity or organization.

The reaction to functionalism's lack of a coherent logical theory came with the cognitive and structuralist revolution, dominated by Piaget within developmental psychology. In turn, the reaction to structuralism, particularly in the past 10 or 15 years, has inspired a new functionalism (or neofunctionalism), which presently dominates research and theory in developmental psychology. The new functionalism has profited from theoretical and methodological advances within and outside of psychology, especially from developments in cybernetics, information and communications theory, and the computer. It has also adopted significant aspects of cognitive theory, although it eschews the critical features of structuralism, system-wide logical models of great scope. The new functionalism, following the lead of information-processing theories but also not bound by them, is based on a conception of humans as symbol processors. The constraints, imposed by computer-based models for symbolic representation, are avoided by others who follow analogue and other computational models. The new functionalism is also characterized by the use of a variety of formalisms such as precise computer languages (e.g., production systems), tangible representations (e.g., flow diagrams), and general structurelike notions (e.g., schemata, scripts, and rule systems). A number of these formalisms, although they appear to be structurelike, serve the purpose of functional description rather than logical causal agents of behavior and lack the properties of wholeness (closure), transformation, and self-regulation that characterize a structural theory.

Present-day functional theories still tend to be bottom-up theories whose constructs are close to the data of observation; they are biased toward associationism and specificity. In the service of process description, functionalist theories of an information-processing type rely on "explanation by synthesis"; other functionalist theories inspired by the information-processing model employ the decomposition processes as their principal method of analysis and seek elementary units that are organized into functional units of structurelike form (e.g., skills, rules, scripts, etc.). A number of contemporary functionalist theories, at their worst, provide little more than functional parallels to structural constructs but, at their best, provide significant insights into functioning systems that differ in kind from the insights provided by a structural analysis. Functionalist theories nonetheless introduce constructs that rival structural theories in "vagueness."

This paper proposes that both functionalist and structuralist metatheories have distinct assets that complement each other and are not incompatible as they are often characterized in tendentious presentations of one or the other view. What is offered is the possibility of a synthesis of both orientations in a theory that integrates functional and structural analysis of development. Piaget's theory in recent years was moving in that direction; other examples show the possibility as well.

ACKNOWLEDGMENTS

This chapter is an expanded version of the address to the Jean Piaget Society 10th Annual Symposium, May 1981, under the title, "Piaget and the New Functionalism." I am indebted to colleagues too numerous to mention individually for making prepublication drafts of their articles available to me and for instructive discussions. I am also grateful to Howard Kendler and Ellin Scholnick for a critical reading of an earlier draft of this chapter.

REFERENCES

Anderson, J. R. *Language, memory, and thought.* Hillsdale, N.J.: Lawrence Erlbaum Associates, 1976.

Anderson, J. R. Arguments concerning representations for mental imagery. *Psychological Review,* 1978, *85,* 249–277.

Anderson, J. R., Kline, P. J., & Beasley, C. M., Jr. Complex learning processes. In R. E. Shaw, P. Federico, & W. Montague (Eds.), *Aptitude, learning, and instruction. Vol. 2: Cognitive process, analysis of learning and problem solving.* Hillsdale, N.J.: Lawrence Erlbaum Associates, 1980.

Angell, J. R. The province of functional psychology. *Psychological Review,* 1908, *14,* 61–91.

Bandura, A. Self efficacy: Toward a unifying theory of behavioral change. *Psychological Review,* 1977, *84,* 191–215.

Beilin, H. Developmental stages and developmental processes. In D. R. Green, M. P. Ford, & G. B. Flamer (Eds.), *Measurement and Piaget.* New York: McGraw-Hill, 1971.

Beilin, H., & Klein, A. *Strategies in geometric problem solving.* Paper presented at the meeting of the Society for Research in Child Development, Boston, April, 1981. (a)

Beilin, H., & Klein, A. *Using what you know: Consistency and adaptability in problem solving strategies.* Paper presented at the meeting of The Psychonomic Society, Philadelphia, November, 1981. (b)

Bereiter, C., & Scardemalia, M. From conversation to composition. In R. Glaser (Ed.), *Advances in instructional technology* (Vol. 2). Hillsdale, N.J.: Lawrence Erlbaum Associates, 1980.

Block, N. (Ed.). *Readings in the philosophy of psychology* (Vol. 1). Cambridge, Mass.: Harvard University Press, 1980.

Bobrow, D. G., & Norman, D. A. Some principles of memory schemata. In D. B. Bobrow, & A. Collins (Eds.), *Representation and understanding.* New York: Academic Press, 1975.

Boring, E. G. *A history of experimental psychology* (2nd ed.). New York: Appleton-Century-Crofts, 1950. (First edition, 1929.)

Bruner, J. S. Afterword. In D. R. Olson (Ed.), *The social foundations of language and thought: Essays in honor of Jerome S. Bruner.* New York: Norton, 1980.

Bruner, J. S., Goodnow, J. J., & Austin, G. A. *A study of thinking.* New York: Wiley, 1956.

Brunswik, E. The conceptual framework of psychology. In *International encyclopedia of unified science. Foundations of the unity of science* (Vol. 1, No. 10). Chicago, Ill.: University of Chicago Press, 1952.

Case, R. Strictures and structures: Some functional limitations on the course of cognitive growth. *Cognitive Psychology,* 1974, *6,* 554–573.

Case, R. Intellectual development from birth to adulthood: A neo-Piagetian interpretation. In R. Siegler (Ed.), *Children's thinking: What develops?* Hillsdale, N.J.: Lawrence Erlbaum Associates, 1978.

Cellerier, G. Information processing tendencies in recent experiments in cognitive learning—Theoretical implications. In S. Farnham-Diggory (Ed.), *Information processing in children.* New York: Academic Press, 1972.

Chomsky, N. A review of Skinner's "Verbal Behavior." *Language,* 1959, *35,* 26–58.

Cooper, L. A., & Shepard, R. N. Chronometric studies of the rotation of mental images. In W. G. Chase (Ed.), *Visual information processing.* New York: Academic Press, 1973.

Dean, A. Patterns of change in relations between children's anticipatory imagery and operative thought. *Developmental Psychology,* 1979, *15,* 153–164.

Dienes, P., & Jeeves, M. A. *Thinking in structures.* London: Hutchinson Educational, 1965.

Fischer, K. W. A theory of cognitive development: The control and construction of hierarchies of skills. *Psychological Review,* 1980, *87,* 477–531.

Flavell, J. H. Concept development. In P. H. Mussen (Ed.), *Carmichael's manual of child psychology* (Vol. 1) (3rd ed.). New York: Wiley, 1970.

Flavell, J. H. *On cognitive development.* Presidential address presented to the Society for Research in Child Development, Boston, April, 1981.

Fowler, W. Cognitive differentiation and developmental learning. In H. W. Reese & L. P. Lipsitt (Eds.), *Advances in child development and learning* (Vol. 15). New York: Academic Press, 1980.

Gagné, R. M. Contributions of learning to human development. *Psychological Review,* 1968, *75,* 177–191.

Gardner, H. *The quest for mind* (2nd ed.). Chicago, Ill.: University of Chicago Press, 1981.

Gelman, R., & Gallistel, C. R. *The child's understanding of number.* Cambridge, Mass.: Harvard University Press, 1978.

Gesell, A., & Ilg, F. L. *Child development: An introduction to the study of human growth*. I. *Infant and child in the culture of today*. II. *The child from five to ten*. New York: Harper, 1949.

Gholson, B. *The cognitive-developmental basis of human learning: Studies in hypothesis testing*. New York: Academic Press, 1980.

Gholson, B., & Beilin, H. A developmental model of human learning. In H. W. Reese & L. P. Lipsitt (Eds.), *Advances in child development and behavior* (Vol. 13). New York: Academic Press, 1978.

Gibson, E. J., Osser, H., Schiff, W., & Smith, J. An analysis of critical features of letters, tested by a confusion matrix. In *On a basic research program in reading* (Final Report. Cooperative Research Project, No. 639). U.S. Office of Education, 1963.

Groen, G. J., & Parkman, J. M. A chronometric analysis of simple addition. *Psychological Review*, 1972, *79*, 329–343.

Heidbreder, E. *Seven psychologies*. New York: Appleton-Century-Crofts, 1933.

Herrnstein, R. J., & Boring, E. G. (Eds.). *A sourcebook in the history of psychology*. Cambridge, Mass.: Harvard University Press, 1965.

Hilgard, E. R. *Theories of learning* (2nd ed.). New York: Appleton-Century-Crofts, 1956.

Inhelder, B., & Piaget, J. Procedures and structures. In D. R. Olson (Ed.), *The social foundations of language and thought*. New York: Norton, 1980.

Inhelder, B., Sinclair, H., & Bovet, M. *Learning and the development of cognition*. Cambridge, Mass.: Harvard University Press, 1974.

Karmiloff-Smith, A. *A functional approach to child language: A study of determiners and reference*. New York: Cambridge University Press, 1979.

Kendler, H. H. *Behaviorism and psychology: An uneasy alliance*. Paper presented at the meeting of the American Psychological Association, September, 1979.

Kessen, W. Stage and structure in the study of children. In W. Kessen, & C. Kuhlman (Eds.), Though in the young child. *Monographs of the Society for Research in Child Development*, 1962, *27*(No. 2).

Klahr, D. Information-processing models of intellectual development. In R. H. Kluwe, & H. Spada (Eds.), *Developmental models of thinking*. New York: Academic Press, 1980.

Klahr, D., & Wallace, J. G. *Cognitive development: An information processing view*. Hillsdale, N.J.: Lawrence Erlbaum Associates, 1976.

Larkin, J. G. Information processing models and science instruction. In J. Lockwood, & J. Clement (Eds.), *Cognitive process instruction*. Philadelphia: Franklin Institute Press, 1978.

Larkin, J. G., McDermott, J., Simon, D. P., & Simon, H. A. Expert and novice performance in solving physics problems. *Science*, 1980, *208*, 1335–1342.

Liben, L. S. Operative understanding of horizontality and its relation to long term memory. *Child Development*, 1974, *45*, 416–424.

Mandler, J. Categorical and schematic organization in memory. In C. R. Puff (Ed.), *Memory organization and structure*. New York: Academic Press, 1978.

Miller, G. A., Galanter, E., & Pribram, K. H. *Plans and the structure of behavior*. New York: Holt, 1960.

Mounoud, P., & Hauert, C. A. The development of sensorimotor organization in the child. In G. E. Forman (Ed.), *Action and thought: From sensorimotor schemas to symbolic operations*. New York: Academic Press, 1982.

Neisser, U. Perceiving, anticipating and imagining In C. W. Savage (Ed.), *Minnesota studies in the philosophy of science* (Vol. 9). *Perception and cognition: Issues in the foundation of psychology*. Minneapolis, Minn.: University of Minnesota Press, 1978.

Nelson, K. How young children represent knowledge of their world in and out of language. In R. S. Siegler (Ed.), *Children's thinking: What develops?* Hillsdale, N.J.: Lawrence Erlbaum Associates, 1978.

Newell, A. A note on process-structure distinctions in developmental psychology. In S. Farnham-Diggory (Ed.), *Information processing in children*. New York: Academic Press, 1972.

Newell, A. You can't play 20 questions with nature and win: Projective comments on the papers of this symposium. In W. G. Chase (Ed.), *Visual information processing*. New York: Academic Press, 1973.

Newell, A. *Physical symbol systems* (Report CMU-CS-80-110). Pittsburgh, Pa.: Carnegie Mellon University, Department of Computer Science, 1980.

Newell, A., & Simon, H. A. *Human problem solving*. Englewood Cliffs, N.J.: Prentice-Hall, 1972.

Overton, W. F., & Reese, H. W. Models of development: Methodological implications. In J. R. Nesselroade, & H. W. Reese (Eds.), *Life-span developmental psychology: Methodological issues*. New York: Academic Press, 1973.

Pascual-Leone, J. Metasubjective problems of constructive cognition: Forms of knowing and their psychological mechanisms. *Canadian Psychological Review*, 1976, *17*, 110–125.

Perner, J., Steiner, G., & Straehelin, C. Mental representation of length and weight series and transitive inferences in young children. *Journal of Experimental Child Psychology*, 1981, *31*, 177–192.

Piaget, J. *Play, dreams and imitation*. New York: Norton, 1962.

Piaget, J. *Structuralism*. New York: Basic Books, 1970.

Piaget, J. *Biology and knowledge: An essay on the relations between organic regulations and cognitive processes*. Chicago, Ill.: University of Chicago Press, 1971.

Piaget, J., Grize, J-B., Szeminska, A., & Bang, V. *Epistemology and psychology of functions*. Dordrecht, Holland: D. Reidel, 1977.

Pribram, K. Some comments on the nature of the perceived universe. In R. Shaw, & J. Bransford (Eds.), *Perceiving, acting, and knowing: Toward an ecological psychology*. Hillsdale, N.J.: Lawrence Erlbaum Associates, 1977.

Pylyshyn, Z. W. Imagery and artificial intelligence. In W. Savage (Ed.), *Perception and cognition: Issues in the foundation of psychology* (Vol. 9). *Minnesota studies in the philosophy of science*. Minneapolis, Minn.: University of Minnesota Press, 1978.

Pylyshyn, Z. W. The rate of "mental rotation" from images: A test of a holistic analogue hypothesis. *Memory & Cognition*, 1979, *7*, 19–28.

Reitman, W. R. *Cognition and thought: An information processing approach*. New York: Wiley, 1965.

Rosch, E. Principles of categorization. In E. Rosch & B. B. Lloyd (Eds.), *Cognition and categorization*. Hillsdale, N.J.: Lawrence Erlbaum Associates, 1978.

Russell, J. Children's memory for the premises in a transitive measurement task assessed by elicited and spontaneous justications. *Journal of Experimental Child Psychology*, 1981, *31*, 300–309.

Schank, R. C. *Conceptual information processing*. Amsterdam: North-Holland, 1975.

Schank, R., & Abelson, R. *Scripts, plans, goals and understanding*. Hillsdale, N.J.: Lawrence Erlbaum Associates, 1977.

Shepard, R. N. The mental image. *American Psychologist*, 1978, *33*, 125–137.

Shepard, R. N., & Metzler, J. Mental rotation of three-dimensional objects. *Science*, 1971, *171*, 701–703.

Siegler, R. S. Three aspects of cognitive development. *Cognitive Psychology*, 1976, *8*, 481–520.

Siegler, R. S. The origins of scientific reasoning. In R. S. Siegler(Ed.), *Children's thinking: What develops?* Hillsdale, N.J.: Lawrence Erlbaum Associates, 1978.

Siegler, R. S. Information processing approaches to development. In P. H. Mussen (Ed.), *Carmichael's manual of child psychology* (4th ed.). New York: Wiley, in press.

Simon, D. P., & Simon, H. A. Alternative uses of phonemic information in spelling. *Review of Education Research*, 1978, *43*, 115–137.

Simon, H. A. On the development of the processor. In S. Farnham-Diggory (Ed.), *Information processing in children*. New York: Academic Press, 1972.

Simon, H. A. The functional equivalence of problem solving skills. In H. A. Simon (Ed.), *Models of thought*. New Haven, Conn.: Yale University Press, 1979. (a)

Simon, H. A. The information storage system called "human memory." In H. A. Simon (Ed.),

Models of thought. New Haven, Conn.: Yale University Press, 1979. (b)

Tanner, J. M. Physical growth. In P. H. Mussen (Ed.). *Carmichael's manual of child psychology* (Vol. 1) (3rd ed.). New York: Wiley, 1970.

Trabasso, T. Representation, memory and reasoning: How do we make transitive inferences? In A. D. Pick (Ed.), *Minnesota Symposium on Child Psychology* (Vol. 9). Minneapolis: University of Minnesota Press, 1975.

Vygotsky, L. S. *Thought and language*. Cambridge, Mass.: MIT Press, 1962. (Originally published in Russian, 1934.)

Vygotsky, L. S. *Mind in society: The development of higher psychological processes*. Cambridge, Mass.: Harvard University Press, 1978.

Wartofsky, M. From praxis to logos: Genetic epistemology and physics. In T. Mischel (Ed.), *Cognitive development and epistemology*. New York: Academic Press, 1971.

Watson, R. I. *Basic writings in the history of psychology*. New York: Oxford University Press, 1979.

Woodworth, R. S. *Contemporary schools of psychology* (2nd ed.). New York: Ronald Press, 1948.

Wozniak, R. Metaphysics and science, reason and reality. The intellectual origins of genetic epistemology. In J. Broughton, & D. J. Freeman-Moir (Eds.), *The cognitive developmental psychology of James Mark Baldwin: Current theory and research in genetic epistemology*. Norwood, N.J.: Ablex, 1981.

Zimmerman, B., & Whitehurst, G. Structure and function: A comparison of two views of the development of language and cognition. In G. J. Whitehurst, & B. J. Zimmerman (Eds.), *The function of language and cognition*. New York: Academic Press, 1979.

Why Are New Trends in Conceptual Representation a Challenge to Piaget's Theory?

Ellin Kofsky Scholnick
University of Maryland, College Park

This book contains a symposium discussing how new formulations of the process of conceptual representation by cognitive scientists and experimental psychologists challenge Piaget's theory. Representation is, of course, the core of every theory because theories provide models to represent and explain selected aspects of a domain, and one cannot understand a theory completely without becoming aware of what aspects of the domain it represents and how that representation is accomplished. Moreover, current cognitive theories view the individual as a theory builder. The goal of a cognitive theory is to describe how people create interpretations and then revise those interpretations as they gain experience with the world and with the implications of their explanatory model. Every debate about theory is a debate about representation, and debates about cognitive processes are debates about representations of representations! At a more specific level representational issues enter into specific challenges to Piaget's data. Piaget measured classification, conservation, seriation, and other concepts in specific tasks. The chapters in this book often discuss tasks requiring sorting blocks into categories and judging whether there are more lions or animals in the world. There are frequent arguments about how to represent those task requirements—at the level of behavior, of linguistic interpretation, or of logical competence. These differences in interpretation lead to different explanations of performance failure such as processing deficits as opposed to encoding deficits. But what is an encoding deficit, if not a failure in adequate representation?

All four levels of debate are present in this book—discussions of the nature of theory, the nature of people as theorizers, the nature of tasks, and the nature of inadequate performance on tasks. The purpose of this chapter is to introduce the issues that ensuing chapters present in greater detail. We begin at the most general level by examining the meaning of representation so as to emphasize how choice of definition reflects the same theoretical biases that enter into choices about the aspects of the world that concepts are designed to represent. Beilin's chapter places the discussion of representation into a historical perspective that begins with the clashes between functionalists and structuralists at the turn of the century and continues to its current expression in this symposium between the new functionalism of cognitive science and experimental psychology and the structuralism of Piaget.

In this and ensuing chapters we move to a discussion of a particular form of representation, concepts, from functionalist and structuralist perspectives. Which form of concept is most basic to thinking: the logical classes described by Piaget, the natural categories described by Rosch, or the event representations Nelson incorporates into her theory? The controversy is not merely about the definition of concepts but the very nature of cognition itself. The debate ranges from the Piagetian position articulated by Neimark and Cocking that concepts are a product of a unitary cognitive mechanism, to arguments by Rosch and Nelson that cognition is more decentralized, to Gleitman's claims that the organization of categorical knowledge tells nothing about cognitive processing.

We then move to more specific issues about the nature of Piagetian tasks and the timetable for their mastery. Precocious task mastery and wide fluctuations in performance across task variations challenge Piaget's stage theory of development and the description of the processes stages represent. We discuss research on class inclusion from this perspective. Markman's chapter explains how variations in the response to questions about class inclusion led her to conclude there is another form of conceptual representation (i.e., collections) whose existence and functions were insufficiently appreciated by Piaget. Scholnick suggests that the debate over collections and classes is really a debate about analogical versus logical reasoning. Similarly, Cohen and Younger's summary of substantial evidence that infants recognize classes and prototype organization within classes leads to a discussion by De Lisi about whether perceptual recognition is the same as the construction of class logic.

Finally, measures of categorical thinking have been used by investigators other than Piaget to examine developmental status and the integrity of the nervous system. These investigations have produced a cohesive set of findings, which are examined by Sigel to summarize the issues that pervade this volume: What should we represent when we talk about categorical knowledge—knowledge of the semantic content of categories, knowledge of categorical logic, or knowledge of the appropriate circumstances for the use of content and procedural knowledge?

REPRESENTATION

What Is Representation?

Any discussion of the nature of representation must begin with an agreement on terminology. However, like other psychological terms, representation has a rich and very vague meaning. Furth (1968) points out that representations serve at least two functions. First, they re-present or re-introduce objects, persons, events, and ideas that are not presently in consciousness. Because we cannot literally call to mind the actual object, person, or event, then representation takes on a second meaning. We call to mind a substitute that stands for the object, person, or event. From that second perspective the debate about representation involves specifying the relation of the event that is being represented and the content that does the representing. Suppose the representation stands for some set of data. To what extent do those data dictate the content of the representation to produce something that is simply a selective but faithful copy of the data set? What provides an organization of the data set—the set itself, the mind, or some mental reworking of the external data set? If we take the view that representations are mental copies of external events, then any theory can be judged in terms of the fidelity of its internal representation to the external data set and in terms of the quantity and quality of the external data encompassed in the internal representation. We can evaluate the representation by determining whether it is an appropriate analogue of the data. Alternatively, the data set is not the "formal cause" of its representation. The data do not constrain their "stand-in" because representations coordinate experiences and derive relations. The act and form of representations may be dictated by the knower who brings to bear past experiences and abstractions derived from reflecting on past experience to form an enriched and personal interpretation of the data.

Rosch, Nelson, and Piaget differ in their stand about representations. Rosch believes the environment determines the content of representation. Nelson suggests the child begins with copies of external data but then quickly evolves an organization of the data that may be due to the inherent properties of human cognition. Piaget believes we construct representations and the procedures to deal with them in a series of qualitatively different stages. Consequently, there are fundamental disagreements about whether modeling is an appropriate synonym for representation, whether representations are static symbols of data sets or procedures for constructing symbols, whether data sets represent facts or relations, and where facts or relations come from.

Piagetian theory does not lend itself to describing representations in terms of models of sets of data, although Rosch, Nelson, and Markman use that definition. What happens when we apply the framework of mental models to the comparison of those functionalist and structuralist theories?

A Taxonomy of Representations

Palmer (1978) describes representations in terms of the domain to be represented (the represented world), the domain that does the representing (the representing world), and the operations that produce a correspondence between the two. Representational models select features and/or relations in the represented world, and mapping operations translate those features and relations into corresponding features or relations in the representing world. Suppose I have the task of sorting an array in which five red and five blue circles are interspersed with three red and three blue squares. I could represent the task in terms of the set of actions to be taken in order to select the objects (e.g., Klahr, 1973; Klahr & Wallace, 1976). In this case I must be concerned with the instructions that start the action, sequence the moves toward a goal, and then stop upon goal completion. Alternatively, I could represent the same task as a matrix with columns describing the shapes, rows describing the colors, and cells for each color-form combination in the array. The two models cannot be compared easily because they select very different aspects of the task and therefore require a processor sensitive to different kinds of data, which will be conducive to different kinds of data reduction or organization. The scripts and schemata described in this volume by Nelson model event representations, whereas in this discussion Rosch and Piaget model category representation. Scripts describe events sequences in which X causes, precedes, or provides the necessary preconditions for Y. In category representations, X is Y or part of Y. Scripts represent time, space, and causal actions by actors on objects, whereas categories preserve some form of object identity and class intersection relation.[1] Because the models select different kinds of information they require different kinds of mapping operations and a different kind of cognitive processor. One cannot automatically make inferences about the cognitive abilities required for event representations from a model that describes category representations.

Even if the same aspects of the array (e.g., color-form combinations) are used to construct a model the data can be represented with different degrees of precision. Although we label certain blocks as red we may ignore perceptible variations in color due to rough handling, uneven lighting, or differences in the batch of paint used to cover each block. We could represent the array focusing only on the difference between red and blue, or the model could represent the array as two focal values around which the blocks vary. Degrees of precision of representation dictate different psychological processes for selecting, mapping, and using the resultant representation. Reduction of the array to a dichotomy places great demands on the selection mechanism. It must ignore dimensional variations

---

[1]Of course Piaget also "models" action sequences, for example, transformations of objects, which get internalized as logical representations. Thus, the initial collection of like objects eventually results in a matrix representing the organization of all possible collections.

other than color or form and it must ignore variations within values such as the differences between reds. However, once the selection (or abstraction) occurs, the representation is so economical it can be used readily. Models that preserve more detail demand less of the selection process, but the resulting representation has to be more elaborate and additional processes may be needed to explain how the individual uses the representation. For example, although the representation may preserve all the data, there may be an additional process by which some parts of the data are selected to stand for the representation. Piaget represents class membership as equivalence, whereas Rosch's model of classes maintains fine gradations of class membership. Therefore, they differ in how they describe the process of forming a class and using class representations.

Even when the same aspects of the represented world are modeled at the same level of detail in the representation, the representation may take different forms. Figure 2.1 describes four ways of representing the array of colors and shapes: Venn diagrams (1a), tree structures (1b), logical equations (1c), and matrices (1d). Class inclusion involves a reciprocal relation between *intension* and *extension*. Intension refers to the defining properties of a class that every object in that class must possess (in this case, color and form). In an inclusion relation, the broader, including class possesses fewer defining properties than the narrower, included class. Although each of the four representations describes the intension of the classes in the display the differences in specification of intensions between included and including class are represented more explicitly by the tree diagram matrix and the logical equations.

Whereas intension is the property of each member, extension is a property of the collective group. Extension refers to the scope or numerosity of the class, its body of members. The including class has more members than the included class. The Venn diagram represents the greater size of the including class most

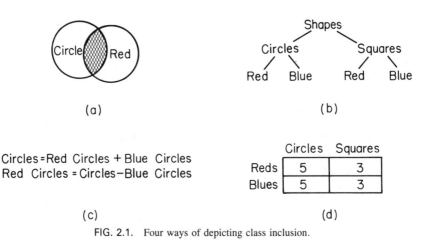

FIG. 2.1.   Four ways of depicting class inclusion.

directly. The size of the circles shows scope of the classes with the whole circle physically including the smaller segment. In class inclusion the superordinate or including class is the union of its subclasses, and the subclasses are partitions of the inclusive set. The tree diagram, matrix and logical equations depict union and partition; they also preserve the identity of each entity (because logically subtraction follows from addition). The four representations differ in how easily they allow us to grasp the fundamental characteristics of inclusion: extension, intension, partition, and union. They also differ in whether the relation is expressed figurally or algebraically and therefore in the kind of mapping and interpretive operations required for their construction and use. The choice of representation of a hierarchy leads to different speculations about the psychological processes that produce the model as well as different applications of the model. Part of the difference between Markman and Piaget is in the choice of representation for class inclusion. Markman chooses a model with properties like the Venn diagram, which emphasizes extensions of the superset class and subset. Piaget uses algebraic equations, which combine explicitly intension, extension, and if one knows arithmetic, the reversibility of union and partition.

ROSCH'S PROTOTYPE THEORY

The preceding discussion of representation suggests that we must analyze every cognitive theory carefully to ascertain what is represented and what does the representing. Up until quite recently conceptual representation was equated with an equivalence response, the designation of diverse stimuli with some common symbol or overt behavior. Flavell (1970) discusses the problems with this definition. Thus for all intents and purposes, conceptual representation involved categorization. In pioneering studies by Hull (1920) and Heidbreder (1947) concept "formation" was assessed by presenting subjects with a set of stimuli varying on a number of dimensions. The subject's task was to learn to classify the stimuli as exemplars or nonexemplars of the experimentally defined concept on the basis of information the experimenter provided about the correctness of the subject's previous classifications (see Bourne, 1966, for a review of this literature). Rosch's theory retains the same associative learning paradigm and the same definition of a concept, making a unique response to a set of diverse stimuli. However, she has different ideas about the set of stimuli the concept learner must categorize and therefore hypothesizes a different kind of mapping or associative process. It is incorrect to reduce the Piagetian perspective on conceptual development to the acquisition of equivalence responses through concept learning. However, one product of the development of logical operations is the evolution of categorical thinking. Therefore, arguments about the kind of world categories represent and the nature of categorical representations have implications for

Piagetian theory, even though Rosch's major challenges were initially directed against experimental psychologists interested in concept learning.

Artificial Categories

Rosch and her colleagues (e.g., Mervis, 1980; Mervis & Rosch, 1981; Rosch, 1978) have contrasted the artificial world of concept-learning experiments with the natural world in which people construct and use concepts. They assert that the two worlds are so different that one cannot use the setting for concept-learning experiments or the models derived to represent that setting (e.g., equivalence categories and truth tables) to represent natural category formation.[2]

In concept-learning tasks the stimuli can be described in terms of constituent dimensions like color, form, and size. Each dimension consists of discrete values like red, blue, and green on the color dimension. In *some* stimulus sets, dimensional variations are independent. Every value on one dimension is paired with every value on the other dimension, producing all possible stimulus combinations. Thus, the set has no internal structure, where structure is defined informationally in terms of greater covariation among some dimensions as opposed to others (e.g., Garner, 1962). The concepts or category system representing the set is defined by a selection mechanism that isolates or abstracts a single dimension or combination of dimensions on which objects vary while ignoring other aspects of the set. Both the lack of structure in the concept set and the nature of the abstraction processes dictate a definition of category intension in terms of necessary and sufficient defining features. All exemplars possess a particular property, and every exemplar that has that property is a member of the concept class. All nonexemplars lack the defining property. Consequently, category boundaries are discrete and sharp. As long as the intensional properties are discrete and conjunctive every instance in the class is equivalent in its qualifications for membership in the category, and each member is an equally good representation of the set.

Concept-learning tasks usually do not tap the construction of elaborate classification hierarchies. However, the stimulus set implies a model of class inclusion. The intensional properties that define a given class determine class inclusion. The more general or inclusive the class, the fewer its defining properties. *A* is included in *B* if the definition of *B* contains some but not all of the properties of *A*. Given a descending hierarchy such as reds, red circles, and large red circles, the inclusion links between red and red circle and between red circle and large red circle are equivalent. Red is no more inclusive of red circles than red circles

---

[2]I would argue that the concept-learning task does not involve category formation at all because the structure of the concept set is already well known to the subject who must merely learn which of the possible forms of representation of that structure are relevant in the task. Thus, concept-learning tasks really measure the logic of concept selection.

is of large red circles. In each pair, we add one intensional criterion as we descend the hierarchy. Thus, there is a uniformity in the logic of set relations because instances within a class are the same and a step down a level of the hierarchy from one starting point is the same as a step from another starting level. The stimulus world consists of discretely valued, unstructured distributions of stimuli. The concept retains the discrete value structure because all instances are treated as if they possessed just the defining property. The representation builds up a set of arbitrary connections, which substitutes for a set where all possible interrelations exist. We call these representations *class logic*. They require a mapping process of abstraction.

Natural Categories

Suppose the concept set or represented world is different. If that concept set is structured with built-in covariation, then we could substitute the natural order of events for the arbitrary rules of logic. Rosch and her colleagues (e.g., Mervis, 1980; Mervis & Rosch, 1981; Rosch, 1978) claim that unlike the shapes or assorted colors that concept learners ponder, the natural world is not an unstructured set of objects described by discrete values. There are continua such as color and size. Dimensions do not vary independently of one another. Like Gibson (1969), Rosch argues that attributes are bundled together or correlated in informative clusters. A hollow-boned, two-legged, feathered creature has wings, whereas creatures with bone marrow have four limbs, fur, and usually are not winged. These clusters are the basis for natural categories. Therefore, we do not need to impose a categorical structure to partition an array but simply to detect the natural partitions already present in nature. Human representations are best accounted for by the structure of the environment rather than by nature of abstractions imposed on the environment. We previously mentioned that Piaget and Rosch differ in the degree of resolution that they think concepts possess. But the difference is much deeper than notions about the represented world. They differ in the extent to which representations are isomorphic with the represented world. Rosch's theory stresses an environmental determinism absent in Piaget (e.g., Rosch, Mervis, Gray, Johnson, & Boyes-Braem, 1976).

Although there are clusters of features to provide the basis for categorization, the covariation among attributes is not perfect. Bats have four limbs and lack feathers, but they have wings. So did pterodactyls. Our winged, beaked, feathered, two-limbed creature category contains animals that sing and fly as well as ones that do neither. Because the world has some but not complete structure, categories lack sharp boundaries. Categories also have an internal structure in which no one intensional property defines the set and creates equivalent instances (Rosch, 1975). It is unlikely that each class member will possess all the properties other members have, and some members will possess more of the characteristic properties of class members than others, creating gradations within the category (Rosch, Mervis, Gray, Johnson, & Boyes-Braem, 1976). Some properties will apply to more members within the category and fewer members outside the category than others. Those properties will have maximal cue validity. Some members of the category will possess more of those valid properties and therefore be more representative and stand as ideal *prototypes* of the category. A prototype can be formed in many ways. It may be the most salient member of the category as is the case with focal colors (Heider, 1971). The category may contain the most frequently found features, or it may be the average member of the category (e.g., Rosch, Simpson, & Miller, 1976). If prototypes are salient instances we must examine the physical characteristics of the organism or the cultural milieu to explain category stereotyping. Averaging, frequency counting, or figuring out the basic structure from which all other instances vary require different processing mechanisms, which are not necessarily compatible with one another.

In summary, natural categories are not defined in terms of a set of necessary and sufficient features but in terms of features that are more or less characteristic of overlapping distributions. Categories are detected, not abstracted. For cognitive economy the learner then selects as representative of the category those instances that have maximal similarity to other members of the category and maximal distinctiveness from contrasting categories. The birdlike bat would not be a good exemplar of the mammal category.

Rosch's description of the nature of inclusion hierarchies follows from her description of category formation (Rosch, Mervis, Gray, Johnson, & Boyes-Braem, 1976). Just as robins may be more representative birds than emus, mammals may be more representative animals than birds. There are gradations in strength of linkages between subclasses and their superordinates. Some levels of a hierarchy are also more informative than others. Rosch adopts the terminology of class logic, which distinguishes between subordinate and superordinate classes, but she adds an intermediate or *basic* level. The learner of hierarchical relations, like the discoverer of a single category, acts so as to maximize within-category similarity while minimizing similarity with contrast classes. Very general or superordinate classes are quite distinct from their contrast classes, but there are few properties the instances within the class have in common. Instances within the class of furniture are very different from items of clothing, but how are a bookcase and a chair alike? (For a counterinterpretation, see Murphy, 1982.) The opposite problem besets subordinate categorization. There are many commonalities within a class but much overlap among categories. For example, how does one distinguish between dining room and office chairs? The ideal intermediate between these extremes is the *basic* category, which contains the largest number of within-class commonalities but the least overlap among contrasting complementary classes. Again, the compromise between distinctiveness and commonality is not arbitrary. The gain in similarity of instances between the basic and superordinate class is slight, but the drop in distinctiveness is dramatic

(Rosch & Mervis, 1975; Rosch, Mervis, Gray, Johnson, & Boyes-Braem, 1976). Nature and the human processor coincide also because the basic level is the easiest one at which to generate a concrete visual or motoric representation of the category.

The Processor

The theory of natural categories leads to a different characterization of cognitive processing than does Piagetian theory. Rosch claims there are real categories out there that the subject learns to detect by maximizing cue validity so as to find the instances that provide the maximum information with the minimum effort. The process is one of perceptual learning of co-occurrences, which is then sharpened by the use of prototypes. Once isolated, the prototype is used to determine whether new instances are analogous to the prototype. It is ironic that the reasoner who is aware of the diversity of experiences boils down that experience to ideal exemplars, which are as much abstractions from and possibly distortions of experience as equivalence classifications! Rosch's chapter in this volume makes explicit human preference for reasoning by analogy or prototypic reference points (see also Rosch, 1978; Rosch, Mervis, Gray, Johnson, & Boyes-Braem, 1976). Although Rosch admits in her chapter that equivalence class logic also exists from infancy, it is hard to know its origin given the nature of her theory.

Instead most of her discussion deals with the origin of natural categories. Prototypes, particularly for perceptual dimensions like color and shape, will be perceptually more salient and will therefore attract the child's attention and serve as the focal instances for category formation and naming (Mervis, Catlin, & Rosch, 1975; Rosch, 1973a, 1973b, 1975). Cultures may structure the daily life of individuals so as to call attention to certain informative aspects of the environment. Rosch (1978) has commented that basic objects usually exist at the level of specification of the props cultures include in scripts. The prototype of a class is often the object we describe as an ingredient of the most normative scripts for a routine activity. Thus, we say we ate dinner with a fork (the prop), not a plastic or salad fork. Fork is a basic category, and salad fork a subordinate level category.

Children and adults detect category membership the same way. They begin at the same point because there are "natural cuts" and natural prototypes. Thus regardless of age, the individual is bound to learn starting with basic categorization and representative instances. The child's acquisition of knowledge parallels the development of expertise by adults who are learning a new domain (Mervis et al., 1975; Mervis & Pani, 1980; Mervis & Rosch, 1981). With experience more peripheral instances of a class are added, more attributes are noticed, and the class is refined by creating subcategories. The basic category for a zoologist is probably a subordinate category to the novice taxonomist.

Two variations of this developmental picture have been proposed. The first changes the notion of basic categories and prototypic instances. Mervis (e.g., 1980; Mervis & Mervis, 1982) claims that children and adults might not have similar basic categories or prototypes. Because the life of the child is different from the adult, the child might attend to different properties or fewer properties than an adult does. Mothers notice their children's unique category structure. When they label objects for their children, they do so from the child's viewpoint and reinforce the child's initial category organization. Then the mother will slowly move the child toward the adult form of categorization. As the child notices a distinction between cars and trucks, for example, the parent will provide labels that call attention to those differences and create subcategories. Alternatively, the parent will take the lead and call attention to a meaningful functional differentiation so that the child will notice it and be ready for a label that will crystallize the difference between classes.

In contrast to Mervis, who stresses developmental differences in experience with category instances, Shepp (1978) and Kemler and Smith (1978; Smith & Kemler, 1978) suggest there are actual changes in perceptual and attentional processes. They draw upon Garner's (1978) distinction between separable and integral perceptual dimensions. For our purposes, integral dimensions are those in which information is combined holistically from several sources such as when we combine frequency and intensity information in making judgments of pitch. Separable dimensions are ones in which information can be analyzed from a single source. Integral dimensions have something in common with natural categories, whereas separable dimensions are used to form equivalence classes. Young children may have a natural propensity to perceive and group objects on the basis of overall similarity (L. Smith, 1979), which facilitates learning natural categories. By kindergarten, perceptual analysis is refined enough for children to separate dimensions (and form equivalence categories) if there is explicit instruction and environmental support. Older children spontaneously perform dimensional analyses and form equivalence classes because our educational system biases them toward taxonomic categorization.

The Representation

Although we know how categories are formed and structured, we do not know much about the nature of representation. Rosch does not specify whether the category is represented by images or propositions nor does she specify how those images or propositions might be structured. These are crucial omissions because we have argued that the form of representation sets limits on the kind of cognitive processor. Given the emphasis on pattern recognition and a format for representation that faithfully mirrors external structure, we might expect that input is structured in images. But dynamic events can also be categorized, so perhaps categories have a propositional structure. Rosch does not imply that the format for representations changes with age, merely that the content knowledge of particular categories does. Thus, Rosch's views contrast with Piaget's descriptions of the emergence of different kinds of representation as the child evolves from the practical actor of the sensorimotor period to the abstract systematizer of formal operations. For Piaget, intellectual development produces changes in representation, which in turn enhance intellectual development.

EVENT REPRESENTATION

Unlike Rosch, Nelson has frequently made her disagreements with Piaget very explicit (e.g., Nelson, 1977, 1979). The starting point for her theory of conceptual development is event representation, which she regards as the fundamental way in which mental life is organized. Her choice may have been influenced by her interest in language acquisition, which leads to competence in using sentences to describe events. Although she claims that children eventually extract classes from those early event representations, the processes underlying the development of classes are very different from the processes underlying the comprehension of events because events are so different from categories. Nelson's ideas about event representations are drawn from the analyses of cognitive scientists (e.g., Bobrow & Norman, 1975; Kuipers, 1975; Rumelhart, 1980; Schank & Abelson, 1977). The cognitive science approach is not very developmental, and therefore the adoption of their framework presupposes a more sophisticated processor than does Piaget's framework for early concept acquisition. Hence, we must carefully examine the concept of representation by focusing on the relations among the external world, the representational model of the world, and the processor who derives the kinds of representations called scripts and schemata.

Whereas Rosch devotes most of her descriptions to the data from the external world and is vague about the internal representation of that world, schema theorists are very explicit about the nature of the internal representation. They say less about the external world but they share with Rosch the belief that thinking involves pattern recognition. The difference is that they believe the recognizer must do more detective work than does Rosch because the clues to structure may be more implicit and incomplete than in Rosch's theory. This means there will be a different kind of processor.

Schemata as Processors

The unit of thinking is a schema. Rumelhart (1980) defines a schema as: "a kind of informal theory about the nature of the events, objects or situations that we face [p. 37]." Each schema embodies an anticipated pattern of events, which is matched to input data. The search for the correct interpretive schema requires analogical reasoning, pattern matching, and theory validiation.

Descriptions of schemata mix content and process. A schema organizes knowledge, applies it, and monitors its application. Theorists (e.g., Kuipers, 1975; Rumelhart & Ortony, 1977) describe schemata as "experts" who make predictions about events, determine whether their expectations are met, and decide to hand over anomalous data to other experts who shunt the problematic data aside temporarily or decide to revise the earlier expectations or formulate a new one. Note this description treats schemata as actors and objects!

Consequently, schemata require the following procedural knowledge: (1) they must know when an interpretation is validated even when the information is ambiguous and incomplete; (2) they must have the self-awareness to monitor their own data interpretation; (3) they must know how to select and use the appropriate analogies to construct their own interpretation and they must know when they cannot make sense of events; (4) they must also be aware of how much time and energy they can devote to the task. The cognitive processing performed by schemata in imposing interpretations on data is similar to Piaget's description of assimilation. The revision of schemata is akin to accommodation. In fact both terms are used liberally by schema theorists. However, while schemata may change in content so as to allow more precise matching, the skill in pattern matching is invariant. Moreover, pattern-matching expertise is localized within the schema. Individual differences arise from the number and detail of schemata available to interpret data but not from a general ability to construct patterns or employ canons of evidence. This is very different from Piaget's theory.

The adoption of schema theory leads to characterizing development in terms of increasing detail and interconnections among schemata. How much initial ability does that ask of the infant? Can they detect patterns without first having some idea about how to differentiate one pattern from another and how to validate their fit? Which comes first, the pattern or the analysis? Nelson, like Gibson (1969) and Rosch, hypothesizes that pattern recognition and analysis evolve very rapidly as the child struggles with the vital task of constructing an orderly, predictable universe. The perceptual processor rapidly gains the power that Piaget claims only evolves gradually during the course of *cognitive* development. Moreover, schematic expertise is somewhat content specific. A chess expert may say nothing to the expert who deals with number schemata. Thus, the real challenge to Piagetian theory is not the centrality of event versus class representation but the rationalism and atomism of schemata.

The Content of Schemata

We have discussed how a schema works, not what it contains. Schemata are relational structures. Objects are represented by their properties and functions and their place in networks of events or semantic hierarchies.

Unlike semantic theories, which characterize objects by essential or defining features, object schemata include encyclopedic knowledge of characteristic features, functions, and contexts. An object is depicted as a node with arrows radiating from it describing functions, properties, and features. Often objects are embedded in event representations, which are structured in a causal framework. The event schema describes how actors act in some way upon actors to cause results that may change the object. For example, the throwing schema depicts moving an object through the air to a new location. Are not some Piagetian schemes also representations of internalized actions that produce transformations? The cognitive scientist's schema represents different kinds of events and represents events differently. The schema of the cognitive scientist presupposes primitive relations like cause, agency, effect, and spatial relations, join the nodes in the schema. Relations like "is a" (classification), "has" (property), agency, or result, which form the framework for the schema, are inherent in the schema. A Piagetian scheme is about cause, effect, or agency—relations that evolve. Schema theories describe semantic networks linked by labeled directional arrows. The system is to a large extent open. In contrast, operational groupings are logical and mathematical, and the system is bidirectional and closed. Again it is apparent that schema theory requires an entirely different kind of cognizer than Piagetian theory.

How much of this apparatus need be present from the beginning? A schema requires grasp of relations like agency, location, and cause. Does the child who perceives mother throwing a ball need to understand agency and causality to register the event and form a schema indicating that the ball not the mother bounces but the mother starts the ball bouncing? We are beginning to understand the kinds of concepts the infant possesses, which might enable the construction of schema, and therefore we do not know yet when schema theory is a useful model of early cognitive development (e.g., Gelman & Spelke, 1981; Golinkoff, 1975, 1981).

Schemata do not represent single events. Even a simple pattern like the letter *A* can vary in size and orientation. Let me use the example of the hiding schema, which underlies object permanence. There are certain constraints in the hiding schema. At the very least the hider must be capable of moving either the object that does the hiding (i.e., the cover) or the object that must be hidden. The cover must be opaque, located correctly, and large enough to obscure the view of the hidden object from some hypothetical viewer. Hiding consists of the movement of one object with respect to another so as to block the viewer's visual access to an object. Any number of variations of the schema are permissible, and a variety of agents can initiate the act. The cover can end up in front of or on top of the hidden object, completely or partly masking its identity. The cover and the hidden object can be made of many materials; the act of hiding can be slow or fast. Thus, each part or *slot* in the schema can be occupied by many fillers. When we build up a schema we discover not just its invariants but also the objects, roles, and activities that can fill each slot. We learn both to extend and limit the range of data covered by each schema. Metaphorically, we can hide not only rattles but feelings. However, if the cover is transparent, we no longer have a hiding schema. Hiding describes the disappearance of objects from view, not their destruction.

Observations also lead to a normalized or modal version of the schema. We learn which actors, activities, and objects are most likely to fill particular slots. Schemata are structured prototypically. For readers of scientific journals, the prototype may consist of Gerald Gratch switching an object from under cover *A* to cover *B,* while mothers of infants think of peekaboo. Adults who are given partial knowledge of an event can use their schema to fill in missing information. In "invisible displacement," when the experimenter puts a hand under the cover that is hiding an object and then moves the hand to a second cover, the adult observer infers by *default* the aim of the movement and the probable new location of the hidden object.

Bower's (1974) analysis of object permanence lends itself to illustrating how schema theory might explain changes in the infant's understanding of object permanence. The child may initially map on the wrong schema, confusing hiding with destruction because the infant's hiding schema is insufficiently detailed. Too broad a range of objects may fill slots so that the child may behave similarly with opaque and transparent covers or be oblivious when the object that is hidden is not the one that is uncovered. Maybe the range of slot fillers is too narrow so that the infant may invoke the hiding schema only when the cover moves slowly, the object is obscured briefly, the cover moves in front of the object, or the object follows the same trajectory when exiting from its hiding place as when entering. Our decisions about when a schema fits, what objects may or may not fill slots, and what organization governs the infant's schema are not simple or obvious. Thus, when we say a child uses an event representation, we must specify the nature of that representation. Schemata also summarize what the infant knows, not why knowledge may be incomplete. We do not know whether we should predict narrow or broad ranges of slot fillers at any particular level of expertise, although Nelson has begun to speculate about some regularities in schema development (e.g., Nelson & Nelson, 1978).

Application of Schemata

Schemata contain not just knowledge but also information about where and how to apply knowledge. The range of fillers for a slot sets the contexts for application of a schema. Because the fillers are organized around prototypes we can predict which situations are easiest to interpret. Schemata even possess motives for interpretation because we are hypothesized to strive for clarification of input and we do not stop applying schemata until we resolve puzzling data or declare the puzzles insolvable. Thus, the schema theorist is not faced with the gap between competence and performance or the explanation of production deficiencies. Schema theorists are not surprised that certain class-inclusion tasks are harder than others. The variability in performance reflects a narrow range of slot fillers based on inexperience or a central processing deficit that may overload the system and prevent smooth application of schemata when the computations are too complex.

Higher Order Schemata

Schemata are elemental theories, but they can exist in different combinations and at different levels of abstraction. Nelson focuses on a particular form of schema called a *script* (Schank, 1975; Schank & Abelson, 1977). A script is a predictable sequence of events organized around achieving a goal (e.g., eating or traveling). Eating is a schema, but the series of events that leads to consumption of food in a restaurant comprises a script. Scripts, like stories, contain a set of entry conditions that identify the script and get the actor to the goal location such as the restaurant for food or the bus station for a trip. Scripts also contain a routine set of actions usually performed to reach a goal such as getting seated, obtaining a menu, ordering food and having it delivered to the table. In the sequence each action is a necessary precondition enabling the next action to occur. For example, to order food one must have (or know) the menu. Because scripts are goal oriented they usually end in goal attainment. Goal-oriented activities are so immediate and intrinsically interesting to children that scripts are good candidates for the initial basis for concept formation. As in the conventional language of drama, scripts specify the actors, who perform in the goal oriented activity, like diners and cooks, and props or instruments used to obtain goals like menus and cutlery. Like schemata, scripts also are flexible because various people and even vending machines can play the role of food deliverers.

There are specific lower order scripts, like eating at McDonald's, which are tracks of more abstract scripts, like the restaurant script. A general structure underlies all scripts, the plan that describes all goal-directed behavior. It includes the conditions that must be met for achieving goals, such as knowledge concerning the whereabouts of the goal, proximity to the goal, and the physical capacities and social influence needed to achieve the goal. Bower, Black, and Turner (1979) have commented that evocation of one level of a script does not necessarily call to mind other levels. The child who knows what to expect when entering McDonald's may be unaware that the sequence of events that ensues is organized to provide the enablement conditions for goal attainment. As with event representations, scripts may be understood at several levels so that it is not clear what the child understands about a script when we invoke it to explain the child's encoding of episodes. Certainly, the script must be sufficiently analyzed to be temporally ordered and differentiated from other scripts. We do not know much about how the child coordinates scripts under the heading of restaurant and then evolves the superscript (i.e., plan). Nelson (1981) suggests children may form superordinate scripts by noting common elements among scripts or by loosening the constraints associated with particular slots. The higher order the scripts, the wider the range of variation. The restaurant script requires food ordering and delivery, but the order can be placed at a counter or at a table.

There may be limits to what we can expect of schema or script abstraction. The domestic cat schema places furry, small, carnivorous pets in homes, whereas the feline schema deletes small, domestic pets to encompass leopards and tigers. Although the possessor of the schemata—animal, cat, and feline—knows the differences among the terms because each schema describes different properties, nothing in the schema can be used to derive the notion of inclusion classes constructed through deletion of intensional constraints. Schemata are linked to one another by overlap in properties, but there may not be a generalized knower who has a schema of schemata. Schema theory includes an executive system, which allocates resources in data interpretation and helps to modify inadequate schema, but there does not seem to be a central logical processor aware of its system of organization. Thus, schema theory differs from Piagetian theory. The difference is not confined to the contrast between representing events or representing classes. As Nelson states in this volume, schemata are static representations of dynamic events, whereas Piagetian schemes are dynamic representations of mental actions. Schemata are decentralized, contextualized concepts, whereas Piagetian schemes are centralized, abstract concepts derived from reflections upon actions.

CLASS INCLUSION

Because schemata are content specific, they do not lend themselves easily to discussions of class inclusion. As Gleitman's chapter in this volume points out, the child who knows that a rutabaga is a vegetable may not know about corn, much less about botany or class relations. That child may not understand the general rule that all members of a subclass are members of a superordinate class but only some members of the superordinate class are members of the subclass. Even Inhelder and Piaget (1964) acknowledge the content specificity of class knowledge. Without knowing something about rutabagas, you can only guess whether vegetables outnumber rutabagas. However, Piaget argues that despite ignorance of some semantic domains, knowledge of inclusion relations applicable to familiar semantic content emerges during the concrete operational period of middle childhood.

If we can accept the existence of this logic and its usefulness in constructing and evaluating inferences, we can turn to how to represent that knowledge. We argue that differences between Piaget and others reflect differences in task representation and that the child's failure is one of representing hierarchies. Inhelder and Piaget (1964) use a logical representation, specifying class relations in terms of intension and extension. At lower levels of inclusion hierarchies, there are at least two contrasting classes that are similar in some respects but different in others. Girls and boys are both young humans, but they differ in sex. The superordinate class, children, has fewer intensional criteria, being defined as young human without reference to sex. The narrower intension of the superordinate class leads to its wider scope or extension. The superordinate class is the union of its subclasses produced by eliminating some intensional criteria. Subclasses are formed by partitioning the superordinate class by the addition of defining criteria unique to each subclass. Union and partition show reversibility and other characteristics of concrete operational logic (Flavell, 1963). This logic is expessed in a variety of class-inclusion tasks, which Piaget acknolwedges vary in difficulty. There are questions about whether some of the superordinate classes are all of the subclass, whether there are more members of the superordinate than of the subclass, and the mind-boggling inverse question comprehensible only to entrants to formal operations: Are there more nonmembers of the subclass than nonmembers of the superordinate class? Though birds outnumber eagles, there are more animals that are not eagles than animals that are not birds!

Class inclusion may also be represented figurally. Ironically, Piaget claims figural representations produce failure, whereas Markman (1973, 1978; Markman & Seibert, 1976) asserts that class inclusion is easier when classes are assigned a figural representation. Markman and Piaget even used the same term, collection, to describe the representation. Piaget hypothesizes that prior to understanding class inclusion logically, the extension of classes is not yet defined by intensional criteria, but by spatial aggregation. Class union or addition is conceptualized as composing a whole, whereas subclass formation is conceptualized as subtracting parts. Logical classes can be imagined simultaneously as wholes and yet parts of classes larger in scope. Perceptual wholes cannot also be parts because spatial separation to produce parts destroys the whole. When classes are treated as objects in a spatial configuration they cannot simultaneously be joined and separated. Dealing with different combinations of intensional criteria permits the same object to be viewed from two levels of abstraction.

Markman's argument is the opposite of Piaget's. Piaget claims that dealing abstractly with intension aids class inclusion, but Markman asserts that abstraction of intension hinders inclusion by weakening the structure of the aggregated whole that children must keep in mind when it is partitioned. Intension is the property of individual objects, whereas extension is the property of the group defining its numerosity, which is the focus of the class-inclusion question. If the wholes were defined purely extensionally by collective terms like forest, family, or bunch rather by individuated intensions, the child would be able to solve class inclusion. Moreover, some part–whole relations having little relevance for classification are easy to compare. We all know a face is bigger than its eye. The two parts of the body each have a definable structure and are linked to each other externally. Oaks are linked to forests by proximity, and forests have a structure.

By calling attention to the figural extension of sets through creating cohesive wholes, collective terms enhance understanding of the quantitative relations among sets underlying both inclusion and number concepts.

Perceptual encoding is often contained in the procedural representations of class inclusion offered by information theorists (e.g., Grieve & Garton, 1981; Klahr, 1973; Klahr & Wallace, 1976; McGarrigle, Grieve, & Hughes, 1978; Trabasso, Isen, Dolecki, McLanahan, Riley, & Tucker, 1978; Wilkinson, 1976). The task of class inclusion is translated into the steps comparing the relative numerosity of two sets. Failures in class inclusion stem from task instructions and stimulus arrangements that fail to specify to the child the sets to be compared. The following example is a modification of Trabasso's (Trabasso et al., 1978) analysis. I use typical Piagetian symbolism and condense the last step in the program:

> Given a physical display of objects that are . . . partionable into a superordinate class (B) with two subordinate classes (A and A'), and given the question, "Are there more A or B?", we can identify at least eight required components.
>
> 1. Representing the physical display.
> 2. Interpreting the question as a request to compare two quantities.
> 3. Finding a referent for A.
> 4. Quantifying A . . . .
> 5 Finding a reference for B.
> 6. Quantifying B . . . .
> 7. Comparing the resulting quantities.
> 8. Responding with a set of decision rules . . . . (Condensed to choose the larger unless they are equal, then guess.) [p. 154].

There is a problem in comparing and evaluating the three different forms of representation of class inclusion because they are not explaining the same thing. If one model successfully accounts for class-inclusion performance, the other model is not eliminated. There may be more than one way to answer a class-inclusion question, but the models may not be testing for the same kind of answer. Many class-inclusion studies test whether non-Piagetian task representations are sufficient to solve class-inclusion problems, but few test whether the Piagetian representation is sufficient and whether it ever gains the status of logical necessity (for some exceptions, see Dihoff, 1975; Inhelder, Sinclair, & Bovet, 1974; Kofsky, 1966; Markman, 1978; Sheppard, 1973).

The task of diagnosis is very difficult because people can use alternate representations to solve a task. Markman (1978) showed that children who solved the "standard form" of class inclusion modeled by Trabasso often failed to understand its logic. They could not answer the same question correctly when the inclusion sets were hidden. They did not know that you could never add enough members to the subclass to make its size exceed the superordinate class. Without added diagnostic testing we cannot know what representation the child is using to solve a particular version of class inclusion and whether that same representation permits solution of the kind of class inclusion specified by Piaget. No wonder Winer (1980) concluded his review of the class-inclusion literature with the opinion that we know very little about the task. We have investigators using different task representations to frame different questions and to train children who are using multiple strategies to solve specific tasks.

Representation in Class Inclusion

Actually that assessment is very gloomy because it is clear the problem lies in the representation of the set and the linguistic terms that encode it. We need merely to ask whether the child's difficulties in representation overlap with or contradict Piaget's analysis. We can de-emphasize quantification skills because if the child knows what to quantify and compare, the counting skills of typical 5-year-olds will usually produce the right answer (e.g., Ahr & Youniss, 1970; Judd & Mervis, 1979; Kohnstamm, 1967). Although counting errors occur (e.g., Trabasso et al., 1978), they are relatively minor in comparison to encoding. Moreover, it is logically necessary that the extension of the superordinate class equals or exceeds the largest subclass no matter what the number of objects in the array.

A Piagetian analysis overlaps with Trabasso's, but there are three crucial differences in interpretation:

1. Trabasso's model is atomistic. Steps 1, 2, 3, and 5 all deal with representation. In Step 1 the child must represent part of the array as a superordinate set B and its subsets A and A'. In Step 2 the child must represent the question as a comparison of the superordinate set B with its subset $A,$ and in Steps 3 and 5 the child must map the linguistic representation of Step 2 onto the perceptual representation produced in Step 1. The processes producing the perceptual and linguistic representation may differ from one another, but the very task of mapping one representation onto the other makes it useful to conceptualize linguistic and perceptual organization as reflective of the same process.

2. Suppose the child does misrepresent the task and therefore fails to make the comparisons the child might be capable of making under other more supportive circumstances. Trabasso could argue that these are artifacts of the array or instructions, whereas Piaget would argue that these failures are symptoms of the child's incapacities.

3. Finally there are differences between Trabasso and Piaget about what must be represented and how. We alluded to these in the previous section.

In class inclusion there is a pervasive tendency for young children to reduce the entities in the question and in the array itself to sets at the same level of abstraction rather than to terms at different levels of abstraction in a hierarchy.

Problems with set organization are not peculiar to the form of class-inclusion task asking whether there are more *A* or more *B*. Adults and children misinterpret "some" and "all" (e.g., Neimark & Chapman 1975), "or" (Braine & Rumain, 1981), and "if" (Braine, 1978) to represent just equivalent or disjoint sets. Inhelder and Piaget noted the problem when they reported that children often reduced the class-inclusion question to a comparison between subsets rather than between superordinate and subordinate classes. It is hard to observe how children encode the class-inclusion questions because their repetition of the question does not specify what they mean by the terms (as in Brainerd & Kaszor, 1974). Some experimenters have asked subjects to count out the subsets they were comparing or have used simplified arrays permitting adequate diagnosis of representation. Grieve and Dow (1981) asked children to compare the numerosity of two arrays described as distances to different locations. When each path was red, the children usually correctly identified the one with more steps. When one array had all red and the other only some red steps, they made many errors. The 3-year-olds compared the length of the all red path with the length of just the red steps in the path containing a mixture of colors. They compared identical sets, not sets with subsets.

Grieve and Garton (1981) asked 4-year-olds to compare subsets with supersets, subsets with one another, and supersets with supersets. In Experiment 1, 90% of the responses compared subsets with one another. The array contained supersets of animals divided into subsets by distinctive coloration. Thus, it was easy for the child to translate: "Are there more cows than black horses?" into "Are there more black cows or black horses?" McLanahan (in Trabasso et al., 1978) showed arrays in which the name of the subset (e.g., pears) differed from the name of the superset (fruit). His subjects were older, yet he still found that one third to one half the errors reflected comparisons of subsets with each other rather than with the superordinate class. Thus children, particularly preschoolers, organize the perceptual array as sets of equally homogeneous, disjoint subclasses. Correct answers to class-inclusion questions increase when one maximizes the encoding of the superset by increasing its salience and cohesion and, to a lesser extent, if one decreases the cohesion and salience of the subsets. Class-inclusion tasks can also be solved if the requirements are translated into comparisons of disjoints sets.

Increasing the Salience of the Superset.   One way to increase the salience of the superset is to include a contrasting hierarchy. Qualitatively different hierarchies like animals and fruits call attention to the similarity of subclasses with one another and their distinctiveness from the other set. They therefore maximize detection of superordinate relations. Trabasso and his colleagues (1978) demonstrated that the inclusion of contrasting hierarchies improved performance. They also unearthed another kind of error. Children often could not compare subsets in one hierarchy with supersets in another. The cross-set comparisons may reflect the same problem as the within-set comparisons. Instead of making cross-set comparisons at two different levels of a hierarchy, the child reduces the task to a comparison between disjoint sets at the same level of abstraction (e.g., Grieve & Garton, 1981).

The perceptual cohesion and salience of the superordinate class can also be enhanced by setting the class apart. Kalil, Youssef, and Lerner (1974) placed bottles in a carton that drew attention to the superset. They then asked if there were more bottles in the carton or green bottles, therefore giving the superset a modifier as distinctive as the subset. McGarrigle et al. (1978) drew attention to the superordinate class by perceptually and/or linguistically adding another distinctive feature to the set (e.g., *sleeping* cows). Consequently, the expanded inclusion question appeared to be a comparison of disjoint sets: "Are there more sleeping cows or black cows?" Both the added perceptual and linguistic specification improved performance slightly, but a combination of the two manipulations greatly affected performance.

Linguistic devices alone can induce proper encoding of the superordinate class by giving it a distinct name thereby making the comparison appear to be among disjoint sets. Markman (1973) and Shipley (1979) assert that most comparisons using "or" are *distributive,* describing properties of individual members. There are linguistic rules against *collective* comparisons of sets with supersets. Class extension is a collective comparison of one group with another. Natural language uses collective adjectives or collective nouns to signal that an unexpected extensional comparison is intended. We ask: "Do you want *all* the cake or *just* a slice? Should I give up *all* alcoholic beverages or *only* martinis? Which has more members, the oaks or the *forest?*" Siegel, McCabe, Brand, and Matthews (1978) tried to enhance the collective identity of the superordinate class by using a more natural form of the class-inclusion question: "Which do you want to eat, the candy or the smarties?" The question improves class-inclusion answers, but the data are ambiguous. Children can choose the candy either because they comprehend inclusion or because they use "candy" to designate the more preferred but smaller subset (Hodkin, 1981). However, the use of collective nouns does improve answers to standard class-inclusion questions and an appreciation of the logical necessity for greater extension of the superordinate rather than the subordinate set. When "all" modifies the superordinate class, class-inclusion answers are also slightly improved (e.g., Hodkin, 1981; Shipley, 1979). Class-inclusion answers also improve when the superset is encoded as a distinctive entity in a story script (Wilkinson, 1976).

Decreasing the Salience of the Subsets.   A less effective manipulation decreases the salience of the subsets. The size of the subsets can be equated so that the disparity between subsets does not draw attention away from the less obvious superset–subset differences (e.g., Ahr & Youniss, 1970; Brainerd & Kaszor, 1974). Naming the superset and subset prior to the inclusion question can clarify that the subsets are each different from the superordinate class. The subsets may only be presented verbally (Winer, 1974; Wohlwill, 1968). Neither manipulation guarantees improvement. So many minor subclasses can be presented that the viewer has no choice but to compare the mentioned subclass and the superset (Trabasso et al., 1978).

Evading Inclusion. Performance can also be improved by turning the inclusion task into something else. The kinds of successful translation or simplification may explain why inclusion is so difficult. For example, take the counting paradigm (e.g., Brainerd, 1974; Judd & Mervis, 1979; Kohnstamm, 1967; Wilkinson, 1976). If the child is instructed to count ten cows of which seven are white and three are black, the child does not have to compare sets at different levels of intension but simply to compare numbers. The inclusion comparison can also be avoided by counting disjoint features rather than objects (e.g., Tatarsky, 1974; Wilkinson, 1976). Imagine an array in which every house has a door but only some houses have one window. The child can count doors and windows to determine whether there are more houses with doors or more with windows. But is that class inclusion? Dean, Chabaud, and Bridges (1981) showed it was not. In their display every house had a door, but some houses had three windows. Although there were fewer houses with windows than houses with doors, there were more windows than doors. Thus, children who were counting features would not answer the class-inclusion question correctly. Inasmuch as many children said there were more houses with windows it was clear they were counting features rather than evaluating sets for their disparate contents.

The class-inclusion task has also been simplified by asking children to count the number of steps in a path to an intermediate destination and to the end (McGarrigle et al., 1978). The shorter distance is included in the longer one, but this is not *class* inclusion. However, the two distances are clearly and distinctly demarcated making the inclusive set as cohesive as the included distance, and there is figural support for the comparison of set extensions.

Class inclusion can also be simplified by separating the location of the superordinate and subordinate classes. This requires two arrays with one designated as the superordinate class and the other designated as the location of the two subclasses. The child is asked to compare the whole of one array with the part located in the other (e.g., Inhelder et al., 1974; McGarrigle et al., 1978; Sheppard, 1973). The physical separation allows the child to think of the two arrays as disjoint sets rather than as part–whole relations. Each "evasion" of class inclusion physically separates the subset from the superset and accords to the whole greater cohesion through its status as a distinctive perceptual entity quantifiable at the same level of abstraction as the part. The simplification strategies resemble the attempts to clarify the language of the question and the structure of the array. Superordinate sets can be made more salient and cohesive by providing contrasting sets or by making one array serve as the superordinate while the other holds the subordinate. One can also make the language appear to describe two non-overlapping subclasses.

Where Is the Failure in Class Inclusion?

Do class-inclusion failures lie in an array arranged so as to obscure its intrinsic structure, in a question that veils its communicative intent, or in the child who perceives the question and the array? After all, not everyone is equally suscepti-ble to the same vagaries in linguistic and perceptual interpretation. Most adoles-cents understand the class-inclusion task. Given all the variables that affect performance on class inclusion (see Winer, 1980, for a thorough review) and the frequent rapid and dramatic improvements when more optimal conditions are provided, there are many different interpretations for the locus of failure. The interpretations are also not isomorphic with the representational model chosen because one can, for example, fail to assemble or employ optimal task pro-cedures for many reasons.

We could conclude that children really understand class inclusion even though their access to their own understanding is hampered by external factors such as the illusory display or the cumbersome unnatural phrasing of the inclusion ques-tion. This explanation fails to integrate the interfering factors or to explain differential sensitivity to interferences. It merely says that children will rely on processing heuristics producing mistaken conclusions because children do not know that the more formal knowledge they possess is more relevant and more adequate (e.g., Gelman & Gallistel, 1978; C. Smith, 1979, 1980). But if the child has such limited access to knowledge, is that knowledge really available? Per-haps the performance constraints on utilization of a skill are not accidental but essential to its application. Underlying the interpretation that very young children possess a skill is a belief in nativism and an acceptance of first inklings as sufficient evidence for full comprehension. These beliefs run counter to Piaget's.

A second interpretation of the data also challenges Piaget. The factors that hamper the child in processing the hierarchical structure of an array are not accidental. They reflect fundamental processing problems in perception and memory (e.g., Pascual-Leone & Smith, 1969), but there is no consensus about the source of the difficulty. It could be that children code objects globally rather than in terms of attributes. Therefore, they have difficulty in switching levels of abstraction while holding each level in mind (e.g., Klahr & Wallace, 1976). Maybe we need to mark subset–superset comparisons linguistically because those comparisons are very difficult to make (e.g., Markman, this volume). Perhaps children can follow a class-inclusion program, but they lack the re-sources to assemble such a program on their own.

Piaget provides yet a third interpretation. Flexibility in composing and recom-posing sets and examining arrays from multiple perspectives is implied by logical reversibility, which is a formal aspect of the organization of concrete operations. However, Piaget (Inhelder & Piaget, 1964) points out that concrete operational thinking has its limits:

> There is no formal mechanism underlying this sort of classification. That is why we call it a concrete operation. The level of reasoning varies with the content to which it applies. Unless the objects fall easily into a nesting set of classes, each of which is readily distinguishable by virtue of an obvious perceptual criterion, the classes break down [p. 114].

The challenge to Piagetian theory is not that variation in performance exists but the cause of the variation. Rosch claims that natural categories provide an inclusion structure, which children can detect at the maximally informative basic level (e.g., Rosch, Mervis, Gray, Johnson, & Boyes-Braem, 1976). Maybe pattern detection depends on perceptual analysis and attention deployment, which develop with age and experience. Alternatively, children may develop through reflecting on their performance and coordinating their shifts in perspective an awareness of the necessary relations between sets. The simple class-inclusion task is not going to tell us which alternative is valid because the data are certainly consistent with more than one alternative. The data consistently show inflexibility in encoding, but they do not show why the child is inflexible, how the child knows flexibility is needed, or what else flexibility implies to the child.

EARLY CATEGORIZATION

Many of the arguments between Cohen and DeLisi (this volume) about the formation of subclasses resemble the arguments about class inclusion. The language or format of the classification task produces underestimation of the child's ability (e.g., Markman, Cox, & Machida, 1981). If young children are given typical exemplars of basic level categories, they will demonstrate considerable expertise in classification (e.g., Rosch, Mervis, Gray, Johnson, & Boyes-Braem, 1976).

Take the case of habituation. Three–month–olds (e.g., Caron, Caron, & Carlson, 1979) habituate to a series containing the same shape at different slants, and they recover if presented with a different geometric form. Cohen and Younger (this volume) review a set of studies showing that in the second half year of life infants can habituate to more diverse stimuli such as different stuffed animals or sets of the same numerosity comprised of different objects (e.g., Cohen & Strauss, 1979; Strauss & Curtiss, 1981). They can extract prototypes and recognize the structure of fuzzy, overlapping sets. One–year–olds will show recognition of superordinate categories, not just basic level categories (Ross, 1980).

These findings generalize beyond habituation. When nine-month-olds are shown an array divisible into two fairly homogeneous categories they consecutively touch all the objects in one of the categories. One–year–olds first touch all the objects in one class and then in the other (e.g., Starkey, 1981). Thirty- to thirty-six–month-olds spontaneously separate arrays into two homogeneous sets (Sugarman, 1981) and match objects belonging to basic level categories (Daehler, Lonardo, & Bukatko, 1979). Three-year-olds can often produce consistent exhaustive groupings of geometric figures and learn discriminations between groups defined by one or a conjunction of attributes (Denney, 1972; Watson, Hayes, & Vietze, 1979).

The data are clear, but their interpretation is not. We do not know what the child is responding to or representing when habituation is demonstrated. We do not know if habituation to similarities is an index of recognition of intension or if dishabituation to noninstances indexes understanding of extension. Although habituation trials present a series of objects and the child may recognize the similarities between adjacent stimuli, does the child recognize that the whole series must be linked by a unitary criterion? We do not know how the recognition abilities indexed by habituation studies contribute to the touching, the sorting, and then the class-inclusion solution the child eventually demonstrates.

The problem is more fundamental than choosing between recognition and production criteria for task mastery. The issue is what classification tasks measure. Flavell (1970) contrasted two notions of classes—as instruments and as objects. Classes as instruments are summaries of the knowledge one has about a particular group of objects. Rosch and Nelson describe classes mainly in these terms. When a class is an instrument, it is necessary to know what belongs in it. This knowledge of natural categories may be gained by pattern recognition and extended by analogy. Preschoolers certainly possess this kind of categorical knowledge, although they spend many years fiddling around with setting class boundaries and achieving the appropriate and useful scope of application (see Nelson & Nelson, 1978). However, though knowledge of the content of categories is fundamental to thought, it may be only a part of thinking. There are logical and abstract categories. Flavell's other aspect of conceptualization—classes as objects—enters here. This is the ability to step back from, be aware of, and gain access to the system by which categories are constructed. The challenges to Piaget presented in this book claim the priority of classes as instruments and the limits of classes as objects. Just as natural categories are not the equivalence classes incorporated into Aristotelian logic, natural logicians do not use class logic to form deductions. They reason by analogy and are not aware of the rules of the class system. There is no class system out there to represent, only bodies of interrelated sets of knowledge.

In summary I have argued that challenges to Piagetian theory discussed in this volume are challenges about the nature of conceptual representation. Rosch accepts the nature of class concepts but suggests that their origin and organization are different from the category logic espoused by Piaget. Nelson claims that categorization is derived from and subordinated to schemata. When we turn to specific measures of categorization, both Markman and information processors represent the class inclusion task differently and claim that the problem of class inclusion lies in the difficulty of representing the class hierarchy and accessing the hierarchy under difficult linguistic and perceptual conditions. Finally, Cohen claims that some form of perceptual recognition of classes is present in infancy, but there is debate about whether that recognition is a recognition of content or a recognition of class logic.

This symposium was dedicated to Jean Piaget, who died while the papers were being written. It is a tribute to his theory that the content of the controversy debated in the symposium goes to the heart of any cognitive theory—the nature of the human cognizer and of human theory building. The ultimate controversy is the opposition between natural reasoning and logical reasoning, and the puzzle of reconciling both, which are surely products of the same human mind.

REFERENCES

Ahr, P. R., & Youniss, J. Reasons for failure on the class inclusion problem. *Child Development,* 1970, *41,* 131–143.

Bobrow, D. G., & Norman, D. A. Some principles of memory schemata. In D. G. Bobrow, & A. M. Collins (Eds.), *Representation and understanding.* New York: Academic Press, 1975.

Bourne, L. E., Jr. *Human conceptual behavior.* Boston, Mass.: Allyn & Bacon, 1966.

Bower, G. H., Black, J. R., & Turner, T. J. Scripts in memory for text. *Cognitive Psychology,* 1979, *11,* 177–220.

Bower, T. G. R. *Development in infancy.* San Francisco, Ca.: Freeman, 1974.

Braine, M. D. S. On the relation between the natural logic of reasoning and standard logic. *Psychological Review,* 1978, *85,* 1–21.

Braine, M. D. S., & Rumain, B. Development of comprehension of "or": Evidence for a sequence of competencies. *Journal of Experimental Child Psychology,* 1981, *31,* 46–70.

Brainerd, C. J. Training and transfer of transitivity, conservation and class inclusion of length. *Child Development,* 1974, *45,* 324–334.

Brainerd, C. J., & Kaszor, P. An analysis of two proposed sources of children's class-inclusion errors. *Developmental Psychology,* 1974, *10,* 633–643.

Caron, A. J., Caron, R. F., & Carlson, V. R. Infant perception of the invariant shape of objects varying in slant. *Child Development,* 1979, *50,* 716–721.

Cohen, L. B., & Strauss, M. S. Concept acquisition in the human infant. *Child Development,* 1979, *50,* 419–424.

Daehler, M. W., Lonardo, R., & Bukatko, D. Matching and equivalence judgments in very young children. *Child Development,* 1979, *50,* 170–179.

Dean, A. L., Chabaud, S., & Bridges, E. Classes, collections, and distinctive features: Alternative strategies for solving class inclusion problems. *Cognitive Psychology,* 1981, *13,* 84–112.

Denney, N. W. Free classification in preschool children. *Child Development,* 1972, *43,* 1161–1170.

Dihoff, R. E. *Multidimensional scaling of Piagetian task performance* (Tech. Rep. No. 316). Madison: Wisconsin Research and Development Center, Feb. 1975.

Flavell, J. H. *The developmental psychology of Jean Piaget.* Princeton, N.J.: Van Nostrand, 1963.

Flavell, J. H. Concept development. In P. H. Mussen (Ed.), *Carmichael's manual of child psychology* (Vol. 1) (3rd ed.). New York: Wiley, 1970.

Furth, H. G. Piaget's theory of knowledge: The nature of representation and interiorization. *Psychological Review*, 1968, *75*, 143–154.

Garner, W. R. *Uncertainty and structure as psychological concepts*. New York: Wiley, 1962.

Garner, W. R. Aspects of a stimulus: Features, dimensions and configurations. In E. Rosch & B. B. Lloyd (Eds.), *Cognition and categorization*. Hillsdale, N.J.: Lawrence Erlbaum Associates, 1978.

Gelman, R., & Gallistel, C. R. *The child's understanding of number*. Cambridge, Mass.: Harvard University Press, 1978.

Gelman, R., & Spelke, E. The development of thoughts about animate and inanimate objects: Implications for research on social cognition. In J. H. Flavell & L. Ross (Eds.), *Social cognitive development: Frontiers and possible futures*. New York: Cambridge University Press, 1981.

Gibson, E. J. *Principles of perceptual learning and development*. New York: Appleton-Century-Crofts, 1969.

Golinkoff, R. M. Semantic development in infants: The concepts of agent and recipient. *Merrill-Palmer Quarterly*, 1975, *21*, 181–193.

Golinkoff, R. M. The influence of Piagetian theory on the study of the development of communication. In I. E. Sigel, D. M. Brodzinsky, & R. M. Golinkoff (Eds.), *New directions in Piagetian theory and practice*. Hillsdale, N.J.: Lawrence Erlbaum Associates, 1981.

Grieve, R., & Dow, L. Bases of young children's judgments about more. *Journal of Experimental Child Psychology*, 1981, *32*, 36–47.

Grieve, R., & Garton, A. On the young child's comparison of sets. *Journal of Experimental Child Psychology*, 1981, *32*, 443–458.

Heidbreder, E. The attainment of concepts: III. The process. *Journal of Psychology*, 1947, 24, 93–118.

Heider, E. R. "Focal" color areas and the development of color names. *Developmental Psychology*, 1971, *4*, 447–455.

Hodkin, B. Language effects in the assessment of class inclusion ability. *Child Development*, 1981, *52*, 470–478.

Hull, C. L. Quantitative aspects of the evolution of concepts. *Psychological Monographs*, 1920, *28*, No. 1(Whole No. 123).

Inhelder, B., & Piaget, J. *The early growth of logic in the child*. New York: Harper & Row, 1964.

Inhelder, B., Sinclair, H., & Bovet, M. *Learning and the development of cognition*. Cambridge, Mass.: Harvard University Press, 1974.

Judd, S. A., & Mervis, C. B. Learning to solve class inclusion problems: The roles of quantification and recognition of contradiction. *Child Development*, 1979, *50*, 163–169.

Kalil, K., Youssef, Z., & Lerner, R. M. Class inclusion failure: Cognitive deficit or misleading reference? *Child Development*, 1974, *45*, 1122–1125.

Kemler, D. G., & Smith, L. B. Is there a developmental trend from integrality to separability in perception? *Journal of Experimental Child Psychology*, 1978, *26*, 498–507.

Klahr, D. An information-processing approach to the study of cognitive development. In A. D. Pick (Ed.), *Minnesota Symposia on Child Psychology* (Vol. 7). Minneapolis, Minn.: University of Minnesota Press, 1973.

Klahr, D., & Wallace, J. G. *Cognitive development: An information processing view*. Hillsdale, N.J.: Lawrence Erlbaum Associates, 1976.

Kofsky, E. A scalogram study of classificatory development. *Child Development*, 1966, *37*, 191–204.

Kohnstamm, G. A. *Piaget's analysis of class inclusion: Right or wrong?* The Hague: Mouton, 1967.

Kuipers, B. J. A frame for frames: Representing knowledge for recognition. In D. G. Bobrow & A. M. Collins (Eds.), *Representation and understanding*. New York: Academic Press, 1975.

Markman, E. M. The facilitation of part–whole comparisons by the use of the collective noun "family." *Child Development*, 1973, *44*, 837–840.

Markman, E. M. Empirical versus logical solutions to part–whole comparison problems concerning classes and collections. *Child Development*, 1978, *49*, 168–177.

Markman, E., Cox, B., & Machida, S. The standard object-sorting task as a measure of conceptual organization. *Developmental Psychology,* 1981, *17,* 115–117.

Markman, E. M., & Seibert, J. Classes and collections: Internal organization and resulting holistic properties. *Cognitive Psychology,* 1976, *8,* 561–577.

McGarrigle, J., Grieve, R., & Hughes, M. Interpreting inclusion: A contribution to the study of the child's linguistic and cognitive development. *Journal of Experimental Child Psychology,* 1978, *26,* 528–550.

Mervis, C. B. Category structure and the development of categorization. In R. J. Spiro, B. C. Bruce, & W. F. Brewer (Eds.), *Theoretical issues in reading comprehension.* Hillsdale, N.J.: Larence Erlbaum Associates, 1980.

Mervis, C. B., Catlin, J., & Rosch, E. Development of the structure of color categories. *Developmental Psychology,* 1975, *11,* 54–60.

Mervis, C. B., & Mervis, C. A. Leopards are kitty-cats: Object labeling by mothers for their 13-month-olds. *Child Development.* 1982, *53,* 267–273.

Mervis, C. B., & Pani, J. R. Acquisition of basic object categories. *Cognitive Psychology,* 1980, *12,* 496–522.

Mervis, C. B., & Rosch, E. Categorization of natural objects. *Annual Review of Psychology,* 1981, *32,* 89–115.

Murphy, G. L. Cue validity and levels of categorization. *Psychological Bulletin,* 1982, *91,* 174–177.

Neimark, E. D., & Chapman, R. H. Development of comprehension of logical quantifiers. In R. J. Falmange (Ed.), *Reasoning: Representation and process.* Hillsdale, N.J.: Lawrence Erlbaum Associates, 1975.

Nelson, K. Cognitive development and the acquisition of concepts. In R. C. Anderson, R. J. Spiro, & W. E. Montague (Eds.), *Schooling and the acquisition of knowledge.* Hillsdale, N.J.: Lawrence Erlbaum Associates, 1977.

Nelson, K. Explorations in the development of a functional semantic system. In W. A. Collins (Ed.), *Minnesota Symposia on Child Psychology* (Vol. 12). Hillsdale, N.J.: Lawrence Erlbaum Associates, 1979.

Nelson, K. Social cognition in a script framework. In J. H. Flavell, & L. Ross (Eds.), *Social cognitive development: Frontiers and possible futures.* New York: Cambridge University Press, 1981.

Nelson, K. E., & Nelson, K. Cognitive pendulums and their linguistic realization. In K. E. Nelson (Ed.), *Children's language* (Vol. 1). New York: Gardner Press, 1978.

Palmer, S. E. Fundamental aspects of cognitive representation. In E. Rosch & B. B. Lloyd (Eds.), *Cognition and categorization.* Hillsdale, N.J.: Lawrence Erlbaum Associates, 1978.

Pascual-Leone, J., & Smith, J. The encoding and decoding of symbols by children: A new experimental paradigm and a neo-Piagetian model. *Journal of Experimental Child Psychology,* 1969, *8,* 328–355.

Rosch, E. Natural categories. *Cognitive Psychology,* 1973, *4,* 328–350. (a)

Rosch, E. On the internal structure of perceptual and semantic categories. In T. E. Moore (Ed.), *Cognitive development and the acquisition of language.* New York: Academic Press, 1973. (b)

Rosch, E. Cognitive reference points. *Cognitive Psychology,* 1975, *7,* 532–547.

Rosch, E. Principles of categorization. In E. Rosch & B. B. Lloyd (Eds.), *Cognition and categorization,* Hillsdale, N.J.: Lawrence Erlbaum Associates, 1978.

Rosch, E., & Mervis, C. B. Family resemblances: Studies in the internal structure of categories. *Cognitive Psychology,* 1975, *7,* 573–605.

Rosch, E., Mervis, C. B., Gray, W. D., Johnson, D. M., & Boyes-Braem, P. Basic objects in natural categories. *Cognitive Psychology,* 1976, *8,* 382–439.

Rosch, E., Simpson, C., & Miller, R. S. Structural bases of typicality effects. *Journal of Experimental Psychology: Human Perception and Performance,* 1976, *2,* 491–502.

Ross, G. S. Categorization in one- to two-year-olds. *Developmental Psychology,* 1980, *16,* 391–396.

Rumelhart, D. E. Schemata: The building blocks of cognition. In R. J. Spiro, B. C. Bruce, & W. F. Brewer (Eds.), *Theoretical issues in reading comprehension.* Hillsdale, N.J.: Lawrence Erlbaum Associates, 1980.

Rumelhart, D., & Ortony, A. The representation of knowledge in memory. In R. C. Anderson, R. J. Spiro, & W. E. Montague (Eds.), *Schooling and the acquisition of knowledge.* Hillsdale, N.J.: Lawrence Erlbaum Associates, 1977.

Schank, R. C. The structure of episodes in memory. In D. G. Bobrow & A. Collins (Eds.), *Representation and understanding.* New York: Academic Press, 1975.

Schank, R. C., & Abelson, R. P. *Scripts, plans, goals and understanding.* Hillsdale, N.J.: Lawrence Erlbaum Associates, 1977.

Shepp, B. E. From perceived similarity to dimensional structure: A new hypothesis about perceptual development. In E. Rosch & B. B. Lloyd (Eds.), *Cognition and categorization.* Hillsdale, N.J.: Lawrence Erlbaum Associates, 1978.

Sheppard, J. L. Conservation of part and whole in the acquisition of class inclusion. *Child Development,* 1973, *44,* 380–383.

Shipley, E. F. The class-inclusion task: Question form and distributive comparisons. *Journal of Psycholinguistic Research,* 1979, *8,* 301–331.

Siegel, L. S., McCabe, A. E., Brand, J., & Matthews, J. Evidence for understanding of class inclusion in preschool children: Linguistic factors and training effects. *Child Development,* 1978, *49, 688–693.*

Smith, C. L. Children's understanding of natural language hierarchies. *Journal of Experimental Child Psychology,* 1979, *27,* 437–458.

Smith, C. L. Quantifiers and question answering in young children. *Journal of Experimental Child Psychology,* 1980, *30,* 191–205.

Smith, L. B. Perceptual development and category generalization. *Child Development,* 1979, *50,* 705–715.

Smith, L. B., & Kemler, D. G. Levels of experienced dimensionality in children and adults. *Cognitive Psychology,* 1978, *10,* 502–532.

Starkey, D. The origins of concept formation: Object sorting and object preference in early infancy. *Child Development,* 1981, *52,* 489–497.

Strauss, M. S., & Curtiss, L. E. Infant perception of numerosity. *Child Development,* 1981, *52,* 1146–1152.

Sugarman, S. The cognitive basis of classification in very young children: An analysis of object ordering trends. *Child Development,* 1981, *52,* 1172–1178.

Tatarsky, J. H. The influence of dimensional manipulations on class-inclusion performance. *Child Development,* 1974, *45,* 1173–1175.

Trabasso, T., Isen, A. M., Dolecki, P., McLanahan, A. G., Riley, C. A., & Tucker, T. How do children solve class inclusion problems? In R. S. Siegler (Ed.), *Children's thinking: What develops?* Hillsdale, N.J.: Lawrence Erlbaum Associates, 1978.

Watson, J. S., Hayes, L. A., Vietze, P. Bidimensional sorting in preschoolers with an instrumental learning task. *Child Development,* 1979, *50,* 1178–1183.

Wilkinson, A. Counting strategies and semantic analyses applied to class inclusion. *Cognitive Psychology,* 1976, *8,* 64–85.

Winer, G. A. An analysis of verbal facilitation of class-inclusion reasoning. *Child Development,* 1974, *45,* 224–227.

Winer, G. A. Class-inclusion reasoning in children: A review of the empirical literature. *Child Development,* 1980, *51,* 309–328.

Wohlwill, J. F. Response to class-inclusion questions for verbally and pictorially presented items. *Child Development,* 1968, *39,* 449–465.

FORMS OF CONCEPTUAL
REPRESENTATION

Prototype Classification and Logical Classification: The Two Systems

Eleanor Rosch
University of California, Berkeley

A logical interpretation of categories in terms of definitions with necessary and sufficient criteria and a prototypical interpretation of categories in terms of clear cases and gradients of membership are normally considered mutually exclusive. So much so that when empirical evidence suggests that both may be operating for a given sample of categories (Gleitman, this volume), that in itself is taken as an argument that we should abandon any search for a general characterization or theory of categorization. In this paper, I would like to situate the discussion of logic versus prototypes in categories in the somewhat broader context of types of reasoning and suggest that there are at least two such types: reasoning using logical structures and reasoning from reference point cases. Use of such a term as *reasoning* is not meant to imply conscious deliberation but rather refers to any form of inferring, deliberate or automatic, in which we go beyond the information given to form categorizations, judgments, or decisions.

After pointing out a few pieces of evidence suggesting that both logical and reference point reasoning arise in infancy and have their own course of development, the bulk of the paper consists of an elaboration of what is meant by reference point reasoning and of how prototype classification is a form of it. Three types of reference point inferences are distinguished: (1) reasoning from specific known cases, events, or examples when this is in opposition to what might be inferred from general knowledge; (2) inference from salient reference points within an organized domain such as the color space; (3) judgment using representativeness, under which fall most of the prototype categorization work. Given this analysis it is possible to indicate what may be general and what may be domain specific to the study of categorization.

LOGIC AND PROTOTYPES IN INFANCY

The nature and generality of logical operations in the abilities of adults has been amply defined and demonstrated through the methods of Piaget as well as by the entire field of study of formal logic and mathematics. In Piaget, the development of logic is dependent on the development of an abstract symbol system (Inhelder & Piaget, 1964). This approach forms the basis of Neimark's argument (this volume) that it is unnecessary to propose more than one type of classification. However, Langer (1980) argues that logical cognition does not require a symbol system at its origin but rather "is rooted in actions that generate pragmatic transformations which have logical properties [p. xi]." In a broad ranging and systematic research program, Langer demonstrates how the actions of infants from 6 to 12 months of age can be interpreted already to include elementary logical and mathematical properties but in pragmatic rather than symbolic form. Langer shows how these pragmatic manipulations are used to produce the fundamentals of logical and mathematical thought such as equivalence, nonequivalence, and reversible relations within and between elements, sets, orders, and quantities. No doubt, Langer's work will not go unmarked by controversy; however, it is at this point quite reasonable to suggest that logical cognition has its origins in infancy antedating the development of abstract symbols.

Formation of categories in infancy that show a prototype structure is perhaps less surprising because such a structure would be predicted even for generalization gradients to a conditioned stimulus (Riley & Lamb, 1979). Demonstration of categorization (or categorylike behavior) in infants is itself of relatively recent origins (Cohen & Gelber, 1975). Prototypelike effects in infants' categories have been shown by Bornstein (1981), Cohen and Younger (this volume), and Golinkoff and Halperin (in press). Finally, the effect of goodness of example on children's learning and development of categories is widely documented (see Mervis & Rosch, 1981, for a review). In short, there is some basis for an argument that in infancy the pragmatic origins of logic and the origins of categorization develop in parallel.

REFERENCE POINT REASONING

By reference point is meant a stimulus or model that other items are seen or judged "in relation to" (Rosch, 1975). Often, when subjects use a basis of judgment such as "vividness" of an event or representativeness within a category in a task where a more logical basis, such as prior probability, could have been used, this is treated as an error or as a heuristic. Heuristic here often has the force of mere heuristic, a shortcut of reasoning that yields errors. This section points to three types of domains in which thinking in terms of reference points seems to be the natural or basic form of cognitive processing.

Reasoning from Specific Known Cases, Events, or Examples

Consider the now classic thought experiment (Nisbett, Borgida, Crandall, & Reed, 1976) in which you have decided to buy a Volvo this week on the basis of *Consumer Reports'* ratings of mechanical excellence and good repair record. In the interim you go to a cocktail party and tell your decision to an acquaintance who reacts with a vivid and detailed account of the trials and ills encountered by his brother-in-law's Volvo. It is obvious that you are unlikely to treat this information as a trivial statistical adjustment to your knowledge about Volvos— as though, for example, the *Consumer Reports'* ratings had included one more bad case.

An actual study of reactions in a situation somewhat similar to this was done by Hamill, Wilson, and Nisbett (1979). Subjects were presented with one of two video-taped ''interviews'' in which a person alleged to be a guard at a state prison discussed his job. In one condition the guard was extremely humane, in the other extremely brutish. Cross-cutting this manipulation subjects were told, before seeing the videotape, either that the guard was typical of prison guards, that the guard was extremely atypical, or they were given no information about typicality. In subsequent ratings of the humaneness of prison guards, subjects were highly influenced by the humane or the inhumane interview and completely uninfluenced by typicality–atypicality information. In a second experiment, subjects read an article about a welfare recipient who was a case study in social pathology. Varying base-rate data about average length of stay on welfare were also provided; again subjects were influenced by the article and uninfluenced by the statistics.

Nisbett and Ross (1980) suggest that cases such as these tend to be influential beyond their legitimate informativeness due to such factors as the extent to which the occurrence is close to the subjects in either space, time, or in a sensory fashion, the extent to which it is of emotional interest to the subjects, and/or the degree to which it is concrete and imagery provoking. The mechanism mediating influence is suggested to be memory; these are all variables that make material highly memorable. A glance at our own memories indicates that they are full of specific events often encoded in vivid detail: experiences that have happened to us or people close to us and accounts we have seen, heard, or read.

In what fashion do such case histories exert their influence? One type of influence may be global. Tversky and Johnson (1981) have found that subjects who read a vivid story about a person who succumbs to some risk (e.g., leukemia) tend to rate all risks (e.g., death from a tornado) as more probable regardless of similarity to the original risk. Another type of influence may be quite specific; inferences about current events may depend on a close match to the remembered event. For example, Abelson and Levi (in press) have reminded us to notice when we consider applicants (e.g., to graduate school) on the basis of their resemblance to successful or unsuccessful graduate students of the recent past rather than on the basis of more formal decision criteria. Tversky (1981) has found an actual effect of this sort in judgment of risk. Although subjects tend to agree that flying out of New York is more dangerous than flying out of Chicago and that a commuter plane is more dangerous than a DC-10, they report that flying out of Chicago in a DC-10 is more dangerous than flying out of New York in a commuter plane. Chicago in a DC-10 matches a recent dramatic accident.

A third type of influence involves representativeness; people may have a strong tendency to consider any experienced event as representative or typical of the population from which it is drawn regardless of indications or even explicit information to the contrary. Certainly the subjects in the Hamill et al. (1979) experiment acted in this fashion in regard to the prison guard and welfare recipient. The assumption that the behavior of a person observed on one occasion is representative of the person in general may be one mechanism behind the persistence of belief in the efficacy of interviews in job and student selection despite the weight of evidence to the contrary (Nisbett & Ross, 1980). (Representativeness is discussed further in a later section.) A fourth type of influence may be general to autobiographical memory. Vivid experiences and cohesive case histories may serve as reference points around which domains of experience become structured—the more bizarre or unidimensional examples of these are what may perhaps be seen on the psychoanalyst's couch. (Reference points of structured domains are discussed further in a later section.)

Is reliance on single cases an irrational or primitive mechanism? Lest you are too hasty in condemning it, it should be pointed out that argument from precedent in the form of individual cases is the basis of Anglo-American common law and, in that sense, a well-established form of social decision making. To be sure, when inference from a single case is experimentally pitted against the correct inference available from simultaneously presented information as in Hamill et al. (1979) or Tversky (1981), reliance on the case study or particular event appears to be simply an error. Viewed in this light Nisbett and Ross (1980) are well justified in taking a normative approach and advising readers to guard against such errors in their own thinking. On the other hand, the tendency to refer back to particular events that have been experienced can be seen as a stubborn empiricism. It is as though subjects were always slightly doubtful of abstract or theoretical information when it contradicts what they have seen or heard. It is precisely the absence of such an attitude that is decried when subjects desert the information of their senses for that of social influence (as in the Asch experimental paradigm, 1952) or when they make judgments on the basis of prior beliefs or (incorrect) causal schema rather than on the basis of the data provided by the experimenter (e.g., Nisbett & Ross, 1980). As such, the use of particular experienced events as reference points in inferencing can be seen as an inductive balance to the tendency to rely on logical deductive inferences from prior schemata. We might tentatively predict that there is a judged *realness* dimension of experiences that will determine the extent to which they will become case reference points for such induction.

Reasoning from Salient Reference Points within an Organized Domain

Concepts do not occur without reference to other concepts, and many concepts occur as part of structured domains. Consider, for example, the pairs red and green, anger and fear, Copley Square and Harvard Square, mass and inertia, president and secretary. Within such structured domains as color or emotion, some points in the domain appear to be salient and to act as reference points around which the domain may become structured and from which inferences tend to be made. There can be various bases for such salience.

Physiological Salience.   One prime example of a domain structured by physiologically salient reference points is the color space. There is accumulating evidence that the semantics of color names follow the outputs of the fundamental hue-response categories in the visual system (as defined in terms of proportional output in the individual hue channel of the opponent process system; see Kay & McDaniel, 1978, for a review). Speakers across languages agree on the best examples of basic color names (Berlin & Kay, 1968; Heider, 1972), and such salient best examples are recognized and recalled better than peripheral examples, even by speakers of a language that does not have basic hue terms (Heider, 1972). In addition, basic hue categories are learned by the speakers of that language more easily when they are structured around the salient best examples, as in natural color language, than when they are artificially structured around peripheral examples (Rosch, 1973). Thus, physiologically salient points of the color space appear to act as reference points for the learning and memory of color terms and for the formation of color names in languages. The reference point nature of best examples of color terms was brought out further in a study by Rosch (1975). Subjects were given sentence frames containing hedges such as "*X* is virtually *Y*" and asked to place a pair of color chips in the slots. Peripheral colors were judged as *virtually, essentially, roughly,* and so forth the best example color but not vice versa. In a second experiment, peripheral colors were judged closer to the best examples than the best examples were to the peripheral colors, a type of asymmetry also found in similarity judgments for other reference point stimuli (Tversky, 1977; Tversky & Gati, 1978). A similar interaction of physiological salience and perception may be operative for horiztonal and vertical in spatial orientation and for good forms such as square and circle in the perception of forms (Rosch, 1973, 1975).

Environmental Salience.   Anyone who has tried to travel in the city of Boston acting as though the streets formed an organized grid, such as in midtown

Manhattan or Lincoln, Nebraska, has had trouble. It is natural to imagine Boston in terms of its squares from which streets radiate and to conceive of one's travel as between squares. Other cities and geographical areas have salient landmarks that can be used as reference points. In fact, it may be difficult and even somewhat unpleasant to navigate in cities that lack reference points (Lynch, 1960).

Salient Environment-Physiological Interactions.   Ekman (1972) has presented evidence that there are six basic emotions with corresponding protypical examples of facial expressions that are universally recognized. A classification of the structure of situations that give rise to basic emotion categories has yielded a somewhat similar set of emotions (Roseman, 1979). Thus, emotions may be an example of a domain in which the most extreme or clearest cases of situational-expressive factors serve as reference points for the structure of the space.

Social Structural Salience.   Social structures have certain positions or roles that are salient because of the nature of the structure. President of a country, most popular girl in a fourth grade class, and a nation which is a world power are examples of such salience. Occupants of these roles exert social influence beyond the influence of other individuals (e.g., the effectiveness of a United States president's wife's breast cancer in persuading women to seek examination and treatment). Advertisers assume such influence when they use prominent people to endorse products. In regard to salient countries, Tversky (1977) has found asymmetry in similarity judgments; for example, North Korea is judged more similar to Red China than Red China is to North Korea.

Salience within Formal Systems.   Within the decimal system of numerical notation, multiples of 10 form reference points. For example, Rosch (1975) found that such numbers acted like the best examples of color categories (e.g., both 97 and 102 were judged *essentially . . .* 100 but not vice versa, and both were considered closer to 100 than 100 was to them). Thus, being a member of a formal system to which logic is clearly applicable does not exclude reference point phenomena.

Scientific-Historical Conceptual Systems.   Kuhn (1981) has argued that scientific conceptual systems must be considered interrelated wholes, which partly determine and are partly determined by what are considered salient attributes within that system. For example, Aristotelian mechanics does not simply make inadequate statements about the variables that Newtonian mechanics better understood; rather it deals with a different set of variables. Carey (1982) has made a similar argument for the development of the child's conception of the animal domain.

The preceding discussion of the bases for salience within domains is not intended to be exhaustive. It does, however, demonstrate that any of the ways in which human perception, thought, and life are organized can give rise to interrelated sets of salient reference points. These are used in interacting with that domain.

Judgment Using Representativeness

Prototypes of categories are an example of the more general relation of representativeness as it has been delineated by Tversky and Kahneman (1982b). Representativeness is a relation between a process or a model M and some instance or event X associated with the model. A relation of representativeness can be defined for:

1. A value and a distribution. Here representativeness is determined by perceived relative frequency or statistical association such as the mean, median, or mode of the distribution. Artificial category research has tended to depend on this type of representativeness relation (see Mervis & Rosch, 1981).
2. An instance and a category.
3. A sample and a population. Research with common semantic categories is of both types 2 and 3; for example, an item such as robin may be treated as an instance of its category, birds, or as a sample of birds. In both cases representativeness is determined primarily by similarity (e.g., of an instance to other instances or of sample statistics to the corresponding parameters of a population). Prototypes as reference points of categories may be representative either because the most representative members of categories are taken as the prototype or because those members are salient points in a domain and the category tends to form around them so that they become representative of it.
4. An effect and a cause. Here representativeness is controlled by (valid or invalid) causal beliefs.

The following sections first review some of the evidence that representativeness affects judgment of probability and then discuss prototypes of categories as a representativeness phenomenon.

1. Representativeness Effects in Probability Judgment. In an impressive program of studies, Tversky and Kahneman have shown that people use representativeness to judge probability (see Kahneman, Slovic, & Tversky, 1982). This heuristic leads to a variety of errors of prediction. In the first place, base rates or prior probabilities are generally ignored. For example, consider the case presented by Nisbett and Ross (1980, following the work of Kahneman & Tversky, 1973). The reader is asked to judge whether a professor friend of the authors who is small, shy, and likes to write poetry is more likely to be a professor of psychology or Chinese studies. We are strongly inclined to judge Chinese studies. This urge uses as a basis of prediction the good fit between the described personality and the stereotype of a Sinologist and ignores prior probabilities—the far greater likelihood that psychologists will have as their friends other psychologists as well as occupation base rates.

The second error generated by use of representativeness to predict probability is that sample bias (e.g., that stemming from sample size) tends to be ignored or underrated. Take the following example from Kahneman and Tversky (1972). Subjects were told that the average heights of adult males and females in the United States were 5 ft. 10 in. and 5 ft. 4 in., respectively. They were asked the odds of each of two samples having been selected from males: (1) if the sample consisted of a single person whose height was 5 ft. 10 in. or (2) if the sample consisted of six persons whose average height was 5 ft. 8 in. Even students who have completed a statistics course are inclined to choose the first case.

Use of representativeness also intrudes into reasoning about causes and effects. Nisbett and Ross (1980) propose (following Mill 1843/1974) that the basic fallacy in causal reasoning is the "prejudice that the conditions of a phenomenon must *resemble* the phenomenon [Mill, p. 765]." For example, the Doctrine of Signature in medicine described by Mill contains reasoning such as that the cause of jaundice or the substance that might cure jaundice should be yellow. Tversky (1981) has shown how causal schemata can intrude into judgments of conditional probability with the force of cognitive illusion. For example, the sequence of coin tosses THHHHTH appears more likely than HHHHTH even though the latter is shorter, less specific, and in fact contained within the former. THHHHTH is more representative of the random process assumed to generate the sequence.

A final set of experiments (Tversky & Kahneman, 1982b) demonstrate how the use of representativeness in judging probability can lead to violation of one of the fundamental axioms of probability itself. In no probability calculus can the conjunction of the probability of two events be greater than the probability of either taken singly; one of the basic laws of probability is that specification reduces probability. It may, however, increase representativeness (e.g., a blue square is more similar to a blue circle than to a circle). Tversky and Kahneman (1982b) have demonstrated that subjects readily rate a conjoint probability as more likely than one of its components. For example, subjects were given the following personality sketch: "Linda is 31 years old, single, outspoken and very bright. She majored in philosophy. As a student, she was deeply concerned with issues of discrimination and social justice, and also participated in anti-nuclear demonstrations [p. 92]." In an appropriately controlled set of judgments, subjects rated Linda more likely to be both a bank teller and active in the feminist movement than simply to be a bank teller.

Representativeness effects such as those outlined in the preceeding section are a prime example of a conflict between logical and reference point thinking. In these problems there are normatively correct answers in terms of the logic of probability. When subjects are debriefed, they readily judge that they have made an error. Yet making judgments on the basis of representativeness is so persuasive that it has been termed a cognitive illusion by Tversky and Kahneman, after its resemblance to perceptual illusions. Even after debriefing with full knowledge of probability and with the full concurrence that judgment based on representativeness in these cases is an error, we still want to say that *this* friend of the authors is probably a Sinologist, that Linda simply would not be a bank teller unless she were also involved in some activity such as the feminist movement, that an individual at the mean of male heights is probably a male, and that a random process such as coin tossing should produce random-looking sequences. The problems do not seem like problems in probability; they seem like judgments concerning individuals about whom information is known. After all, if Linda actually is both a bank teller and feminist, the probability of this event is 1.

In these situations models appear to be the reference points from which reasoning is performed, and as in the case of reasoning from particular cases described in the first section, the degree of specificity of match to the model determines inferences. If models serve as reference points, then logical factors that affect probability (e.g., base rates) should affect judgment to the extent that they are incorporated as features into the model and not otherwise. The differential effects of causally and noncausally motivated base rates (Tversky & Kahneman, 1982a) can be interpreted in this fashion. Such differential effects can be illustrated by the following example. If subjects are told merely that 85% of the taxis in a city are blue and 15% are green, they fail to use this information in judgment of the validity of the report of a witness of an accident; however, if told that there are an equal number of taxis but that 85% of the accidents are caused by blues, such information is incorporated. Presumably statistics about differential accident rates (but not differential taxi frequency) are seen as information about the characteristics of the drivers and thus part of the model to which the incident of a single accident will be matched.

2. Prototypes of Categories as a Representativeness Phenomenon.   Prototypes of categories are reference points based on representativeness. According to the logic of classes, categories should have definitions specifying necessary and sufficient criteria for membership; all category members should be logically equivalent, and categories should otherwise obey the laws of class logic (as outlined by Neimark, this volume). Or if categories are conceived as simple probabilistic phenomena, they should consist of differential weightings of members according to their frequency. However, by now there is a growing amount of empirical evidence pointing to the fact that categorization is better conceived as a representativeness phenomenon than as a matter of class logic or of simple probability. Subjects are highly consistent in their ratings of how good an example an item is of its category, and such ratings have been shown to affect virtually all of the major dependent variables used as measures in psychological research: speed of processing, free production of exemplars, set or expectation, natural language use of category terms, asymmetries in similarity relationships between category exemplars, and learning and development (Mervis & Rosch, 1981; Rosch, 1977, 1978).

Prototypes of categories can be considered equivalent to models of the category in relation to which instances and noninstances are judged; they may stand for or represent the category as a whole in reasoning tasks. Such a model is the reference point for the category. It may consist of: (1) salient points of a domain (as with colors); (2) the most typical instances of the category based on features (Rosch & Mervis, 1975) or statistical parameters (Reed, 1972; Rosch, Simpson, & Miller, 1976); or (3) types considered ideal types either because they are never actually seen (Franks & Bransford, 1971; Posner & Keele, 1968) or because they embody the essence but not the typicality of the category (Tversky & Kahneman, 1982b). The mode of *representation* of the category does not matter for this formulation: The model can be in the form of images, propositions, or any other current suppositions about representation.

We may now see how research on prototype effects in categories can be formulated in a language consonant with representativeness effects in probability judgments. When asked to verify whether or not an instance is a member of a category, subjects do so according to similarity of the instance to the model; consequently, reaction times decrease the more representative the instance. When subjects are asked to produce category exemplars, they do so in an order that matches similarity to the model. When the model is invoked by priming with the category name, subjects generate the most representative instances and are blocked from generating the less representative instances. Because of the nature of representativeness itself, it can be seen how subjects will be facilitated in forming a category model, and thus learning the category, by training on the most representative instances first. Because the most salient, representative, or ideal type that forms the category reference point can stand for the category, it is not surprising that representativeness ratings for members of categories predict the extent to which the member term is substitutable for the category name in sentences (see Mervis & Rosch, 1981; Rosch 1977, 1978, for reviews of these phenomena).

Of greatest interest for purposes of the present paper is the effect of category reference points and representativeness on reasoning. In regard to inductive reasoning, the evidence is that subjects infer from the most representative members of categories in ways which they do not from less representative members. Rips (1975) found that new information about a category member was generalized asymmetrically; for example, when told that the robins on an island had a disease, subjects were more likely to decide that ducks would catch it than that robins would catch a disease which the ducks had. Carey (1979) found that young children generalize asymmetrically in the domain of animals. When told that a human has a new organ called a spleen 4–year–olds will assume that any animal, including a bee, has a spleen, whereas when told that a bee has a spleen they do not infer that *any* animal, even a bug, has one. We are presently finding this phenomenon to be general and to apply to reference points in domains such as social structure as well as to common semantic categories. Effects of representativeness on deductive reasoning using syllogisms have also been demonstrated (Cherniak, in preparation). Perhaps the phenomenon that most closely relates reasoning from reference points in categories to effects of representativeness in judgments of probability is the finding that the representativeness of items in categories appears to be used by subjects in judging the frequency of those items, rather than vice versa (Barsalou, 1981; Rosch, 1981).

By now it should be apparent why it is quite reasonable to expect Gleitman's subjects to act as they did in relation to categories that do have formal definitions. Subjects may know the mathematical definition of an odd number and the biological definition of a woman, just as Tversky and Kahneman's subjects know elementary rules of probability; however, neither is evidence that categories do not also have a representativeness structure. We could conjecture that categories with formal definitions are not required to have a representativeness structure because the definition and potentially clear-cut category boundaries that can be generated from it could provide a means of categorization. And we might prefer it if categories, such as woman, did not have a representativeness structure. However, the fact of the matter is that categories, even categories with definitions, do have a representativeness structure. And clearly, subjects perform processing tasks with categories in relation to that structure rather than by use of the concurrently available class logic.

Both logic and representativeness are abstract formulations. They do not tell us about the attributes and contingencies relevant for particular domains of categorization. Gleitman is correct in stating that such knowledge can come only from studying the particular domains. However, this is a separate issue from the fact that both logical and representative structures can apply to the same category and that both forms of reasoning can tell us something about the structure and processing of categories.

CONCLUSIONS

This paper has attempted to situate the discussion of categorization in the context of types of reasoning. I have suggested that there are at least two such types— logical reasoning and reasoning from reference points—both of which may have their origins in infancy. In many tasks both kinds of reasoning are possible. Making inferences on the basis of representativeness is one kind of reference point reasoning; prototype effects in categories are largely of this nature. Although categories that do not have definitions or determinate boundaries can perhaps only be understood by means of their representativeness structure, categories with clear definitions are subject to both types of reasoning. Reference point reasoning is often considered irrational (Nisbett & Ross, 1980); however, both types of reasoning may lead to errors: reference point reasoning when it is used in a domain where it is inappropriate (e.g., judgment of probability) and logical reasoning when the facts or presuppositions on which the reasoning is based are incorrect. We might conclude with the speculation that reference point reasoning is somewhat more empiricist and logical thinking more rationalist in flavor, and we might wish to investigate further the interaction of these two propensities.

ACKNOWLEDGMENTS

The writing of this paper was supported in part by a grant from the National Institutes of Mental Health 1 RO1 MH24316–03.

REFERENCES

Abelson, R. P., & Levi, A. Decision-making and decision theory. In G. Lindzey & E. Aronson (Eds.), *Handbook of social psychology*. Reading, Mass.: Addison-Wesley, in press.

Asch, S. E. *Social psychology*. Englewood Cliffs, N.J.: Prentice-Hall, 1952.

Barsalou, L. W. *Determinants of graded structure in categories*. Unpublished doctoral dissertation, Stanford University, 1981.

Berlin, B., & Kay, P. *Basic color terms: Their universality and evolution*. Berkeley: University of California Press, 1968.

Bornstein, M. H. Two kinds of perceptual organization near the beginning of life. In W. A. Collins (Ed.), *Minnesota Symposia on Child Psychology* (Vol. 14). Hillsdale, N.J.: Lawrence Erlbaum Associates, 1981.

Carey, S. *The child's conception of animal*. Paper presented at the annual meeting of the Psychonomics Society, San Antonio, Texas, November 1979.

Carey, S. Semantic development: State of the art. In L. Gleitman & E. Wanner (Eds.), *Language acquisition: State of the art*. New York: Cambridge University Press, 1982.

Cherniak, C. Manuscript in preparation, Tufts University.

Cohen, L. B., & Gelber, E. R. Infant visual memory. In L. B. Cohen & P. Salapatek (Eds.), *Infant perception: From sensation to cognition: Basic visual processes*. New York: Academic Press, 1975.

Ekman, P. Universals and cultural differences in facial expressions of emotion. In J. Cole (Ed.), *Nebraska Symposium on Motivation* (Vol. 19). Lincoln: University of Nebraska Press, 1972.

Franks, J. J., & Bransford, J. D. Abstraction of visual patterns. *Journal of Experimental Psychology*, 1971, *90*, 65–74.

Golinkoff, R. M., & Halperin, M. S. The concept of animal: One infant's view. *Infant Behavior and Development*, in press.

Hamill, R., Wilson, T. D., & Nisbett, R. E. *Ignoring sample bias: Inferences about collectivities from atypical cases*. Unpublished manuscript, University of Michigan, 1979.

Heider, E. R. Universals in color naming and memory. *Journal of Experimental Psychology*, 1972, *93*, 10–20.

Inhelder, B., & Piaget, J. *The early growth of logic in the child*. London: Routledge & Kegan Paul, 1964.

Kahneman, D., Slovic, P., & Tversky, A. (Eds.). *Judgment under uncertainty: Heuristics and biases*. New York: Cambridge University Press, 1982.

Kahneman, D., & Tversky, A. Subjective probability: A judgment of representativeness. *Cognitive Psychology*, 1972, *3*, 430–454.

Kahneman, D., & Tversky, A. On the psychology of prediction. *Psychological Review*, 1973, *80*, 237–251.

Kay, P., & McDaniel, C. K. The linguistic significance of the meanings of basic color terms. *Language*, 1978, *54*, 610–646.

Kuhn, T. *From revolution to salient features*. Paper presented at the annual meeting of the Cognitive Science Society, Berkeley, Cal., August 1981.

Langer, J. *The origins of logic: Six to twelve months*. New York: Academic Press, 1980.

Lynch, K. *The image of the city*. Cambridge, Mass.: Harvard University Press, 1960.

Mervis, C. B., & Rosch, E. Categorization of natural objects. In M. R. Rosenzweig & L. W. Porter (Eds.), *Annual review of psychology* (Vol. 32). Palo Alto, Cal.: Annual Reviews, 1981.

Mill, J. S. *A system of logic ratiocinative and inductive*. Toronto: University of Toronto Press, 1974. (Originally published, 1843.)

Nisbett, R. E., Borgida, E., Crandall, R., & Reed, H. Popular induction: Information is not always informative. In J. S. Carroll & J. W. Payne (Eds.), *Cognition and social behavior*, Hillsdale, N.J.: Lawrence Erlbaum Associates, 1976.

Nisbett, R., & Ross, L. *Human inference: Strategies and shortcomings of social judgment*. Englewood Cliffs, N.J.: Prentice-Hall, 1980.

Posner, M. I., & Keele, S. W. On the genesis of abstract ideas. *Journal of Experimental Psychology*, 1968, *77*, 353–363.

Reed, S. K. Pattern recognition and categorization. *Cognitive Psychology*, 1972, *3*, 382–407.

Riley, D. A., & Lamb, M. R. Stimulus generalization. In A. D. Pick (Ed.), *Perception and its development: A tribute to Eleanor J. Gibson*. Hillsdale, N.J.: Lawrence Erlbaum Associates, 1979.

Rips, L. J. Inductive judgments about natural categories. *Journal of Verbal Learning and Verbal Behavior*, 1975, *14*, 665–681.

Rosch, E. On the internal structure of perceptual and semantic categories. In T. E. Moore (Ed.), *Cognitive development and the acquisition of language*. New York: Academic Press, 1973.

Rosch, E. Cognitive reference points. *Cognitive Psychology*, 1975, *7*, 532–547.

Rosch, E. Human categorization. In N. Warren (Ed.), *Studies in cross cultural psychology* (Vol. 1). London: Academic Press, 1977.

Rosch, E. Principles of categorization. In E. Rosch & B. B. Lloyd (Eds.), *Cognition and categorization*. Hillsdale, N.J.: Lawrence Erlbaum Associates, 1978.

Rosch, E. *Typicality effects on judgments of frequency*. Manuscript in preparation, University of California at Berkeley, 1981.

Rosch, E., & Mervis, C. B. Family resemblances: Studies in the internal structure of categories. *Cognitive Psychology*, 1975, *7*, 573–605.

Rosch, E., Simpson, C., & Miller, R. S. Structural bases of typicality effects. *Journal of Experimental Psychology: Human Perception and Performance*, 1976, *2*, 491–502.

Roseman, I. *Cognitive aspects of emotion and emotional behavior*. Paper presented at the annual meeting of the American Psychological Association, New York, Sept. 1979.

Tversky, A. Features of similarity. *Psychological Review*, 1977, *84*, 327–352.

Tversky, A. *Cognitive illusions*. A series of lectures delivered at a symposium of the Cognitive Science Program, Berkeley, 1981.

Tversky, A., & Gati, I. Studies of similarity. In E. Rosch & B. B. Lloyd (Eds.), *Cognition and categorization*. Hillsdale, N.J.: Lawrence Erlbaum Associates, 1978.

Tversky, A., & Johnson, E. J. *Affect and the perception of risk*. Paper delivered at the meeting of the Cognitive Science Society, Berkeley, August 1981.

Tversky, A., & Kahneman, D. Evidential impact of base rates. In D. Kahneman, P. Slovic, & A. Tversky (Eds.), *Judgment under uncertainty: Hueristics and biases*. New York: Cambridge University Press, 1982. (a)

Tversky, A., & Kahneman, D. Judgments of and by representativeness. In D. Kahneman, P. Slovic, & A. Tversky (Eds.), *Judgment under uncertainty: Heuristics and biases*. New York: Cambridge University Press, 1982. (b)

4 On Doubting the Concept 'Concept'

Lila R. Gleitman
University of Pennsylvania

Sharon Lee Armstrong
Wesleyan University

Henry Gleitman
University of Pennsylvania

Recently, psychologists have become interested in concepts and their learning—so interested in fact that the 1981 Jean Piaget Society meetings were wholly given over to this awesome topic. As always, part of the reason for this new-found interest has to do with some apparently positive findings that make a topic investigatable. We believe a central positive finding is the fascinating line of investigation of prototypicality structure as discussed and empirically demonstrated by Eleanor Rosch and her colleagues.[1]

The present paper continues discussion of prototypicality structure and its interpretation in light of some further experimental work we have done (Armstrong, L. Gleitman, & H. Gleitman, in press). We begin by sketching the family resemblance or prototypicality theory of concepts and its classical opponent, the theory of definitions. Thereafter, discussion centers on how the experimental literature, including our own work, can be reconciled with these descriptions of conceptual structure. To hint at the start where we will end up in our conclusions, we believe our experiments suggest that the prototypicality descriptions of concepts, though real, are less of the whole picture than might have been hoped.

---

[1]See Rosch (1973, 1975, 1978), Rosch and Mervis (1975), Caramazza, Hersch, and Torgerson (1976), Rips, Shoben, and Smith (1973) and Tversky and Gati (1978). For review, see Mervis and Rosch (1981) and the elegant general discussions in Smith and Medin (1981).

THEORIES OF CONCEPT STRUCTURE

By *concept* we mean a mental category. We take the lexical items of a language to be linguistic labels for certain concepts.[2] To the extent this is correct, those who are studying concepts and categories and those who are studying lexical semantics overlap considerably in what they study; hence, for present purposes, we make no fine distinction between theories of word meaning and theories of concept structure.[3]

The theories of word meaning divide naturally into two main types: the componential (or featural) and the holistic. Prototype theory has been interpreted both ways, but we begin here with the interpretation that places it among the componential theories; this is because the experimental work has usually been interpreted on a componential, featural, view (though Rosch, 1975, and others, e.g., Smith & Medin, 1981, have considered analogue, imagistic, positions, etc. For detailed discussion, see Armstrong et al., in press).

The componential theories hold that a word is not usually simple semantically, but rather is the lexical label for a bundle of semantic elements (usually called features, properties, or attributes). For example, maybe what we call in English "a bird," is, mentally, an *animal*, that *flies*, has *feathers, wings*, lays *eggs*, and so forth. One-feature words (e.g., perhaps, "male" or "animal") are

---

[2]In detail, we distinguish a number of terms. All the real and projected creatures in the world that fall under a category (concept) are termed the *extension* of that category. The English word "dog," for example, is standardly used to refer to dogs out there (the extensions) and to the category 'dog.' The *category* 'dog' is the mental representation, whatever this will turn out to be, that fixes the conditions under which we use the word "dog." However, whether or not the mental category/concept "properly" fixes the extension of the English word is left open, though this issue comes up in later discussion. It could be that there is a fact of the matter about the extension of the term unknown to the users (i.e., not given as a simple consequence of the structure of the mental representation). For example, on at least some views (cf. Locke, 1690/1968) there are *real essences* ("to be found in the things themselves [p. 288].") and *nominal essences* (that "the mind makes [p. 288]"). Our use of concept/category, then, has to do with the nominal essences, the mental structure of the concept that may or may not properly fix the extension (e.g., our concept of 'gold' may have the consequence for sorting that we pick out only certain yellow metal in the world to call "gold," but the internal structure of the sort of thing we mean to be talking about when we talk about gold may include some of the instances we identified as gold, on the basis of their yellowness, and exclude some other instances that were white in appearance but still—really—gold (for discussion, see Kripke, 1972). As for the *lexical items*, say, "dog," we take them to be the linguistic titles for concepts, or nominal essences. Notationally, we use italics for features, single quotes for concepts, and double quotes for words, in what follows.

[3]Of course, certain concepts are labeled by phrases, so the study of linguistic semantics involves combinatorial rules defined over either the lexical items (if these have no substructure) or over those substructures. But similarly, the theories of concepts also require combinatorial rules. For example, the concept 'All dinosaurs who have turned into oil' is likely conceptually, as well as linguistically complex. So again the appropriate theories of semantic structure and conceptual structure overlap considerably.

FIG. 4.1   The robin, a birdy bird.

just a special case. On the classical or definitional view, a smallish set of such features are individually necessary and severally sufficient to pick out all and only the birds (i.e., the extension of 'bird') from amongst all the things and creatures in the world. Membership in the class is categorical, for all who partake of the right semantic elements are in virtue of that equally birds; and all who do not, are not. No other distinctions among the class members are relevant to their designation as birds. The familiar creature in Fig. 4.1 is a bird because it has the feathers, wings, and so forth. But the peculiar creature in Fig. 4.2 is on the definitional view no more or less a bird than that in Fig. 4.1, again in virtue of exhibiting the stipulated features.

FIG. 4.2   The pelican, a not so birdy bird.

It is reasonable to ask why this theory of word meaning has seemed attractive for so long. There are two main reasons. First is the desire to limit the primitive base, the set of atomic concepts or discriminations with which each human must be assumed to be endowed if concept development is to get off the ground at all. The idea is not to populate neonates' heads with thousands of pregiven concepts to explain how they could learn the myriad words they will learn. Rather, the complex knowledge is built up by recognizing that some simple elements occur together recurrently in the encounters of the sensorium with the external world, and so get bundled together through the mechanism of association. This program, the empiricist program, is usually identified with Locke (1690/1968). It is continued by cognitive psychologists such as Rosch (1975) who holds that it is the "correlated structure of the world," the co-occurrence of the simple concepts in real-world objects, that gives rise to the complex categories. It is the fact that, in our world, what has feathers tends to fly and so forth that gives rise to the complex category 'bird.'

The second main attraction of the classical theory of definitions is that it gives hope of understanding how we reason with words and solve the problem of compositional meaning. (By reasoning with words is meant how, e.g., we determine that "this vixen is a fox" is true, whatever the attendant circumstances. The problem of compositional meaning is related. This is the problem of understanding the phrase and sentence meanings that derive from combining the lexical items.) For example, the definitional theory has, at least programmatically, an explanation of word-to-phrase synonymy; that is, how we know that "bachelor" and "man who has never married" mean about the same thing. It does so by claiming that in the language of the mind "bachelor" explodes into such semantic elements as *man* and *never married,* just the same items that occur in the semantic representation of the phrase. More generally, the definitional theory programmatically has an answer to how we understand the infinitely many phrasal categories (e.g., "all the carpenters who drink three beers a day") that we might not have experienced directly and stored mentally. We do so, on this position, in terms of the underlying simple feature vocabulary, and a combinatorial theory defined on this vocabulary (see Katz & Fodor, 1963; Katz, 1972, for further explication; and Fodor, 1975, for a pessimistic review and a countertheory).

Given the not inconsiderable virtues of this classical theory in describing how we could begin humbly, with a minimum number of innate categories, and yet come to know such complicated things in the long run, the question becomes: Why is there now some doubt as to its validity? The answer is only the difficulty of making it work, in detail. No one has succeeded, after hundreds of years of earnestly trying, in finding the supposed primitive features. For instance, it is not so clear after all that *feathers, wings,* and other features into which "bird" is to explode, are closer to sensation than "bird" (rather, its concept 'bird') itself.

What is worse, it rarely seems to be the case that words *can* be defined as necessary and sufficient lists of such conjectured elements. For example, baby male ostriches are down covered and so have no feathers; they cannot fly; and they do not lay eggs; still, they are birds. Symmetrically, the trouble is that all that glitters is not gold. Finally, the conjectured elements seem not to be a list of properties that simply ''are'' the complex categories; rather, the postulated features seem related to their category in varying ways. For example, birds *are* animals, but they *have* wings, and they *lay* eggs. This suggests that something more complex than a list may be required to describe categories in featural terms (see Collins & Loftus, 1975, for a feature theory that responds to this last defect in some measure).

Recently, there has been interest in a variant decompositional theory, perhaps first alluded to by Wittgenstein (1953), though he might be surprised at some of its modern guises. Wittgenstein took as an important example, challenging the definitional description of words, the category 'game.' He defied anyone to think of a definition in virtue of which all and only the games in the world could be picked out from among all things and events. This being impossible on the face ot it, Wittgenstein conjectured that the word ''game'' named a cluster concept, held together by a variety of gamey attributes only some of which each game instantiated. His analogy was to the structure of family resemblances. It is such a position that Rosch and her colleagues have adapted and refined, and brought into psychology through a series of compelling experimental demonstrations.

We sketch here the properties of such a theory by using the example of the Smith Brothers, of cough drop fame, and their family resemblances (Fig. 4.3). Notice that all these brothers have some Smith features in common—the eyeglasses, the light hair, the bushy moustache, and so forth. But not all Smith

FIG. 4.3   The Smith brothers.

brothers have all the same Smith features. The brother at 11 o'clock is a poor exemplar of Smithness for he has only a few of the attributes and thus may share attributes with the Jones family or perhaps the James family. But the brother in the center is a prototypical Smith because he has all or most of the Smith attributes. One final characteristic of a family resemblance structure does not appear in Fig. 4.3. Namely, there is no sharp boundary delimiting where the Smith family ends and the Jones family starts; rather, the family demarcation line is indistinct. (We have left this detail out of the figure because we do not wish to indulge in public gossip about the Smith family.)

What are the virtues of this new proposal about the organization of human concepts? To the extent the prototype view is still componential, it still gives hope of limiting the primitive basis, the set of innate concepts. Second and most useful, it allows us to account for the (alleged) fact that membership in a concept may be graded; for example, to explain why the robin in Fig. 4.1 seems a birdier bird than the pelican in Fig. 4.2. Keep in mind, however, that the description of reasoning with words, for example understanding analytic truths of the vixen-is-a-fox variety and understanding compositional meaning, become titanically more difficult if the prototype view is accepted. The problem is not so much whether the extensional set coded by the words and phrases is fuzzy rather than exact; perhaps it is. The problem is getting the compositional theory of meaning to work—as we know it does, passing well, for we understand each other when we speak and listen. For example, if the description of the lexical concepts is prototypical (e.g., if for some single instance of use of the word "bird," there is no clear telling which possible *bird* features are intended by the speaker) and you combine "foolish" and "bird" together into the phrase "foolish bird," it is no longer a fixed matter—rather, it is variable—which *foolish* elements and which *bird* elements are intended to be combined. It goes almost without saying that to fix this one could not have stored prototypes for the set of phrasal categories, there being infinitely many of these. (For a discussion of such problems, see Osherson & Smith, 1981).

In light of this extreme difficulty, it seems surprising that psychologists have usually been pleased, rather than depressed, by experimental findings that tend to support a prototype theory of the concepts and the word meanings. Since we speak in whole sentences rather than in single words, the chief desideratum of a theory of word meaning would appear to be promise of a computable description for the infinite phrase and sentence meanings.

THE EXPERIMENTAL EVIDENCE
FOR (AND AGAINST) PROTOTYPE THEORY

On the other hand, a singular virtue of the prototype theory appears to be that it has a good deal of experimental evidence going for it. For example, Table 4.1 shows four everyday superordinate concepts—'fruit,' 'sport,' 'vegetable,' and

TABLE 4.1
Categories, Category Exemplars, and Mean Exemplariness Ratings
for Prototype Categories[a]

| | Rosch, 1973 | Armstrong et al., in press | | |
		(Set A)[b] n = 31	(Set B) n = 32	
Fruit				
Apple	1.3	1.3	Orange	1.1
Strawberry	2.3	2.1	Cherry	1.7
Plum	2.3	2.5	Watermelon	2.9
Pineapple	2.3	2.7	Apricot	3.0
Fig	4.7	5.2	Coconut	4.8
Olive	6.2	6.4	Olive	6.5
Sport				
Football	1.2	1.4	Baseball	1.2
Hockey	1.8	1.8	Soccer	1.6
Gymnastics	2.6	2.8	Fencing	3.5
Wrestling	3.0	3.1	Sailing	3.8
Archery	3.9	4.8	Bowling	4.4
Weight lifting	4.7	5.1	Hiking	4.6
Vegetable				
Carrot	1.1	1.5	Pea	1.7
Celery	1.7	2.6	Spinach	1.7
Asparagus	1.3	2.7	Cabbage	2.7
Onion	2.7	3.6	Radish	3.1
Pickle	4.4	4.8	Peppers	3.2
Parsley	3.8	5.0	Pumpkin	5.5
Vehicle				
Car	1.0	1.0	Bus	1.8
Boat	2.7	3.3	Motorcycle	2.2
Scooter	2.5	4.5	Tractor	3.7
Tricycle	3.5	4.7	Wagon	4.2
Horse	5.9	5.2	Sled	5.2
Skis	5.7	5.6	Elevator	6.2

[a]Adapted from Armstrong, Gleitman, and Gleitman (in press).
[b]Set A items are as in Rosch (1973).

'vehicle'—and some exemplars of each. In one experiment, Rosch (1973) asked subjects to rate such exemplars, for these and many other categories on a 7-point scale, as to how good an instance each exemplar was of its category. As the obtained ratings in the first column of the table show, people respond that apples are very good fruits and deserve a score of 1, while figs or olives are poor examples of fruits and deserve lower ratings. The second column shows a set of ratings given by subjects we have run with the same stimuli, closely replicating this finding from Rosch. The third column shows our replication of the findings with yet another set of exemplars of the same categories.

Most interesting, as Rosch has pointed out, is not just that subjects can and will rate exemplars, but that their ratings are in close agreement, with split-group correlations of subjects' mean rankings generally on the order of .9. Table 4.2, using this same method, shows the split-group correlations we obtained in our replication of these effects.

Note that we have adapted' Rosch's materials directly for comparability and constructed new lists by following her methods, so that the items on the lists share the virtues and warts of the earlier choices. For example, you might object that horses and skis are vehicles by courtesy only, accounting for the graded results. But Rosch (1975) and Komatsu (in preparation) have shown that the graded or fuzzy character of responses will not go away by removal of problematic items nor even by providing strenuous clarifying instructions to the subjects.

More important, the Rosch group has developed a variety of experimental paradigms, and in each the same results keep cropping up. As one more example, subjects respond faster in a verification task to items with high exemplariness ratings than to those with lower ones. That is, reaction time to "A robin is a bird" is faster than reaction time to "An ostrich is a bird" with word frequency controlled across the list of test items. Notice that the definitional view simply cannot accommodate these graded findings, if they are findings about the structure of concepts. So, since they are achieved in paradigm after paradigm including many that we have not mentioned (for a review of the evidence, see Smith & Medin, 1981), we might conclude that something like a family resemblance structure for these everyday concepts has been established beyond reasonable doubt.

However, a necessary extension seemed to Armstrong, Gleitman, and Gleitman (in press) to be missing from these experiments, making them hard to

TABLE 4.2
Question: How Good an Example of the
Category Is _____?

	Split-Group Correlations on Mean Ratings of Items in a Category	
	Set A	Set B
Fruit	1.00**	.94**
Vegetable	.94**	.94**
Sport	.89*	1.00**
Vehicle	1.00**	1.00**

*p < .05.
**p < .01.

interpret. The problem is this. If you believe that certain concepts are nondefinitional just because of graded responses to them in these experimental paradigms, that must be because you believe that definitional (all-or-none) categories, *whose definitions were known to and accepted by the experimental subjects,* would not have yielded these results under these paradigms. But this has never been explicitly shown.

Are there classical concepts to test? Of course. For example, consider the superordinate concept 'odd number.' This seems to have a clear and nonfuzzy definition, namely, *an integer not divisible by 2 without remainder.* No integer seems to sit on the fence, undecided as to whether it is quite even, or perhaps a bit odd. No odd number seems odder than any other odd number. Then in experiments that purport to show 'bird' is prototypical to the extent that responses to "ostrich" and "robin" are unequal, these paradigms should fail on the same reasoning to yield differential responses to "5" and "7" as exemplars of 'odd number.' Similarly, such well-defined concepts as 'geometric figure' and 'female' ought not to yield the response characteristics that were the experimental basis for organizing the concept 'bird' as a family resemblance structure. We performed both the exemplar-rating and the reaction-time experiment described earlier, using in addition to the everyday concepts these well-defined concepts and some of their exemplars.

Table 4.3 shows what happened when the subjects were asked to rate two sets of exemplars each, of the categories 'even number.' 'odd number,' 'plane geometry figure,' and 'female' on the usual 7-point scale. Note that for the well-defined items we were here asking subjects, e.g., to distinguish *among* the odd numbers, *for* oddity, and common sense asserts that one cannot do so. But the subjects could, and did. They didn't even raise objections to the task. Moreover, as Table 4.4 shows, split-group correlations on mean ratings of items in these categories were about as powerful as for the everyday concepts described earlier[4] (see also Wanner, 1979, for related results concerning prime numbers, using a different paradigm).

As if this were not enough, we also ran a version of the reaction time to verification task with these same stimulus materials, again using items equated for word frequency. For example, subjects were asked to verify, as quickly as possible, the truth of sentences such as "Seven is an odd number," "A waitress is a female," and so forth (see Table 4.5). Again we found an effect of exemplariness on these reaction times, independent of word frequency, for the well-defined categories just as for the allegedly prototypic ones (see Table 4.6).

---

[4]In retrospect, the choice of 'odd number' was a mistake. In interviews our subjects later told us that they sometimes took the liberty of interpreting 'odd number' to mean 'strange number.' Such ambiguities lower correlations obtained in this kind of study for obvious reasons (as shown formally in McCloskey & Glucksberg, 1978). Notice that the correlations for 'even number' are in the expected range.

TABLE 4.3
Categories, Category Exemplars, and Mean Exemplariness Ratings
for Well-Defined Categories[a]

Set A (n = 31)		Set B (n = 32)	
Even number			
4	1.1	2	1.0
8	1.5	6	1.7
10	1.7	42	2.6
18	2.6	1000	2.8
34	3.4	34	3.1
106	3.9	806	3.9
Odd number			
3	1.6	7	1.4
7	1.9	11	1.7
23	2.4	13	1.8
57	2.6	9	1.9
501	3.5	57	3.4
447	3.7	91	3.7
Female			
Mother	1.7	Sister	1.8
Housewife	2.4	Ballerina	2.0
Princess	3.0	Actress	2.1
Waitress	3.2	Hostess	2.7
Policewoman	3.9	Chairwoman	3.4
Comedienne	4.5	Cowgirl	4.5
Plane geometry figure			
Square	1.3	Square	1.5
Triangle	1.5	Triangle	1.4
Rectangle	1.9	Rectangle	1.6
Circle	2.1	Circle	1.3
Trapezoid	3.1	Trapezoid	2.9
Ellipse	3.4	Ellipse	3.5

[a]Adapted from Armstrong et al., (in press).

Summarizing, exemplariness ratings and differential reaction times to verification often are as reliable and as powerful for well-defined, even mathematical, concepts as they are for the everyday concepts that seem to intuition to be ill-
defined or prototypic. Moreover, this is not just a case of asking a silly question
and getting a silly answer, for this latter explanation cannot account for why the
subjects agreed with each other in rating and in reacting.

What can we conclude from these strange outcomes? Many psychologists we
have talked to conclude that Wittgenstein's position was more general than he
supposed—that, psychologically speaking, odd numbers as well as birds and

TABLE 4.4
Question: How Good an Example of the
Category is _____?

*Split-Group Correlations on Mean
Ratings of Items in a Category*

	Set A	Set B
Even number	.94**	.94**
Odd number	.81*	.80
Female	.83*	1.00**
Plane geometry figure	.94**	.89*

$*p < .05.$
$**p < .01.$

TABLE 4.5
Categories and Category Exemplars Used in Sentence
Verification Study[a]

	Good Exemplars	Poorer Exemplars
Prototype categories		
Fruit	Orange, banana	Fig, coconut
Sport	Baseball, hockey	Fishing, archery
Vegetable	Peas, spinach	Onion, mushroom
Vehicle	Bus, ambulance	Wagon, skis
Well-defined categories		
Even number	8, 22	30,18
Odd number	7, 13	15, 23
Female	Aunt, ballerina	Widow, waitress
Plane geometry figure	Rectangle, triangle	Ellipse, trapezoid

[a]Under each rubric (e.g., fruit, good exemplar), high-frequency exemplars are listed first, low-frequency ones second (from Armstrong et al., in press). Note that frequency counts for the integers chosen were taken from the Kucera and Francis listings (1967).

vegetables are represented mentally by family resemblance structures. We reject this conclusion. We believe that many human reactions to the concept 'odd number' (such as the fact that none are divisible by 2 without remainder, that one can find whether a given number belongs to the class simply by looking at the rightmost digit within it, that 9 no more and no less than 39 is odd, and so on) hang together on the usual, arithmetic, definition of the concept. The new finding (that odd numbers can be graded according to their oddity) threatens these myriad, consistent, old facts as forming the basis for description of the mental representation. For coherence, we believe the threat should be rejected. It cannot

TABLE 4.6
Verification Times for Good and Poorer
Exemplars of Several Prototype and Well-
Defined Categories (in msec)[a]

	Good Exemplars	Poorer Exemplars
Prototype categories		
Fruit	903	1125
Sport	892	941
Vegetable	1127	1211
Vehicle	989	1228
Well-defined categories		
Even number	1073	1132
Odd number	1088	1090
Female	1032	1156
Plane geometry figure	1104	1375

[a]From Armstrong et al. (in press).

be rejected by saying the experimental outcomes are not factual. Rather, we will end up by saying the graded responses to odd numbers derive from a mental source other than the mental structure of that concept. Briefly, we will distinguish between *concept structure* and *exemplariness*.

Note that the foregoing is not any kind of claim about the structure of such everyday concepts as 'fruit.' Rather, we have a general result that tells us the graded results are achieved regardless of the structure of the concept tested. To assent to this, readers need only believe that the structure of 'odd number' and the structure of 'fruit' differ from one another. If this is agreed to be so, and it is agreed also that subjects know and organize these two concepts differently, then it seems to follow that a paradigm that cannot distinguish between them is not describing the structure of concepts very satisfactorily. We conclude, thus far, that we are back at square one, not only in determining the structure of 'odd number' but also in determining *experimentally* the structure of 'fruit.' This is because the experiments previously alleged to display the structure of 'fruit' fail to distinguish among concept structures, and so tell us no more about 'fruit' than about 'oddness.' All issues again seem to be up for grabs.

However, our subjects and Rosch's subjects were orderly in their response styles under these paradigms, so they must be telling us something. If not the structure of concepts, what are they telling us about? As a step toward finding out, we now asked a new pool of subjects to tell us straight out whether membership in the class was graded or categorical for a variety of the definitional and putatively prototypic concepts. We asked them, essentially, whether you could be more or less of a bird, or more or less odd an odd number, or whether each was an all-or-none matter as the classical theory would have it. The summary of the results appears in Table 4.7.

We found that people always say for the mathematical concepts and usually say for 'female' that membership in the category is all-or-none and that it is absurd to think otherwise. Rather more surprisingly, they say about half the time that membership in the everyday categories is all-or-none. In light of these assertions, we now asked these selfsame subjects to rank exemplars of these categories, as the earlier subjects had done. That is, the selfsame subjects who said it was absurd to say some odd numbers were odder and some fruits fruitier than others were now asked to rate exemplars of these categories on the usual 7-point scale.

Table 4.8 shows that these subjects were again able to provide the exemplariness ratings. The leftmost column shows the responses for the Experiment 1 subjects (redisplaying the relevant results from Tables 4.1 and 4.3 for comparison) and only those responses from the current experiment that represent ratings for categories that the individual new subjects said were all-or-none. That is, the ratings for some subject are included in this table if and only if, for the category in question, he previously asserted that it was well defined. As Table 4.8 shows, not 5 minutes after saying it was absurd to suppose the concept 'odd number' or 'vegetable' was graded, these subjects rated odd numbers and vegetables and gave graded responses. To be sure, inspection of the numbers in this table reveals that the subjects genuflected slightly to their prior responses. They now used less

TABLE 4.7
Subjects' Responses When Asked: "Does It
Make Sense to Rate Items in This Category for
Degree of Membership in the Category?"
($n = 21$)

	Percentage of Subjects Who Said NO
Prototype categories	
Fruit	43
Sport	71
Vegetable	33
Vehicle	24
Well-defined categories	
Even number	100
Odd number	100
Female	86
Plane geometry figure	100

[a]From Armstrong et al. (in press).

TABLE 4.8
Mean Exemplariness Ratings[a]

	Experiment I All Subjects		Experiment III Subjects who said NO (out of 21)	
Prototype Categories	n	X̄	n	X̄
Fruit				
Apple	31	1.3	9	1.3
Strawberry		2.1		1.7
Plum		2.5		1.9
Pineapple		2.7		1.3
Fig		5.2		3.3
Olive		6.4		4.2
Vegetable				
Carrot	31	1.5	7	1.1
Celery		2.6		1.1
Asparagus		2.7		1.4
Onion		3.6		3.1
Pickle		4.8		4.1
Parsley		5.0		3.1
Sport				
Football	31	1.4	15	1.1
Hockey		1.8		1.5
Gymnastics		2.8		1.6
Wrestling		3.1		1.9
Archery		4.8		2.5
Weight lifting		5.1		2.6
Vehicle				
Car	31	1.0	5	1.0
Boat		3.3		1.6
Scooter		4.5		3.8
Tricycle		4.7		2.6
Horse		5.2		2.8
Skis		5.6		5.2
Even number				
4	31	1.1	21	1.0
8		1.5		1.0
10		1.7		1.1
18		2.6		1.2
34		3.4		1.4
106		3.9		1.7

(continued)

TABLE 4.8
(*Continued*)

Prototype Categories	Experiment I All Subjects		Experiment III Subjects who said NO (out of 21)	
	n	X̄	n	X̄
Odd number				
3	31	1.6	21	1.0
7		1.9		1.0
23		2.4		1.3
57		2.6		1.5
501		3.5		1.8
447		3.7		1.9
Female				
Mother	31	1.7	18	1.1
Housewife		2.4		1.8
Princess		3.0		2.1
Waitress		3.2		2.4
Policewoman		3.9		2.9
Comedienne		4.5		3.1
Plane geometry figure				
Square	31	1.3	21	1.0
Triangle		1.5		1.0
Rectangle		1.9		1.0
Circle		2.1		1.2
Trapezoid		3.1		1.5
Ellipse		3.4		2.1

[a]From Armstrong et al. (in press).

of the rating scale than did the original subjects. That is, they acted as though, even if some odd numbers are odder than others, no odd number is so awfully unodd as to deserve a rating of "7." Nonetheless, what is central is that subjects still gave graded responses, the rank orders of the ratings agree very closely between the first experiment and this new one, and the subjects still agreed with each other about how to do so (for extensive further discussion of these findings, see Armstrong et al., in press).

ATTEMPTING TO DESCRIBE THE CONCEPTS

So again we must ask how to interpret these results. One response is to claim that subjects are happy to contradict themselves if it pleases their experimental masters. This seems unlikely to us. Rather, we believe the subjects responded differently because two different questions were asked. It is one thing to think about membership *in* a category, quite another to judge a good exemplar *of* a category. Exemplariness, in short, is not the same as class membership, a distinction that we discuss in more detail later. Here, we conclude that what has been shown in the prototypicality experiments over and over again is that exemplars differ as to how well they exemplify some concept, and people agree with each other in making this judgment. But the structure of the concept does not much affect subjects' abilities to tell good exemplars from less good ones (though, to be sure, the *bases* for such judgments differ from concept to concept), nor are the exemplar ratings the conceptual structure itself.

Now the first likely hypothesis we considered, which could account for subjects' ability to think about exemplars, on the one hand, and to reason about concepts using definitions, on the other hand, would be to grant them dual representations for some concepts—one representation definitional, the other prototypic. Note that according to this view, it is the same concept that has the two representations. As Landau (1982) has recently shown, it often seems useful to have the two representations.

For example, suppose you want to find a grandmother in Yankee Stadium. It pays to have a workable representation of likely grandmother candidates for these rough identification purposes. You ought to look around for a gray-haired lady with a twinkle in her eye, preferably one dispensing brownies. This is faster than making geneological inquiries. But to reason about the concept 'grandmother' (e.g., to decide whether somebody's grandmother might be a virgin), you had better refer to a representation that stipulates that grandmothers are mothers of parents. (For discussion, see Armstrong et al., in press; also Miller, 1977).

It is even possible to guess where the identification function comes from, in language learning. When someone is first introduced to you as "grandmother," she hardly wears her definitional structure on her sleeve. The only pro tem move, it seems, is to store that this word was used to refer to the kindly gray-haired lady (and hence might mean—including humanly natural concepts only!—either 'kindly,' 'gray-haired,' 'lady,' 'elderly,' even 'grandmother') and wait for dissociating circumstances to choose among them as the true meaning (e.g., it might be helpful to meet little Howie Gabor's grandma, Zsa Zsa, in the current case). Presumably, the set of wrong choices, ordered according to the frequency with which they were paired in experience with the right one, now hang on to be used for rough-and-ready identification purposes. The "real" description would be used to find the lexical and phrasal entailments.

Despite what we think are some tempting aspects, we now hastily back off from the dual theory of concept organization. One reason is that dual theories have the disagreeable property of being able to explain their failures by referring to their partners. At worst, they become like the old story of the man who said that between his brother and himself they knew everything. But every time you asked this man a question, he responded that this was the part his brother knew.

The serious issue is that we do not relieve the prototype theory of its various woes by saying that in some cases and for some concepts there lurks a definition, usable when convenient. The real problem in our opinion is that the prototype theories say no less but no more than that all concepts have central and peripheral instances. Even if all concepts are organized so as to reflect this common-sensical fact (a fact about objects in the world, not necessarily about the concepts under which they are organized), what is to distinguish *among* the extensional sets and among the concepts themselves? If *any* featural account is to describe the concepts, the first big job is to identify the particular features that are relevant to each one, so as to pry them apart.

For example, referring back to Table 4.3, notice that apparently the *smallest* even number is taken to be the prototypical even number, by and large. But looking at the same table, it is not the case that the smallest female is taken to be the prototypical female. Size is not relevant as a feature for 'female,' despite the fact that it has some cue validity for this category (i.e., at least for mammals, females tend to be smaller). As a matter of fact, a sheer sexism metric organizes the ratings of females, as is also easy to see from the tabulated results. One problem here is that these properties, which predict the ratings, seem tangential to our understanding of these concepts. A second problem is that each concept seems to require a new set of features: The list of all required features threatens to be as large or larger than the list of lexical items themselves. If so, a featural substrate (besides being unobservable and, on known techniques, uninferrable) does not economize on the list of base (innate) discriminations.

Restating our position, neither the definitional nor the prototypical feature view is attractive unless we can specify the features and the latitude of allowed variability on each feature for each concept. This has been remarkably difficult to do, whether the features are neat or fuzzy.

Most important of all, the problem of feature theories is that the lists of attributes never seem to add up to the concept itself. This is shown by the fact that subjects are willing to have most of their cherished attributes removed, while maintaining that the instance is in the category, all the same. As one example, Alice maintained correctly that she remained 'a little girl,' and not 'a serpent' despite massive changes in her superficial size and shape, and despite Pigeon's argument to the contrary (''I've seen a good many little girls in my time, but never *one* with a such a neck as that!''). Similarly, the man on the street has no trouble agreeing that an albino, tame, three-legged tiger is a tiger all the same, despite his abnormalities. Certainly he is less prototypical, but what keeps him a tiger? Moreover, as Quine (1960) has pointed out in a different context, not all the features (of most tigers) in the world can distinguish between 'tiger' and 'undetached tiger parts.' When one of these descriptions is veridical, so is the other. Only to the extent that the features are bound together as 'tiger' under one description and not under the other can we distinguish between them. But if there is an essence of tiger, distinct from the featural content, what share of the burden of explanation does the latter successfully bear? This question is the one for which the features were devised in the first place, and they fail to answer to it.

Symmetrically, addition of features does not simply change the categorial assignment of an exemplar, nor the description of the category itself. As usual, the best demonstration of these problems comes from Lewis Carroll. Recall the Queen's gardeners, who were asked to plant red rose bushes, but had planted white ones instead. They attempted to repair the error by painting the blooms, but Alice (and we) know that adding the feature *red* does not make white rose bushes into red rose bushes—only, red white rose bushes.

Since neither adding nor subtracting features affects the categorial essence of things in any simple way, it is not clear that feature descriptions are the concept descriptions. We have argued such difficulties of feature theories elsewhere (see again Armstrong et al., in press) as have many others (particularly, Fodor, 1975, 1981; Fodor, Garrett, Walker, & Parkes, 1980). Thus, we do not argue here for the definitional view over the prototype view, nor the reverse. Rather, we believe it is hard to make good on *any* featural description. This is part of the reason why we reject the tempting dual theory, which has the double trouble of requiring two feature lists, neither of which can currently be discovered or exhaustively described.

ALTERNATIVE VIEWS

Since the feature theories have many troubles, perhaps we should give holistic theories their chance. These theories urge, for example, that ''grandmother'' is mentally represented as 'grandmother.' This immediately resolves the difficulty of finding the component features, for on this view 'grandmother' is an unanalyzable Gestalt. But notice that the cost of this move is high indeed. It seems to involve repopulating the neonate's head with a huge set of innately given concepts, as Fodor has again pointed out.

Let us be clear about why this at least seems to be the cost. One way of explaining the myriad lexical concepts is on empiricist principles. The learner is endowed with the simplest discriminations—in fact, the atomic sensory attributes—and he builds the complex ones by combining these, by association. But if lexical concepts are not after all feature combinations, the primitive base becomes approximately the set of concepts one can ever, in principle, discriminate and encode lexically. This position avoids total absurdity because it need not assert that there are *no* lexical items with substructure (''grandmother'' has substructure, if any lexical concept has) and also because it acknowledges that phrasal concepts are constructional. Nevertheless, the idea of hundreds of thousands of primitive discriminations is somewhat repugnant.

Consequently, it is possible to believe that the psychological study of concepts is on the wrong track. Possibly, there is no spoor where we are looking. We believe there is room to wonder whether there is a general psychological domain encompassing "all concepts" parallel to, say, a general psychological domain of "all sensory experiences," "all emotions," and so forth. Perhaps when we refer generally to *concepts* and their development, we are referring to a general theory of mental organization that exists only in our collective professional imagination.

Let us press this pessimism about studying "concepts in general" or "meanings in general" a few steps further. We turn to the uncomfortable possibility that in the matter of concepts there may be less in common among individuals than is often supposed. Many philosophers, chief among them Weinstein (personal communications), have led us to wonder whether our usually successful communication is explainable only by granting that members of a linguistic community necessarily share most of the same concepts as well as most of the same words. Less than this might do, after all, for successful communication. The speakers need only more or less share views about which words refer to which things. It does not necessarily follow that, because this can be done, what individuals have in mind to pick out these referents (i.e., what the concepts are) must be the same across persons.

An example of the problems here comes from work being done by Landau and L. Gleitman on the sighted vocabulary of children blind from birth. It turns out that blind children say such words as "look" and "see" at the time usual for sighted children, namely before the third birthday. And the mothers of blind children often use these words with them in fairly normal ways (i.e., to mean 'see with the eyes') just because it is hard to remember not to do so. So it turns out that the mother may be holding a doll and will say to the blind child, "Look at this doll." And the blind child then walks over to the mother, takes the doll, manipulates it manually, and answers, "I see." We have shown that the child's intention in using "look" or "see" is 'explore by hand,' but the mother's meaning does not change. Yet, for some time, there seems to be no trouble in communicating.

Recognition that there is a partial mismatch of concepts in mind comes late and as something of a shock to both parties. The mother is astonished when Landau tests the children on such commands as "look up," and the child raises her hands instead of her face. The mother is astonished further when the blind child responds differently when told to "touch" the doll (whereupon she taps or scratches it) and when told to "look at" it (whereupon she explores it manually). The blind child, in turn, comes late to the realization that the mother is using the sighted terms differently from herself. This happens, for example, when the two, along with sighted others, are looking at family photographs. Unable now to see by exploration of the various flat papers any distinction that others are making between pictures of Mommy and pictures of a xylophone, the blind child finally asks, "Mommy, because my eyes don't work?" Up until these catastrophic events, blind learner and sighted caretaker seem hardly ever to have reflected that they are using the same words to code partly different concepts. This is presumably because the two different concepts both mapped almost identically onto scenes, activities, objects, or events in the world.

Such varying matches of the concepts to the words by different people seem to be all around us. We can discuss iron with metallurgists and rabbits with biologists, but it is no more than sand in your eye to assert that experts and laymen have the same concepts of 'iron' or of 'rabbits.' All that is required for communication, perhaps, is that each of us have some function from the word "rabbit" to the world that picks out the same or mostly the same referents. But it does not have to be the same function.

To the extent this might be so, one might wonder why we don't all mean wildly different things by all the words we are saying, resulting in such major breakdowns of communication as Alice observed in Wonderland. Maybe you recall the confrontation between Alice and the Queen, in the garden playing croquet. They disagreed intractably as to whether upside-down flamingos could be mallets or whether rolled-up hedgehogs could be croquet balls. On the empiricist story, what keeps communication in hand is just that we are *not* in Wonderland. In our own land, nature so carves the world as to make certain inductions about the conceptual distinctions obvious to the point of irresistability. But such a position has trouble explaining why we do not encode the rabbits as 'undetached rabbit parts,' as we previously noted. A different claim for how we adjudicate among such logically possible choices might be a store of richly specififed innate concepts (or else what might come to much the same thing, a rich and highly constrained inductive machinery, rather than an open-minded one) that we hold in common in virtue of our neurophysiology and that misleading circumstances can hardly distort. For instance, it is not so radical to suppose that we are biased to code whole objects, not collections of parts.

To illustrate this view, we again consider the blind language learner. We have so far emphasized that the blind child *differs* from the sighted mother in what she intends by "look" and "see." The blind child means 'apprehend by manual exploration,' while the sighted mother means 'apprehend by visual exploration.'[5] But these descriptions are even more remarkable for their sameness than for their differences. Both parties use "look" and "see" as perceptual terms. Both have other expressions such as "touch" and "set eyes on" that refer to

---

[5]Of course the mother has other interpretations for "see" and the child might too. "See" sometimes means 'perceive' (without reference to any modality). The sighted terms are also used metaphorically, as when the mothers says to the blind child clad in overalls, "You look like a kangaroo today." Landau and Gleitman's work with blind children and blindfolded sighted controls suggests that these latter interpretations are developmentally late. Whatever these developmental facts, the important point here is that there is a modality-specific meaning for both the adult and the learner. The mismatch is between these.

'contact, as opposed to apprehension' in their differing dominant modalities. It seems that the explanation for the similarities, in the face of vastly different encounters with the world, must be a richly specified, modality independent, bias about perceptual representation.

Where we have made progress in studying concept acquisition and where we believe significant progress is likely to be forthcoming is with respect to such richly structured perceptual and conceptual domains. Examples that come to mind are the study of number (e.g., Gelman & Gallistel, 1980), objects (e.g., in the infancy work of Spelke, 1982), speech (e.g., Eimas, Siqueland, Jusczyk, & Vigorito, 1971), space (e.g., Landau, Spelke, & Gleitman, 1981), and face recognition (Carey, 1978). Then of course there is the study of language acquisition by a large group of investigators who derive their theoretical framework from the thinking of N. Chomsky (for a review, see Gleitman & Wanner, 1982). Discoveries concerning these conceptual domains suggest that nothing so simple as a featural, listlike structure of any kind offers an adequate description of human organization or functioning in any of them. Rather, in each domain, the units, their patterning, their development, their environment dependence, are all different and all remarkably complex. The findings in these areas, taken together, suggest that no single theory of concept acquisition is likely to account for them all.

Outside the rule and representation systems that subserve these specific domains, how are we to think about the everyday concepts at large (e.g., concepts such as 'rhubarb,' 'wimple,' and 'aardvark')? Perhaps we are fooling ourselves if we believe they are organized by a general theory of categorization or concept development that will subsume and therefore illuminate them. Concepts like 'rhubarb,' as these are mentally stored, are likely ad hoc derivatives of experiential vagaries, without clear fundamental interest to psychology. And if we do trouble to do the required studies of 'rhubarb' and 'wimple' so as to understand them and even find a single theory that covers both, this theory is likely to require radical revision when we decide—as we then must—to study the 'aardvarks' too. Surely the simple statement that all have a central tendency (defined on different elements, in each case) is too impoverished and undifferentiated to describe our mental life.

SUMMARY

We have argued there is little hope that we can describe conceptual development as a matter of joining together the rock-bottom sensory elements of experience; hence, one serious reason for believing in a definitional view of concepts is diluted. Second, we tried to argue that an alternative prototype theory, which would preserve some of the virtues of such a theory (viz., limiting the primitive base), fails to provide a ready basis for explaining lexical and phrasal entailments. Worse, we presented findings that suggest the prototype view has not been demonstrated experimentally. This was because nonprototypical concepts yielded the same experimental outcomes as allegedly prototypic concepts, suggesting that current experimental lines are consistent with *any* theory of the concepts. Moreover, we argued that the descriptions of known domains offered by prototype findings are often inadequate and tangential descriptions of these domains. (As one more example, consider the theory of language that might emerge if it were constructed on the basis of subjects' rankings of the prototypicality of sentences.)

In later comments, we argued that some of the confusion in identifying the real concepts resides in the fact that for the mass of them we may be communicating in the presence of differing internal representations for them, deriving from our slightly differing experiences in the world. The greater the difference among experiences, the greater the differences among such ordinary language concepts. For experts and novices, for those who confront the world visually and those who cannot, experience has been materially different, with the consequence of materially different mental contents and structures. Should one fall down a rabbit hole, one may find oneself in a world where many old concepts are no longer serviceable. To the extent this view is defensible, communication is successful insofar as we agree to call the same things by the same names, whatever their varying descriptions (cf. Kripke, 1971, 1972, for discussions).

But symmetrically, we asserted that such conceptual anarchy could not be the whole story or else we would really be in Wonderland, unable to understand each other any better than Alice and Humpty Dumpty. To find out what we importantly have in common and where we are all the same by way of conceptions, we argued that the promising route is by examination of the richly structured domains, singly and in great detail.

In conclusion, we merely recall that a host of thinkers from Aristotle to Wittgenstein, from Katz to Fodor, from Rosch to Osherson and Smith, have shown us that there is enormous difficulty in explicating so simple and concrete a concept as 'bird.' They have shown that the difficulty becomes greater by orders of magnitude when our theories are confronted with the requirement to describe an abstract functional concept like 'game.' We believe psychologists are more than a little overexuberant to suppose it will be easier to explicate the concept 'concept.'

ACKNOWLEDGMENTS

A number of colleagues read and commented on prior drafts of this paper, as well as aided in the conception of the whole work. The present version is based on Armstrong, Gleitman, & Gleitman (in press). We thank B. Armstrong, J. Fodor, J. Hochberg, F. Irwin, B. Landau, E. Newport, E. Shipley, E. Spelke, and E. Wanner for their generous help.

Particularly, Spelke helped us search *Alice in Wonderland* for its delightful insights into word and concept structure. All of us, but especially Lila Gleitman, thank Scott Weinstein not only for innumerable readings of our work on concepts but for teaching us whatever we know about semantics. A grant from the National Foundation for the March of Dimes to Lila Gleitman and Barbara Landau helped to support the work discussed herein and the writing of this report; we thank the foundation for this support. A postdoctoral fellowship from the National Institutes of Health to Sharon Armstrong also helped to support this work, and we thank this agency as well.

REFERENCES

Armstrong, S. L., Gleitman, L. R., & Gleitman, H. What some concepts might not be. *Cognition,* in press.

Caramazza, A., Hersch, H., & Torgerson, W. S. Subjective structures and operations in semantic memory. *Journal of Verbal Learning and Verbal Behavior,* 1976, *15,* 103–118.

Carey, S. A case study: Face recognition. In E. Walker (Ed.), *Explorations in the biology of language.* Montgomery, Vt.: Bradford Books, 1978.

Carroll, L. *Alice's Adventures in Wonderland,* 1862.

Collins, A., & Loftus, E. F. A spreading activation theory of semantic processing. *Psychological Review,* 1975, *82*(6), 407–428.

Eimas, P. D., Siqueland, E. R., Jusczyk, P., & Vigorito, J. Speech perception in infants. *Science,* 1971, *171,* 303–306.

Fodor, J. A. *The language of thought.* Cambridge, Mass.: Harvard University Press, 1975.

Fodor, J. A. *Representations.* Cambridge, Mass.: MIT Press, 1981.

Fodor, J. A., Garrett, M. F., Walker, E. T., & Parkes, C. Against definitions. *Cognition,* 1980, *8*(3), 1–105.

Gelman, R., & Gallistel, C. R. *The child's concept of number.* Cambridge, Mass.: Harvard University Press, 1980.

Gleitman, L. R., & Wanner, E. Language acquisition: The state of the state of the art. In E. Wanner & L. R. Gleitman (Eds.), *Language acquisition: The state of the art.* New York: Cambridge University Press, 1982.

Katz, J. J. *Semantic theory.* New York: Harper & Row, 1972.

Katz, J. J., & Fodor, J. A. The structure of a semantic theory. *Language,* 1963, *39,* 170–210.

Kripke, S. Identity and necessity. In M. K. Munitz (Ed.), *Identity and individuation.* New York: New York University Press, 1971.

Kripke, S. Naming and necessity. In D. Davidson & G. Harman (Eds.), *Semantics of natural language.* Dordrecht, Holland: Reidel, 1972.

Kucera, H. K., & Francis, W. N. *Computational analysis of present-day American English.* Providence, R.I.: Brown University Press, 1967.

Landau, B. Will the real grandmother please stand up? *Journal of Psycholinguistic Research,* 1982, *11*(2).

Landau, B., Spelke, E., & Gleitman, H. Spatial representation in a blind child. *Science,* 1981.

Locke, J. *An essay concerning human understanding.* Cleveland, Ohio: World Publishing Co., 1968. (Originally published, 1690.)

McCloskey, M., & Glucksberg, S. Natural categories: Well defined or fuzzy sets? *Memory & Cognition,* 1978, *6*(4), 462–472.

Mervis, C. B., & Rosch, E. Categorization of natural objects. *Annual Review of Psychology*, 1981, *32*, 89–115.

Miller, G. A. Practical and lexical knowledge. In P. N. Johnson-Laird & P. C. Wason (Eds.), *Thinking: Readings in cognitive science*. New York: Cambridge University Press, 1977.

Osherson, D. N., & Smith, E. F. On the adequacy of prototype theory as a theory of concepts. *Cognition*, 1981, *9*(1), 35–58.

Quine, W. V. O. *Word and object*. Cambridge, Mass.: MIT Press, 1960.

Rips, L. J., Shoben, E. J., & Smith, E. E. Semantic distance and the verification of semantic relations. *Journal of Verbal Learning and Verbal Behavior*, 1973, *12*, 1–20.

Rosch, E. On the internal structure of perceptual and semantic categories. In T. E. Moore (Ed.), *Cognitive development and the acquisition of language*. New York: Academic Press, 1973.

Rosch, E. Cognitive representations of semantic categories. *Journal of Experimental Psychology: General*, 1975, *104*, 192–233.

Rosch, E. Principles of categorization. In E. Rosch & B. B. Lloyd (Eds.), *Cognition and categorization*. Hillsdale, N.J.: Lawrence Erlbaum Associates, 1978.

Rosch, E., & Mervis, C. B. Family resemblances: Studies in the internal structure of categories. *Cognitive Psychology*, 1975, *7*, 573–605.

Smith, E. E., & Medin, D. L. *Categories and concepts*. Cambridge, Mass.: Harvard University Press, 1981.

Spelke, E. S. Perceptual knowledge of objects in infancy. In J. Mehler, M. Garrett, & E. Walker (Eds.), *Perspectives in mental representation*. Hillsdale, N.J.: Lawrence Erlbaum Associates, 1982.

Tversky, A., & Gati, I. Studies of similarity. In E. Rosch & B. B. Lloyd (Eds.), *Cognition and categorization*. Hillsdale, N.J.: Lawrence Erlbaum Associates, 1978.

Wanner, E. *False identification of prime numbers*. Paper presented at the annual meeting of The Society for Philosophy and Psychology, New York, N.Y., March, 1979.

Wittgenstein, L. *Philosophical investigations*. New York: Macmillan, 1953.

5 There Is One Classification System with a Long Developmental History

Edith D. Neimark
*Rutgers, The State University
of New Jersey*

Rosch (this volume) makes the provocative assertion that there are two classification systems—prototypical and logical—each of which has its origins in infancy and an independent course of development thereafter. Unfortunately, she does not go on to support the assertion but, rather, shifts to a different question concerning the influence of one system upon reasoning.

That there should be two independent classification systems, each applicable to the same instances and serving the same cognitive function, running along in parallel throughout life seems at first blush to make no sense. What useful purpose could be served by having two different systems, both applicable in a given context but capable of leading to different consequences? If there is a Creator and if She created us in Her image, then She must be a Neurotic to create us with so inescapable a basis for conflict in decision making. If, on the other hand, the human mind is a product of evolution, what kind of selection process would select for two parallel but different systems? Because they are not redundant safeguards such as two eyes, ears, kidneys, lungs, and so on but, are rather, potentially competing systems, a serious theory incorporating the two parallel systems would seem to need, in addition, a selection and control system for adjudicating between the two classification systems (much like a central commisure bridging the right and left hemispheres of the brain: some homunculus or homuncula). Such a theory is too strong a violation of the laws of parsimony to be accepted without a struggle. This chapter represents my attempt at the requisite struggle.

Empirical evidence for the existence of two classification systems is now—thanks in large part to the efforts of Rosch and her co-workers—too compelling to be denied. The theoretical problem is to account for that evidence. Rosch suggests that each system is a type of organization characterized by its own psychological laws. In the discussion that follows I suggest several alternative means of reducing the two proposed systems to one general set of principles with other systems constituting modifications of or approximations to it. Basically, I offer a defense of the traditional view that logical classification is the most comprehensive, general, optimal approach to classification.

WHY ONE SYSTEM IS PREFERRED
AND HOW IT MAY BE ATTAINED

Gleitman's (this volume) statement: "Maybe when we meet to study and discuss *concepts* and their development, we are discussing a general theory of mental organization that exists only in our collective professional imagination" forces us to face up to our strong implicit preference for a monistic theory. When confronted with conflicting explanations for what we believe to be phenomena subsumable under a unitary principle we tend to invoke the tired allegory of the blind men and the elephant. It is probably apt in this instance, but it also illustrates a firm implicit conviction that *there is an elephant*. Therefore, let us consider what the elephant assumption might impose by way of requirements for a psychological theory.

The strong form of the elephant assumption requires that a general theory—in this instance, of classification—applies: (1) to all concept classes of (2) all persons in (3) all contexts at (4) all times and development stages. These are powerful requirements; existing evidence suggests that they are not met. For example, Gleitman (this volume) presents compelling evidence that within individual subjects the same class—odd number—appears to have an Aristotelian structure in one context and a prototypical structure in another. Rosch (this volume) comes to a similar conclusion in her exploration of conditions under which reference point reasoning occurs. How is this evidence to be interpreted? One possibility is to consider one of a family of weaker elephant assumptions generated by removing, one at a time, the four previously mentioned constraints, then removing pairs, and so forth. The data just cited, for example, might suggest removal of the context constraint. Another approach is to examine the criteria for identification of differences in phenomena demanding different theoretical explanation (i.e., what properly constitutes "different systems").

The usually accepted criterion for distinguishing different phenomena as *truly* different is that they cannot be accounted for by the same explanatory principle (i.e., they are not reducible to the same class). In the case of classification and concept attainment there has been little searching, critical examination of proposed theories in relation to their data base. This is not a purely academic point because over the long course of experimental study of classification the directing questions, experimental paradigms, and implicit assumptions have changed so much that it seems impossible to establish a common universe of discourse to encompass all the existing evidence. The trend among contemporary theorists is to differentiate concepts with respect to their assumed structure, for example, whether the class is defined with respect to similarity to some central best exemplar (a prototype) or whether or not it possesses the necessary and sufficient criterial property required of a logical class. By far the best critical comparison of structural theories is presented by Smith and Medin (1981) who consider three theoretical views, one of which has three possible interpretations. After detailed scrutiny of the three views they conclude that the views are not so clearly different as first appeared (e.g., some alternatives of their probabilistic view meld, and the modified probabilistic view is quite similar to the exemplar view). They do, however, conclude that the classical (Rosch's logical and Gleitman's Aristotelian) view must be rejected. Although the Smith and Medin analysis follows from their organizing principles, I personally find it hard to accept those organizing principles. The structural criterion does not seem to be adequate as a necessary and sufficient criterion for differentiation of concept categories.

What other differentiating criteria are there? Because I want to argue for a monistic view, I shall not enumerate all possible criteria for differentiation of concept categories here. However, one logical candidate, which is apparently overlooked by contemporary theorists is worth noting: the hypothesized nature of the computing mechanism. The analogy of the computer as a model for human information processing is now so familiar as to be part of our collective thinking. But to say *the* computer is to ignore all the potential variation among possible computer analogues of human thought processes. Not so long ago students were taught that there were *two* kinds of computer, analogue and digital. The digital allows only two possible element states, on or off, whereas the analogue allows for a full continuum of possibilities. The first makes for elegant theory and simple mechanics, although the second appears to be a more accurate model of reality.

Perhaps Rosch's two systems might be directly coordinated to two different kinds of computing mechanisms: prototypical classification to analogue computation and logical classification to digital. Before pursuing the implications of the proposed coordination, however, it is salutory to recall that the "difference" between the two computational mechanisms can be broken down. It is possible to create a digital approximation to any desired degree of accuracy of an analogue computation. That is why current computers are digital. It seems to me that there is a lesson here for the student of classification. People may not seem to behave according to the rules of classical two-value logic in all situations, but they can do so under certain conditions. In other words, logical models appear to be more useful as a normative model of behavior than as a descriptive one. But, as in the case of digital approximations to analogue, perhaps it is also possible to reconcile a logical approximation (as a more elegant and powerful computing system) with more analogue/prototypelike observed performance.

There are many possible explanatory devices one could invoke to account for why a single system, or process, manifests itself differently on different occasions and contexts. In the following discussion I briefly consider a few alternative possibilities.

Experimenter Focus

The first consideration has to do with the question the experimenter is asking, how he or she goes about answering it experimentally, and the preferred level of analysis adopted in theory construction. It is, in a sense, the blind men and the elephant explanation. Starting first with the level of analysis of the theory, it is now common practice to differentiate *competence* from *performance* theories of behavior. With respect to Rosch's proposed two classification systems, I would suggest that a single system, the logical system, is adequate to account for classification at the competence level, whereas a prototype system often does a better job at the performance level. The distinction between competence and performance models parallels the differentiation raised earlier between normative and descriptive theories: A theory addressed to competence leads to a normative approach, whereas one addressed to performance leads to a descriptive approach. Although this distinction was not made at the time of the earlier work on classification and concept attainment, it is reasonably accurate to classify much of that work as normative in intent. The work of Piaget and his associates is now recognized as directed toward a competence theory. Although most English speaking investigators seem more temperamentally disposed toward an empiricist approach, their favored directing framework (information processing and computer analogues) would also seem to be normative in its formalized version (e.g., Newell & Simon, 1972).

The Subject's Task

The experimenter's theoretical bias and experimental interest, of course, influence the nature of the task he or she devises for the subject as well as the way that task is presented. For example, one standard procedure used in the study of prototypical classification is to ask the subject to rate exemplars with respect to goodness as a member of the class (e.g., pigeons, pelicans, penguins, partridges, and peregrines as instances of the class "bird"). Differences in ratings are reliably obtained, suggesting that some exemplars are better instances than others. But suppose one asked the subject to sort exemplars into those which are class members and those which are not, and to defend the sorting. They would have little difficulty in deciding that all the foregoing examples are birds because they have wings, feathers, lay eggs, and so forth, whereas pitchers, pomeranians, pillars, and prototypes are not. Similarly, Gleitman's (this volume) subjects know the rule differentiating odd and even numbers at the same time that they regard some numbers to be odder or evener than others.

Similar instances of subtle task differences predisposing to one kind of data or another appear in the study of logical reasoning and problem solving. The literature is full of evidence of illogical reasoning by well-trained adults (probably even this volume is not totally free of illustrative instances of illogic). Rosch describes some instances from her own work and from the work of others (e.g., Nisbett & Ross, 1980; Tverksy & Kahneman, 1982). Why do people who should know better reason illogically? It ssems to me that it occurs in part because the experimenter invites (entraps) them into doing so by raising questions of *empirical* rather than *logical* truth. With respect to the latter, by the rules of the game a proposition is completely true or it is false; when computation of probabilities and maximizing desirable outcomes or minimizing undesirable ones are at issue then two-value logic is no longer directly relevant. A related issue in the realm of problem solving has to do with whether one asks the subject for *a* solution, for *the best* solution to a problem, or for a method of solution that will always work (i.e., an algorithm vs. a heuristic). Even the most committed academic probably does not look for, or apply, an algorithm in all contexts and at all times. Most mortals are realists and will use any heuristic conveniently available. Prototypical classification, it seems to me, is a marvelously useful heuristic for many of the problems of everyday life (cf. Flavell, 1970). It is no surprise that it is so widely used in such a variety of contexts—it works. But, on those occasions where a logical classification is called for it generally can be, and is, produced. Even where the logical classification is not ultimately forthcoming (e.g., Wittgenstein's, 1953, demand for a logical classification of "game") one is well aware of what form the solution must take (e.g., a game is a rule-governed activity engaged in for purposes of diversion). Why else use one word, game, for the great variety of disparate activities?

To summarize the point I have been developing in this section, the two logical classification systems proposed by Rosch may be viewed as adaptations to different task demands upon the individual and different levels of analysis imposed by the theorist. At the more abstract level of analysis, however, when one focuses upon the optimal competence of the individual for creating and applying algorithms, the logical classification system constitutes a more powerful and adequate explanatory system. It can subsume the prototypical explanation, but the reverse is not true. The prototypical classification system, in this view, is a defective, heuristic approximation to logical classification, although for practical purposes it often provides a more accurate description of observed behavior. It is, so to speak, a default processing system.

Individual Style Differences

Might it perhaps be the case that the two alleged classification systems are not so much independent strategies of information processing as alternative styles, both available to the same individual? If so, there might be individual differences in preference for one style over another, which would be manifest in contexts permitting choice (e.g., a free-sorting task of the type widely used for developmental and for clinical research). An early study by Kagan, Moss, and Sigel (1963) did reveal classification styles among both adults and school-age children; those styles were correlated with other cognitive measures. In fact, clinical uses of free-sorting classification tasks (e.g., Goldstein & Scheerer, 1941: Hanfmann & Kasanin, 1937) derive from their diagnostic utility.

The roots of preferred classification styles might go back to early childhood. Nelson (1981) has presented impressive evidence for the existence of two styles of language acquisition, referential and nonreferential; both are available to the child, but they are reflected in different proportions for any given individual. It seems reasonable that the referential style, which by its very nature is focused upon acquisition of word classes and algorithms for combining words into sentences, would lead naturally to a preference for logical classification systems. Both seem to be analytic and abstractive in intent. A nonreferential style, on the other hand, with its emphasis upon whole phrases and compressed sentences for expressive or social functions, is by its very nature organized around prototypical reference points. It would, therefore, seem to be a natural origin for a prototype-based classification style. Both the nonreferential style and the prototype preference style use a unitary formula or exemplar as the central reference for organization of classes rather than a defining property; they are holistic in orientation.

Other widely used style typologies such as reflection/impulsivity (Kagan, Rosman, Day, Albert, & Phillips, 1964) or field dependence/independence (Witkin & Goodenough, 1981) might or might not be correlated to the proposed classification style dimension. The expected coordination of the poles of the various style typologies should be fairly obvious: Reflectivity, field independence, and other manifestations of an analytic and abstractive approach should be related to a preference for logical classification. Correlation at the opposite extreme, that is, impulsivity, field dependence, and holistic, global impressionistic, or context-tied approaches, with preference for prototype-based classification is not quite so obvious. Certainly, the nature and effects of classification style differences are worth experimental study. I have elsewhere (Neimark, 1981) analyzed the effects upon reasoning of cognitive style differences. An interesting illustration of the effect of classification style preferences, it seems to me, is provided by comparison of the organization and presentation style of the present chapter with Rosch's. It is left as an exercise for the reader to decide which chapter reflects which style preference.

Developmental Differences

A final possible means of relating the two proposed classification systems is to assume that the prototypical system is a developmentally earlier form of the logical system. This is counter to Rosch's explicit assertion that each system has its origin in infancy with an independent course thereafter. There is, however, a sizable body of literature on the development of classification (e.g., Bruner, 1966; Inhelder & Piaget, 1958; Vygotsky, 1962) demonstrating reliable, orderly changes in behavior in the direction of emergence of logical classification in middle childhood (concrete operations). Although there is little research on changes in classification during adolescence, what little evidence exists is compatible with the assumption of a formal operational level (cf. Neimark, 1975). Most of this research derives from a classical view of classification and employs free classification procedures.

Evidence concerning the development of prototype-based classification is not yet as widely available. Evidence of the structure of some natural language classes, although relevant, is hard to interpret at this point. At the early stages of development (Anglin, 1977; Rescorla, 1981) the child's first classes seem to derive from an exemplar-based core, but the mode of generalization from it is unclear. Rosch and Mervis (1975) show that most common categories of natural language (e.g., food, animals, clothing, etc.) are well described as prototype based. Some developmental studies of the organization of natural language classes find little difference between children and adults, whereas others obtain developmental differences (e.g., Neimark, 1974; Nelson, 1974; Rosch, Mervis, Gray, Johnson, & Boyes-Braem, 1976; Rosner & Hayes, 1977; Saltz, Soller, & Sigel, 1972). The specific class and the nature of experimental procedure seem to have some effect. For the few studies directly varying age, instructions, and exemplar structure in a single experiment (Horton & Markman, 1980; Kossan, 1981) results are consonant with the interpretation that a prototype/exemplar approach is used by younger children from whom logical, feature-based classification is difficult under all conditions and that logical classification is used by older children.

A growing number of investigators purport to show that adultlike concepts are evidenced even in infancy (Nelson, 1973a; Ricciuti, 1965; Starkey, 1981; Sugarman, 1981) and that even nursery schoolers are more sophisticated than they have been credited to be (Gelman, 1978; Markman, Cox, & Machida, 1981). Extrapolation from the interpretation of that line of research would lead to a conclusion that developmental changes in the nature of classification behavior and resulting concept classes are almost negligibly small. That conclusion, it seems to me, is not warranted in view of large differences in procedure and definitional criteria (e.g., habituation or successive-touching definition of classes treated as equivalent to sorting, labeling, justifying behaviors). DeLisi (this volume) considers these issues in greater detail.

The remainder of this chapter views classification from a broad developmental perspective in order to: (1) suggest the ontogeny of logical classification and (2) support the view that prototypical classification is ontologically earlier and phylogenetically more primitive than logical classification.

DEVELOPMENTAL CONSIDERATIONS

When Does Classification Begin?

To a large extent the answer to this question depends on one's definition of "class" or "concept" (a thorny problem beyond the scope of this chapter, but cf. Flavell, 1970, or Miller & Johnson-Laird, 1976, for a thoughtful consideration of it). Most accepted definitions (e.g., a definition proposed by Cohen & Younger, this volume) require two properties of classification behavior: (1) the same response is made to a variety of stimuli; (2) in other contexts, those stimuli can be shown to be discriminably different for the organism. The second property is essential if one is to differentiate classification from failure of discrimination, which obviously should not qualify for inclusion. Even with that exclusionary requirement, it is clear that behavior satisfying the definition occurs in most, if not all, living organisms and, possibly, in nonliving systems as well. On purely a priori grounds it seems inescapably obvious that no organism—or, even, inanimate mechanism—whose operation was contingent on a tightly circumscribed range of stimulus energies could survive in a multifactorial, changing, and variable universe. To cite a trivial example, automobiles will run not only on the recommended grade of gasoline, regardless of brand, but also on other grades, kerosene, alcohol, or some combination of these substances. However, it would be a travesty to conclude that, therefore, automobiles have a fuel concept. At that mechanistic level it is more parsimonious to speak of a tolerance range characteristic of the system.

At lower phyletic levels discriminative repertoires and the range of effective stimuli controlling them are probably determined by properties of the receptors and nervous system of the organisms. For example, the visual receptors of the frog are triggered by motion but discriminate poorly for other features such as shape. The class "food" for a frog, as defined by the response of striking and ingesting, is evoked by objects displaying an appropriate range of motion and an appropriate size range (for other examples in moth and octopus cf. Fenton & Fullard, 1981; Wells, 1961). At progressively higher phyletic levels the effective range is modifiable by experience through the mechanisms of habituation, sensitization, conditioning, associative learning, and so on (Hinde & Stevenson-Hinde, 1973; Razran, 1971). In some instances (e.g., imprinting in precocial birds) there is evidence for the existence of a critical period for modification. The existence of categories not so readily explained in terms of organism structure or species characteristics is evidenced by the work of Herrnstein and his associates (Herrnstein, 1979; Herrnstein & Loveland, 1964) demonstrating that pigeons have what might be called a "people" class, a "water" class, and so forth, as demonstrated by differential pecking to photographs of what we would call "people" or "water" as compared to foils. It is not yet known how these pigeon categories are acquired (if they are), how they are modified, or whether they are organized in a prototypical or logical fashion. I introduce them to highlight the fuzziness of the boundary between discrimination and classification.

That even the classificationlike behavior of Herrnstein's pigeons may have a simple biologically determined basis is suggested by a large variety of comparative evidence. In most species discriminations differ in speed of acquisition: Food aversions, for instance, are learned much more rapidly than the usual laboratory discrimination (Garcia, Hankins, & Rusiniak, 1974). Some discriminations, for example, diagonal orientation for the octopus (Wells, 1961), seem impossible to learn. And, in still other instances, learned behavior patterns seem to break down over time because of intrusion of primitive instinctual patterns (Breland & Breland, 1961). Thus, although many behavioral phenomena observed at subhuman levels seem to satisfy the definitional criteria for classification, they can usually be accounted for in terms of simpler principles of discrimination, generalization, and instinctive behavior.

It seems reasonable to assume that a primitive form of classification is present in human infants at or before birth and that it constitutes the starting point for later ontological elaboration. Most psychologists would accept the assumption. Rosch, however, posits two classification systems arising in infancy. On the basis of phylogenetic evidence, I can find no basis for more than one kind of classification behavior, which is more prototype based than logical.

Early Categorization Is Heavily Influenced by Stimulus Properties

The role of stimulus salience in control of infant behavior has been widely noted and abundantly documented. With respect to what is asserted to be early classification, Ricciuti (1965) and his recent replicators (Starkey, 1981; Sugarman, 1981) all find that some sets of four objects of one type and four of another, randomly arranged in reach of the infant, are more likely to evoke successive touching of each member of one type category (or three out of four as criterion for classification) than others. Sets that do not work are, presumably, not used as experimental material. Although there has been a good deal of research on infant attention, especially visual attention (cf. Haith, 1980; Kessen, Haith, & Salapatek, 1970), it is not yet possible to characterize a stimulus salience continuum in any systematic way that sheds light on Rosch's proposed two classification systems. Although there is some research on the development of prototypes, especially the face schema (e.g., Kagan, 1970), most investigators tend to use stimulus properties (e.g., form, color, size, etc.) of the sort traditionally used in the definition of logical classes as independent variables in the investigation of salience. Whether or not it will some day be possible to specify what makes a salient stimulus salient, it is sufficient for present purposes to note that early human classification behavior, as well as the presumed categories resulting from it, seem to be dictated by the nature of immediately encountered stimuli in a way that the categories of older children and adults are not. The research of Cohen and his students (Cohen & Younger, this volume) promises to provide more systematic evidence not only on the role of stimulus properties but, more importantly, on the basis of classification rules and dimensions of abstraction. It is unfortunate that groups of older children or adults are not included in their research design to provide further data on the possible limitations of infant classes.

In the foregoing discussion I assume that infant categories are built upon a foundation of biological predisposition modified by simple processes of habituation, conditioning, associative learning, and exercise of circular reflexes. Two predictions seem to follow from that assumption: (1) early categories should be stimulus driven (that is, their core should be heavily influenced by initial experiential context), which makes infant categories appear more similar to Rosch's prototype-based classes than to logical ones; (2) later extensions from the core should be dependent on basic learning parameters such as frequency, salience, and generalization gradients. To the extent that early one-word utterances reflect the child's early natural categories, evidence concerning them is compatible with the predictions. For example, Nelson (1979) notes that objects (e.g., toys) actively manipulated by the child constitute early vocabulary items, whereas invariant features of the environment (e.g., wallpaper) or common objects manipulated only by caretakers (e.g., diapers) do not. Huttenlocher (1974) notes a similar effect in learning the names of significant family members and pets.

The Advent of Symbolic Representation Leads to a Qualitative Change in the Nature of Categorization

Liberation from the dominance over early categories by external contextual features, or by the child's own action schemes, is provided by the symbol as a new stimulus entity. The child (or chimp, if one admits them to the realm of symbol users) can now classify and think about classes in the absence of instances or relate symbol to symbol (e.g., word to picture) as well as symbol to object. Moreover, the repertoire of symbols itself becomes part of the behavioral context within which subsequent experience is evaluated and new categories are formed. The systematic structuring of knowledge as a deliberate goal has begun (as beautifully evidenced by the frequency of questions in early language).

With the shift toward symbolic control of classification systems comes the potential for greater interindividual variation in both content and structure of the category or system of categories. Another contributing factor to interindividual variation among categories is variation in the form of the symbols themselves. They may take the form of internalized imitation, anticipatory sequences, or images, as well as words. Nelson's (this volume) description of the origin of early categories and concepts provides a good picture of the richness of this early stage. A limit on the potential range of variation is provided by the fact that many classes are socially shared and acquired in a social context of communication with other individuals; for example, early words that are not understood by others appear to drop out.

Are the new symbolically represented categories organized logically or prototypically? It is difficult to say, especially because none of the available evidence was explicitly addressed to that question, but the answer seems clearly to be that both types of organization are now evidenced. As noted earlier, Nelson's (1981) proposed two styles of language acquisition provide a possible basis (or counterpart) for individual differences in preferred style of classification, which might find their origin at this stage of development.

Concrete Operations Provide a General Algorithm for Logical Classification

The attainment of concrete operations enables the classifier to employ a higher level of classification that differs from preceding levels in two respects: (1) the nature of the definitional rule; (2) the rule system or calculus for organizing and relating classes. The new definitional rule is possession of a necessary criterial property, relation, or combination of them independent of the exemplars embodying it (e.g., a requisite form, size, behavioral or structural characteristics, consanguinity, etc.). Prototype-based classes, in contrast, do not have an explicit intensive property but, rather, are defined on the basis of similarity to a most representative exemplar, the prototype, which is the core of the class structure. As one gets away from the core to poorer and poorer examples, the class boundary becomes "fuzzy." Definition of a class in terms of presence or absence of a criterial property or properties, on the other hand, implies that class boundaries are clearly identifiable and important in defining the class.

The second characteristic of a logical class, its calculus, derives from the nature of classification as a concrete operation, that is, its status as a reversible mental transformation whose rules are described in terms of a loose quasi-mathematical structure of groupments (Flavell, 1963). Some of the criteria for a logical class (Inhelder & Piaget, 1964) are listed here to give a clearer idea of the role of boundary and complement in the class definition:

1. Each and every element must be uniquely assigned to its class with none unassigned (e.g., every number is even or odd). A singular element constitutes a class in itself.
2. Every class, A, characterized by its property, a, implies its complement, A', characterized by a'. $B = A + A'$ (numbers = odd + even).
3. A class, A, includes all elements with property a and only those elements.
4. All classes of the same rank are disjoint; that is, $A \cap A' = \phi$, their intersect is a null set (e.g., for plants and nonplants, i.e., animals, there is no living thing that is both a plant and an animal).

5. A complementary class has its own characteristics not possessed by its complement (cf. animals and plants in item 4; animals have their own defining properties).
6. A class, A, is included in every higher ranking class that contains all its elements: All A are some B and $B > A$.
7. Additional criteria include extensional and intensional simplicity and symmetrical subdivision.

At the concrete operations level of development it is clear that Rosch's proposed two classification systems have different descriptive properties, but as I suggested in the first part of this chapter, they need not require different explanatory principles. The logical classification system described earlier in Piagetian terms has the theoretical status of an optimal level of competence or a general algorithm potentially available to the concrete operational thinker. For many everyday classifications, that algorithm is adequately approximated by the practical heuristic of Rosch's second classification system. A related conclusion is reached by Osherson and Smith (1981) on the basis of their detailed formal analysis of the adequacy of prototype theory as a theory of concepts.

What differentiates classification at the concrete operations level from earlier levels is the higher level of abstraction at which classification proceeds: The class is defined in terms of properties or relations and their calculus rather than exemplars possessing those properties. For example, bird is defined by criterial properties of feathers, wings, egg-laying, and so on rather than by resemblance to robins and sparrows. Although most older children, adolescents, and adults are capable of classifying in this manner, they may not do so in a given instance for a variety of reasons, among them task demands, situational constraints, and stylistic factors (cf. Overton & Newman, 1982). Thus, if asked whether an apteryx is a bird, it may not seem worth the time or effort to look up accepted biological criteria and run through them systematically, so, as a quick expedient, one might just decide if it looks like a bird. Presumably, the higher the level of abstraction involved, the greater the potential gap between hypothesized competence and observed performance.

At the Highest Levels of Abstraction an Algorithm Is Less Likely to Be Manifest in Behavior

Inhelder and Piaget (1958) identify a level of competence, formal operations, beyond concrete operations in level of abstraction. Classification at the formal operational level probably proceeds in a different fashion from concrete operational classification. It is more likely to proceed deductively from the highest level down rather than inductively from familiar instances and to focus on identification of differentiating features most readily distinguished at the boundary of complementary classes. To return to the apteryx example, a formal operational classifier would probably focus on the least birdlike features of the apteryx (e.g., tiny wings incapable of flight) and determine if they would qualify as nonbird properties. They do not. Therefore, if it is not a nonbird, it is a bird. Classificatory behavior at this level of abstraction is the professional concern of judges, taxonomists, theorists, and systematizers of mores and beliefs, and they may be the only individuals who devote a substantial proportion of their time to it. Even at this exalted level, however, there are clear stylistic differences in preferred approach as evidenced by, for example, the variety of theoretical approaches in psychology (e.g., associationists vs. Gestaltists, Piagetians vs. information processors, etc.).

Rosch (this volume) has presented a sample of the wealth of evidence for reference point reasoning among even sophisticated adults. However, this evidence, along with a similarly large body of evidence showing that most adults do not exhibit formal operational reasoning, should not lead to the conclusion that because so many intelligent persons do not reason logically that they are incapable of doing so. It simply is not the case; given clarification of task demands, introductory illustrative examples, or even explicit instruction and demonstration, people can and do reason logically (cf. Neimark, 1981, for a review of some of this literature).

The Development of Expertise May Provide a Horizontal Analogue of Longitudinal Development of Higher Levels of Abstraction

Early studies of the development of motor skills in code sending (Bryan & Harter, 1899) and in typing (Book, 1908) both provided evidence of a clear change in the organization of performance as skill increased. Change in this case was in the direction of development of larger processing units: to words or phrases instead of individual letters. Recently there has been a return of interest in the development of skill, first in studies of chess players (Chase & Simon, 1973) and, more recently, in acquisition of knowledge about physics (Chi, Glaser, & Rees, 1982). As was found with motor skills, here, too, skilled performers seem to organize their knowledge in bigger chunks. More importantly, there is a change with advancing skill in the nature of the organizing principle, in both cases to a more abstract form of organization. For example, beginning physics students seems to encode and access their knowledge (e.g., in order to solve problems) in terms of the class of phenomena in question (as defined by situational features), whereas their instructors dealt with the same problems in terms of the physical principles relevant to their solution. The behavior of the beginning students appears closer to the reference point reasoning described by Rosch than does that of their instructors.

Some of my own unpublished data shed additional light on changes in the form of classification behavior over the course of development of expertise.

Students in an introductory psychology course were asked in an individual interview session to define 10 terms randomly selected from a larger pool of terms drawn from text and lecture material (e.g., reinforcement, motivation, perception). The purpose of the study was to see how students went about defining terms. By way of initial orientation they were asked to define familiar everyday terms like "fruit." In that phase they were pushed to explore the boundaries of their definition by means of questions such as: "Is the tomato a fruit?" One major finding, which considerably complicated our problems of data analysis, was that introductory psychology students are not very good at defining even familiar terms. There were a distressing number of psychological terms that they could not define at all. For terms they could define many definitions seemed to be based upon a class or text example and were, in spirit, essentially prototype definitions. Although other students did attempt definition in terms of criterial properties, their knowledge base often appeared too limited to provide the correct property. Students in the author's senior level course in thinking were also asked to provide definitions of psychological terms, two per week selected by them from lectures and reading assignments. Material on development of classification as well as theories of concept attainment and relevant research evidence were covered fairly extensively during the middle of the semester. In this instance the quality of the definitions was somewhat better, but it did not change appreciably during the course of the semester. Once again, definitions using an example as a prototype were fairly common, but there were also many definitions in terms of criterial properties. Students did not, however, often spontaneously anchor a term in relation to its superordinate class in such a way as to explore the bounds of the class, for example, reinforcement is: (1) a class of stimulus consequences of behavior—either positive or negative; (2) a theoretical principle to account for effects of those contingencies; and so on. The data suggest to me that beginning students, as well as poorer students at more advanced levels, tend to classify psychological concepts in a prototypical fashion and that logical classification types of definitions become more likely at a more advanced stage of knowledge. They also suggest to me that we do not do a very good job of teaching students about the process of classification and its application to the organization of knowledge.

SUMMARY AND CONCLUSIONS

How many kinds of classification behavior are there? It depends on the criteria selected for their differentiation. By currently employed structural criteria there are at least the two classification systems proposed by Rosch—sometimes coexisting within the same person for the same class, as Gleitman has so convincingly demonstrated. These findings suggest that perhaps one should suspect that strong contextual effects of task demand or material operate to determine which class structure is manifest. Some other possible determining factors such as preferred classification style or developmental level have also been considered. If, however, one differentiates classification systems with respect to the theoretical principles needed to account for them and proceeds by a process of exclusion (i.e., introducing new principles only for what cannot be dealt with by the theory), then it seems to me that all the putative variety may be encompassed within a framework of developmentally determined, progressively higher levels of abstraction. These levels, if viewed as normative descriptions of optimal competence, are assumed to be described better by logical classification systems. Those optimal levels, however, may not be attained in practice because of the operation of a variety of moderating factors such as situational constraints, economic considerations, cultural conventions, or individual differences in cognitive style. At the descriptive level, observed approximations to logical classification, which were described as heuristics or default options, are characterized better by a prototype classification system. The account closed with a developmental consideration of the two classification systems directed at determining whether there is sound evidence for Rosch's assertion that the two systems originate in infancy and follow independent courses thereafter. It was concluded that there is not compelling evidence for two systems.

REFERENCES

Anglin, J. *Word, object, and conceptual development*. New York: Norton, 1977.

Book, W. F. *The psychology of skill*. Missoula, Mont.: University of Montana Press, 1908.

Breland, K., & Breland, M. The misbehavior of organisms. *American Psychologist*, 1961, *16*, 681–684.

Bruner, J. S. On cognitive growth. In J. S. Bruner, R. R. Olver, & P. M. Greenfield (Eds.). *Studies in cognitive growth*. New York: Wiley, 1966.

Bryan, W., & Harter, N. Studies on the telegraphic language: The acquisition of a hierarchy of habits. *Psychological Review*, 1899, *6*, 345–365.

Chase, W. G., & Simon, H. A. Perception in chess. *Cognitive Psychology*, 1973, *4*, 55–81.

Chi, M. T. H., Glaser, R., & Rees, E. Expertise in problem solving. In R. Sternberg (Ed.), *Advances in the psychology of human intelligence*. Hillsdale, N.J.: Lawrence Erlbaum Associates, 1982.

Fenton, M. B., & Fullard, J. H. Moth hearing and the feeding strategies of bats. *American Scientist*, 1981, *69*, 266–275.

Flavell, J. H. *The developmental psychology of Jean Piaget*. Princeton, N.J.: Van Nostrand, 1963.

Flavell, J. H. Concept development. In P. H. Mussen (Ed.), *Carmichael's manual of child psychology* (3rd ed.). New York: Wiley, 1970.

Garcia, J., Hankins, W. G., & Rusiniak, K. W. Behavioral regulation of the milieu interne in man and rat. *Science*, 1974, *185*, 823–831.

Gelman, R. Cognitive development. *Annual Review of Psychology*, 1978, *29*, 297–332.

Goldstein, K., & Scheerer, M. Abstract and concrete behavior. *Psychological Monographs*, 1941, *53*(2, Whole No. 239).

Haith, M. *Rules babies look by*. Hillsdale, N.J.: Lawrence Erlbaum Associates, 1980.

Hanfmann, E., & Kasanin, J. A method for the study of concept formation. *Journal of Psychology*, 1937, *3*, 521–540.

Herrnstein, R. J. Acquisition, generalization, and discrimination reversal of a natural concept. *Journal of Experimental Psychology: Animal Behavior Processes,* 1979, *5,* 116–129.

Herrnstein, R. J., & Loveland, D. H. Complex visual concept in the pigeon. *Science,* 1964, *146,* 549–551.

Hinde, R. A., & Stevenson-Hinde, J. *Constraints on learning.* New York: Academic Press, 1973.

Horton, M. S., & Markman, E. M. Developmental differences in the acquisition of basic and superordinate categories. *Child Development,* 1980, *51,* 708–719.

Huttenlocher, J. The origin of language comprehension. In R. Solso (Ed.), *Theories in cognitive psychology: The Loyola Symposium.* New York: Wiley, 1974.

Inhelder, B., & Piaget, J. *The growth of logical thinking from childhood to adolescence.* New York: Basic Books, 1958.

Inhelder, B., & Piaget, J. *The early growth of logic in the child.* New York: Norton, 1964.

Kagan, J. Attention and psychological change in the young child. *Science,* 1970, *170,* 826–832.

Kagan, J., Moss, H. A., & Sigel, I. E. Psychological significance of styles of conceptualization. *Monographs of the Society for Research in Child Development,* 1963, *28*(2), 73–112.

Kagan, J., Rosman, B. L., Day, D., Albert, J., & Phillips, W. Information processing in the child: Significance of analytical reflective attitudes. *Psychological Monographs,* 1964, *78*(1, Whole No. 578).

Kessen, W., Haith, M. M., & Salapatek, P. H. Infancy. In P. H. Mussen (Ed.), *Carmichael's manual of child psychology* (3rd ed.). New York: Wiley, 1970.

Kossan, N. E. Developmental differences in concept acquisition strategies. *Child Development,* 1981, *52,* 290–298.

Markman, E. M., Cox, B., & Machida, S. The standard object-sorting task as a measure of conceptual organization. *Developmental Psychology,* 1981, *17*(1), 115–117.

Mervis, C. B., & Rosch, E. Categorization of natural objects. *Annual Review of Psychology,* 1981, *32,* 89–116.

Miller, G. A., & Johnson-Laird, P. N. *Language and perception.* Cambridge, Mass.: Harvard University Press, 1976.

Neimark, E. D. Natural language concepts: Additional evidence. *Child Development,* 1974, *45,* 508–511.

Neimark, E. D. Intellectual development during adolescence. In F. D. Horowitz (Ed.), *Review of child development research* (Vol. 4). Chicago: University of Chicago Press, 1975.

Neimark, E. D. Explanation for the apparent nonuniversal incidence of formal operations. In I. Sigel, D. Brodzinsky, & R. Golinkoff (Eds.), *Piagetian theory and research: New directions and applications.* Hillsdale, N.J.: Lawrence Erlbaum Associates, 1981.

Neimark, E. D. Adolescent thought: Transition to formal operations. In B. Wollman (Ed.), *Handbook of developmental psychology.* Englewood Cliffs, N.J.: Prentice-Hall, 1981.

Nelson, K. Some evidence for the cognitive primacy of categorization. *Merrill-Palmer Quarterly,* 1973, *19,* 21–39. (a)

Nelson, K. Structure and strategy in learning to talk. *Monographs of the Society for Research in Child Development,* 1973, *38*(1–2, Serial No. 149). (b)

Nelson, K. Variations in children's concepts by age and category. *Child Development,* 1974, *45,* 577–584.

Nelson, K. The role of language in infant development. In M. Bornstein & W. Kessen (Eds.) *Development in Infancy.* Hillsdale, N.J.: Lawrence Erlbaum Associates, 1979.

Nelson, K. Individual differences in language development: Implication for development and language. *Developmental Psychology,* 1981, *17,* 170–187.

Newell, A., & Simon, H. A. *Human problem-solving.* Englewood Cliffs, N.J.: Prentice-Hall, 1972.

Nisbett, R. E., & Ross, L. *Human inference: Strategies and shortcomings of social judgment.* Englewood Cliffs, N.J.: Prentice-Hall, 1980.

Osherson, D. N., & Smith, E. E. On the adequacy of prototype theory as a theory of concepts. *Cognition*, 1981, *9*, 35–58.

Overton, W. F., & Newman, J. L. Cognitive development: A competence-activation/utilization approach. In T. M. Field, A. Huston, H. C. Quay, L. Troll, & G. E. Finley (Eds.), *Review of human development*. New York: Wiley, 1982.

Razran, G. *Mind in evolution*. Boston, Mass.: Houghton Mifflin, 1971.

Rescorla, L. A. Category development in early language. *Journal of Child Language*, 1981, *8*, 225–238.

Ricciuti, H. Object grouping and selective ordering in infants 12–24 months old. *Merrill-Palmer Quarterly*, 1965, *11*, 129–148.

Rosch, E., & Mervis, C. B. Family resemblances: Studies in the internal structure of categories. *Cognitive Psychology*, 1975, *7*, 573–605.

Rosch, E., Mervis, C. B., Gray, W. D., Johnson, D. M., & Boyes-Braem, P. Basic objects in natural categories. *Cognitive Psychology*, 1976, *8*, 382–430.

Rosner, S., & Hayes, D. A developmental study of category item production. *Child Development*, 1977, *48*, 1062–1065.

Saltz, E., Soller, E., & Sigel, I. E. The development of natural language concepts. *Child Development*, 1972, *43*, 1191–1202.

Smith, E. E., & Medin, D. L. *Categories and concepts*. Cambridge, Mass.: Harvard University Press, 1981.

Starkey, D. The origins of concept formation: Object sorting and object preference in early infancy. *Child Development*, 1981, *52*, 489–497.

Sugarman, S. The cognitive basis of classification in very young children: An analysis of object-ordering trends. *Child Development*, 1981, *52*, 1172–1178.

Tversky, A., & Kahneman, D. Judgments of and by representativeness. In D. Kahneman, P. Slovic, & A. Tversky (Eds.), *Judgment under uncertainty: Heuristics and biases*. New York: Cambridge University Press, 1982.

Vygotsky, L. S. *Thought and language*. Cambridge, Mass.: MIT Press, 1962.

Wells, M. J. What the octopus makes of it; our world from another point of view. *American Scientist*, 1961, *49*, 215–227.

Witkin, H. A., & Goodenough, D. R. *Cognitive styles: Essence and origins*. New York: International Universities Press, 1981.

Wittgenstein, L. *Philosophical investigations*. New York: Macmillan, 1953.

6 The Derivation of Concepts and Categories from Event Representations

Katherine Nelson
*City University of New York Graduate School
and University Center*

One basic problem for psychology is to describe the interface between the external world of physical and cultural reality and the individual's internal representation of that reality. The problem for the developmental psychologist is to describe how the internal representation changes with development.

Concepts and categories constitute some of the mental representations of reality that psychology is concerned with. In this paper I discuss some hypotheses as to how these entities in the head come to be formed in the first place and how they relate over time to the child's activities in the world. Because our ways of assessing what is in the head depend on making inferences based on the child's activities in the world, it has not always been easy or even possible to distinguish the two empirically. However, for the construction of theory it is necessary to keep them clearly separated. Moreover, the clearest expression of conceptual knowledge is through the language, and nonverbal behaviors are inherently ambiguous as indicators of internal concepts and categories. Thus, any discussion of preverbal or nonverbal concepts is necessarily speculative. Nonetheless, I am going to attempt here to trace the development of such conceptual knowledge from its nonverbal beginnings to its more adultlike stages in middle childhood. In doing this, I am going to try to bring three areas together into a single coherent description, the areas being memory for events, formation of concepts, and concept–word relationships. The present account grows out of converging findings in these areas. Although I do not detail the data base here, I hope to persuade the reader of the sense of this description or at least to present some problems worth speculating about.

129

The traditional way of viewing the development of cognitive representations is in terms of pieces or elements that are extracted from a perceptual array and then, through a series of usually unspecified cognitive operations, are combined into wholes that ever more faithfully represent reality. The problem for such theories is to find the *basic units* from which larger wholes are made, an enterprise that has deep philosophical roots emerging during the 19th century in various conceptions of mental chemistry based on primary and secondary sensations. In recent decades the units have been identified as attributes of percepts, features of words, and components of concepts. Various theories have been put forth to show which features, attributes, or components are acquired in what order and how they are combined at different stages of development (e.g., Anglin, 1977; Clark, 1973; Gentner, 1978; Smith & Kemler, 1977). These theories, whether concerned with percepts, concepts, or word meanings, all basically view the child as extracting salient features from the perceptual array to build mental copies of the world. Such a view is of course at odds with Piaget's theory of the child's interiorization of action schemes as the basis of mental representation.

However, the conception of conceptual representation that I want to outline here deviates in some ways from both these positions. I call it a contextualized account of conceptual representation. I do not claim great novelty for this view of cognitive development. It is related to certain ideas in anthropology (Ardener, 1980), to Gibson's (1979) perceptual theory, and to the ideas of George Herbert Mead (1934), Werner (1957), Vygotsky (1962), and Bruner (1966), although it does not derive directly from any of these theorists.

A contextualized view of cognitive representation rests on the assumption that pieces of reality are never experienced apart from their context, whether these pieces are attributes, features, components, words, objects, or what have you. Indeed a basic proposal of this thesis is that the experience of parts is a cognitive achievement, *not* a primitive building block.

Rather than elaborating the contextual framework itself, I want to address some central issues of conceptual development within this framework. I hope that, in this way, salient aspects of the view emerge with enough clarity to suggest its utility for further theorizing. Briefly, the issues to be raised are: What are we to call a concept? When does a child have a concept? What is the conceptual context, and how does it change? What different kinds of conceptual representations and relations are there? How do they develop? What is the relation of conceptual representations to words and word meanings, and how do these change? What cognitive processes are involved in conceptual acquisition and development? Obviously, my discussion of these questions cannot be exhaustive, but I hope to sketch enough of the story to convince you of the usefulness of this approach. I begin the story very early—at the point where the child is just beginning to learn words.

WHAT IS A CONCEPT?

Any discussion of concept development is made difficult by lack of agreement on the meaning of central terms, a problem that has been noted with despair by many authors and that received an extensive analysis in Flavell's (1970) review of concept development research. I need not repeat this analysis here. Rather, I briefly set forth the way in which I intend to use the term, namely, in the sense of a mental object. In this mental-object sense, concepts make easy contact with the language, an important characteristic. For, as Bronowski and Bellugi (1972) state: "What language expresses specifically is the *reification* by the human mind of its experience, that is, an analysis into parts (including actions and properties as well objects) which, as concepts, can be manipulated *as if they were objects* [p. 670, emphasis added]."[1]

There are two essential interconnected parts to this important observation. The first is the move mentally to separate parts from the whole; the second is the reification or mental construction of stable *objects* from a less stable, more dynamic context. It is interesting that Piaget (1962) viewed the progression from sensory-motor intelligence to conceptual intelligence in a way that is almost opposite to this: "Sensory-motor intelligence thus functions like a slow-motion film, representing one static image after another instead of achieving a fusion of the images [p. 238]." In this view the problem is to achieve "the speeded up film of the behavior" to become the interior representation. As in later developments (e.g., images) Piaget thus saw the problem as one of moving from static to dynamic representations. I am proposing that at least in the beginning the problem is rather one of mentally stabilizing an ongoing dynamic reality.

Implicit in this view is the assumption that experience is first represented in the head holistically; concept formation and language, then, are the result of processes that reify certain aspects of the whole and make them separately accessible to mental manipulation as if they were objects. I believe this to be an important and basic function of conceptual development.

This conception of the concept rules out the use of the term in the sense of a cognitive principle. In contrast, Flavell (1970) states:

> The concept may have only the status of a vehicle or instrument of adaptation, or it may also have in varying measure the status of a well-articulated and fully coded object of thought. An individual could not be said to have a concept if he could not in some sense think *with* it; he might well be said to have it, however, even though he could not in the slighest degree think *about* it [p. 989, emphasis added].

---

[1]Reification is being used here in a different sense than it is used in Marxist analysis (see Sampson, 1981), where it refers to the abstraction of a process from its sociohistorical context to grant it a timeless, objective quality. In this paper the reference is to the formation of a mental object from a less bounded mental experience.

Unfortunately, to my way of thinking this view of the concept conflates a tool of thinking with an object of thought, a distinction that I believe is important to maintain. Moreover, this conflation has pernicious consequences for our view of mental development, for example, when the child is said to have a "concept" of the permanent object, because it is obvious that this concept is in no sense an *object* of thought as the child's concept of *mother* or *cup* may be. Flavell was quite clear in stating that the child does not think *about* such a concept, although he may think *with* it. However, applying the term concept to achievements of this kind has the unfortunate effect of appearing to reify them, and thus giving them the status of mental "thingness," a status that in turn unwarrantedly suggests their achievement in some definite and fixed sense. Confining the term concept to only objects of thought—stable wholes that have at least the *potential* of being named—avoids these problems.

It is important to note also the implications contained in the assertion that the concept is an object of thought, a whole that is indivisible. That is, it is not a collection or a category of equal members. The instances of a concept that appear in the world do not ordinarily retain their individuality in the head but are assimilated to the general concept. Their identity is merged with the whole. The concept may have internal structure, but this internal structure is the intension of the concept: It specifies the conditions under which the concept applies—its functions, properties, and relationships. It should be noted here that the prototype concept I refer to is the *basic object concept* in Rosch's (Rosch & Mervis, 1975) terms. Like her, I distinguish basic concepts from *categories*. The exemplars of categories do retain their individual identity as part of the mental representation. Indeed, categories in this sense are composed of basic concepts, a point that I return to.

Concepts, then, are here considered to be stable cognitive wholes with structure but without individuated members. This is not to claim that a concept such as "dog" is not applied to different instances of the dog class but only that, as a mental object, it is not a collection of dogs but a single whole. (I should comment in passing that the notion of a prototype fits easily here, although it is not necessary.) It is interesting to note that because of this holistic status the basic object concept (Rosch, 1978) or natural kind term (Putnam, 1975) has more in common with such cognitive abstractions as "justice" and "peace" than it does with general concrete categories such as "furniture."

There are of course cognitive representations that are not basic concepts in this sense. Superordinate categories are one type, as I have just indicated. Superordinate categories combine two or more basic concepts into a higher order collection of mental objects. This is in my view a semantically based distinction rather than a basic cognitive one.[2] What defines a superordinate term is not its

___

[2]In this sense I am using the term categories in a different way than Cohen (this volume) and others (including myself) use it when speaking of the infant's perceptually based categories. We can

generality or abstractness but the fact that it dominates terms at a lower level. For example, young children may use very general terms that are not superordinate (e.g., "bug" applied across virtually the entire class of insects) for the same real-world domain as an adult uses a superordinate term (i.e., "insect"). The difference is that "insect" stands in a hierarchical relation to terms such as "ant" and "bee." Unless the young child applies the general term *and* a specific object term to the *same* individual, there is no indication that a superordinate relation had been set up. This distinction is essentially the same as the logical distinction of the relationship between a class and its members ($x \in X$) and its subclass ($\{x\} \in X$). As Lyons (1977) states: "A class contains its members but includes its subclasses [p. 157]." We might note that this is equivalent to Piaget's test for the child's understanding of logical class relationships. Because this is a semantic relationship according to the present analysis, understanding of these relations should be better in the purely linguistic realm than when concretized with objects. For the same reason children may also be confused by the particular phrasing of the questions.

The structure of superordinate categories in the head is not the same as that of basic objects. Superordinate categories combine elements that retain their cognitive individuality and participate equally in the category structure (although this is not to deny that there are better or poorer members as Rosch, 1978, has amply demonstrated). Different structures imply different processes. I hypothesize that the intension of a superordinate category is derived from the abstraction of common elements among its mentally represented member concepts (its extension), whereas the extension of a basic concept (the real-world instances) is derived by applying the *intension* of the concept to possible candidate instances. Given this possibility, different principles of formation and development will be likely to apply to these different conceptual levels.

Subordinate categories may be differentiated from the basic concept by a process of analysis, which is likely to be primarily perceptual and which, like superordination, is likely to be guided by language use in the community. Subordination is the least studied and least understood of conceptual processes. Note that subordination is not the same as dividing the concept into single instances, but rather into subconcepts. However, individual concept members may be given proper names when it is important that they retain their individuality in the face of the indivisibility of the concept as a whole. The different relations among levels of the hierarchy proposed here suggest that no single conceptualizing process will explain conceptual development.

The foregoing comments are derived from and are applicable primarily to object concepts and categories, as is typical of most of the work in concept

---

speak of categories$_1$ (perceptual) and categories$_2$ (conceptual). The first reflects a basic ability to group discriminable things for functional purposes. The latter reflects the ability to form conceptual hierarchies. The confusion of terms is unfortunate.

formation and semantic development. However, for a complete theory of concept development we need to take into account people and social relationships, actions, states, properties, and relations of all kinds as well as various levels of abstract thought. We need, in fact, a framework within which all of these can be derived. Part of my purpose here is to propose such a framework.

THE CONTEXT OF CONCEPTS

At the outset it was claimed that no pieces of experience exist outside of some context. This is as true of concepts as it is of objects, attributes, and so on. As adults we appear to use many different kinds of conceptual representations and relationships, some of which have been studied and modeled in different ways in recent years. We represent events, states, logical classes, similars, attributes, words, grammatical categories, and any number of other types and relations. Thus, our conceptual context is extraordinarily rich. We call it into play whenever we think, act, speak, listen, or dream. Recent research suggests that our prior conceptual schemata are extremely powerful in shaping our interpretations of ongoing events (e.g., Bransford & McCarrell, 1974). That is, "what happens" is always interpreted in terms of prior conceptual context. What about the young child? Where is the context, and what role does it play?

To begin to examine this question, we turn to a consideration of the child's knowledge of *events* on the assumption that in order to understand conceptual development it is necessary to analyze knowledge of events, as well as objects. The reason for this is that objects are embedded in events, and they may have no privileged status therein. Indeed, there is good reason to believe that for the very young child objects are substitutable one for another (e.g., in give-and-take games) but that events are not substitutable. One may not shift with impunity from peekaboo to bye-bye, for example. But at similar ages (8 to 12 months) one can substitute different objects in object-hiding tasks (Le Compte & Gratch, 1972; Nelson, 1979) and elicit little reaction from the infant. I have been startled to observe the equanimity with which a 15-month-old child will shift from one ball that has rolled out of sight to another having quite different perceptual characteristics. In this case, object permanence was not in question because the second ball was retrieved from an out-of-sight but known location in the toy box. This is an area that needs intensive investigation; I believe it to be important to understanding development from infancy to childhood.

If events are the context within which objects reside, it seems clear that *event representations* must form the context of concepts of objects. We need then to examine what an event is and how it is represented in the head. We are all familiar with the idea of an action scheme and the role it is assumed to play in the child's understanding of the object world. The event representation as we view it includes action schemata and much more, in particular, representation of objects, persons and person roles, and *sequences* of actions appropriate to a specific scene. In other words, it includes specific social and cultural components essential for carrying through a particular activity. If children understand to any degree the ongoing activities of their world such that they can take their role in them, they must have formed some sort of representation of these activities.

We start then with the proposition that in order to participate in social activities young children must represent their own roles and the roles of others and be able to reciprocate the actions of others with appropriate actions of their own. That is, event representations must be built up to guide interactions in recurrent situations. We have been calling these representations social *scripts*. There is considerable evidence (e.g., Ashmead & Perlmutter, 1980; Bruner, 1975; Nelson, 1978; Schank & Abelson, 1977) that by 1 year of age the child has a number of scripts for guiding action and interactions in familiar routines. These routines are the child's first exposure to the surrounding culture, embedding notions of how to eat, how to play, and so forth.

The proposal here is that the child's *initial* mental representations are in the form of scripts for familiar events involving social interaction and communication. A script, like a concept, is a structured whole. It represents a sequential activity involving roles that people play and objects that they interact with in the course of the activity. It is a *generalized* representation of an activity that has occurred more than once, rather than a collection of particular experiences. Because of the generalized, holistic quality, we could say that the child's first *concepts* are of events. However, in order to keep the terminology straight, I speak of event representations as scripts and of concepts as derived from scripts by a further process of analysis or partitioning.

The whole event as a basic unit in the child's initial cognitive representations was implicit in the model of the functional core concept I put forth some years ago (Nelson, 1974), in which objects were said to be represented in terms of the relations—actions and reactions primarily—into which they entered. The *concept* as outlined there was essentially an event representation or rather the abstraction of relationships across a number of different scripts. The present description can be viewed as a simple extension of that model.

There is ample evidence for the psychological reality of scripts for young children. My associates and I have assembled a large body of evidence showing that children as young as 2 articulate their familiar experiences in a wholistic, sequentially ordered, generalized form (Nelson, 1978; Nelson, Fivush, Hudson, & Lucariello, 1982; Nelson & Gruendel, 1981). At younger ages we have to rely primarily on nonverbal evidence, and the evidence at this point is primarily informal. Children's responses to words and many of the first words themselves present evidence that in fact they are using words to refer to a whole event at the beginning of speech. For example, Church (1961) reports the case of a 12-month-old girl who responds to the word "bath" by going to the bathroom, taking off clothes, turning on water, and so on. Bloom (1973) and several other observers have cited the child's use of the word "car" for the activity of looking out the window and watching the cars go by.

It is important to note that events and event representations come in different sizes. The child's throwing a ball is an event (it is also an action scheme); the reciprocal game of rolling a ball back and forth to another is also an event. I call the representation of the latter a script because it involves roles that people play—in this case interchangeable and reciprocal roles of rolling and catching. It also involves actions that in fact define the roles and are sequentially and causally related and an object, ideally a class of objects including different particular objects as instances. But ball rolling is still a small and simple script (it might be better thought of as a scene, see Abelson, 1981). Larger scripts that may be mentally represented include eating a meal, going to bed, dressing, and being taken on outings of various kinds. At the present time we do not know how large or small a child's scripts typically are at the age of 1 year, nor how many scripts a child of this age may have.

Let me emphasize again that the proposal is that events themselves are represented as wholes at first, not as part constructions. That is, playing ball is a scripted *activity;* so is looking at picture books with mother. As observers we can specify the parts—its roles, props, and so on—but for the child these may not be separable. Ball *implies* throwing, book *implies* reading (or chewing), and cup *implies* drinking.

Conceptualizing the parts of the script as separate entities (i.e., separating out objects, actions, and properties in order to treat them as mental objects that can be manipulated) requires a further step of analyzing the original script into its component parts and the relations that hold between them. This process marks the beginning of the conceptual system per se. Studying the various types of concepts and relations that develop therefrom is our next task.

CONCEPTUAL RELATIONS

To introduce this discussion let me quote first from de Saussure (1915/1959):

> In a language-state everything is based on relations. . . . Relations and differences between linguistic terms fall into two distinct groups, each of which generates a certain class of values. . . . They correspond to two forms of our mental activity, both indispensable to the life of language.
> In discourse, on the one hand, words acquire relations based on the linear nature of language because they are chained together. . . . The elements are arranged in sequence in the chain of speaking. Combinations supported by linearity are *syntagms* . . . in the syntagm a term acquires its value only because it stands in opposition to everything that precedes or follows it, or to both [p. 122].

For example, an adjective-noun phrase is syntagmatic. The *relation* between the two words establishes the categories. If we say "the bear cub," "bear" belongs to the adjective category and "cub" to the noun. However, if we say "the baby bear," the relation is reversed—"bear" is the noun. It is for these reasons that parts of speech cannot be defined out of context. De Saussure (1915/1959) continues:

> Outside discourse . . . words acquire relations of a different kind. Those that have something in common are associated in the memory, resulting in groups marked by diverse relations . . . co-ordinations formed outside discourse . . . are not supported by linearity. Their seat is in the brain; they are a part of the inner storehouse that makes up the language of each speaker. They are *associative relations* [p. 123].

Note that these associative relations are not taken from the world but are constructed in the head.

This description of the two types of relations in the language fits neatly into the analysis of relations in event representations and concepts. Since de Saussure, associative relations have been transmuted in linguistics into *paradigmatic* relations, specifying relations between units that can occur in the same context. Although the term is most often used in psychology to refer to words from the same form class (e.g., nouns, verbs, and adjectives), it may refer to many different domains and to more specific types as well (e.g., all animate nouns, all food terms, etc.). For example, bears, cows, and dogs share paradigmatic relations through their common membership in the animal class. They can occur in the frame "X is running" but do not all usually occur in this frame simultaneously.

Syntagmatic and paradigmatic relations are best known in psychology for their use in the analysis of free word associations. It is well established that younger children give more syntagmatic than paradigmatic word associations, whereas older children and adults give more paradigmatic associations (e.g., Entwisle, 1966; Ervin, 1961; Woodrow & Lowell, 1916). For example, in response to the stimulus word "table" younger children are likely to say "eat," whereas older children and adults will respond "chair." There are of course alternative explanations of this development in the production of different types of word associations (Nelson, 1977). It is not my intention, however, to discuss these or to draw an exact parallel between this phenomenon and conceptual development, although I believe that they are related (see Petry, 1977).

To begin the discussion of conceptual relations, note that just as words can be described in terms of their syntagmatic and paradigmatic relations in and between sentences, so the objects, actions, and persons in real-world events that sentences describe can be so identified.

The script model of event representations suggests three sorts of general relations pertaining to the objects or actors in the script:

1. An actor or an object may recur throughout the event taking part in different actions (e.g., mother and ball in the ball-rolling script). Thus, the

object or person may take on a number of different relationships within a single event context.

2. On the other hand, different objects may alternatively occur in the same position in the event—they may be alternative tokens or slot fillers (e.g., tennis balls and red rubber balls).

3. Or a single object or category of objects may recur in a number of different events, in similar or different relationships (e.g., balls at the beach and on the tennis court).

These different types of relations may lead to, respectively, concepts of a single object, concepts of functionally similar objects, and general contextfree concepts and categories. Let us examine each of these in more detail.

First note that the relation between the various elements in a given instance of a script—the actions, actors, and objects—are syntagmatic relations, that is, relations between elements of contrasting types that occur in a sequential structure. In contrast to the intrascript relations, the various cross-script object relations that we are going to consider here are paradigmatic relations, that is, relations between elements of the same type occurring in similar contexts in different structures. (Whether the type comes before the relationship or vice versa is a problem that, it is hoped, this analysis can help to untangle.) At the start we should note that establishing paradigmatic relationships of even the simplest type requires more abstracting from both real-world and conceptual context than do syntagmatic relationships, which are apparent as events unfold in the real world.

Concepts of the Single Object

The recognition that a single object plays a role in different relations within a given situation can lead the child to form a concept of that object that will include a number of different actions and relations and perhaps different actors. In this way the script (the internal event representation) can form the basis for a *situationally specific concept* of an object. Turning the script structure around and respecifying it in terms of the object, we then get something that looks very much like the concept that I first proposed in terms of a functional core model (FCM) (Nelson, 1974). For example, the concept of ball at time 1 was defined in terms of its spatiotemporal parameters and of such actions as:

"Mother throws, picks up, holds."
"I throw, pick up, hold."
"Ball rolls, bounces."

To restate some of the claims of the FCM model, the concept of ball will be formed because it is a focal object in a dynamic situation of some interest to the child. It is the situation, event, or script that determines *what* objects will be conceptualized. In turn, the objects so conceptualized will be analyzed for their identifying characteristics and will therefore become identifiable as concept members by the child outside the original context. Note that participation in more than one action or relationship is assumed for the separation of the object concept from its syntagmatic context-defined relationships in the event representation. This assumption is related to Piaget's theory because action-object schemes are not sufficient for establishing knowledge of the object independent of the action.

Because we assume that the event structure, not the object structure, is primary in the conceptualization process, it becomes clear why function or action should be important to the child's formation of concepts and word meanings. It is not simply because the child's own actions are fundamentally defining (as one reading of Piaget would suggest) but because conceptual representation is in the first instance the representation of event structures, and objects are known in terms of their relation to the events of which they are a part.

To clarify another point, the discussion here is in terms of conceptual representation, not perception. Children may know what a ball looks like before they know what it does. This level of world knowledge enables object recognition but not knowledge at a deeper conceptual level. Clearly, perceptual information and categorization are important to human functioning in general and to language learning in particular. However, the argument here is that the place of the object in the pattern of activity represented by the child's event scripts must be established for the child to confer meaning on the object within his or her own conceptual system. It is in this sense that we must at the outset abandon the notion of the concept as a category of objects in favor of the object representation in terms of a system of relationships. An object concept may then be seen as an achievement by way of the abstraction of the consistent appearance in an event representation of a particular object or set of objects in a system of recurrent relationships. Creation of an object concept involves the establishment of a decontexted unit apart from its relationally contexted particulars.

Categories of Objects

In many situations objects that are perceptually quite diverse and therefore clearly distinguishable as different object types recur in the same "slot" in a script over different occurrences of the event. For example, mother may offer chopped liver and spinach for dinner on one day and fried chicken and peas on another. The child may hate liver and spinach but love chicken and peas; thus, the two are distinguishable, but both occupy similar slots in the dinner-eating sequence. Here is an ideal situation for forming a simple category, namely *food*.

Moreover, we have good evidence that children do possess such categories very early. Not only do preschool children report that they "eat food" or "have dessert" when asked about what happens at lunch, but even the 1½-year-old begins to use general terms for items that recur in the same event sequence, sometimes the category terms such as "fruit," but more often the name of a particular fruit such as "apple" (Rescorla, 1980, 1981). This kind of "error" appears to verify the psychological reality of "slot-filling." What the child must do in order to learn *appropriate* lexical terms, however, is distinguish, on the basis of perceptual characteristics, those objects that were identified as equivalent on the basis of their similar place in an event script. Later the child will have to relearn some of the same general categories on the same essential basis, that is, that the category members serve similar functions.

Note that this type of category formation on the basis of scripts is based on substitutability within an event rather than grouping of similar members. It requires the recognition that different elements occupy the same position in a given structure at different times and therefore necessarily involves an abstraction from mental representations. This is quite a different matter from the process of simultaneous grouping that is usually assumed to underlie the child's formation of hierarchical categories and, in fact, is often used as a test of that skill.

Contextfree Concepts and Categories

If an object (e.g., "apple") or a category of objects (e.g., "food") occurs in more than one script it may come to be recognized by the child as the same concept or category serving similar or different functions in different situations. This move will obviously be easier if the same object serves similar functions in different scripts. For example, the breakfast, lunch, and dinner scripts all require cups and spoons. It is likely to be more difficult to see that the same object serves different functions in different scripts (e.g., that a cup can be used to hold pencils as well as milk). In the latter case, the cup might not in fact be recognized as the same object in the new script.

Whereas the basic object concept has identifying characteristics that enable the child to recognize an instance in novel circumstances, higher level object categories are usually quite diverse perceptually, without invariant perceptual characteristics. Although categories such as animals, money, and fruit are functionally similar, they are not usually perceptually similar enough to provide for contextfree identification of perceptually novel examples. Thus, some mechanisms beyond private experience may be needed to insure that the child who sees animals at the zoo and feeds turtles and gerbils in the preschool classifies both as "animals." Generally, adults make the connection for the child by calling both "animals." However, the child may resist this classification, deny that some animals are animals, or call them by subordinate terms such as "wild animals" or "pets." If there is overlap in the membership of the categories in the two scripts, these connections may be made directly. However, as the conceptual structure grows more complex, the connections become less certain because objects may belong to more than one category.

Categories that are extracted across scripts become more general and less tied to spatiotemporal context than slot-filler categories because the script, although general, is essentially spatially and temporally context bound. The formation of contextfree categories then represents a very powerful conceptual move, where paradigmatic relations are extracted from syntagmatic ones, not within a single script or context but across contexts, that is, across event representations. One necessary basis for this move is the ability to recognize same or similar procedures or functions in different scripts. Even when the adult in effect picks out or defines the contextfree category, as for example, when an adult tells children that both gerbils and elephants are animals, the category may lack psychological reality for the children until they can see what *functions* are similar to both.

Thus, it seems clear that across all three types of concepts and categories syntagmatic relations are basic to conceptual development. Different types of concepts and categories are built up depending on which relationships they·share. Note that what is not involved in any of the operations outlined thus far is an analysis in terms of the *similarity* of object types independent of their functional relations. The analysis assumes instead that the child operates for a very long time with a conceptual representation that defines object categories in terms of their relationships and not in terms of their internal qualities (see also Markman, 1981 and this volume, on this point). The establishment of similarity relations is assumed to be a more advanced cognitive operation that takes place only after the basic categories have been formed. This is as true for general categories as it is for basic object concepts.

To recapitulate, the initial representations are in terms of syntagmatic relations, including actions, between people and objects. Objects then are known in terms of these relations and actions. At the same time language is beginning to be used and understood in terms of situational representations.

In contrast to the standard Piagetian position and to abstraction (of internal qualities) theory, this view of conceptual development proposes that representation is first and basically neither of objects nor of object attributes but of situations in which objects are a part. The move to symbolization through language is a move that involves decontextualization of aspects of the situation. In the course of this decontextualization, objects and actions become conceptualized and named.

CONCEPTUAL AND SEMANTIC DEVELOPMENT

Once the child has acquired language, conceptual development may be studied through the analysis of word meanings and relationships. In fact, it is a basic part of this proposal that conceptual and semantic development are inextricably entwined through most of early childhood.

Let me make this explicit. Events are first represented whole, and names or other bits and pieces of language are mapped onto these representations. Through a process of extraction and mapping, the syntagmatic event representation yields individual concepts that require names. Thus at the outset, the child appears to attach words directly to the conceptual structure. In the course of decontextualization of object and action concepts from their embedding event representations, the language terms and constructions also become freed from context. No doubt these progressions are interactive, taking place usually around the period from 18 to 24 months. Then, during the 3rd, 4th, and 5th years, the child gradually builds up a distinct grammatical system that is not mapped directly onto the conceptual system but rather acts as an interpreter of it, as well as a lexical system that interacts with but is not a direct mapping of the conceptual system. That is, this period of semiotic development appears to be one of the simultaneous development of semi-independent but interacting language and conceptual structures.

The child's first language constructions (of the "mommy sock" type) are assumed to be direct mappings of the primitive conceptual representations. This is not to say that these representations dictate anything like regular word order or categories such as actor, action, and object. The order in an event representation derives from its relation between actions, not from the relation between action and its instigators or its objects.

What is the relation of lexical terms to the conceptual representation? At the outset, it is assumed that the lexical relations will be mapped onto the conceptual relations. The early categorical overextensions that are found in the child's early lexicons often reflect substitutability within an event frame. For example, in Rescorla's (1980) data, a child named all fruits "lardi," a name taken from the greengrocer who delivered fruits to her house. Or children may name all vehicles that they play with "truck" or "car," although they are able to distinguish between these types on perceptual grounds (Nelson, Rescorla, Gruendel, & Benedict, 1978; Rescorla, 1981).

At some point children may identify lexical categories as they are reflected in the language used around them and rely less on the concepts and categories they have defined in terms of substitutability in event slots. At that point each object category that receives a distinct name in the adult language used with the child will come to be given a distinct name by the child. Fortunately, there will be considerable overlap in the two systems.

The continuing effect of the initially defining event frame can still be seen in the types of relations that are established between words at the emerging lexical level, as the word-association data referred to earlier show. Indeed, analysis of these data is highly consistent with the notion of a lexical system initially mapped onto a conceptual representation that is based in event structures. Petry's (1977) analysis of Entwisle's (1966) data demonstrated that the earliest associations from the 5-year-olds in her sample (which she characterized as evidencing "primitive noun responses") were based on *situational* associations of a script (or episodic) type, for example, "night-moon." Subsequently, the syntagmatic responses appeared to be based more on lexical relationships, ones that could appear together in speech (although not necessarily contiguously), as for example, "dog bark." Only in the school years did they begin to reflect the categorical or paradigmatic responses that are typical of adults, for example, "night–day" or "dog–cat." That is, the system Petry describes moves from relationships based in a context-bound conceptual system organized according to event structures to a lexical system that becomes increasingly decontextualized, and therefore removed from its basis in the event representation level, and reflects more and more the categories that are derived from the paradigmatic relationships of the event structures. There are now increasing amounts of data from children's use of language to indicate that relations between words are being established during the preschool years. Bowerman's (1976, 1978) reports are most conclusive in this respect.

As outlined, the most basic object category is the type that can fill a particular slot (or a number of slots) in an event sequence. If these types are recognized as having perceptual features that are relevant to their similar functions with the sequence, they will be categorized as "the same" and given the same name by the child. It may happen that they are also given the same name by the language community or culture, as is the case with "dog," "car," and "ball." However, in some cases, objects that fit into the same slot in an event do not look alike and are not given the same names in the language. This is the case with food items such as apple and banana. In this case, the child may learn a general category word to fit the slot, as well as the distinct names that differentiate the members able to fill that slot. Thus, category names such as "food," "fruit," "toys," and "games" are learned early and are used by the child in event-appropriate contexts. Often, they are used as alternates to the more specific terms rather than in hierarchical dominance relations. Thus, children may talk readily about animals, and if you ask what some of the animals are they may be able to tell you, but they will resist telling you that, for example, a dog *is* an animal. No independent classification of this kind exists at this point. On the other hand, if the adult tells the young child that a wombat is a kind of animal, the child knows what functional relationships to insert wombat into. Markman's (1981) analysis suggests that the child may interpret the class (animal) as a collection; in this case, to say a dog *is* an animal would be wrong (see Markman, this volume). This alternative view complements the present account. Future research will determine the circumstances under which each of these may apply. Note, however, that both rely on the child's understanding of relations between objects.

A more abstract level is reached when the child combines categories across scripts. As noted earlier, this might be the case because some of the same instances occur in more than one script, that is, rabbits are seen both in the preschool and in a children's zoo. As long as *animal* does not exist as a dominating class, these need have no effect on the child's general category but only on his or her concept of rabbit. However, noticing the existence of particular instances in more than one event context is likely to have greater repercussions. First, if the child has acquired two separate sets that overlap in membership, one of which fits context A and the other context B, there may be a cognitive disposition to combine the two into a single set, especially if the functional relations defining them are similar. The effect of language is to support this cognitive disposition. In the case of animal, for example, the language community will apply the word ''animal'' to both sets.

The next move is to note that ''animal'' can be used not only to fill a slot in an event sequence as an alternative to a particular instance, but also that it constitutes a category itself, which subsumes all the members of the sets that fit into the various frames where animal is the general term. I am suggesting that *this move is dependent on language*—that it does not take place conceptually without language. It becomes possible only because of the possible abstract manipulation of symbols. It is the unique result of the decontextualization process. At this point a network of relations has become established that is specifically lexical. The lexicon is no longer mapped onto or organized directly in terms of the underlying conceptual event representation but is organized in terms of relations between words.

We have recently collected data that support this view of the formations of categories using the free recall of categorized word lists paradigm.[3] If scripts are important in the way indicated to the formation of categories, we believed that we should be able to manipulate their use in recall lists by varying the script relations contained therein.

For this experiment we first elicited lists of words from 3- and 4-year-olds in the categories clothes, food, and animals. We asked children to tell us the clothes they put on in the morning, those they wore outside, and those they wore to bed. We also asked for zoo animals, pets, and farm animals. And we asked for lunch, breakfast, and dessert foods. Next we took the most frequently mentioned word for each subcategory and composed a taxonomic list of three each of animals, food, and clothes. We also composed a script-based list of zoo animals, lunch foods, and clothes you put on in the morning.

Different groups received either the taxonomic list or script-based list in either free or constrained recall. The script-based list was tested under two types of constrained recall, when children were asked either to tell all the animals (clothes, food), as with the taxonomic lists, or to tell all the things you could eat for lunch, put on in the morning, or see at the zoo.

The results are straightforward. There is a difference in the predicted direction among all conditions. Script lists are better than taxonomic in both free and constrained recall and clustering, and the script cues are better than categorical cues for amount of recall.

---

[3]This experiment was designed and carried out by Joan Lucariello at CUNY. It and a follow-up study will be reported in full in a forthcoming report.

All of the objects used in the script-based lists are ones that are associated with a single action in a given script, that is, they are Type I slot fillers, all potentially fitting into the slot provided by "put on X," "look at X in cage," supporting the assumption that such slots are of use in categorical construction for the child.

Thus, this initial evidence supports the hypothesis outlined here that scripts serve as the basis for generating more abstract forms of conceptual organizations such as taxonomic categories that reflect paradigmatic relations.

The general conceptual developmental scheme proposed here can be summarized as follows: An undifferentiated event representation yields to the cognitive analysis of its parts, forming concepts that are related to one another syntagmatically. Syntagmatic relations are revealed in the events that are represented as well as in the speech that is used in connection with those events. Further cognitive analysis reveals paradigmatic relations between the concepts, thus setting up conceptual systems of related elements. Learning hierarchical language terms in turn sets up semantic hierarchies that may operate semi-independently of the conceptual system.

DEVELOPMENTAL PROCESSES

Are concepts learned? Do they develop spontaneously? I have tried here to stress that concepts and categories come in different types and are therefore subject to different courses of aquisition. At this point I try to sketch what processes are necessary to concept acquisition and development.

As stressed throughout, representation of events in the world is basic to the process, implying perception and memory for complexly structured, sequentially ordered information. I believe that informal evidence is in hand (and that more systematic studies will back it up) to support the assertion that the pre-linguistic child operates on this basis. Note that I am not claiming complex sequences of differentiated *parts* but rather a complex whole whose parts are not yet individuated.

In order to form concepts from these representations, the system must employ analysis of the whole (or if you prefer, differentiation). Once analyzed into parts, the system needs to learn rules of recombination (or integration into a new whole). But this does not end the matter. The process of analysis then operates on the parts and their combination as well, setting up new conceptual systems of relations that are revealed only indirectly. Thus, the system *achieves* conceptual context in addition to the original event context. The contexts possibly available in which any event or object can be seen grow unceasingly. The conceptual relation to the real world is thus always indirect and abstract but also always contingent.

Of course, children do not stop representing and amending old representations on the basis of new experiences. Nor are they immune to the structuring of experience through language. Representation (and the exchange of representation through symbolic forms) is the basic interface between mind and world, but it is far from the end of the matter. The system itself takes over and through a never-ending process of analysis and synthesis continues to evolve in more complex directions. Thus, we conclude that concepts are not learned in any conventional sense. Nor are they innate. Rather they are the product of a powerful set of cognitive operations on the contexted array that the culture presents to the child. As such they are both individual and conventional, tied to the world and to the language, but also potentially independent of them.

In this section I have gone far beyond any data now available to us in part to indicate why I believe development—of concepts or anything else—is so difficult to study. So much of it is underground, inaccessible to us and to the child. The process is, in Campbell's (1979) words, cryptic, or in Reber and Lewis' (1977) terms, implicit. Piaget and Inhelder (1973) gave us a clue to all this in their intriguing studies of changes in memory over time. My description is more mundane than theirs, relying not on logical systems but on simple processing mechanisms. Nonetheless, I believe I am operating in the same spirit in proposing that development is at least in part an exercise in making the implicit (i.e., the structure) explicit (revealing its parts).

And I think there is equal developmental truth in the notion that a large part of the developmental process is involved in differentiating pieces from their dynamic wholes in order to construct more complex integrations. Here, of course, I echo Werner. It is difficult—indeed impossible—to be an original developmental psychologist.

SUMMARY AND CONCLUSION

The general argument set forth here can be summarized as follows. The basic form of conceptual representation is that of the event representation. This basic form provides data for further internal analysis in terms of patterns of relationships and substitutability of objects, actors, and actions. Concepts of particular objects are conceptual achievements that require cumulating relational information within and across event structures, extracting paradigmatic categories from syntagmatic representations. The learning of language terms at first maps onto the event representation and constructed conceptual structures directly, determining both early word use and semantic categories and semantic relations in early (presyntactic) language. Although syntactic structures soon become decontextualized with respect to the semantic structure, the semantic structure continues to map the conceptual structure directly well into the preschool period. Eventually, however, the lexical system itself becomes decontextualized so that word and concept become less tightly entwined and an independent (but interacting) level of lexical relationships is built up and is reflected in the increasingly language-specific responses in verbal tasks. This developmental course is conceived to represent a process of differentiation and integration. Earlier representational processes (e.g., event scripts) are not lost but are supplemented by more abstract levels of functioning.

ACKNOWLEDGMENTS

Preparation of this chapter was supported in part by NSF Grant # BNS 79–14006. Thanks to Joe Glick for helpful comments on an earlier version of the paper. Parts of the chapter are based on a paper prepared for presentation at the Developmental Section of the British Psychological Society, Edinburgh, September 6, 1980, and on a chapter by Nelson (1982).

REFERENCES

Abelson, R. P. Psychological status of the script concept. *American Psychologist,* 1981, *36,* 715–729.

Anglin, J. M. *Word, object and conceptual development.* New York: Norton, 1977.

Ardener, E. Some outstanding problems in the analysis of events. In M. L. Foster & S. H. Brandes (Eds.), *Symbol as sense.* New York: Academic Press, 1980.

Ashmead, D. H., & Perlmutter, M. Infant memory in everyday life. In M. Perlmutter (Ed.), *Children's memory.* San Francisco: Jossey-Bass, 1980.

Bloom, L. *One word at a time.* The Hague: Mouton, 1973.

Bowerman, M. Semantic factors in the acquisition of rules for word use and sentence construction. In D. Morehead & A. Morehead (Eds.), *Directions in normal and deficial child language.* Baltimore, Md.: University Park Press, 1976.

Bowerman, M. Systemizing semantic knowledge: Changes over time in the child's organization of word meaning. *Child Development,* 1978, *49,* 977–988.

Bransford, J., & McCarrell, N. S. A sketch of a cognitive approach to comprehension: Some thoughts about understanding what it means to comprehend. In W. B. Weimer & D. S. Palermo (Eds.), *Cognition and the symbolic processes.* Hillsdale, N.J.: Lawrence Erlbaum Associates, 1974.

Bronowski, J., & Bellugi, U. Language, name and concept. *Science,* 1972, *168,* 669–673.

Bruner, J. S. On cognitive growth. In J. S. Bruner, R. R. Olver, & P. M. Greenfield (Eds.), *Studies in cognitive growth.* New York: Wiley, 1966.

Bruner, J. S. The ontogenesis of speech acts. *Journal of Child Language,* 1975, *2,* 1–20.

Campbell, R. N. Cognitive development and child language. In P. Fletcher & M. Garman (Eds.), *Language acquisition.* Cambridge, England: Cambridge University Press, 1979.

Church, J. *Language and the discovery of reality.* New York: Random House, 1961.

Clark, E. V. What's in a word? On the child's acquisition of semantics in his first language. In T. E. Moore (Ed.), *Cognitive development and the acquisition of language.* New York: Academic Press, 1973.

Entwisle, D. R. *The word associations of young children.* Baltimore, Md.: Johns Hopkins University Press, 1966.

Ervin, S. M. Changes with age in the verbal determinants of word associations. *American Journal of Psychology,* 1961, *74,* 361–372.

Flavell, J. Concept development. In P. H. Mussen (Ed.), *Carmichael's manual of child psychology* (3rd ed.) (Vol. 1). New York: Wiley, 1970.

Gentner, D. On relational meaning: The acquisition of verb meaning. *Child Development*, 1978, *49*, 988–998.

Gibson, J. J. *The ecological approach to visual perception*. Boston: Houghton Mifflin, 1979.

Le Compte, G. K., & Gratch, G. Violation of a rule as a method of diagnosing infants' level of object concept. *Child Development*, 1972, *43*, 385–396.

Lyons, J. *Semantics* (Vol. 1). Cambridge, England: Cambridge University Press, 1977.

Markman, E. M. Two different principles of conceptual organization. In M. Lamb & A. Brown (Eds.), *Advances in developmental psychology* (Vol. 1). Hillsdale, N.J.: Lawrence Erlbaum Associates, 1981.

Mead, G. H. *Mind, self and society*. Chicago: University of Chicago Press, 1934.

Nelson, K. Concept, word and sentence: Interrelations in acquisition and development. *Psychological Review*, 1974, *81*, 267–285.

Nelson, K. The syntagmatic–paradigmatic shift revisisted: A review of research and theory. *Psychological Bulletin*, 1977, *84*, 93–116.

Nelson, K. How children represent knowledge of their world in and out of language: A preliminary report. In R. S. Siegler (Ed.), *Children's thinking: What develops?* Hillsdale, N.J.: Lawrence Erlbaum Associates, 1978.

Nelson, K. Explorations in the development of a functional semantic system. In W. A. Collins (Ed.), *Children's language and communication*. Hillsdale, N.J.: Lawrence Erlbaum Associates, 1979.

Nelson, K. The syntagmatics and paradigmatics of conceptual representation. In S. Kuczaj II (Ed.), *Language, thought, and culture*. Hillsdale, N.J.: Lawrence Erlbaum Associates, 1982.

Nelson, K., Fivush, R., Hudson, J., & Lucariello, J. Scripts and the development of memory. In M. T. H. Chi (Ed.), *What is memory development the development of?* In J. A. Meacham (Ed.) *Contributations to Human Development Monograph Series*. Basil, Switzerland: S. Karger, A. G., 1982.

Nelson, K., & Gruendel, J. Generalized event representations: Basic building blocks of cognitive development. In M. Lamb & A. Brown (Eds.), *Advances in developmental psychology* (Vol. 1). Hillsdale, N.J.: Lawrence Erlbaum Associates, 1981.

Nelson K., Rescorla, L., Gruendel, J., & Benedict, H. Early lexicons: What do they mean? *Child Development*, 1978, *49*, 960–968.

Petry, S. Word associations and the development of lexical memory. *Cognition*, 1977, *5*, 57–71.

Piaget, J. *Play, dreams and imitation in childhood*. New York: Norton, 1962.

Piaget, J., & Inhelder, B. *Memory and intelligence*. New York: Basic Books, 1973.

Putnam, H. *Mind, language and reality: philosophical papers* (Vol. 2). Cambridge, England: Cambridge University Press, 1975.

Reber, A. S., & Lewis, S. Implicit learning: An analysis of the form and structure of a body of tacit knowledge. *Cognition*, 1977, *5*, 333–361.

Rescorla, L. A. Overextension in early child language development. *Journal of Child Language*, 1980, *7*, 321–335.

Rescorla, L. A. Category development in early language. *Journal of Child Language*, 1981, *8*, 225–238.

Rosch, E. Principles of categorization. In E. Rosch & B. Lloyd (Eds.), *Cognition and categorization*. Hillsdale, N.J.: Lawrence Erlbaum Associates, 1978.

Rosch, E., & Mervis, C. B. Family resemblances: Studies in the internal structure of categories. *Cognitive Psychology*, 1975, *7*, 573–605.

Sampson, E. E. Cognitive psychology as ideology. *American Psychologist*, 1981, *36*, 730–743.

de Saussure, F. *Course in general linguistics*. New York: McGraw-Hill, 1959. (Originally published, 1915.)

Schank, R., & Abelson, R. A. *Scripts, plans, goals and understanding*. Hillsdale, N.J.: Lawrence Erlbaum Associates, 1977.

Smith, L. B., & Kemler, D. G. Developmental trends in free classification: Evidence for a new conceptualization of perceptual development. *Journal of Experimental Child Psychology*, 1977, *24*, 279–298.

Vygotsky, L. S. *Thought and language*. Cambridge, Mass.: MIT Press, 1962.

Werner, H. *Comparative psychology of mental development*. New York: International Universities Press, 1957.

Woodrow, H., & Lowell, F. Children's association frequency tables. *Psychological Monographs*, 1916, *22*(5, Whole No. 97).

7

Early Concept Formation: Models from Nelson and Piaget

Rodney R. Cocking
National Institute of Education
Washington, D.C.

INTRODUCTION

A recurrent theme in recent developmental research, and particularly in the Piaget Society's symposia, has been issues of behavioral continuities and discontinuities. At the level of theory construction, the continuity–discontinuity theme has been presented at length in a comparison of Piaget as the functional Constructivist and Piaget as the Structural theorist (Cocking, 1981). In the present volume, Beilin discusses a prevailing contemporary interest in continuities of function. In the discussion of Katherine Nelson's work, the subject of this chapter, we see an exemplary body of research that is directed toward the issue of functional continuity in her analysis of concepts, classes, categories, and context as the critical elements during the emergence of children's symbolic functioning.

The purpose of this chapter is to highlight differences between two explanations of concept formation: Piaget's model and Nelson's model as presented in this volume. At the same time, the chapter also discusses the strengths of each model. The aim, therefore, is not to build a case for or against either approach.

It becomes apparent that the theoretical approaches of Piaget and Nelson share many common aspects. In some instances, in fact, the only real differences appear to be the way an issue is discussed. Unique terminologies are retained and at times compared so that the reader can see that some differences are more apparent than real.

Although the theoretical approaches of Piaget and Nelson have many commonalities, certain underlying differences in their respective philosophies of science bear mentioning. The discussion of differences in these philosophical traditions make the Structuralist/Functionalist labels, so frequently used to characterize each theorist, more meaningful. Within the context of Structuralism and Functionalism discussions two theoretical issues are also considered: (1) developmental continuities and discontinuities; (2) competence versus performance criteria in developmental models. These two theoretical issues (continuity–discontinuity; competence–performance) are considered briefly and only as they relate to the data, methods, and interpretations each theorist utilizes in discussions of concept formation.

This chapter takes a look at the developmental problem of early concept formation in which the major goals of scientific research on the topic are considered. In the course of considering what needs to be known in order to understand how concepts develop in young children, we also have to look at the major methods and troublesome aspects of conducting research on the topic. Inasmuch as this discussion focuses only on two models, these comparisons are necessarily limited. They should, however, help in clarifying where Nelson's and Piaget's models differ, as well as the ways in which they overlap.

The treatment of topics in this chapter may sometimes appear very intertwined when a more linear approach might be desirable. Issues, unlike definitions, however, involve a network of concepts and terms, and for this reason, it is sometimes necessary to refer back to previous remarks and to preface other parts that follow. For example, as the discussion moves through the issues of continuity and discontinuity, the term *action* (in the Piagetian sense) is referred to. Discussions of processes of representation also make reference to *action,* and when Piaget's functionalist leanings are considered, the term again enters the discussion. This occasional volleying forth and back should actually aid the reader in seeing that although differences do exist between these theorists' accounts of development, the two are not in direct opposition to each other. Each theorist sees his or her account as comprehensive, so it is the intent here to assess the relative emphases of the two different models. This assessment requires us to look at the interconnectedness of issues.

STRUCTURALISM, FUNCTIONALISM, AND REPRESENTATION

The labels Structuralist and Functionalist do not apply to Piaget and Nelson in the most orthodox sense of the definitions. However, Piaget, because of his emphasis on cognitive organization (cognitive structures), is generally termed a Structuralist (Piaget, 1970). Likewise, Nelson is usually grouped with latter-day Functionalists because she chooses to study the continuity of function within given periods of development. Adopting the methods of functionalism is not the only critical departure Nelson makes from mainstream Piagetians, however. Her chapter in this volume clearly sets forward her performance account of development, preferring to dispense with Structuralist obsessions over competence. As noted in her comments, efficacy and even classification skills only remotely become necessary considerations in her account of understanding concept formation. We return to the competence–performance issue later, but for the present characterization of Structuralists and Functionalists it is sufficient to say that the latter are generally more interested in performance skills, whereas Structuralists speak and write in terms of cognitive competence.

The distinctions between who is a Structuralist and who is a Functionalist are not always clear-cut. When Piaget writes about the move from action schemes to concepts in early cognitive growth, he himself falls into the functionalist category (Cocking, 1981). This characterization is especially apparent in his discussions in *The Principles of Genetic Epistemology* (1972). As an example, Piaget sees representation as an important function because it accounts for a critical shift in development: to the existence of events in thought, rather than their existence resting solely in action. In this shift, Piaget tells us, the child must re-construct everything that was acquired at the level of actions. That is, everything that was previously constructed in terms of external sensorimotor and internal action schemes has to be *re*constructed in *conceptual* terms and, in turn, will have to be reconstructed again at the concrete operational level. A retrospective of Piagetian theory reveals that a major goal was to *integrate* structural and functional aspects of development (i.e., how structures are constructed). Piaget the theorist, however, still is classified principally as a Structuralist because of his interest in cognitive operations as a system of transformations, one of the basic tenets of Formal Structuralism (cf. Cocking, 1981). Similarly, Nelson's interest in the *structure* of the social event should not be misinterpreted: For her, the social event is functionally defined by the relationships that the child perceives and that are eventually mapped syntagmatically and paradigmatically.

CONTINUITY AND DISCONTINUITY
IN DEVELOPMENT

The Structuralist/Functionalist differences emerge in bold relief when discussing the issue of continuity and discontinuity in development. The Functionalist tends to look for continuities of function. Nelson, specifically, concentrates on the development that occurs *within* a given developmental time frame (during concept formation) as opposed to the broader period of concept development. This within-period focus emphasizes the continuity picture she paints. The Structuralist, by contrast, looks across developmental periods for evidence of growth toward competent functioning, specifically in the growth of cognitive competence. Structuralists often cite as evidence of the discontinuities in cognitive growth the disparities in related types of thinking across various periods of development, explaining that structures undergo major reorganizations. Such discussions invariably invoke a second issue of development—the ever-present competence versus performance theories of development. As mentioned previously, Functionalists tend to look at the development of skills and see the child's smoothing out of performance as the index of development. Structuralists, by contrast, try to determine the underlying understandings of concepts that children have at various points in development. Because understanding appears to be very different at different times in development, Structuralists characterize children's mental growth in terms of levels of understanding (competence). In the structuralist position, performance is epiphenomenal: Cognitive competence is what the cognitive scientist strives to know. Some observers boil down the controversy to a difference between practitioners and theoreticians, in which educational psychologists are the functionalists who wish to know more about specific skills so that they can implement training programs. Research psychologists, by comparison, are seen as prone to dwell on the larger picture of theory and model building. This pragmatic distinction, however, is not a widely shared view.

In terms of the continuity–discontinuity distinction, it might seem that Nelson should emerge as a Structuralist because her focus is on the structure of the social event, especially with regard to the structure of the relationships she maps. Piaget, with his focus on *action,* by like analysis, appears to be the Functionalist. It is important, therefore, to keep in mind the critical features of Functionalism and Structuralism as *continuity of function* and *reorganizational changes of structures.* The Structuralist or Functionalist label is useful for characterizing the theories and the courses of development, but it does not characterize what the child does, as in the erroneous conclusion mentioned earlier, which assumes that an "action" theory is necessarily a functionalist perspective.

Before considering how each approach deals with the issue of representation, it is first necessary to consider what is meant by the *nature of representation* itself. This consideration, in turn, forces us to take up the issue of *internal* versus *external* representation. It must be noted, however, that this is not a discussion of whether representation itself is internal or external, but only which type of representation is critical in the two models of concept formation. In order to see more clearly how this issue emerges in the present comparison, a few comments need to be made about the philosophical traditions represented in the two models of development.

The major differences between Nelson and Piaget are in the basic *research model* (not method) each adopts. Nelson appears to adhere more closely to what is identified as a model of "logical empiricism" (Piaget, 1973). This model studies knowledge in two forms: (1) knowledge gained by experience (both sensory and learning); (2) logical thinking *after the event,* in which language plays a central role.

By contrast, Piaget adopts a model that poses hypotheses in a different way: (1) at every level in the acquisition of knowlege, including perception and learning, the child's activities prepare logical structures; (2) because of the preparatory coordinations at every initial level, logical structures are in evidence, in some degree, in even the earliest elements of intellectual functioning. The point is clarified by recalling Piaget's definitions and distinction between figurative and operative intelligence. Representational thought consists of both figurative and operative components. According to Piaget (1973), the figurative aspect is "everything related to the configurations [p. 75]," as opposed to transformations. The preoperative child reasons on configurations of events and compares the events or objects directly without any intermediary system, such as a system of transformations. The operative aspect relates to transformations, which are the mental activities that modify objects or events. The operative structures that emerge early are seriation, correspondences, classifications, and so forth. But just because preschool children can *perform* along these lines (e.g., create a number series) by no means implies that they are operational thinkers. Piaget (1973) points out that "a large number of logical, mathematical, and physical operations develop . . . in the child aged six or seven . . . [p. 76]." This, by the way, is an example of one of the discontinuities of development that Structuralists like to point out.

As we proceed with a detailed look at the two models, we can see that the distinction between logical empiricism and developmental discontinuity boils down to a difference in characterizing the process in terms of either *external events* or *internal action*. We see that, in terms of representation, the difference is between representing the relationships of external "events" and "scripts" on the one hand and the internal representation through imitation (mental imagery) on the other. The vehicles of representation are discussed by Nelson as "event representation" and by Piaget as "action schemata." Although these are two concepts that should not be pulled from the contexts of their respective models, they serve to highlight the external–internal issue when the models are compared. The larger picture of each model is needed in order to make such comparisons, however.

EVENTS VERSUS ACTION SCHEMES

Functional Core Model and Representation (FCM)

Nelson's functional analysis of event representation in conceptual development begins with the recurring, familiar events in the lives of children as the basis of single-object concepts. This is much the same as Piaget's account of repeatable, generalizable actions. Nelson labels these events as "scripts" and assigns a major role to the social character of the events. She tells us that in representing the familiar social event, script elements of *actors–actions–objects* stand in syntagmatic relationship to one another. That is, script elements are "understood" only as elements of the particular event, not as elements having class memberships that give them defining or unique features.

According to Nelson's analysis, three different types of relations lead to: (1) concepts of single objects; (2) categories of objects; (3) generalized, contextfree concepts and categories. Type I relations give rise to *concepts*. These relationships involve single objects and actions that are situation-specific, and the objects or actions are "known" by their contextually defined relationships within the event. *Categories* of objects are represented as Type II relations, in which the event representation is characterized by substitutability of objects in a script. Categories, thus, are more extensive than concepts. Finally, in Type III relations, objects and acts are less dependent on the context for their meaning. Although Type III representation of relationships is still functionally based, the script elements are increasingly grouped as members of more than a single category. The interscript relationships of Type III are characterized as paradigmatic.

In summary, Nelson's model is an account of how the child moves from representation of an event to concepts. Event representation is analyzed into three types of relationships among actors, actions, and objects, which are syntagmatically linked to one another. From these syntagmatic representations, paradigmatic relations are extracted. The Functional Core Model (FCM) prescribes that representation is first and basically of action *situations* of which objects are part. In this characterization, representation is neither initially nor basically of objects or of object attributes. The model also prescribes that functional syntagmatic relations are basic to concept formation across all three types of relationships that are mapped.

Perception and Conception

Events are *perceived* relationships in the model Nelson presents. A basic assumption of Piagetian theory is that conceptual thought is not simply a buildup of knowledge through perceptual experience or that it is a series of corrections and readjustments to perceptual errors made in the course of development. According to Baldwin (1980), Piaget's is a theory in which concepts are "constructed *de novo* in the course of development [p. 190]." In this view, conceptual thinking in young children is less accurate than their perceptions.

The mental image is the basis for mental schemata within Piaget's system. The "action scheme" is an *internal* schema for 'picturing' the external situation. The external expression of the internal schema is called the sensorimotor scheme. Thus, Piaget incorporates both internal and external factors into his system of representation. The emphasis, however, is on the internal schemata because a symbol, for Piaget, is not representational until it has meaning for the individual. Thus, perceptions are not meaningful until they have been internalized and can be separated, conceptually, from the perceptions themselves. In this system, the mental image is not useful as a symbolic tool until it can be separated from the perception. One indication of such a separation is when children can imitate a model after the model has been removed, so-called deferred imitation (Baldwin, 1980). Thus, the image, in Piaget's system, is not an afterimage of a perception, but rather something that must be constructed, and the construction of the image is an *internal* act.

Nelson's "event representation" and Piaget's "action schema" can be compared as mechanisms of similar purpose. One is struck in such a comparison by the apparent similarity in the two theorists' concepts. But the major difference— varying emphases of focus on perception and conception of internal and external representations—is not the only one. Another distinction is in terms of the "size" of the event. For Nelson and Piaget, *throwing a ball* is both an event *and* an action scheme. Nelson points out that the situation is a little different for a script than for an event because the latter is socially defined. Hence, the reciprocal roles define *throwing a ball* between child and adult as a script. Scripts, then, involve socially defined roles that people play. Piaget, by contrast, maintains that the defining features of the events are the child's own actions; that is, the child's action schemes define events. It is important to recall that, for Piaget (1973), an action (praxis) is not some sort of movement, but rather "a system of *coordinated* movements [p. 63; emphasis added]." The event *structure,* not the child's actions alone, constitute the basis of conceptual representation according to Nelson. The two theorists clearly depart from one another on this point.

Forming Versus Representing Concepts

Much to its credit, Nelson's analysis helps break apart two developmental issues: (1) issues of concept formation; (2) issues of representation. Her analysis of concept formation separates concepts, categories, and contexts; her analysis of Representation shows the coordination of Event Representation with Lexical Represenation—or with Language, as the issue becomes after further development by the child.

The broad FCM may be characterized as a superordinate model that describes how second-order representation (e.g., language) is mapped onto events and then eventually separated from specific events (decontextualized) in order to function abstractly. As we consider what the FCM has to offer, we also need to weight Piaget's alternatives by asking: If the FCM rejects abstraction theory, how are the relations "extracted" by the child? How are the relations generalized or transferred? What is the mechanism for extracting relations?

In the FCM, words are applied directly to the conceptual structure, and during the decontextualization of object concepts and action concepts, the language terms (lexicon) are also freed of the context. The semantic aspect (meaning), however, remains linked to the conceptual structure. The representational systems, then, are developing semi-independently. At the same time we cannot overlook the interactive nature of the language and conceptual structures. Certainly, the message from the roles of syntagmatic and paradigmatic relations in concept formation is that paradigmatic relations in concept formation is that paradigmatic relationships, as represented across scripts, are at a more abstract level *because* the child combines categories across scripts. In this model language is an essential vehicle for representing paradigmatic relations; the relationships are *re*-structured through language. In the course of the re-structuring, language representation is no longer mapped directly onto a representation of the event. That is, just as actions were gradually replaced by concepts, language functioning is no longer restricted to the event.

Piaget also states that such structuring and restructuring—that is, construction and reconstruction—are essential to conceptual development. But, the question is whether or not the restructuring is due to language. Piaget tells us that learning is based on how the child *acts* on the environment and changes that environment through his or her actions (Gallagher & Reid, 1981). During the sensorimotor stages of development and before the advent of language, the child organizes and reorganizes information *spatially,* in terms of durability (permanence), and in terms of *causal* relations. All of this organization, which in effect is event representation, occurs prior to semiotic functioning when a second phase of development begins: preoperational thought (Gallagher & Reid, 1981). The move into a preoperational phase brings about a shift in the character of children's thinking, and they become capable of representing thought because of the development of a symbol system. Piaget, unlike Nelson, does not insist on the centrality of language for this shift to occur. Rather language is classed as one of the important "coordinating functions."

What Issue Does the FCM Address?

With the details of how Nelson's model functions spelled out, it is now possible to ask more directly what issue it is that the FCM addresses. Is the issue: (1) how do we represent events as human information processors? or (2) how do we form concepts, with event representation constituting an initial step in the process? It would seem that the second question—How do we form concepts?—is the issue in Type I relations of this model. Category substitutions (Type II) and even decontextualized relations (Type III) *may be* formed syntagmatically, but Type I relations, in which concepts are linked to the specific events, are exclusively syntagmatically based (e.g., the elements of "I eat oatmeal" are defined by the event of breakfast, but they are not substitutable in the supper event). This concept/category distinction is important. However, the question of how we form concepts seems to shift once we get into the controversy surrounding the role of language in contextfree concept and category functioning. At that point, the question of *how* we represent events becomes intimately tied to the role of language or some other second- or third-order representational system.

If the issue for Type I relations is how we form concepts, then it would seem as if Types II and III in the FCM require a different system for representing relations analytically (II) and for decontextualizing the relations (III). Piaget, (1972) views language as merely one of several representational options for internal symbolic functioning. However, on another topic—reflexive abstraction—Piaget acknowledges the *functions* that Nelson presents for us to consider: the function of collateral representational systems and how they develop semi-independently but eventually come to function independently and are free of any specific context; in other words, how they become conceptual tools.

Concept complexity, in Nelson's analysis, appears to be related to the ability to link diverse events across scripts, and some additional tools are required for this to happen. The role of language is clearly specified at this point: Language facilitates generating new concepts (it facilitates structuring and restructuring), and language promotes a sort of liberation of thought from specific events, as explained by Nelson in her account of decontextualization.

PROCESSES, FACILITATORS, AND PROMOTERS OF REPRESENTATION

The FCM is a broader model that others describe separately as event representation and linguistic representation (e.g., Gibson & Levin, 1975; Menyuk, 1971; Sigel & Cocking, 1977; Tough, 1973). In the FCM, events are the first concepts to be represented, and a fine analysis of the kind described by Nelson leads to the three types of relations that are represented. The elements of those relations are linked or understood (not associated) in those relationships either syntagmatically (context bound) or paradigmatically (across contexts). But, if the issue is split between how concepts are formed and how events are represented, the most central "functionalist" question is: What promotes representation?

What promotes the act of representing? Nelson states that language is the facilitator. However, because language is a type of representational system itself, can we assume that it is also the process? Nelson is inclined to reject abstraction theories, but in order to account for the child's shift from syntagmatic to paradigmatic comprehension of event components (script elements), she states that the child "*extracts* paradigmatic categories from syntagmatic representations [p. 24, emphasis added]." Both she and Piaget state that the child does not "extract" single attributes or attributes of single objects to form concepts, but Piaget uses the term "abstract" instead of "extract." Perhaps if we briefly consider how Piaget uses this term, we can determine whether or not it is fair to classify his as an abstraction theory and if his explanation avoids the problem of shifting back and forth between linguistic and/or conceptual representation as in the functional model. Then, finally, we can assess whether or not Piaget's structuralist approach overlooks functional components that the New Functionalism (Beilin, this volume) is trying to rectify.

Nelson and Piaget appear to be in agreement on the point that children do not learn concepts by extracting or abstracting singular objects or attributes. Piaget's view, however, is that the child abstracts from action rather than from events, and it is on this point that we see a critical difference between the two theorists. Nelson's system does not account for the role of action in concept formation, but for Piaget, action is a sine qua non for learning, especially for concept formation. For example, logical and mathematical knowledge are derived forms of knowledge and reflect abstract thought. Physical knowledge, by contrast, is concrete and is learned through *acting* on the physical world. That is, the physical world is learned through actions performed on some physical properties of the objects. Math concepts, by comparison, do not derive from any property of the objects. A child learns numerosity initially by counting objects, but the concept of number is not inherent in the objects. The abstraction is drawn from the action of counting, not from the attributes of the objects themselves (Evans, 1973). Thus, although Piaget and Nelson seem to agree that single-object attributes are not the basis of concept learning, they seem to differ in the importance they assign to the role of the child's action in the process.

Piaget points out that the rudimentary structures are derived from actions that are repeated and generalized. Nelson categorizes these as Type I syntagmatic relationships between actors, actions, and the objects of the event. Piaget calls such repeatable and generalizable actions a *scheme*. Schemes have a logic when they are coordinated with one another. Thus, each scheme may not have any prescribed logic, but when schemes are coordinated there is a coordination of action, as in the "pulling scheme," and this coordination of schemes is referred to as the *logic of action*.

The practical logic of action becomes internalized (action schemes) before the appearence of language. Events come to exist in thought rather than solely in action, as in the cases we pointed to previously: causality, permanence, and spatial organization. This is representation. According to Gallagher and Reid (1981): "Language learning is based on how the child *acts* on the environment and changes that environment through action . . . [p. 79, emphasis added]." It is clear that Piaget's model points to the collateral development of these domains, but we have to question whether Nelson's model was designed for asking how concepts develop or if it best fits a design that describes how language develops. The manner in which concepts are learned is a reconcilation between the child's actions and the child's understanding. We are then led to ask two additional questions with regard to Nelson's model: (1) how does "action" fit into event representation? (2) what is the role of awareness? Piaget, of course, speaks to both of these questions, but the Functionalist approach appears to deal with only the first of the two.

Action and Abstraction

In the Piagetian system, logic derives from the coordination of action schemes. Piaget strongly asserts that the roots of logical thought are not to be found in language alone. Evans (1973) notes that although language eventually becomes an important coordinator, the roots of the concepts are in the coordination of actions that ''are the basis of reflexive abstraction . . . [p. xlvii].''

In contrast to the Piagetian account, Nelson contends that symbolic representation is of the event, not of the action. The initial representations are of early events, and these early concepts of single-object relations are useful (functional) to the child as a way of dealing with recurring experiences. The functional purpose of the concept is to represent the event, and the representational relations that are established may be analyzed into simple syntagmatic groupings. Gradually, events are spanned, and the relationships are represented paradigmatically. This shift is accomplished primarily through the facilitating vehicle of language. Nelson accounts for the linkage of represented events in these two ways (syntagmatic and paradigmatic). Piaget, on the other hand, maintains that the linkage among represented events is through the vehicle of reflexive abstraction—that it is, in fact, a reflexive-abstraction *coordination.*

As stated previously, abstraction is drawn from action, not from objects (as in the counting example). Piaget distinguished two types of abstraction. *Simple abstractions* are based on individual actions that would be classed as Type I relations in Nelson's syntagmatic relational analysis. The script elements, for Nelson, are *actor–throw–ball,* and they all constitute the event. Piaget, on the other hand, states that something about the toy ball is abstracted from the actions that are performed on the ball. These things that are learned about toy balls, then, are simple abstractions, acquired empirically.

Reflexive abstractions, the second type, are not based on individual actions, as in the case of simple abstractions. Instead, they are *coordinated* actions. Various kinds of coordinations are additive (joined), temporal (ordered or sequenced), and correspondences (Evans, 1973). All of these coordinated actions are represented in Nelson's Type III relations. The one-to-one correspondences that are described by Nelson as Type I (e.g., ball) become categorical (e.g., toy) through reflexive abstraction, such as ''ball *is a* toy.'' This establishes a set of ''is a . . .'' relations.

Reflexive abstraction consists of two essential aspects: (1) a projection of knowledge from a lower to a higher level; (2) a reorganization or reconstruction of knowledge within a level. Thus, the functional benefits of reflexive abstraction can result in one of two courses: Either the cognitive conflict is sufficient to cause a rethinking of the event, which results in *pushing* the child to a higher level of thinking, or if no discrepancy is detected by the child, the reflection may result in a reorganization and *consolidation* of knowledge at that particular level of thought. Thus, what happens in the paradigmatic shift in Type III relations described by Nelson is a move from simple abstraction to a coordination of actions. This reorganization and reconstruction moves the child from simple, contextually defined comprehension *categories* of experience to higher levels that we call *contextfree concepts.*

As a functionalist, Piaget offers the construct of reflexive abstraction. The process is useful to the system because it promotes the paradigmatic shift Nelson describes. What, then, aids syntagmatic learning? Piaget has another term for this: simple abstraction. The function of simple abstraction is to learn the properties of acting on objects, to be an actor, to learn the properties of objects, and to learn the properties of action. That is, aspects of the physical world are learned through empirical abstraction, alias, simple abstraction (Gallagher & Reid, 1981).

Awareness and Understanding

Finally, we have to ask if we are satisfied solely with a performance account of behavior. At this point, we come to the problem of where notions of *awareness* or *understanding* fit into Nelson's functionally based model. Nelson, citing Flavell's work, eschews the approach that distinguishes concepts as *objects* of thought and *vehicles* of thought. Piaget, by contrast, scrutinizes closely the idea of *levels* of thought. For him, the first form of knowledge is a form of *doing*. But in the course of development, "doing" is eventually distinguished from "knowing about the doing" (e.g., Lefebvre-Pinard, 1981) or "knowing" and "knowing how the doing was done" (e.g., Forman & Kuschner, 1977), the latter making a temporal distinction. The progression is from practical (functional) forms of action to cognizance of action. Piaget (1978) says that this is the transformation of action schemata into concepts and operations, moving from successful performance toward understanding one's actions. Nelson is concerned with the growth of contextfree functioning, and Piaget, likewise, speaks to the autonomous and cognitive character of action. He, however, asks how conceptualization catches up with action. In this sense, Piaget moves from performance to competence, whereas Nelson presents only the performance account of concept acquisition.

We have seen a body of research emerge over the past few years that addresses this precise issue of performance differences, which at one time were erroneously interpreted as competence differences. For example, Orasanu, Lee, and Scribner (1979) found performance differences in category organization (in this case, taxonomic vs. functional organization). These performance differences within developmental levels were not predictive of later behavior. Thus, although performances may differ, understanding of the event at a later time point (e.g., exercising memory) is not affected by the initial organizing performance. Such differences are, perhaps, best viewed as individual or ethnic–group–membership differences in performance that do not relate to metacognitive awareness. Thus, Piaget's approach moves from performance toward competence, whereas the functional analysis reduces the competence–performance controversy to little more than a distinction between acquisition versus development or use in concept formation.

NOTE

This chapter was written by R. R. Cocking in his private capacity. No official support or endorsement by the National Institute of Education, U.S. Department of Education is intended or should be inferred.

REFERENCES

Baldwin, A. L. *Theories of child development* (2nd ed.). New York: Wiley, 1980.

Cocking, R. R. Continuities and discontinuities in structuralism and constructivism. In I. E. Sigel, D. Brodzinsky, & R. Golinkoff (Eds.), *New directions in Piagetian theory and practice*. Hillsdale, N.J.: Lawrence Erlbaum Associates, 1981.

Evans, R. I. *Jean Piaget: The man and his ideas*. New York: Dutton, 1973.

Forman, G., & Kuschner, D. S. *The child's construction of knowledge: Piaget for teaching children*. Monterey, Cal.: Brooks/Cole, 1977.

Gallagher, J. M., & Reid, D. K. *The learning theory of Piaget and Inhelder*. Monterey, Cal.: Brooks/Cole, 1981.

Gibson, E. J. & Levin, H. *The psychology of reading*. Cambridge,MA.: The MIT Press, 1975.

Lefebvre-Pinard, M. *Understanding and auto-control of cognitive functions: Implications for the relationship between cognition and behavior*. Paper presented at the sixth biennial meeting of the International Society for the Study of Behavioral Development, Toronto, August 1981.

Menyuk, P. *The acquisition and development of language*. Englewood Cliffs, N.J.: Prentice-Hall, 1971.

Orasanu, J., Lee, C., & Scribner, S. The development of category organization and free recall: Ethnic and economic group comparisons. *Child Development*, 1979, *50*, 1100–1109.

Piaget, J. *Structuralism*. New York: Basic Books, 1970.

Piaget, J. *The principles of genetic epistemology*. New York: Basic Books, 1972.

Piaget, J. *The child and reality*. New York: Grossman, 1973.

Piaget, J. *Success and understanding*. Cambridge, Mass.: Harvard University Press, 1978.

Sigel, I. E. & Cocking, R. R. *Cognitive development from childhood to adolescence: A Constructivist perspective*. New York: Holt, Rinehart & Winston, 1977.

Tough, J. *Focus on meaning*. London: G. Allen, 1973.

8 Two Different Kinds of Hierarchical Organization

Ellen M. Markman
Stanford University

It would be a rare student of cognitive development who was not deeply influenced by Piagetian theory and research. Even those who strongly disagree with the theory still worry about many of the issues and phenomena that Piaget introduced. I have been interested in discovering and analyzing different principles of conceptual organization and in determining the consequences of these differences. Although the work I summarize here was not for the most part designed to test Piagetian theory, the influence of Piaget can be readily seen.

People must form categories in order to cope with the complexity of the world. There are an overwhelming number of distinct objects in the world, far too many to deal with as unique individuals. So, to simplify this problem and cope with this diversity, we form categories. That is, we mentally group objects, treating them as instances of a category instead of as unique. Many natural categories are organized into class-inclusion hierarchies (e.g., poodle, dog, animal; oak, tree, plant; rocking chair, chair, furniture), with some categories being superordinate or subordinate to others. Much psychological research on human concepts focuses on this type of organization. Research on the structure of natural categories by Rosch and her colleagues (Rosch, Mervis, Gray, Johnson, & Boyes-Braem, 1976) and on the organization of semantic memory (Smith, 1976) deals with nested class-inclusion relations.

Much developmental research is concerned with whether or not children have taxonomic organization and in what contexts they can use it. There is a great deal of evidence that there are developmental differences in the use of taxonomic categories. I cannot review all of this work here, but many studies of categorization, classification, and clustering in memory all suggest developmental differences in the use of taxonomic organization. For example in classification tasks, which are largely inspired by Piagetian research (Inhelder & Piaget, 1964), children are shown objects that belong to one of several common categories (e.g., animals, vehicles, furniture, and food). They are then told to put the things that are alike together. Older children group the objects according to taxonomic category, putting all and only the animals together, the vehicles together, and so forth. In contrast, younger children sort on some nontaxonomic basis. Although there is some debate about how to interpret these results (Huttenlocher & Lui, 1979; Markman & Callanan, in press; Markman, Cox, & Machida, 1981), traditionally they have been taken as evidence for differences in the organizational principles children use for classification of objects (Bruner, 1966; Inhelder & Piaget, 1964; Vygotsky, 1962).

In another well-known task introduced by Piaget, the class-inclusion problem, children are shown objects that comprise a hierarchy with one superordinate set (e.g., trees) consisting of two mutually exclusive subordinate sets (e.g., oaks and pines). One of the subordinate sets is larger than the other, and the children are asked whether the superordinate set or the larger subordinate set contains more members. For example, a child might be shown pictures of five oaks and two pines and asked, "Are there more oaks or trees?" Though there are alternative interpretations (Klahr & Wallace, 1972; Trabasso, Isen, Dolecki, McLanahan, Riley, & Tucker, 1978; Wilkinson, 1976), according to Inhelder and Piaget (1964) the ability to answer the class-inclusion problem is one of the major accomplishments of the stage of concrete operations. They argued that to solve the problem children must simultaneously add two classes (oaks + pines = trees) and subtract two classes (trees − pines = oaks). That is, the child must be able to subtract oaks from the whole set of trees and simultaneously include it in the whole set in order to make this part–whole (oaks–trees) comparison. This is extremely difficult for young children, who consistently answer that there are more in the larger subordinate class (e.g., oaks) than in the superordinate class (e.g., trees). These incorrect answers do not however, mean that a child does not know that oaks are trees. In fact, one should insure that children know the inclusion relations because otherwise they could fail the class-inclusion question out of lack of knowledge rather than because they lack concrete operations. Thus, this task does not measure children's knowledge of a hierarchical inclusion relation but rather their ability to operate upon that relation, adding and subtracting classes and comparing parts to wholes.

Although there is a great deal of evidence that young children fail to use categorical structure where it is appropriate or useful, we still do not fully understand why such an organization is so difficult for children. Because of the importance and prevalence of class inclusion, it has overshadowed the investigation of other relations. In ignoring the differences between class inclusion and other relations, we may be overlooking important differences in principles of organization. I have been studying one type of concept, collections, which differs in its organization from another type of concept, classes. The organization of collections is of interest in its own right but gains additional importance in providing a contrast to class inclusion. By contrasting with inclusion, collections help us understand why children find hierarchical classification so difficult. I summarize some of this work in this paper (but see Markman, 1981a, for further discussion).

DIFFERENCES BETWEEN CLASSES
AND COLLECTIONS

Collections are the referents of collective nouns, such as forest, pile, family, army. To determine membership in a collection, one must consider more than properties of individual objects; the relationship between objects is also critical. There are at least four related ways in which classes and collections differ: (1) the manner in which membership is determined; (2) the nature of their part–whole relations; (3) their internal structure; (4) the nature of the whole that is formed. These differences are discussed in the following sections.

How Membership Is Determined

Membership in a class can be determined by evaluating an object against the defining criteria of the class. To know whether an object is a toy block, for example, one must examine it for size, shape, material, function, and so on. That is, the object's intrinsic properties must be analyzed. To know whether an object is a member of a collection, however, one needs to know something about its relationship to the other possible members of the collection. The object's extrinsic relations must be analyzed. To determine whether a block is part of a pile of blocks, for example, one must examine its relation to other blocks in the pile. Spatial proximity is not necessary for membership in a family, a team, or a club, but some type of relationship is still required.

The Nature of Their Part–Whole Relations

Collections have more literal part–whole relations than do classes. A dog, for example, is a kind of (or type of or example of an) animal, not part of an animal. In contrast, children are parts of families, not kinds of (or types of or examples of) families.

Internal Structure
and the Nature of the Whole Formed

The internal structure of collections results in their greater psychological coherence compared to classes. This may be best illustrated by comparing physical objects to classes and collections. To result in a physical object, component parts must be appropriately organized. A random set of car parts does not form a car. Only when parts of objects are properly assembled do they result in a well-formed whole. Classes do not have the internal organization of objects, nor do they result in good psychological units. Collections, however, do have an internal organization that results in a coherent structure. A random set of people does not make a family. To be a family, the people must be related to each other. Intuitively it seems fairly natural to consider a family, a pile, or a crowd as a single thing. English captures this intuition in that collective nouns are singular in form.

It may seem surprising to argue that by being relational collections could simplify hierarchical organization. Having to take relations into account could just as well complicate rather than simplify the problem. But noticing relations may not necessarily be an additional requirement. It may be that having to ignore relations rather than notice them is the cause of difficulty. In common everyday situations, objects are found in spatial, temporal, and causal contexts. To treat an object solely as a member of a class requires abstraction away from this contextual information to consider only what is relevant for the category. To treat an object as a member of a collection involves noticing relations that exist between the objects. In this regard collections are similar to events or themes that also have relational organizations (see Mandler, 1979; Nelson, this volume). These eventlike, meaningful structures might be a more spontaneous, natural way of organizing information. Probably little time is spent cataloging objects, in trying to generate the taxonomies to which objects belong. Because stories have relational organizations, there are few cross-cultural or developmental differences in the principles people use to understand stories (Mandler, Scribner, Cole, & DeForest, 1980). In marked contrast, many cross-cultural and developmental differences are found in the use of taxonomic organization. Thus, the relational structure of collections does not necessarily have to be more difficult for children to understand.

To summarize, collections and classes are both hierarchically organized concepts, but they differ in their structural principles. The part–whole structure of collections is a type of relational structure that confers psychological coherence on the higher order aggregate formed. If this analysis is correct, then organizing items into collections should help children solve problems that depend on psychological coherence. Some of the findings presented later demonstrate that children become able to pass some of the Piagetian milestones of cognitive development (e.g., part–whole comparisons and number conservation) when they think of objects as collections. Yet they typically fail these problems when they think of the same objects as classes. If we understand how the collections help the child, then we will better understand why class inclusion is so difficult.

Contrasting classes and collections enables us to study organizational differences in a controlled way because no literal rearrangement or reorganization of the materials is needed. The identical objects can be thought of as a class (trees) or a collection (forest). If changes in the conceptual organization occur, they would be due simply to relabeling the array and thereby mentally imposing one of two different principles of organization on the identical objects. In this way, the studies to be reported explore some of the consequences of organizing materials into class-inclusion relations versus the part–whole structure of collections.

The Piagetian Class-Inclusion Problem

Some evidence for the greater coherence of collections over classes comes from work on the Piagetian class-inclusion problem described earlier, where children are asked to make a quantitative comparison between a superordinate set and the larger of its subordinate sets (Inhelder & Piaget, 1964). For example, a child might be shown pictures of five boys and three girls and asked, "Are there more boys or more children?" Children younger than 7 or 8 years usually find the class-inclusion problem very difficult (Ahr & Youniss, 1970; Inhelder & Piaget, 1964; Kohnstamm, 1963). Though children are asked to make a part–whole comparison (boys versus children), they make part–part comparisons (boys versus girls) instead. To answer the class-inclusion question correctly, children must maintain the whole class in mind while simultaneously attending to its subclasses. This division of the superordinate class into subordinate classes weakens the psychological integrity of the superordinate class. If collections have greater psychological integrity, they should be less vulnerable to this weakening.

In several studies children have consistently revealed a superior ability to make part–whole comparisons with collections than with classes (Markman, 1973; Markman & Seibert, 1976). In each of the studies the objects children viewed and the questions they were asked in the two conditions were identical. The only difference in the two conditions was in the description given the higher level of the hierarchy. As one example, for the boys–children comparison in the class condition children were told, "Here are kindergarten children. These are the boys, and these are the girls, and these are the children. Who would have a bigger birthday party, someone who invited the boys or someone who invited the children?" As usual, young children often answered incorrectly, claiming that there were more boys. The collection version of this question was identical except that "Here are kindergarten children" was changed to "Here is a kindergarten class" (note "class" is a collection term). So the question became: "Who would have a bigger birthday party, someone who invited the boys or someone who invited the class?" With this change of just one word in the question, children became able to solve the part–whole comparison that they usually find so difficult.

I know that many investigators interpret these findings as evidence against Piaget. Because collections simplify the problem, children can now solve the part–whole comparisons, the argument goes, thus demonstrating that children have the abilities Piaget claimed they lack. In this case I do not agree with this line of argument (but see the discussion of number abilities later). The point of these studies was to demonstrate the differences between the part–whole structure of collections and classes. Thus, an ability to make part–whole comparisons on collections is not evidence for the same ability for classes.

Cardinal Number

In his work on number Piaget (1965) argued for the importance of the relation between classification and an understanding of number. In fact the class-inclusion problem was discussed at length as part of the study of the child's conception of number. For Piaget number requires integrating the logic of classes and the logic of asymmetrical relations: "Number is at the same time a class and an asymmetrical relation, the units of which it is composed being simultaneously added because they are equivalent, and seriated because they are different from one another. . . . Since each number is a whole, born of the union of equivalent and distinct terms, it cannot be constituted without inclusion and seriation [p. 184]." In the work I am about to describe, I emphasize a different way in which number and classes are related.

The cardinal number of a given set of items is not a property of the individual items themselves. Number is a property of the set taken as a whole, not a property of the elements that compose the set. To see why, consider the following syllogism: "Men are numerous. John is a man. Therefore, John is numerous." The syllogism is absurd because numerosity does not distribute over each element of a set, but is a characteristic of sets themselves. To take another example, "There are five books" does not imply that any one of the books is five. "Five" applies only to the group, not to the individuals in it. Of course, one cannot ignore individual members when calculating the numerical value of a set. Individuals must be counted or otherwise enumerated, but it is not enough just to focus on the individuals. One must also consider the set taken as a whole. Because collections should promote conceptualization of individual objects as aggregates and because cardinal number applies to aggregates, not individuals, collections should facilitate numerical reasoning about discrete objects. There are many well-known problems that young children have in dealing with cardinal number (e.g., number conservation). Young children should be better able to solve these problems when the objects are thought of as collections rather than classes. This hypothesis was investigatcd in the following studies which focused on different aspects of a full appreciation of cardinal number (Markman, 1979).

Number Conservation: Understanding the Irrelevance of a Length Transformation.   In the standard conservation task (Piaget, 1965) two equal rows of pennies or other items are lined up in one-to-one correspondence. A 4- to 5-year-old child will usually claim that the rows are equal. One of the rows is spread out in front of the child who then typically judges that the lengthened row now has more pennies, even though no pennies have been added or subtracted from either row. There are several ways in which the spreading of the pennies could prevent children from judging that the rows still have the same number of objects. First, it could draw the child's attention to individuals rather than to the aggregate as the individuals are moved about. Second, the one-to-one correspondence between rows has been disrupted, forcing the child to rely on more abstract notions of numerical equality (Gelman & Gallistel, 1978). Third, other quantiative dimensions (i.e., length and density) have been changed, although number remains invariant. A child must correctly interpret the original judgment in terms of number and must attend to number per se throughout the physical transformation in order to override these other misleading factors. Collection labels, by making it easier for children to think about the aggregate and thus about number, might help them to conserve.

This hypothesis was tested by having 4-year-olds solve conservation problems where the objects were given either class or collection labels. Half of the children received class questions and half received collection questions. Each child was given four conservation problems. The only difference between conditions was that a collection label (e.g., army) was substituted for a class label (soldiers) for the rows. For example, a child in the class condition saw two rows of soldiers lined up in one-to-one correspondence and heard: "These are your soldiers and these are my soldiers. What's more: My soldiers, your soldiers, or are they both the same?" A child in the collection condition saw the identical two rows and heard: "This is your army and this is my army. What's more: My army, your army, or are they both the same?" Then the experimenter spread out one of the rows and asked, "What's more: My army (soldiers), your army (soldiers), or are they both the same?" depending on the condition.

The children in the two conditions were presented with identical perceptual information and asked virtually identical questions. Yet, simply relabeling the objects as collections helped children to conserve. Children hearing the objects described as classes correctly answered an average of only 1.46 out of 4 problems. Children hearing objects described as collections correctly answered an average of 3.18 problems.

Understanding the Relevance of Addition and Subtraction. The next study addressed whether children who have heard objects described as collections would be more likely to realize that the addition or subtraction of an object does in fact change the number. After a child has seen someone add or subtract an object from one row, he or she will strongly tend to judge that two initially equal rows differ. Even in the standard conservation task, children judge that the rows are different even though the rows are in fact the same. The conservation procedure leads children to respond "different" erroneously because: (1) children make an initial judgment that the two quantities are equal, witness a change, and then are requestioned; these demand characteristics call for a "different" response (Hall & Kingsley, 1968; McGarrigle & Donaldson, 1975); (2) there are misleading perceptual differences that the child must resist in order to judge the rows to be equivalent; (3) the rows do in fact differ on other quantitative dimensions (e.g., length). All of these factors would lead a child to judge that the two rows are not equal. When an object is added or subtracted from a row, all of these factors remain and still call for a judgment of difference. Now, however, "different" is the correct answer, so children could respond correctly without attending to number per se. One way to determine whether or not children base a judgment on number is to examine their justifications for their responses. Though children hearing arrays described as collections are predicted to be more sensitive to numerical change, this difference may appear only when their justifications are taken into account.

This hypothesis was tested by having children solve addition and subtraction problems where the objects were given either class or collection labels. Half the 4-year-olds participating in the study were in the class condition and half were in the collection condition. The procedure was identical to the conservation procedure in the previous study except that instead of lengthening a row the experimenter added or subtracted an object from a row.

As expected, after witnessing an addition or subtraction, children almost always judged that the two rows were no longer equivalent. The mean number correct for children hearing class descriptions was 3.14 out of 4 compared to 3.55 for children hearing collection descriptions.

The fact that children in the collection condition are so willing to say the rows are different rules out an alternative explanation for the results of the conservation study. Children were not better able to conserve because of any type of "same" bias that a collection term might have introduced. Children hearing collection labels are quite ready to respond "different" when it is appropriate.

The children's justifications for their judgments were scored as to whether or not they were basing their answers on numerically relevant information. The modal justification for correct answers was to say that an item had been added or subtracted. The main difference in the justification between the two conditions was that collection children mentioned number relatively more often, whereas class children gave relatively more irrelevant explanations. Overall, collection children were significantly more likely to base their judgments on numerically relevant information. They correctly answered and justified a mean of 3.36 responses compared to 2.53 for children hearing class descriptions.

Children's Initial Judgments of Equality. Earlier, I argued that there are many factors that could lead children to answer the addition–subtraction questions correctly without basing their judgments on number per se. That is why children's justifications of their judgments were thought to be critical. A similar argument can be made for the pretransformation "same" judgments. These are not the conservation judgments but rather the first judgments children make when the two equal rows are lined up in one-to-one correspondence. Children could base these initial "same" judgments on the perceptual similarity of the row, on their equal length or density, or even on some nonquantitative, qualitative identity. Because these factors would all lead to a judgment of sameness, a correct answer may not necessarily reflect a judgment of numerical equality.

To test this possibility, children's justifications for these initial pretransformation "same" judgments were coded as to whether they were numerically relevant or not. When only their judgments are taken into account, children in both conditions are close to perfect on these simple "same" judgments. The mean correct out of 4 was 3.64 for children in the class condition and 3.69 for children in the collection condition. When children's justifications are taken into account, children in the collection condition can be seen to have been basing their judgments on number more than children in the class condition. Children hearing class labels correctly answered a mean of only 1.14 of 4 problems compared to 2.33 for children hearing collection labels.

In summary, in this study children made two quite simple comparisons. Two equal rows of objects were lined up in one-to-one correspondence, and the child judged which was more or whether they were both the same. Then an object was added or subtracted from one row, and the child was requestioned. Because children could be correct for a variety of reasons, their justifications were used to help clarify the basis for their judgments. Children hearing objects described as classes were unable to offer much beyond "they look the same" as explanations for their judgments. Children hearing the identical objects described as collections more often offered numerically relevant explanations, indicating their judgments were in fact based on number.

Selection of Equivalence Based on Number Versus Length.   In another study children were presented with three rows of items and explicitly asked to select the two that were numerically equivalent. In each triad two of the sets of objects were equated for number but differed in length, whereas two were equated for length but differed in number. When length is pitted against number in this way, kindergarten children often base their selection of equivalence on length rather than number, especially for numbers greater than 5 (Miller & Heller, 1976). This procedure was used to determine whether children would be more likely to select on the basis of number when the sets had been described as collections.

Kindergarten children participated in the study, half in the collection condition and half in the class condition. Pictures of objects that could be given either collection or class labels (e.g., forest, trees) were pasted in horizontal lines onto strips of poster paper. For each object type, four cards were constructed, two with five pictures and two with eight pictures. Each card with five pictures was equated for length with one of the cards having eight pictures. Cards that were numerically identical differed in length. As it was presented, each card was labeled for the child "Here are some trees" or "Here is a forest" depending on the condition. Once the three cards were visible, the children in both conditions were asked, "Which two cards have the same number of things on them?"

An answer was considered correct if the child selected on the basis of number and was able to justify that selection with a numerically relevant explanation. Children hearing class descriptions for the objects almost always chose on the basis of length, not number. They correctly answered only 1.25 of 12 items. In marked contrast, children hearing collection descriptions quite often chose correctly on the basis of number. They correctly answered 6.23 items. Again, by helping children conceptualize the elements as an aggregate, collections labels helped children to attend to number per se.

The Cardinality Principle.   Three- and four-year-old children are generally able to count an array of five toys. However, when they are then asked, "How many toys are there?" they often count again rather than answering "five." This is a reflection of the child's difficulty with the cardinality principle, the failure to appreciate that the last number counted becomes the cardinal number of the set (Gelman & Gallistel, 1978; Schaeffer, Eggleston, & Scott, 1974). If part of the child's problem with the cardinality principle is a difficulty in thinking of the individual items as a set to which cardinal number applies, then helping the child think of the arrays as collections might promote correct use of this principle.

In a study designed to test this hypothesis half of the 3- and 4-year-old children were assigned to the class condition and half to the collection condition. In both conditions children viewed some objects, were instructed to count the objects, and then were asked how many objects there were.

When children heard a class description, for example, "Here are some pigs, count the pigs," they counted, "1, 2, 3, 4, 5." When they were then asked, "How many pigs are there?" they tended to count again, "1, 2, 3, 4, 5." They correctly gave the cardinal number only 1.85 out of 4 times. In marked contrast, when children in the collection condition heard, for example, "Here is a pig family, count the pigs in the family," they counted. But when asked, "How many pigs are in the family?" they very often correctly responded "five." These children gave the cardinal number a mean of 3.46 out of 4 times.

In summary, I argued that number is a property of a set of objects and not of objects themselves. If thinking about individuals as collections helps children focus on the aggregate as well as on the individual, it should thus facilitate numerical reasoning. As predicted, thinking of objects as collections helped children solve numerical problems they otherwise would have failed. It helped them conserve number in the face of an irrelevant change. It helped them access and verbalize a numerically relevant basis for their judgments of equality and of difference. It allowed them to judge equivalence on the basis of number rather than length, and it promoted their use of the cardinality principle.

This is, of course, by no means the first demonstration that children's performance can be improved during an experimental session. However, when training, feedback, modeling, or other types of practice are used, it is less surprising that children improve. Or when the problems are modified so as to simplify the task demands, improvement would be expected. In the present work, however, there is no obvious way in which the problems, such as conservation task, would be simplified by relabeling trees as a forest or soldiers as an army. There is certainly no way in which we trained children or induced any abilities or knowledge that they did not already possess before they participated in the studies. To take the clearest case consider the study on the cardinality principle in which after children counted an array of objects they were asked how many objects there were. Children hearing the objects described as classes tended to count again, whereas children hearing the objects described as collections correctly gave the cardinal number. Relabeling trees as forest could not possibly have taught children that the last number in a count series becomes the cardinal number of the set. They must have already possessed this principle, yet been prevented from accessing it. The general point that young children's abilities may be underestimated by traditional procedures has been forcefully argued by Gelman and her colleagues (Gelman, 1978; Gelman & Gallistel, 1978).

Numerical Classifier Languages.   I have argued that dealing with number requires a kind of part–whole analysis. Individuals in a set must be enumerated, but number is a property of the set itself. Collections help children conceptualize number by allowing them to maintain the whole set in mind. This analysis might have some bearing on the linguistic curiosity that occurs in some languages called "numerical classifier" languages.

English, which is not a classifier language, draws a distinction between count and mass nouns. Count nouns can be counted directly, for example, "one pencil, two pencils, three pencils." Mass nouns cannot be counted directly as in "one water, two waters, three waters." Instead, some other unit or measure is mentioned, and then that unit is counted, for example, "one drop of water, two drops of water, three drops of water." Because mass nouns typically refer to undifferentiated masses (e.g., milk, clay, rice), they cannot be counted until some unit or measure is imposed on them. What is of interest is that some languages express quantity by using a construction that is similar to the mass construction, even when the objects being referred to are not masses (Greenberg, 1972). In fact, they require such a construction for virtually all expressions of quantity. Thus, in these languages one would have to say something like "two long-things of pencil" rather than "two pencils."

Of course there must be many forces that determine the structure of a language. However, I would like to raise the possibility that there is a functional explanation than can help account for classifier languages. The explanation is related to my argument as to why collections help children conceptualize number.

Although mass nouns and collective nouns differ in some ways (as is mentioned in the discussion of mass nouns in the section on hierarchical organization), they are similar in referring to the whole rather than to the individuals that comprise it. By using mass nouns and then requiring a classifier, quantitative expressions in classifier languages provide an explicit representation of both levels of analysis that are needed for cardinal number. "Two long-things" refers to the individuals, whereas "of pencil" provides a representation of the whole. Greenberg reviewed over 100 classifier languages and found that there was wide variation in the types of linguistic constructions for which use of a classifier was mandatory. Some languages use classifiers in many different constructions including adjectives and demonstratives, for example, whereas others use them in only one construction. Yet, even with considerable diversity of numerical classifier languages, all of them require classifiers when mentioning number (Greenberg, 1972).

A historical analysis of the languages indicated that regardless of how many different classifier constructions the modern language contains, classifiers originated for use in quantitative expressions (Greenberg, 1972). I am suggesting that they may have originated in order to express quantity better. One untested prediction of this analysis is that one would expect that, if cultural and social differences could be controlled, children learning a classifier language should exhibit accelerated number development.

LEARNING HIERARCHICAL RELATIONS

Children must eventually learn hierarchically organized class-inclusion relations (e.g., that chairs are furniture, that poodles are dogs, that oaks are trees). In first learning terms, children learn common labels for objects often at the basic level (Anglin, 1977; Brown, 1958; Rosch et al., 1976). Once these labels are learned, the child must cope with the fact that now the car will also be labeled "vehicle," the dog "animal," and so on. As Macnamara (1979) points out, children must learn how one object can have multiple labels and figure out what the relations between them are. Many opinions are possible, including that the terms be synonymous, overlapping, or hierarchical. If the terms are taken to be hierarchical, one might suppose that class inclusion would be a likely hypothesis, especially for older children, because class terms are far more frequent in the language, and children must have encountered many more of them. Though collective nouns are scarce relative to class terms, it still could be that the collection hierarchy is easier for children to construct. When children are relatively free to impose their own structure on a novel hierarchy, they might prefer a collection to a class organization.

This hypothesis was tested by contriving a situation where children were presented with only minimal information about a hierarchical relation (Markman, Horton, & McLanahan, 1980). We wanted to see how children would spontaneously interpret the relations when given relative freedom. In actuality the relations were novel class-inclusion hierarchies, analogous to the relations between oaks, pines, and trees. Ostensive definition (pointing and labeling) was used to achieve a minimal specification of the relationship. To illustrate, imagine that oaks and pines are lined in a row in front of the child. As the experimenter points to the oaks he says, "These are oaks"; as he points to the pines he says, "These are pines"; and as he points to the trees he says, "These are trees." When he describes trees in the plural, "These are trees," it means that each individual tree is a tree. Thus, the use of the plural establishes the class-inclusion relation. The singular would have to be used in order to establish a collection such as, "This is a forest." Though the ostensive definition provides only minimal information, it does establish that the objects presented form a class-inclusion hierarchy.

Suppose children misinterpret the class-inclusion relation as a collection hierarchy. What errors should they make? They should erroneously believe that several of the items together form an instance of the concept at the higher level of the hierarchy (trees in the example) and should not believe that any single item is an instance. To see why, consider what the correct response would be had children actually learned a collection (e.g., "forest"). If asked to point to the forest, the child should point to many trees but deny that a pine or any other single tree is itself a forest.

Children aged 6 to 17 years participated in the study. Each child learned four novel categories, one at a time, each composed of two subcategories. All of the category exemplars were small construction-paper figures of novel shapes or novel animate figures. Nonsense syllables were used as names for the novel figures.

The results of this study revealed that children, until a surprisingly late age, tend to misinterpret class-inclusion relations as collections when only minimal information is provided. When novel class-inclusion relations were taught by ostensive definition, children as old as 14 often mistakenly interpreted the relations as collections. When asked what would be analogous to "Show me a pine," children correctly picked up a single pine. When the experimenter pointed to a pine and asked, "Is this a pine?" children responded correctly. The errors occurred almost exclusively on the upper level of the hierarchy. When asked, "Show me a tree", children scooped up a handful rather than just one. When the experimenter pointed to a tree and asked, "Is this a tree?" children often said "No." Children averaged 3.49 errors at the upper levels compared to .18 errors at the lower level. This is exactly as one would expect if children were answering questions about a collection.

Because collections form more stable hierarchies, it may be easier for children to keep the two levels of the hierarchy distinct. At least in the somewhat artificial conditions of the present study, children apparently found it simpler to impose a collection structure on a novel hierarchy than to interpret it correctly as inclusion.

This is true despite the fact that children must certainly have more experience learning inclusion relations, as collective nouns are relatively rare. Because this was an unusual way to learn novel concepts, collection errors may be unlikely in natural situations. However, there is some anecdotal (Valentine, 1942) and experimental (Macnamara, 1979) evidence suggesting that such errors may be found in a naturalistic context.

Callanan and I have conducted a more controlled study to investigate this possibility further (Callanan & Markman, in press). We questioned 2- and 3-year-olds about five categories: toys (balls and dolls), animals (horses and cows), drinks (milk and juice), children (boys and girls), and cars (racing cars and Volkswagens). In general there was a very low error rate in part because these category terms were pretested to ensure that children knew them (in the plural). However, there was a significant tendency for children to interpret the terms as collections. Children agree, for example, that a set of toys is toys, but they deny that a single toy (e.g., a doll) is itself a toy and pick up several toys when asked for one. We were able to rule out a possible alternative explanation for these findings. Children might pick the best label for a given array and then reject any other label. Thus, they would deny that a doll is a toy because "doll" is a better label than "toy." To test this hypothesis, we asked children whether the superordinate label applied to a plural but homogeneous set of objects. For example, children were asked, "Are these toys?" for two dolls. If this alternative hypothesis was correct, then children should deny that the dolls were toys because the best label for the two dolls as with a single doll would be "dolls" not "toys." The results argue against this hypothesis and support the collection interpretation. Children accepted the higher level labels (e.g., toys) for groups of homogenous objects (e.g., dolls) but not for a single object. These findings suggest that in first acquiring superordinate terms young children distort some class-inclusion relations into collections. Thus, even in naturally occurring contexts, very young children may find it simpler to impose a collection structure on inclusion hierarchies that they are trying to learn.

Superordinate Terms and Mass Nouns

I have noticed something puzzling about many superordinate terms in English, which this work on the learning of hierarchical relations may help explain. There are many common superordinate terms in English that are mass nouns, yet they shouldn't be. Ordinary mass nouns in English typically refer to relatively homogeneous masses (e.g., clay, water, grass). In contrast to count nouns, mass nouns cannot be counted directly; one cannot say "one or two clays." Instead, one must speak of "pieces of clay," "drops of water," or "blades of grass" when referring to individual components or parts of the more or less homogeneous substance. Some terms that refer to categories of discrete objects are nevertheless mass nouns. These include: furniture, clothing, money, jewelry, silverware. One cannot speak of one or two furnitures, silverwares, or jewelries. Rather, one must say a piece of furniture, a piece of jewelry, a piece of silverware. Yet, the objects to which these mass terms refer are not masses. Even though we must say "A fork is a piece of silverware," "A chair is a piece of furniture," "A bracelet is a piece of jewelry," certainly these are class-inclusion relations. Chairs *are* furniture, forks *are* silverware, and bracelets *are* jewelry. The relation between chairs and furniture, forks and silverware, and bracelets and jewelry is not conceptually different from the relationship between hammers and tools or cars and vehicles.

I would like to speculate about why these categories would be referred to by mass terms. The findings just reported suggest that if superordinate category terms were represented by collective nouns, then children would find them easier to learn. But collective nouns cannot themselves serve as superordinate terms for the very reason that they express a different relation. And these differences are extremely important when one considers the function of taxonomies. One of the main purposes of taxonomies is to support inductive and deductive inferences. Large amounts of knowledge can be organized efficiently and with little redundancy if taxonomies are used. So, for example, if I know something that is true of all mammals (e.g., that they breathe, eat, bear their young live, are warm-blooded, etc.), once I learn that an unfamiliar animal is a mammal I can transfer all of this knowledge to the newly learned animal. Collections do not support inferences in the same way. Properties true of the forest may not be true of the individual trees. Nor will similarities that exist between the trees allow an inductive inference that the properties will also be true of the forest. Thus, although the part–whole organization of collections is simpler for children to learn, it is not a useful substitute for the inclusion relation that defines taxonomies. Mass nouns, however, may provide the appropriate substitute. They may provide some of the benefits of collective nouns while maintaining an inclusion relation.

In the studies about learning hierarchically organized categories, it was argued that the part–whole organization of collection may be more stable than that of class inclusion. It is easier to keep the two levels of the hierarchy distinct when the higher level has greater psychological coherence. Superordinate categories (e.g., furniture) in contrast to basic level categories (e.g., chairs) are at the top node (or relatively high node) of a given natural language hierarchy (Rosch et al., 1976). I am suggesting that mass nouns may serve a function similar to collective nouns in helping to keep that top node more stable and distinct. In a sense, mass nouns can be viewed as a compromise between collections and classes or, to be more precise, as a compromise between *part–whole* and *is a* relations. Consider a typical mass such as clay. A piece of clay is part of the whole mass of clay. This is similar to the part–whole organization of collections where each tree, for example, is part of the forest. On the other hand, each piece of clay is itself clay. This is more like the *is a* relation of class inclusion in which each oak is a tree.

Although collective nouns reflect more stable hierarchical structures, they could not themselves serve as superordinate terms for the very reason that they express a different relation. However, by referring to discrete objects with mass terms, a language might be able to provide some of the stability that the part–whole organization of collections would have achieved, yet remind the speaker that an inclusion relation is still involved.

This analysis has several empirical consequences. First, the analysis predicts that this peculiarity should not be limited to English. Other languages with a count-mass distinction should also have this type of aberration. Second, if these aberrations serve the purpose of helping to give stability to hierarchically organized categories, then such "inappropriate" mass terms should occur only on what speakers would judge to be relatively high or superordinate levels of the hierarchy, not on relatively low levels. That is, languages should contain terms that require one to say "a piece of furniture" or "a piece of vehicle" when what one means is "a furniture" or "a vehicle." But they should not require speakers to say "a piece of chair" or "a piece of car" when what one means is "a chair" or "a car."

I have tested this hypothesis in 19 languages including Afrikaans, Greek, Ukranian, Urdu, Japanese, and Hebrew (Markman, 1981b). The predictions have held up in every language, suggesting that languages distort count nouns into mass nouns to serve some psychological function.

There are parallels between these speculations about language and those I made earlier about classifier languages. In both cases I am suggesting that languages distort count nouns into mass nouns in order to serve some psychological function. In both cases evidence from developmental studies indicates that the part–whole structure of collections helps children in those domains where the languages contain some peculiarity. Collections help children conceptualize number (Markman, 1979), and classifier languages use the classifier construction for number. Hierarchical relations of collections are in some respects simpler for children compared to class-inclusion relations (Markman et al., 1981), and it is in the designation of hierarchical relations that this peculiarity with mass nouns arises. The common hypothesis is that in both cases the compromise structure of mass terms may serve a function related to that of collections. These speculations suggest an interesting way in which psychological functions contribute to the forces that bear on the evolution of linguistic structure.

DISCUSSION

Summary

I have argued that when objects are viewed as forming a collection, such as an army or a forest, the objects are related to each other and thereby form a higher order aggregate with good psychological integrity. Once children organize objects into collections, they become better able to solve problems that require attending to the set as well as the individuals in the set. On the Piagetian class-inclusion problem, children were better able to make part–whole comparisons for the part–whole organization of collections than for the inclusion relations of classes. Because number is a property of sets themselves, not just the members of the sets, collection organizations should help children solve numerical problems. Younger children were better able to conserve number, to evaluate when a transformation changed the number of objects, to judge equivalence on the basis of number rather than length, and to use the cardinality principle when arrays of objects were thought of as collections rather than classes. Finally, when trying to learn a novel hierarchial relation, children erroneously impose a part–whole structure of collections on the inclusion relation classes.

In most of these studies, collection terms and class terms were used to describe physically identical displays. Yet, they nevertheless induced different organizations. When success on a task depends on the unity or coherence of an array, or requires keeping two levels of a hierarchy in mind at once, collections helped children solve the problem.

Class Inclusion Versus Relational Structures

Once of the major differences between collections and classes is that collections are defined by interrelationships of their elements, whereas classes are not. There are other domains that seem to provide a relational contrast to inclusion. In particular, there is evidence that relational organizations unify arrays and that they are simpler for children to use (see Markman, 1981a).

Linear Versus Classical Syllogisms.   The distinction between linear and classical syllogisms may in some ways be analogous to the collection-class distinction. For both collections and linear syllogisms, elements that are explicitly related to each other become organized into a unified representation. Consider the following two arguments:

1. A is smaller than B.
   B is smaller than C.
   Therefore, A is smaller than C.
2. All As are Bs.
   All Bs are Cs.
   Therefore, all As are Cs.

The first is a linear syllogism that contains a relational term (smaller) in both premises. A simple transitive inference is made from the information in the two premises to deduce the conclusion. The second is a classical syllogism that specifies class-inclusion relations in both of the premises. This too is a transitive relation, and a simple transitive inference is sufficient to deduce the conclusion.

Despite this similarity, subjects represent and solve these problems in very different ways. People seem to use some type of a linear ordering to represent the information given in the premises of the linear syllogism (Potts, 1972; Trabasso, 1975). The evidence for this stems from contrast between what would be expected if people were storing the premises and then drawing transitive inferences to judge the truth of a conclusion versus what would be expected if subjects were constructing a linear ordering to represent the information and then "reading" the answer off this ordering. If subjects stored information about pairwise comparisons and made transitive inferences at the time they were questioned, they should be faster at comparing the adjacent items they had learned and memorized (e.g., B is smaller than C) than at comparing more remote elements that would require them to draw inferences (e.g., A is smaller than C). In fact, however, the verification of transitive inferences is faster the more distant the items (Potts, 1972; Trabasso, 1975). In summary, when individual terms are explicitly related to each other via relations terms (e.g., smaller), they appear to be represented as a linear ordering rather than as discrete pairs.

People behave very differently when solving syllogisms containing class inclusions. Subjects are less accurate in their judgments of class-inclusion comparisons than of the relational comparisons (Griggs, 1976; Potts, 1976), and accuracy *decreases* and latency *increases* with distance (Carroll & Kammann, 1977). Across several studies the evidence indicates that most untrained subjects do not spontaneously represent classical syllogisms as linear orderings (Griggs, 1976; Mynatt & Smith, 1979; Potts, 1976). There are other differences between the two types of syllogisms that make it difficult to know why subjects solve the problems differently. Yet, there may be an interesting analogy between the collection-class differences and the linear versus classical syllogism. People do not construct unified representations for classical syllogisms, although in principle they could. In contrast, just as the relational structure of collections results in a coherent representation of the whole, the relational structure of linear syllogisms results in a unified representation of the ordering.

There are other examples of contrast between relational and class-inclusion organizations that make a similar point. The shift from syntagmatic to paradigmatic word associations and the developmental change from thematic to taxonomic organization in children's object sorting are two other examples (Markman, 1981a). I do not mean to argue that all relational organizations are equivalent to collections. Rather the point here is that the class-collection contrast may be viewed as an instance of a more general distinction with wider ranging implications for cognitive functioning.

As I pointed out earlier, there are many ways in which this work has been influenced by Piagetian issues. I would like to conclude by mentioning one important Piagetian insight that this work builds on. Many psychologists and philosophers have recognized that classification and categorization are fundamental to human cognition. I think a major contribution of Piaget's was his insight about the special importance and difficulty of hierarchical classification. The class-inclusion problem is based on that insight as is much of Piaget's analysis of number. This implies that the important developmental question may not be how children form categories but, rather, may lie in how children interpret, represent, and utilize hierarchical organizations.

ACKNOWLEDGMENT

This work was supported by PHS research grant MH 28154.

REFERENCES

Ahr, P. R., & Youniss, J. Reasons for failure on the class-inclusion problem. *Child Development*, 1970, *41*, 131–143.

Anglin, J. M. *Word, object, and conceptual development*. New York: Norton, 1977.

Brown, R. *Words and things*. New York: The Free Press, 1958.

Bruner, J. S. On cognitive growth. In J. S. Bruner, R. R. Olver, & P. M. Greenfield (Eds.). *Studies in cognitive growth*. New York: Wiley, 1966.

Callanan, M. A., & Markman, E. M. Principles of organization in young children's natural language hierarchies. *Child Development*, in press.

Carroll, M., & Kammann, R. The dependency of schema formation on type of verbal material: Linear orderings and set inclusions. *Memory & Cognition*, 1977, *5*, 73–78.

Gelman, R. Cognitive development. *Annual Review of Psychology*, 1978, *29*, 297–332.

Gelman, R., & Gallistel, C. R. *The child's understanding of number*. Cambridge, Mass.: Harvard University Press, 1978.

Greenberg, H. H. Numerical classifiers and substantial number: Problems in the analysis of a linguistic type. *Working Papers on Language Universals*, 1972, *9*, 1–39.

Griggs, R. A. Logical processing of set inclusion relations in meaningful text. *Memory & Cognition*, 1976, *4*, 730–740.

Hall, V. E. & Kingsley, R. Conservation and equilibration theory. *The Journal of Genetic Psychology*, 1968, *113*, 195–213.

Huttenlocher, J., & Lui, F. The semantic organization of simple nouns and verbs. *Journal of Verbal Learning and Verbal Behavior*, 1979, *18*, 141–162.

Inhelder, I., & Piaget, J. *The early growth of logic in the child*. New York: Norton, 1964.

Klahr, D., & Wallace, J. C. Class-inclusion processes. In S. Farnham-Diggory (Ed.), *Information processing in children*. New York: Academic Press, 1972.

Kohnstamm, G. A. An evaluation of part of Piaget's theory. *Acta Psychologica*, 1963, *21*, 313–356.

Macnamara, J. Unpublished manuscript, Names for Things McGill University, 1979.

Mandler, J. M. Categorical and schematic organization in memory. In C. R. Puff (Ed.), *Memory organization and structure*. New York: Academic Press, 1979.

Mandler, J. M., Scribner, S., Cole, M., & DeForest, M. Cross-cultural invariance in story recall. *Child Development*, 1980, *51*, 19–26.

Markman, E. M. Facilitation of part–whole comparisons by use of the collective noun "family." *Child Development*, 1973, *44*, 837–840.

Markman, E. M. Empirical versus logical solutions to part–whole comparison problems concerning classes and collections. *Child Development*, 1978, *49*, 168–177.

Markman, E. M. Classes and collections: Conceptual organization and numerical abilities. *Cognitive Psychology,* 1979, *11,* 395–411.

Markman, E. M. Two principles of conceptual organization. In M. E. Lamb & A. L. Brown (Eds.), *Advances in developmental psychology.* Hillsdale, N.J.: Lawrence Erlbaum Associates, 1981. (a)

Markman, E. M. *Why superordinate terms can be mass nouns.* Unpublished manuscript, Stanford University, 1981. (b)

Markman, E. M., & Callanan, M. A. An analysis of hierarchical organization. In R. Sternberg (Ed.), *Advances in the psychology of human intelligence* (Vol. 2). *In Press.*

Markman, E. M., Cox, B., & Machida, S. The standard object sorting task as a measure of conceptual organization. *Developmental Psychology,* 1981, *17,* 115–117.

Markman, E. M., Horton, M. S., & McLanahan, A. G. Classes and collections: Principles of organization in the learning of hierarchical relations. *Cognition,* 1980, *8,* 561–577.

Markman, E. M., & Seibert, J. Classes and collections: Internal organization and resulting holistic properties. *Cognitive Psychology,* 1976, *8,* 561–577.

McGarrigle, J. & Donaldson, M. Conservation accidents. *Cognition,* 1975, *3,* 341–350.

Miller, P. H., & Heller, K. A. Facilitation of attention to number and conservation of number. *Journal of Experimental Child Psychology,* 1976, *22,* 454–467.

Mynatt, B. T., & Smith, K. H. Processing of text containing artificial inclusion relations. *Memory & Cognition,* 1979, *7,* 390–400.

Nelson, K. How children represent knowledge of their world in and out of language: A preliminary report. In R. S. Siegler (Ed.), *Children's thinking: What develops?* Hillsdale, N.J.: Lawrence Erlbaum Associates, 1978.

Piaget, J. *The child's conception of number.* New York: Norton, 1965.

Potts, G. R. Information processing strategies used in the encoding of linear orderings. *Journal of Verbal Learning and Verbal Behavior,* 1972, *11,* 727–740.

Potts, G. R. Artificial logical relations and their relevance to semantic memory. *Journal of Experimental Psychology: Human Learning and Memory,* 1976, *2,* 746–758.

Rosch, W., Mervis, C. B., Gray, W. D., Johnson, D. M., & Boyes-Braem, P. Basic objects in natural categories. *Cognitive Psychology,* 1976, *8,* 382–439.

Schaeffer, B., Eggleston, V. H., & Scott, J. L. Number development in young children. *Cognitive Psychology,* 1974, *6,* 357–379.

Smith, E. E. Theories of semantic memory. In W. K. Estes (Ed.), *Handbook of learning and cognitive processes.* Hillsdale, N.J.: Lawrence Erlbaum Associates, 1976.

Trabasso, T. Representation, memory, and reasoning: How do we make transitive inferences? In A. D. Pick (Ed.), *Minnesota Symposium on Child Psychology* (Vol. 9). Minneapolis: University of Minnesota Press, 1975.

Trabasso, T., Isen, A. M., Dolecki, P., McLanahan, A. G., Riley, C. A., & Tucker, T. How do children solve class inclusion problems? In R. S. Siegler (Ed.), *Children's thinking: What develops?* Hillsdale, N.J.: Lawrence Erlbaum Associates, 1978.

Valentine, C. W. *The psychology of early childhood.* London: Methuen, 1942.

Vygotsky, L. S. *Thought and language.* Cambridge, Mass.: MIT Press, 1962.

Wilkinson, A. Counting strategies and semantic analysis as applied to class inclusion. *Cognitive Psychology,* 1976, *8,* 64–88.

9 Classes, Collections, and Other Connections

Ellin Kofsky Scholnick
University of Maryland, College Park

Matthew Lipman (1981) created a fictionalized account of a child's struggles with mastering logical relations to use as a text in his course teaching philosophy to children (described in Lipman, Sharp, & Oscanyan, 1980). In his story (Lipman, 1981) the heroine, Pixie, visits her friend, Isabel, and Isabel's younger sister, Connie. Connie is excited because she and her sister are going to visit their grandmother for Thanksgiving. Pixie innocently asks who else Connie will visit. When Isabel replies "the family," Pixie persists:

> "Like who? . . . Your aunts and your uncles?"
> "Oh, sure" Isabel replied. "And my cousins". . . . "And the family." said Connie. . . .
> "Oh, no Connie" Isabel said. "Don't say, '*and* the family'. The family isn't in addition to us and grandma and our cousins. . . ." Connie looked real hard at Isabel and Pixie could tell she couldn't understand what Isabel was saying. . . . [So Pixie added] "When all your relatives are together, they're called your 'family' ". [Note this is a *collective* definition.] Connie said . . . [rejecting that definition] "What about when they're not together. Are they still the family?"
> "Of course". Isabel said.
> "So my family is made up of people who are related to me?", Connie asked.
> "That's right—all your relatives and only your relatives.", Pixie said [supplying a *class* relation].
> Connie looked at Pixie. "Do you have a family, too?" Pixie said, "Of course. Everyone in my family is a relative of mine, just like everyone in your family is a relative of yours".
> [Connie replied], "They're your aunts and uncles and cousins? . . . But they're different from my relatives? . . . So does that mean . . . that all families are alike but they just have different people in them?" . . .

[Isabel said], "I guess what you mean is the people in different families are different but the relationships are the same. . . . Pixie has a mother-daughter relationship in *her* family and we have a mother-daughter relationship in *our* family. . . . Don't you see, Connie, we're members of *our* family and Pixie's a member of *hers*?" . . .

Then Connie asked, "The whole family will be at the Thanksgiving dinner, will the members be there, too?" [pp. 18–20].

THE PROBLEM OF CLASS INCLUSION

Pixie is not alone in her difficulty in explaining class inclusion and in differentiating class inclusion from other concepts. After reviewing recent class-inclusion research Winer (1980) came to the conclusion that we still have no acceptable explanation of why children readily concede that brothers and sisters are members of a family but fail to infer that there are more family members than brothers or sisters. Inhelder and Piaget (1964), who called attention to the phenomenon, provided many reasons for the failure to make correct quantitative class-inclusion comparisons. The one that has attracted the most attention, perhaps wrongly, involves addition of the extension of subsets. The child answers quantitative class-inclusion questions by constructing a set of logical equations defining the extension of both subclasses (usually labeled A for the majority and A' for the minority subclass) and the superordinate class (B) to which they both belong. These equations are coordinated through the operation of reversibility. The extension of the superordinate class B is given by adding or combining its subclasses A and A' ($B = A + A'$). The extension of either subclass, for example, A, is derived by subtracting from the superordinate class the complementary subclass A' ($A = B - A'$). The coordination of the two equations leads to the inference that the superordinate class has a greater extension than the subclass.

The explanation that comparison of the extension of classes at different levels of a hierarchy depends on the reversible operations of addition and subtraction of class extension has dissatisfied many psychologists. Class inclusion is mastered later in development than many other concrete operational tasks like conservation and seriation, which are also thought to depend on logical reversibility for their solution. The ease of class inclusion varies so much depending on a host of other conditions, such as the linguistic form of the questions, the perceptual arrangement of the array (see Winer, 1980, for a review), and the typicality of the class members (Carson & Abrahamson, 1976; Scholnick & Johnson, 1981), that perhaps those sources of variation are more important than the underlying logical relation. In addition, the solution to the task of class inclusion can be enhanced by teaching behavioral algorithms like counting (Wilkinson, 1976), and these rapid gains in performance suggest that the formal Piagetian analysis of class inclusion does not represent how children conceptualize the relation and solve the quantitative class-inclusion task.

Yet, ultimately, all those alternative explanations are unsatisfying (see Larsen, 1977, for similar points). No matter how one simplifies the task there is an age where even the simplest version cannot be solved, and we are left explaining the sources of early failure. Behavioral strategies like keeping track of objects already counted (Klahr & Wallace, 1976; Wilkinson, 1976) or using devices that dissociate subsets from superordinate sets (Trabasso, Isen, Dolecki, McLanahan, Riley, & Tucker, 1978) are often so task specific that they trivialize class inclusion. If all that underlies class inclusion is keeping straight some vocabulary, making appropriate divisions, or double tagging, then why are these skills of interest to the course of cognitive rather than linguistic, perceptual, or arithmetic development? Finally, class inclusion often seems to suffer the same fate as conservation and object permanence. The logic of class relations is reified in a single task, and mastery of that task has become the focus of scientific inquiry rather than the processes that class inclusion is thought to embody. Class inclusion is a very complex relation in terms of what it implies and how it can be understood. Not only have we tended to narrow our attention to a small range of tasks embodying the relation, but we have also focused on a small range of logical implications of that relation.

Markman's Approach

It could be argued that Markman's (1978, 1979, 1981; Markman, Horton, & McLanahan, in press; Markman & Seibert, 1976) work on collections summarized in this volume falls into the category of simplification strategies. However, her analysis has much broader ramifications. She has produced an elegant and creative line of experiments that call attention to another form of conceptual organization, collections, which are interesting in their own right. Her work deals with knowing not only how children compare the extension of classes, but also how they make other quantitative comparisons such as conservation of number and magnitude estimation. Thus, her explanations are not confined to a single task. She also implicitly espouses a particular approach to cognitive development that has provided many challenges to Piagetian theory. At the risk of over-simplifying subtle distinctions that Markman often makes and at the risk of caricaturing her theory, let me summarize that theory and its implications so that I can discuss what it does or does not reveal about class inclusion.

Many cognitive scientists (e.g., Anzai & Simon, 1979; Klahr & Wallace, 1976) have used analogical problem solving as an analogy itself for development. In the course of development individuals encounter new tasks and retrieve old procedures, which they adapt to the new demands. Although this sounds very Piagetian or Wernerian (e.g., Werner & Kaplan, 1963), the explanation for the search for old procedures is different. Success in finding and adapting procedures depends on situational constraints, which provide clues about what to access and which provide easy or difficult problem spaces in which the old routine must be adapted and applied. There are also individual differences in retrieval skill reflecting the individual's knowledge of the situation and criteria for suitable analogies. There are additional individual differences in skill in adapting routines based on the availability of operations to do the transformation and the efficiency of the transformation process. Young children may not understand which routine is a good fit and may lack the variety of transformation skills adults possess. They may not be able to perform many transformations because they lack the computing space. They may be unable to fine tune routines as well because they are inefficient.

This developmental model is implicit in Markman's explanation of class-inclusion performance. The operation of part–whole comparison is available to children for class-inclusion judgments. That operation has been applied in the past to simpler domains, which make fewer demands. If we analyze those simpler tasks to discover what makes them simpler, we will discover what is missing when the child approaches class inclusion. That lack will not be the availability of a solution procedure, but the task or person constraints on accessing and utilizing the procedure (see Gelman & Gallistel, 1978, for a similar argument).

Let us return to the model of analogical problem solving. The analogous procedure for comparing the extension of class and superordinate class is part–whole comparison. Markman extends Piaget's (Inhelder & Piaget, 1964) discussions of sublogical strategies to characterize the early procedures children could use to solve class-inclusion tasks and why the use of those procedures is so difficult. The initial procedure derives from comparing the extent of an object to the extent of a part. That comparison, of hand to finger or tree to branch, is very easy because there is perceptual support for it. The part is physically distinct from the whole. The whole has an external perceptual integrity, and there is an external linkage between the part and the whole, some physical juncture between the two in most cases.

The child could use this part–whole analysis to reason by analogy to the next step, the collection, which is the focus of Markman's work and which also came to the attention of Piaget who called the relation figural (or graphic) collections. A collection is a grouping of objects according to some conventionalized, external physical relation. Piaget usually defined collections as aggregates based on spatial proximity or belongingness. Although he acknowledged that children often use part–whole relations in the formation of classes and in the construction of class hierarchies (see also Kofsky, 1966), he argued that the reliance on external physical relations interferes with understanding the logic of classes. This argument is consistent with his claim that logical relations cannot be derived from perception, although the child may sometimes use perceptual supports to solve a task, which in reality is not understood. The attempt to separate perceptual from logical bases for task solution led to devising the complicated logical tasks Piaget used. In contrast Markman says that perceptual supports actually form the bridge for understanding logic. Moreover, she has widened the definition of collections to include other kinds of aggregates with a different kind of belongingness than perceptual proximity, membership, which was the focus of little Connie's confusion. Thus, although forest, clumps, bunches, armadas, and crowds owe their identity to physical proximity, academic classes, families, clubs, and military groups are structured through membership. The size of collections is easy to compare with the size of groups of objects for many of the same reasons that promote easy object–part comparisons. The members of a collection are physically distinct from the collective entity. At least in spatially organized collections, trees can exist outside of forests, groups can exist outside of bunches, and people can exist in isolation from crowds. The collection is constituted through an external relation that gives the whole cohesiveness, making it easier to see as an entity not dependent for its existence on any one part. Moreover, the part–whole relation is concretized. The spatial or membership criterion that defines the whole also defines the relation of the whole to the parts.

Markman has argued that part–object relations and collection–subgroup relations exist on a continuum. The same techniques of comparison are applicable to both relations, and similar perceptual mechanisms give integrity to the whole and to the parts yet differentiate and integrate the part and whole. The physical integrity of the whole in each case facilitates the task of holding in mind simultaneously the two terms of the comparision while operating on them. Class–subclass comparisons demand the same routine but under more adverse conditions. The task of comparing extensions is the same, but the terms of the comparison are different. The child must still compare one entity with another, but the two entities are defined by similarity or *intensional* criteria. It is harder to isolate those criteria because they do not refer to external relations; rather they refer to similarities that are often conceptual, not perceptual. Because it is harder to identify the internal criteria, it is also harder to retrieve the part–whole scheme or even know if it is applicable. Once retrieved, the part–whole scheme is harder to apply because the terms of the comparison are no longer sets of objects with another set but one set of attributes abstracted from objects with another set of attributes. Sets of attributes have no physical boundaries that differentiate parts from wholes. The very abstractness of intensional similarity destroys the perceptual integrity of the part and its whole. The routines for part and whole comparison are available to the child, but the child has difficulty in abstracting the intensions and using the part–whole routines to compute the extensions of sets defined by those intensions.

Markman's arguments make sense. Part–whole comparisions could be used to solve class inclusion even though it is hard to apply a perceptual routine to contextfree entities. Linguistically, the singular noun by which collections are labeled certainly may help focus attention on the relative size of collections. Dean, Chabaud, and Bridges (1981) suggest that the assumption that collective nouns always designate large quantities so simplifies the inclusion task that children automatically decide that collections are more extensive than subclasses.

However, although the routine of part–whole comparisions might enable the child to solve class-inclusion problems, it may not be a reasonable, necessary, or sufficient route. Because collections are easier to deal with than class inclusion, it is tempting to think that collections are natural cognitive organizations. But even in Markman's classification studies, kindergartners and first graders have trouble with collective and part–object comparisions. No wonder. When a collection is already constituted it may be easy to compare objects and collections. However, because collections lack definite intension and extension, they are not so easy to construct. Take intension. Trees in a forest are in spatial proximity to one another, but the trees are also close to the moss that grows on them, the animals that live in them, and the rocks on the forest floor. Which objects constitute the forest? Although the preceding example deals with spatially constituted groups, the problems of intensional definition are much greater when we deal with groups defined by membership criteria. Given the prevalence of divorce, premarital, and extramarital relations, it is hard to define who belongs to a family.

Extensional problems also abound. Two armadas meet in combat. During the course of the battle the two fleets become interspersed. Are they now one armada? You are flying in a plane looking out at the vegetation below. As the density of the trees increases at what point do you go from looking at a cluster of trees, to scanning a copse, to examining a forest? Although collections may be easier to compare in some tasks, they may not be so easy to define or compare in other tasks. The problems of part–whole definitions are not entirely avoided with collective entities, particularly when one collection must be compared with another (as in Dean's study).

Second, class inclusion does not really lie on a continuum with collections. The description of class inclusion as nothing but a part–whole comparison of extensions defined by internal criteria focuses attention on the similarities between collections and classes, but it neglects the real importance of the difference. The acquisition of abstraction as a task demand (see Nelson, this volume) is central to theories of cognition. Classes may be analogous in some respects to collections, but they are not collections. Children must differentiate the two, or they will fail to appreciate the power classification provides them. That power is not merely that by providing equivalence groups we simplify the diversity we encounter. We can call oaks and pines, trees wherever they are located and what we know about trees applies to each kind of tree. Classes provide the connections which allow inferences. As Markman readily acknowledges, many tasks are not amenable to valid solutions through part–whole reasoning. Once formed a collection may have organizational coherence, but the collection lacks temporal stability. Crowds scatter, bands disperse, and members of a fleet drift away. Thus, the generalizations one can make about the collection itself or the properties of things in a collection are limited. One cannot even learn much about part–whole relations because the properties that characterize collective aggregates (like proximity) are so global as to be uninformative. Collections are often unrelated to one another. That is why one cannot readily decide which collection contains more members. In collections, the characteristics of a whole cannot be generalized to its parts. Parts can exist in isolation. A forest is defined by proximity, but an oak is not. In contrast, classes have permanence. You may think of an aunt in terms of sex or relation to one's parent, but she is always female and a sister of a parent. The characteristics of the superordinate class usually[1] define its subordinate class members so that one can generalize from the whole to the part and make inferences. Moreover, the creation of any class defines potential class complements and the potential superordinate class to which the subclass and the complement could belong. If the child only acted as if each class were a collection, the child would lose much. It is a matter of emphasis whether the interesting cognitive phenomenon is discovery of how the child uses the collective analogy to deal with classes or discovers that the analogy fails and builds a new model.

My third problem with Markman's analysis is that I do not think part–whole comparisons of the extension of classes are a complete explanation of class inclusion. Winer (1980) made a telling point when he described the relevance of simplification strategies as ultimate explanations of class-inclusion performance: "The very processes which underlie the ability to include the less difficult items might be irrelevant to or play a small role [in the more difficult tasks] [p. 323]." Examine the literature on addition. It might appear that the same counting forward strategy used to add 2 to 8 might also be used to add 2 to 18, but the latter addition ultimately requires knowing something about the base 10 structure of our number system. Similarly, it might appear that part–whole strategies can be applied to collections and classes, but the latter involves an additional property, which entirely transforms how adults understand class inclusion.

I have always thought the Piagetian equations discussed earlier are misleading if taken in isolation. Piaget has emphasized that those equations are only part of the story because they describe the formal logic of extensional comparison alone. Those equations are applicable to many extensional comparisons such as collection-subcollections, but classes are unique in that they involve both intension and extension. Each property uniquely defines the other. Once you know a set's intension you know its extension and vice versa. The problem of class inclusion is a coordination of intension and extension. Intension does not refer to sets of objects but to sets of properties, and the operations of addition (composition) and subtraction (decomposition) discussed with reference to extensions work differ-

---

[1]Of course Rosch (e.g., Rosch, Mervis, Gray, Johnson, & Boyes-Braem, 1976) claim this is not the case.

ently when they are applied to sets of properties rather than to sets of objects. A subclass possesses a set of specific intensional criteria, whereas superordinate sets are defined by more general criteria. Boys are defined by age and gender but males just by gender. To define a subset one adds intensional criteria to the superordinate class definition. To define a superordinate class one deletes a differentiating attribute from the subclass definition. Thus, the reversibility of classes refers to intension as well as extension. In discussing extension we refer to sets of objects, but in discussing intension we deal with sets of properties that must be taken one or two at a time. That makes class inclusion sound formal operational, and indeed class logic is a structural precursor of formal thought. Moreover, again as in formal operations, one must coordinate intension and extension as complementary, opposite processes. The more specific the intension of a class, the narrower its extension. When you add an intensional criterion, you descend the inclusion hierarchy to a class narrower in extensional scope. When you delete an intensional property, you add to the extension of a class.

You can solve class-inclusion tasks by an extensional part–whole algorithm, but that does not mean that you understand the full implications of class inclusion, a relationship between extension and intension that is irrelevant to collections, which lack definite intension and extension. The collection analogy is not all there is to class inclusion. Many Piagetian tasks are quite complex and could be solved in a variety of ways. Thus, conservation may be initially comprehended in terms of identity relations, but it may be only later that the role of compensation enters into conservation. In one experiment Markman (1978) demonstrated that children who could solve the standard class-inclusion task still failed to appreciate that the intensional relation between nested classes necessitates the outcome of comparisons of extension. Markman has made a very real contribution in describing a way of looking at one partial solution to class inclusion. However, we lack two important pieces of data. We know it is easier to solve an extensional class-inclusion task if the terms used are collective. But we do not know if the children who use collective strategies then go on to apply those strategies to standard class-inclusion tasks. That is, we do not know how the old routine is applied to the new task. Second, we do not know how adults evolve, if they ever do, a richer and qualitatively different way to answer class-inclusion questions.

Let me end by returning to the information-processing literature. Sometimes I imagine the psychology department at Carnegie-Mellon as a Tower of Hanoi factory. Construction of the Tower of Hanoi involves transferring a stack of rings from one post to another without ever violating the initial principle of constructing the tower—small rings rest on larger ones. Subjects who solve the problem of construction in the same number of steps do not necessarily do so with the same routine. First, they concentrate on how to get one ring out of the initial stack, then they realize that each transfer involves a repetitive series of activities, and finally they conceptualize the task as a nested set of recursions (e.g., Anzai &

Simon, 1979; Klahr & Robinson, 1981). It would be a mistake to assume merely by examining the tower builder's moves that a particular conception of the tower motivated those moves. Simon examined task encoding through his subject's verbal description of her thought processes just as Piaget has used clinical interviews. It might also be a mistake to think that the earlier solutions were the analogies on which the latter solutions were based. In fact they were not because the solution process became hierarchically organized. The earlier solutions preceded but were different from the later stacking-transfer attempts. Simon simulated each stage of performance in a computer program. The later stages made more demands on memory but handled the outcomes of more extended transfers more efficiently. The program accounted for the demands of each successive solution attempt, but it does not yet explain the means by which the subject met those demands or the means by which the subject knew the problem was being handled better. Although the Tower of Hanoi is not analogous to many tasks cognitive psychologists study, unless one thinks cognition involves multiple embeddings, some of the points made about its solution and how to conceptualize it surely apply to the tasks that tap the logic of classes.

Some difficult questions remain to be addressed. Does early conceptualization of classes as collections lead to the solution of class-inclusion tasks? Does collective organization provide an algorithm that so decreases the processing load for the child that the class-inclusion task becomes manageable? Once the child finds the task manageable, does the child then begin to think of the logical implications of the inclusion relationship? If so, where do those implications come from? Are they also borrowed by analogy from other domains, and which might they be? Are they the domains Piaget claims, or is the notion of collection a fundamental challenge to Piagetian theory?

ACKNOWLEDGMENTS

This discussion of the paper by Ellin Scholnick in this volume was presented at the Eleventh Jean Piaget Society Symposium in Philadelphia, May 1981. The chapter was written while its author was at the National Institute of Education.

REFERENCES

Anzai, Y., & Simon, H. A. The theory of learning by doing. *Psychological Review*, 1979, *86*, 124–140.

Carson, M. T., & Abrahamson, A. Some members are more equal than others: The effect of semantic typicality on class inclusion performance. *Child Development*, 1976, *47*, 1186–1190.

Chi, M. H. T. Knowledge development and memory performance. In M. Friedman, J. P. Das, & N. O'Connor (Eds.), *Intelligence and learning*. New York: Plenum Press, in press.

Dean, A. L., Chabaud, S., & Bridges, E. Classes, collections and distinctive features: Alternative strategies for solving class-inclusion problems. *Cognitive Psychology*, 1981, *13*, 84–112.

Gelman, R., & Gallistel, C. R. *The child's understanding of number*. Cambridge, Mass.: Harvard University Press, 1978.

Inhelder, B., & Piaget, J. *The early growth of logic in the child: Classification and seriation*. New York: Harper & Row, 1964.

Klahr, D., & Robinson, M. Formal assessment of problem-solving and planning processes in preschool children. *Cognitive Psychology*, 1981, *13*, 113–148.

Klahr, D., & Wallace, J. G. *Cognitive development: An information processing view*. Hillsdale, N.J.: Lawrence Erlbaum Associates, 1976.

Kofsky, E. A scalogram analysis of classificatory development. *Child Development*, 1966, *37*, 191–204.

Larsen, G. Y. Methodology in developmental psychology: An examination of research on Piagetian theory. *Child Development*, 1977, *48*, 1160–1166.

Lipman, M. *Pixie*. Montclair, N.J.: First Mountain Foundation, 1981.

Lipman, M., Sharp. A. M., & Oscanyan, F. S. *Philosophy in the classroom*. (2nd ed.). Philadelphia, Pa.: Temple University Press, 1980.

Markman, E. M. Empirical versus logical solutions to the part–whole comparison problem concerning classes and collections. *Child Development*, 1978, *49*, 168–177.

Markman, E. M. Classes and collections: Conceptual organization and numerical abilities. *Cognitive Psychology*, 1979, *11*, 395–411.

Markman, E. M. Two different principles of conceptual organization. In M. Lamb & A. Brown (Eds.), *Advances in developmental psychology* (Volume 1). Hillsdale, N.J.: Lawrence Erlbaum Associates, 1981.

Markman, E. M., Horton, M. S., & McLanahan, A. G. Classes and collections: Principles in the learning of hierarchical relations. *Cognition*, in press.

Markman, E. M., & Seibert, K. J. Classes and collection: Internal organization and resulting holistic properties. *Cognitive Psychology*, 1976, *8*, 561–577.

Rosch, E., Mervis, C. B., Gray, W. D., Johnson, D. M., & Boyes-Braem, P. Basic objects in natural categories. *Cognitive Psychology*, 1976, *8*, 382–439.

Scholnick, E. K., & Johnson, J. W. *Knowledge and conceptual structure in semantic memory*. Paper presented at the meeting of the Society for Research in Child Development, Boston, April 1981.

Trabasso, T., Isen, A. M., Dolecki, P., McLanahan, A. G., Riley, C. A., & Tucker, T. How do children solve class-inclusion problems? In R. S. Siegler (Ed.), *Children's thinking: What Develops?* Hillsdale, N.J.: Lawrence Erlbaum Associates, 1978.

Werner, H., & Kaplan, B. *Symbol formation*. New York: Wiley, 1963.

Wilkinson, A. Counting strategies and semantic analysis as applied to class inclusion. *Cognitive Psychology*, 1976, *8*, 64–85.

Winer, G. A. Class inclusion reasoning in children: A review of the empirical literature. *Child Development*, 1980, *51*, 309–328.

THE PROBLEM OF TIMING

10 Perceptual Categorization in the Infant

Leslie B. Cohen

Barbara A. Younger
University of Texas at Austin

The field of infant perception has made great progress over the past 20 years. Much of that progress is unknown to those in developmental psychology or even to those interested in cognitive development in young children or infants. For the most part this lack of knowledge or perhaps, more precisely, lack of communication between two apparently related research areas is understandable. As long as those of us in infant perception were examining how well an infant could see or why an infant preferred to look at a circle rather than a square, there appeared to be little overlap with those trying to explain how a child acquires a notion of an object or forms a concept or category.

However, as the field of infant perception has evolved and expanded, we are finding that the division between perceptual development and cognitive development is arbitrary at best. As our research questions have changed from whether or not infants can see anything to what types of information infants can process, organize, and remember, we have learned that many of the same theoretical issues confronting those in cognitive development confront us as well.

The purpose of the present paper is twofold: (1) to explain the procedures we have been using with infants; (2) to describe how we have adapted these procedures to answer basic questions about infant categorization such as: What is the earliest age at which infants can categorize? Can they categorize at different levels of abstraction? And what types of mechanisms best represent how they do it?

DEMONSTRATION OF INFANT CATEGORIZATION

We probably should start by explaining what we mean by a category. We define a category as a recognized equivalence among stimuli, objects, or events that are

197

discriminably different. We pick this definition to be consistent with the one usually used in the child and adult literature. Two parts of the definition need to be stressed. The first is that in order for individuals to be responding categorically, the various exemplars comprising the category should be responded to equivalently. The second is that this response equivalence should occur even though the exemplars are clearly different from one another.[1]

Consider, for example, one simple type of categorization task often used with children or adults. In the training phase of these tasks subjects are given a variety of exemplars and learn that they are all members of the same category. They are then tested with novel exemplars from the category and with nonexemplars. Their ability to select the new members from the nonmembers is taken as evidence of categorization. The appropriate selection of new exemplars satisfies the equivalence portion of the definition, and because these new exemplars usually are physically quite different from the old exemplars received in training, the discriminability portion of the definition can also be assumed.

We have been able to use an analogous procedure with infants. However, in many of these studies we have felt it necessary to make an explicit test for discriminability as well as for equivalence. Our procedure takes advantage of a well-known phenomenon in the infant perception literature called habituation. When infants are repeatedly shown the same visual stimulus, their fixation times to that stimulus usually decrease or habituate. If the infants subsequently are given a test with the familiar and with a novel stimulus, their fixation times increase again (or dishabituate) but only to the novel stimulus. Figure 10.1 provides an idealized example of habituation and dishabituation. The fact that infants decrease their response with repeated exposures to the same stimulus is an indication they are remembering that stimulus. And the fact that they respond more in the test to the novel stimulus than to the familiar one is an indication they can discriminate the novel from the familiar test stimulus. This habituation procedure has been used effectively many times by many investigators to show that infants can perceive, remember, and discriminate colors, shapes, sizes,

---

[1]We recognize that our definition of categorization, or for that matter any definition, will have certain limitations (see Flavell, 1970, for a discussion of this issue). We defined a category as a response equivalence to multiple exemplars. One could counter with the argument that some concepts or categories have only one or even no exemplar. That argument hinges on the distinction between a concept and a category. But even if it held for a category, our definition need not be exhaustive. It need only include a subset of those cases most would agree represent categorization.

Another more serious argument could be made about cases in which infants respond equivalently to discriminable stimuli but do not seem to be forming a category. A good example might be their responding in the same way to different views of the same object. At a later point in this chapter we also note some similarities between infant categorization, on the one hand, and object permanence or perceptual constancy, on the other. It could well be that common processes are involved in all three abilities, and that by investigating the development of infant categorization we shall be learning more about the development of object permanence and perceptual constancy as well.

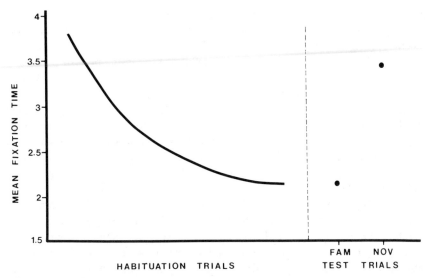

FIG. 10.1   Idealized habituation curve showing both reduction in fixation time during the habituation phase and dishabituation to the novel stimulus in the test phase.

textures, and numerous other characteristics of specific stimuli or objects (Cohen, DeLoache, & Strauss, 1979; Cohen & Gelber, 1975).

We have modified the procedure slightly to show that infants can also perceive categories. The design of one of our early experiments on infant categorization (Cohen & Caputo, 1978) is given in Table 10.1. This was an experiment to demonstrate that 7-month-old infants could form the category of toy stuffed animals. During a pretest all infants were shown a picture of a checkerboard (CH), a stuffed animal (SA_N), and a rattle with an overall configuration resembling that of the stuffed animal. The same three pictures were shown again in the test following habituation. The purpose of the checkerboard was to examine whether any lack of responding in the test resulted from nonspecific fatigue. In fact the infants looked as long at the checkerboard in the test as they had in the pretest, thereby ruling out a fatigue explanation. The purpose of the other two

TABLE 10.1
Experimental Design for Stuffed Animal Study

Conditions	Pretest	Habituation	Test
Same	CH, SA_N, Rattle	SA_{10}, SA_{10}, SA_{10}, . . . SA_{10}	SA_N, Rattle, CH.
Changing	CH, SA_N, Rattle	SA_1, SA_2, SA_3, . . . SA_{10}	SA_N, Rattle, CH.
Object	CH, SA_N, Rattle	O_1, O_2, O_3, . . . SA_{10}	SA_N, Rattle, CH.

pretest pictures was to see if there was any initial preference for the stuffed animal or rattle, which might complicate interpretation of the test data. Fortunately, no initial preference appeared. The infants looked at the stuffed animal and rattle for approximately the same amount of time in the pretest.

Following the pretest infants were assigned randomly to one of three habituation conditions. Those in the same condition were repeatedly shown the same picture of a single stuffed animal (SA_{10}) for 10 trials. Those in the change condition were shown a different stuffed-animal picture on each habituation trial. And those in the objects condition were shown pictures of totally unrelated objects like a telephone, a ball, a bottle, and a stuffed animal. Following habituation all three groups were given the test with the novel stuffed animal and with a nonstuffed animal, the rattle.

Figure 10.2 shows the habituation data for the three groups. It is apparent that if the infants saw either a single stuffed animal or multiple stuffed animals, they habituated quite rapidly. On the other hand, if they saw unrelated objects, they displayed little if any habituation. Our interpretation was that if the infants could abstract any invariant features from the set of stimuli they had seen, they would remember those features and would habituate to them. Inasmuch as the unrelated objects had little in common, there was little to habituate to (other than to the fact that they were pictures), and in this group fixation times should remain high.

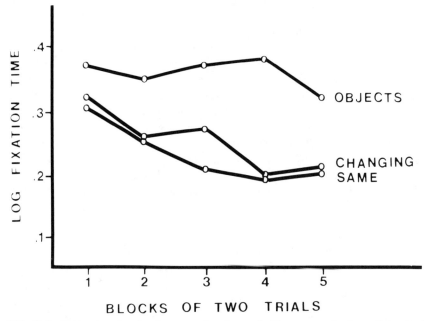

FIG. 10.2   Habituation data for the same, changing, and objects groups in the stuffed animal experiment (from Cohen & Caputo, 1978).

The test data are given in Fig. 10.3, which shows fixation times to the last habituation stimulus, to the novel stuffed animal, and to the rattle. As can be seen, the same group dishabituated both to the stuffed animal and to the rattle in the test. Both were novel, and the infants could discriminate the test stuffed animal from the one they had seen during habituation. In contrast the change group dishabituated only to the rattle. For them the test stuffed animal was familiar enough to be treated as something they had seen before. As might be expected, the objects group continued to look a long time at the last habituation stimulus as well as at the two test stimuli. Because they did not habituate, one would not expect them to have short looking times to any of the stimuli.

This experiment provided one bit of evidence that by 7 months of age infants can respond categorically. However, there are many questions the experiment did not answer, such as: Are there age differences in this categorical ability? Can infants form categories at different levels of abstraction? And if they can, on what basis do they do it?

We ran the same experiment with infants 5 months of age and obtained uninterpretable results. The change group habituated but then dishabituated to both the novel stuffed animal and the rattle. The same group showed little habituation and then looked longer in the test at the rattle than at the novel stuffed animal. Whatever the reasons for their unpredictable behavior, it certainly was not consistent with the view that the 5-month-old infants were responding in terms of a category.

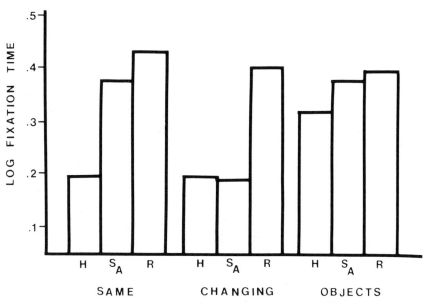

FIG. 10.3   Test data in the stuffed animal study for the same, changing, and objects groups. H, S_A, and R refer to the last habituation, novel stuffed animal, and rattle stimuli, respectively.

Another experiment has just been completed in our laboratory (McDonough, 1981) in which older infants were given the change condition. The experiment compared the performance of normal infants versus those with cerebral palsy. We found that normal infants at 12 to 18 months and at 18 to 24 months learned the stuffed-animal category quite easily, but the cerebral palsied infants did not learn it until they were 18 to 24 months of age.

Several tentative conclusions can be reached from this one set of studies. First, it is clear that our habituation procedure can be used to investigate infant categorization. Second, it can be used over a fairly wide age range, at least from 5 months to 2 years. Third, we have evidence, at least with stuffed animals, that a developmental change occurs sometime between 5 and 7 months of age. Normal infants under 7 months have considerable difficulty forming the category, whereas those over 7 months have much less difficulty. Finally, we have a suggestion from our infants with cerebral palsy that, in at least one handicapped population, our categorization procedures may be sensitive to certain delays in cognitive development.

However, before the importance of these results can be determined, it is necessary to replicate and extend the findings from our stuffed-animal studies. In another experiment (Cohen & Strauss, 1979) we wanted to replicate the age differences we had found, but with a different category. In this study we also wanted to see if we could get infants to respond at different levels of abstraction by habituating them to different invariant properties. Our experiment was based upon an earlier study reported by Cornell (1974); our study's design is given in Table 10.2. Infants were habituated and tested with photographs of female faces. In Group 1 the infants were repeatedly shown the same photograph (F_{11}) during habituation. The first subscript denotes that it was Person 1, and the second that the person was in a particular orientation (e.g., looking to the upper left). Following habituation, the infants were tested with Face 1, (F_1) for the first time looking straight ahead and with a novel face (F_n) also looking straight ahead. Group 2 also received a single face during habituation, however, for them the orientation of the face varied from trial to trial. Sometimes the face was looking to the upper left, sometimes to the lower right or lower left, and so on. Group 3 received different faces in different orientations on each habituation trial. Both Groups 2 and 3 were also tested with F_1 and with F_n.

TABLE 10.2
Experimental Design for Cohen and Strauss (1979)
Face Concept Study

Group	Pretest	Habituation	Posthabituation	Test	Posttest
1	Checkerboard	F_{11}, F_{11}, F_{11}	F_{11}, F_{11}, F_{11}	F_1, F_N	Checkerboard
2	Checkerboard	F_{11}, F_{12}, F_{13}	F_{17}, F_{18}, F_{19}	F_1, F_N	Checkerboard
3	Checkerboard	F_{11}, F_{22}, F_{33}	F_{77}, F_{88}, F_{99}	F_1, F_N	Checkerboard

Different groups of infants were tested at 18, 24, and 30 weeks of age. We expected that if the infants could discriminate the habituation from test faces, Group 1 should dishabituate to both test faces. Both faces were in a different orientation from the habituation face, F_{11} and prior research has shown that infants at all of these ages should be able to discriminate among different orientations. The story should be quite different for Group 2. During habituation they saw the same face, but the orientation varied from trial to trial. If they were habituating to the same face regardless of orientation, their response should remain low to the familiar face in the test, and they should dishabituate only to the novel face. Finally, Group 3 received different faces in different orientations during habituation. If they were habituating to faces in general, their response should be low to both test faces.

The results are shown in Fig. 10.4. As can be seen from the bottom of the figure, at 30 weeks of age the infants performed just as expected. Group 1 dishabituated to both test faces, Group 2 only to the novel face, and Group 3 to neither face. We interpreted these results as showing that by 30 weeks of age infants could abstract different levels of invariant information from a set of related stimuli. Depending on what they had seen during habituation, they were responding in the test in terms of either a particular face in a single orientation, a particular face regardless of orientation, or faceness in general.

The results were quite different at the younger ages. As shown in the top two sections of Fig. 10.4, both 18- and 24-week-old infants dishabituated to both test stimuli regardless of what they had received during habituation. The only change in stimulation from habituation to test that occurred consistently over all three groups was a change in orientation. Apparently the younger two groups of infants were able to perceive this change in orientation and responded only on that basis.

We consider both the stuffed-animal and face studies primarily to be demonstrations that infants can categorize. These studies indicated that there are age differences in this categorization ability, with 7 months of age in normal infants being the turning point. The face study also showed that infants can form categories at different levels of abstraction, although it does not tell us much about how they do it.

LEVELS OF ABSTRACTION

Before we describe what we have learnad about the mechanisms underlying infant categorization, we would like to discuss more fully the issue of levels of abstraction. The types of levels we tested for in the face study were different from the subordinate, basic, and superordinate levels usually associated with categorization tasks (Rosch, 1978). For example, according to Rosch's system, bassinets, beds, and furniture would represent subordinate, basic, and superordi-

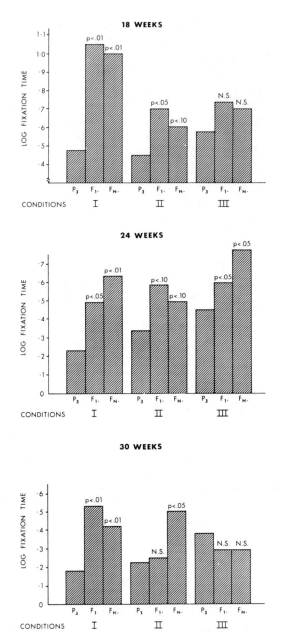

FIG. 10.4   Test data for the face concept experiment. P_3 refers to the last trial in the habituation phase, F_1 to Face 1 looking straight ahead, and F_N to a novel face looking straight ahead (from Cohen & Strauss, 1979).

nate, categories respectively. We too have begun to investigate superordinate categorization in infants and are finding that at between 18 and 24 months of age infants will respond to the superordinate, "toys," as a single category. Although numerous questions remain about infants' formation of superordinate categories, at the present time we are more curious about the formation of subordinate categories.

Categories are usually thought of as groupings of distinct objects, and subordinate categories as groupings of highly similar, yet distinct, objects. Bassinets, highchairs, and baby bottles would be examples of different subordinate categories most infants have experienced. But how do young infants tell the difference between separate objects comprising a subordinate category and different examples of a single object? When an infant experiences a baby bottle at two different times and possibly in two different locations, is the infant perceiving a single object displaced in time or two objects that are members of the same subordinate category? In the face study reported earlier, when the infants were habituating to the same face in different orientations, were they grouping what they perceived as different faces into a common subordinate category, or were they grouping different views of the same face into the notion of a single object? Without delving too deeply into the metaphysical question of the meaning of "similarity," it is clear that the dividing lines between categorization, object permanence, and perceptual constancy are not very precise. Just because we as experimenters usually have little trouble distinguishing between the same object at different times or places and different objects at the same time or place, it does not mean that the infant makes the same distinctions.

Before we can hope to disentangle categorization, permanence, and constancy, we have to learn much more about the processes infants use to group things together. The demonstration experiments we have reported so far have shown that infants are capable of abstracting invariant information, but little attempt was made to discover what type of information they were abstracting or how they were using this information. In order to understand the processes underlying the infant's ability to perceive some equivalence among members of a category, it is necessary to ask what types of invariant features the infant is capable of abstracting and if these features are integrated in some way into a unique representation of the category.

PROTOTYPICALITY

Fortunately, we were able to look to the adult categorization literature to help guide our efforts in addressing these questions. Rosch and her colleagues (Rosch, Mervis, Gray, Johnson, & Boyes-Braem, 1976) have suggested that most natural categories do not have criterial attributes (i.e., there is no single feature or set of features necessary or sufficient to define category membership). Instead, it has been suggested that categories are structured as "family resemblances" (Rosch & Mervis, 1975; Wittgenstein, 1953). Category members are related by a series of overlapping attributes. Those members having the most in common with other members of the category are the best examples or prototypic members of the category (Rosch, 1978).

A good deal of literature exists examining the process of abstracting a prototype from experience with category exemplars. Two important and consistent results have emerged from this adult work on prototype abstraction. First, adults can abstract a prototypical representation consisting of either the averaged or the most frequently occurring values of experienced exemplars even though the prototype itself has never been seen before (Goldman & Homa, 1977; Homa & Chambliss, 1975; Neumann, 1977; Posner & Keele, 1968, 1970). And second, recognition and classification of prototypes is very resistant to forgetting and may even be better than previously experienced exemplars (Goldman & Homa, 1977; Posner & Keele, 1970).

As one might expect, adults abstract a modal representation of values varying along discontinuous dimensions; however, values varying along continuous dimensions are sometimes "counted" to yield a modal prototype and at other times averaged to yield a mean prototype (Goldman & Homa, 1977; Neumann, 1977). In general, it has been found that adults "count" and form modal prototypes when featural values are easily discriminated, whereas they tend to average the values when the discrimination is more difficult.

If one were interested in understanding the processes involved in infant categorization, a reasonable starting point might be to ask if infants, like adults, abstract some type of prototypic representation of experienced exemplars of a category and if this representation is based on the mean or mode of the experienced values.

Using a police Identikit, Strauss (1979), in our laboratory, constructed two sets of faces varying along four continuous facial dimensions—eye separation, nose width, nose length, and head length. There were five values on each dimension. As can be seen in Table 10.3, one set consisted of highly discriminable values (1, 3, and 5) along each dimension. The other set, not shown in the table, consisted of less discriminable values (2, 3, and 4). In each set, the end point values (e.g., 1 and 5) occurred six times on each dimension, and the middle value (3) only twice. In an adult study, Strauss confirmed that, with these stimuli, adults in the highly discriminable condition formed a prototypical representation by "counting" the most frequently occurring features, whereas those in the less discriminable condition formed an average representation.

The procedure used in the infant study differed slightly from the habituation procedure we described earlier. A visual preference paradigm was used in which two stimuli were presented side by side in front of the infant. During familiarization the same stimulus was presented on both sides. During the test the infant was

TABLE 10.3
Experimental Design for Strauss (1979) Prototype Study

Familiarization

	Facial Dimension Values			
Familiarization Faces	*Eye Separation*	*Nose Width*	*Nose Length*	*Head Length*
1	1	1	5	5
2	5	3	1	5
3	1	1	5	3
4	1	3	1	5
5	5	5	3	1
6	5	1	1	5
7	1	5	1	5
8	3	5	1	1
9	5	5	1	1
10	3	1	5	5
11	1	5	5	1
12	1	5	3	1
13	5	1	5	1
14	5	1	5	3

Test Pairs
Pair 1   3333 vs. 1111 or 5555
2   3333 vs. NNNN
3   NNNN vs. 1111 or 5555

shown two different stimuli; for example, a familiar stimulus paired with a novel stimulus. The observer simply recorded the amount of time the infant spent looking at each stimulus.

Strauss familiarized 10-month-old infants with the set of 14 faces described in Table 10.3. Each face was shown for 5 seconds. After the infants had seen all 14 familiarization stimuli, they received three pairs of test stimuli. In one, the average prototype (Face 3333) was paired with one of the modal prototypes (e.g., 1111 or 5555). In a second pair, the average prototype was paired with a totally novel face (NNNN). And finally, in the third pair, one of the modal prototypes was paired with the novel face.

The test pairs were designed to determine whether infants would form a prototypical representation of the experienced exemplars, and if so, whether they would do so by averaging the values they had experienced or by "counting" the most frequently occurring values. It was expected that, if the infants were abstracting an averaged representation, the average prototype would be more familiar than the modal prototype, and as a consequence, the infants should spend a greater proportion of time looking at the more novel modal prototype. In contrast, if they were "counting" values, the modal prototype should be more familiar, and the averaged prototype should elicit a greater proportion of looking.

The results were consistent with the notion that infants were forming an averaged representation of the experienced exemplars in that they exhibited a greater proportion of looking time toward the modal prototype when it was paired with the average prototype. They also exhibited a greater proportion of looking time to the totally novel face when it was paired with the average prototype. However, they did not show any differential looking in the contrast between the modal prototype and the novel face. Unlike the results with adults, the infants formed an average prototype with both sets of faces.

In a second study Strauss (1981) tested for memory of prototypic information and specific item information. Again, the face category was constructed in the same manner and varied along four dimensions. The eight faces used during familiarization contained the values 1, 2, 4, and 5. As can be seen in Table 10.4, each value occurred twice on each dimension. In this study the average value, 3, was never seen during familiarization. Ten-month-old infants were familiarized with the faces shown in the table. Each was presented until the infant had accumulated 5 seconds of looking time. Following familiarization the infants received three test pairs: the average prototype, P, (3333) paired with a novel category member, N; the average prototype paired with either the first or last

TABLE 10.4
Experimental Design for Strauss (1981) Prototype Study

| | Familiarization | | | |
| | Facial Dimension Values | | | |
Familiarization Faces	Eye Separation	Nose Width	Nose Length	Head Length
1	1	1	5	5
2	1	5	1	5
3	2	4	2	4
4	2	2	4	4
5	4	4	2	2
6	4	2	4	2
7	5	5	1	1
8	5	1	5	1

Test Pairs
Pair 1   P vs. N
2   P vs. SP1 or 8
3   N vs. SP1 or 8

familiarization stimulus, SP1 or 8; and finally, the novel category member with the familiarization stimulus.

As in the previous study infants looked longer at the novel face when it was paired with the average prototype. They also looked longer at the old familiarization faces than at the prototype. This pattern of results indicates that, as in Strauss' previous study, infants had formed an averaged prototype from their experience with the familiarization stimuli and also that memory for the prototype, which the infants had never seen before, actually was better than memory for the individual exemplars that they had seen.

Together, these Strauss experiments provide fairly strong evidence that by 10 months of age infants can abstract a prototypical representation from experienced exemplars of a category; this representation is formed by averaging the values experienced during familiarization.

ATTRIBUTE SALIENCE AND ILL-DEFINED CATEGORIES

Even though these studies have shown that infants do abstract and store categorical information of some kind, they have been limited in that they have not provided information concerning such questions as the number of attributes infants use in forming categories, the relative weights assigned to the attributes, or how they are combined. The procedures we have discussed thus far are not well suited to addressing these kinds of issues in that they deal with the acquisition of only a single category. These questions involve the validity of particular cues in determining category membership—a concept that is defined in terms of at least two contrasting categories.

In an effort to address the question of the specific attributes used in category learning and the weights assigned to these attributes, Husaim and Cohen (1981) adopted an operant head-turn conditioning procedure that enabled the simultaneous learning of two contrasting categories. In addition to examining the question of specific attributes, an attempt was also made to assess the infant's ability to learn ill-defined categories. As we mentioned earlier, most natural categories are considered ill-defined in that there is no simple set of features necessary or sufficient to define category membership (Rosch et al., 1976). Studying ill-defined categories in infants is important because they frequently confront categories in the world structured in just this way.

The stimuli used in the study were schematic drawings of animals varying on four dimensions—body size, neck length, leg length, and number of legs. The binary values on each dimension are shown in Table 10.5. Two categories were constructed from the 16 possible combinations of these animals. The structure of the categories is presented in abstract notation in Table 10.6. As can be seen, the categories are ill-defined in that there is no single feature or set of features determining all and only the instances of either category. For example, each

TABLE 10.5
Stimulus Dimension Values for Ill-Defined Category Study

Dimension Values	Body Size (a)	Neck Length (b)	Leg Length (c)	Number of Legs (d)
0	Small	Short	Short	2
1	Large	Long	Long	4

feature in Category A has a value of 1 three times and 0 once. An example of one stimulus from each category is shown in Fig. 10.5.

Ten-month-old infants were trained to turn left to members of one category and right to members of the contrasting category. Electronically operated animated toys served as reinforcers. The procedure consisted of three phases. The first phase involved a single blocked presentation of the eight training stimuli.

TABLE 10.6
Design for Husaim and Cohen (1981) Ill-Defined Category Study

				Response Shaping and Training					
	Category A					Category B			
		Dimension Values					Dimension Values		
Stimulus Number	a	b	c	d	Stimulus Number	a	b	c	d
1	1	1	1	0	5	0	0	0	1
2	1	1	0	1	6	0	0	1	0
3	1	0	1	1	7	0	1	0	0
4	0	1	1	1	8	1	0	0	0

				Transfer					
	Group 1					Group 2			
		Dimension Values					Dimension Values		
Stimulus Number	a	b	c	d	Stimulus Number	a	b	c	d
9	1	0	1	0	10	0	1	0	1
11	1	1	0	0	12	0	0	1	1
13	1	0	0	1	14	0	1	1	0
15	1	1	1	1	15	1	1	1	1
16	0	0	0	0	16	0	0	0	0

Note: The letters a, b, c, and d stand for body size, neck length, leg length, and number of legs, respectively.

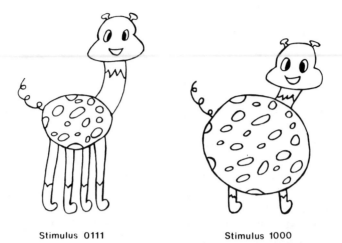

Stimulus 0111   Stimulus 1000

FIG. 10.5   Some examples of the stimuli used in the Husaim and Cohen (1981) ill-defined categories experiment.

For example, the four members of Category A were followed by the four members of Category B. Reinforcement was administered if the infant made a head-turn response in the appropriate direction or if the infant failed to respond at all at the end of the 10-second trial. This phase was designed to familiarize the infant with the location of the reinforcers and the contingency between a head turn and activation of the toys.

The second phase consisted of repeated randomized blocks of the eight training patterns. In this phase reinforcement was totally contingent upon a correct response. Upon reaching a criterion of seven of eight correct responses within a block, infants proceeded to the third and most important phase of the experiment. During this transfer phase infants were presented the transfer stimuli shown in Table 10.6. All infants were presented with the modal prototypes, 1111 and 0000, for each of the categories in addition to three other novel patterns. During transfer a head turn in either direction was reinforced because for most patterns there was no "correct" response.

Classification performance on the transfer stimuli was used to assess the infant's ability to generalize to novel patterns and to estimate the weights they assigned to each of the four dimensions. The infants correctly classified the modal prototypes with very little difficulty (95% correct), whereas performance on most of the other transfer patterns did not differ from chance.

In order to estimate the weight assigned to each dimension, equations were derived for each transfer pattern from two models of categorization: an independent cue model (Posner & Keele, 1968, 1970) and the context model (Medin & Schaffer, 1978). The independent cue model assumes that categorization is a function of the overall similarity of a pattern to a summary representation (or prototype) of a given category. Similarity is derived for this model by combining features independently using an additive rule, so the more shared features a pattern has with the prototype, the better example it is of the category. In contrast, the context model assumes that patterns are categorized on the basis of their similarity to stored exemplars rather than to a summary representation. This model treats similarity as a multiplicative function of feature matches between stored exemplars and the pattern to be categorized. The weightings derived from the two models were in general agreement. (The study was not designed to pit one model against the other.) The infants relied most heavily on neck length, followed by the number of legs, body size, and least of all, leg length.

In summary, this study has shown that 10-month-old infants are capable of learning two contrasting ill-defined categories. Further, it provided a technique for investigating the specific attributes infants use in learning categories and how these attributes are combined. The results also suggested that individual infants used multiple dimensions in learning and using ill-defined categories.

CORRELATED ATTRIBUTES

We have seen that infants are able to use multiple dimensions in learning categories, and another question we might ask is how relationships among attributes might be involved in categorization. Natural categories are presumed to be formed in such a way as to take advantage of the highly correlated structure of perceived attributes in the world (Rosch, 1978). The world is structured in such a way that all combinations of attributes are not equally likely to occur. Co-occurrences of some sets of attributes are highly probable, whereas others are very rare or do not occur at all. For example, wings are very likely to occur with feathers but are much less likely to occur with fur. If the correlated attribute structure of the world plays an important role in categorization, we might ask if the infant makes use of correlated clusters of attributes in forming categories. Implicit in this question is the infant's ability to process the relationship among the attributes of an object.

In a recently completed study in our laboratory (Younger & Cohen, 1982), we addressed the question of whether infants perceive correlations among attributes. The stimuli we used were schematic drawings of animals varying along five dimensions—body, tail, feet, ears, and number of legs. Each dimension could have one of three values as shown in Table 10.7. So, for instance, infants might be shown a two-legged giraffe with a fluffy tail, antlers, and webbed feet. Some examples of the drawings we used are shown in Fig. 10.6.

Infants aged 4, 7, and 10 months were habituated to two categories of animals, each defined by the correlational structure of the attributes. The stimuli we used are represented in abstract notation in Table 10.8. In each case the first three dimensions (body, tail, and feet) were correlated. In examining the design of this

TABLE 10.7
Stimulus Dimension Values for Correlated Attribute Study

Dimension Values	Body (a)	Tail (b)	Feet (c)	Ears (d)	Legs (e)
1	Giraffe	Feathered	Webbed	Antlers	2
2	Cow	Fluffy	Club	Round Ears	4
3	Elephant	Horse	Hoofed	Human Ears	6

experiment for the moment consider only Group 1. For that group a value of 1 on the first dimension was always accompanied by a value of 1 on the second and third dimensions. Similarly, a 2 on the first dimension always occurred with a 2 on the second and third dimensions. The remaining two dimensions (ears and number of legs) were irrelevant, and their values varied independently across the four stimuli. The same pattern of correlations existed for Group 2, except for them the correlations were 122 instead of 111 and 211 instead of 222.

The infants were shown each of the four habituation stimuli twice in 20-second trials, followed by three 20-second test trials. As can be seen in the table, the correlated test stimulus contained one of the correlations present in the habituation stimuli (for Group 1 it was a 222, and for Group 2 it was a 211). In

11121

22212   33333

FIG. 10.6   Some examples of the stimuli used in the Younger and Cohen (1982) correlated attribute experiment.

TABLE 10.8
Experimental Design for Younger and Cohen (1982) Correlated
Attributes Study

	Habituation									
	Group 1					Group 2				
	Dimension Values					Dimension Values				
Trial	a	b	c	d	e	a	b	c	d	e
1	1	1	1	1	2	1	2	2	1	2
2	1	1	1	2	1	1	2	2	2	1
3	2	2	2	1	1	2	1	1	1	1
4	2	2	2	2	2	2	1	1	2	2
5			.					.		
6			.					.		
7			.					.		
8			.			.				

| | Test | | | | | | | | | |
	a	b	c	d	e	a	b	c	d	e
Corr	2	2	2	1	2	2	1	1	1	2
Uncorr	2	1	1	1	2	2	2	2	1	2
Novel	3	3	3	3	3	3	3	3	3	3

Note: The letters *a, b, c, d,* and *e* stand for body, tail, feet, ears, and legs, respectively.

the uncorrelated test stimulus, the values on the previously correlated dimensions were familiar to the infants, but they occurred in a novel combination. Finally, the novel test stimulus contained a novel value on each of the five dimensions.

We expected that, if the infants perceived the correlation, the uncorrelated test animal would appear sufficiently novel to the infants to elicit an increase in looking, whereas the correlated test animal would not. In contrast, if the infants were only remembering something about the specific attributes but not the relationship among them, the uncorrelated animal should look as familiar to the infants as the correlated animal. The results were quite clear. As can be seen in Fig. 10.7, the 10-month-old infants dishabituated to both the novel and the uncorrelated test stimuli but did not dishabituate to the correlated test stimulus. This pattern of results indicated that by 10 months of age infants are not responding to the attributes in isolation. They can perceive the correlation among attributes and can base their novelty preferences solely on those correlations. In contrast, as can be seen in Fig. 10.8, the 4- and 7-month-old infants dishabituated to the novel test stimulus but did not dishabituate reliably to the correlated or

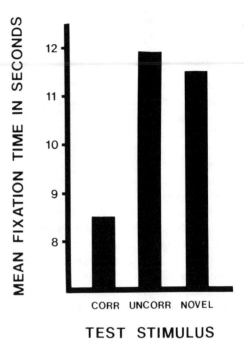

MEAN FIXATION TIME IN SECONDS

CORR   UNCORR   NOVEL

TEST STIMULUS

FIG. 10.7   Test data from the 10-month-old subjects in the Younger and Cohen (1982) correlated attribute experiment.

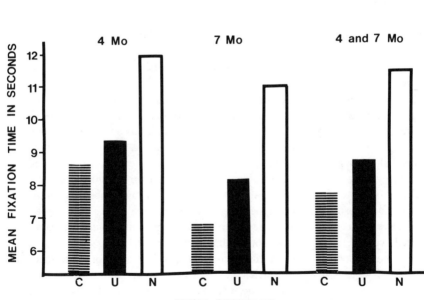

MEAN FIXATION TIME IN SECONDS

4 Mo   7 Mo   4 and 7 Mo

C   U   N   C   U   N   C   U   N

TEST STIMULUS

FIG. 10.8   Test data from the 4-month, 7-month, and combined 4- and 7-month-old subjects in the Younger and Cohen (1982) correlated attribute experiment.

the uncorrelated test stimuli. Unlike the 10-month-olds, the younger infants seemed to be responding more on the basis of specific attributes than on the basis of the correlation among attributes. These results suggest a possible developmental shift from processing a set of stimuli or a category in terms of independent attributes to processing in terms of relationships among attributes.

It may be an understatement to say that over the past 2 or 3 years our knowledge of infant categorization has increased considerably. We now know that simple habituation and conditioning techniques can be used effectively to investigate complex issues related to infant categorization. We know that by 7 months of age infants can acquire certain categories, and we know some of the means by which they do it. By familiarizing infants to different invariant properties we can get them to categorize at different levels of abstraction. Furthermore, the processes 10-month-old infants use to generate categories seem quite similar to those used by older children and adults. When attributes vary along a continuous dimension, the infants will form a prototype, which is based upon the average values they have seen. Even if they have never experienced this prototype before, it will still be more familiar to them than an exemplar they did experience. Finally, the mechanism they use to form categories seems quite sophisticated. As our research on ill-defined categories and correlated attributes indicates, infants are capable of learning categories that have no single attribute or set of attributes in common. They also are capable of using multiple attributes to form categories and even of taking the correlation among these attributes into account.

UNRESOLVED ISSUES

Even though we know much more now about infant categorization than we did 3 or 4 years ago, there is much we do not know. Recent research on infant categorization has generated as many questions as it has answered. A couple of examples should illustrate fruitful avenues for future research. One involves the fact that although the ability to pick out invariant features or attributes from a set of changing pictures or objects clearly is important for category acquisition, it cannot be the whole story. How can the principle of invariance explain the fact that infants respond to prototypes they have never seen before as more familiar than exemplars they have seen? Or how can infants learn ill-defined categories that have no criterial features or attributes in common?

Just as the presence of invariant features is not necessary for the formation of a category, it is also not sufficient. We can all think of instances in which invariant information would be present in a set of stimuli, but infants just could not or would not pick it up. Our initial research on superordinate categorization indicated that 12- to 18-month-old infants did not learn the category "toys", whereas 18- to 24-month-old infants did learn it. The same invariant information was present for both groups. It was sufficient for the older group but not for the younger.

Even more dramatically, in our "face" concept study the 30-week-old infants in the latter two groups responded to faces in general or to a particular face regardless of orientation. They did not respond to a change in facial orientation, although that was also invariant during habituation. But the younger, 18- and 24-week-old infants, who could not process these more abstract concepts, did respond to orientation. It is obvious that much more research is needed to determine under what conditions infants will or will not pick up a particular invariance and to what extent failure to pick up an invariance results from processing limitations at any particular age.

Another example of a question requiring more research was mentioned earlier in this chapter: the relationship between perceptual constancy, object permanence, and categorization. At that time we indicated that the borderline between categorization and permanence was difficult to draw. It depended on the factors infants use to distinguish between the same object in different locations or times and different objects in those locations or times. The same argument can be made for the distinction between categorization and constancy, only in this instance the problem is made more dramatic by the similarity of the techniques used to investigate the two phenomena. For example, McGurk (1972) reported an experiment in which 3- to 12-month-old infants were habituated to a simple form, a vertical line with a circle on top. In one condition the orientation of this form remained constant. In another condition the orientation varied from trial to trial. Subsequently, the infants were tested with the old form in a novel orientation, the line with the circle on the bottom, and with a totally new form, the line with an upside down "v" at the bottom. If the infants had been in the constant habituation condition, they dishabituated to both test stimuli. If they had been in the varied condition, they dishabituated only to the new form. This pattern of results was clear for the 6-, 9-, and 12-month-old infants and was in the right direction although not significant for the 3-month-olds. A subsequent study by Caron, Caron, and Carlson (1979) has now demonstrated a similar effect with 3-month-olds.

There are at least two ways to interpret the findings from these studies. One is in terms of form constancy. It was clear that the infants in the varied condition responded to the form as the same even though the orientation and therefore the proximal image of the form changed from trial to trial. Responding to the objective or distal image rather than to the proximal image is usually how form constancy is defined.

The other interpretation is in terms of categorization. You may recall we defined the existence of a category as a recognized equivalence among stimuli, objects, or events that were discriminably different. The paradigm McGurk used was almost identical to the one we have been using in our categorization experiments. It included a constant condition that showed the infants could discriminate the form in one orientation from the form in another orientation. Nevertheless, when the orientation was varied from trial to trial during habituation, the infants responded to the same form in a novel orientation in the test as equivalent to what they had seen before. Both essential elements of our definition of categorization, discrimination and equivalence, were met by the study. Should we then conclude that McGurk's infants were forming a category?

One major difference between the results obtained in the constancy studies and those on infant categorization is the age at which infants can pick out the relevant invariance. In our categorization research the earliest age is about 7 months. In the constancy experiments it is 3 months and possibly somewhat earlier. Additional research is needed to find out the meaning of that age difference, and the research should examine just what is varying as well as what remains invariant. One relevant factor may be that in the constancy studies a single form or object was presented during habituation, whereas in the categorization studies multiple objects were presented. That certainly is how we, as adults, would distinguish between constancy and categorization. But do infants make the same distinction? In order to answer this question, future research must examine the nature of the transformations we perform on forms or objects and how those transformations are perceived by infants. In a recent series of studies, Strauss and Cohen (1980) have shown that certain perceptual dimensions such as color or form are remembered better by 5-month-old infants than are others such as orientation or size. Perhaps those dimensions more integral to the identification of an object are those that are most salient. It may be that early in life infants learn that some transformations of objects destroy the objects' integrity more readily than do other transformations. If what is varying during an habituation sequence destroys an object's integrity, the infants may be confronted with a much more difficult task than if the object's integrity is maintained. The infants would have to integrate and abstract information from multiple objects rather than from a single one. As a result, the infants may not be able to process this information until they are somewhat older.

If infant categorization, and perhaps infant perceptual constancy, is ever to be explained, it is clear that we as researchers in the area must go beyond simply demonstrating that infants can acquire categories. As our two examples illustrate, we must gear our efforts toward finding ages at which categories cannot be formed as well as ages at which they can be formed. We must look to the types of information infants process at different ages and try to use what we learn to explain developmental changes in categorization. We must try to design experiments that examine these processes more carefully—processes like the abstraction of invariance, the formation of prototypes, or the relationships among relevant attributes. Finally, we should make better use of the information already available from categorization studies on children and adults. Both the results and the theories used to explain them can provide clues on how infants form categories. The techniques are now available to examine rather sophisticated questions about infant categorization, and the answers researchers come up with should be of benefit not only to those interested in infant development but to those interested in later development as well.

ACKNOWLEDGMENTS

An earlier version of this paper was presented at the Eleventh Annual Jean Piaget Symposium, Philadelphia, May 1981. The research presented in this paper was supported in part by grants HD-03858 and HD-15035 from the National Institute of Child Health and Human Development.

REFERENCES

Caron, A. J., Caron, R. F., & Carlson, V. R. Infant perception of the invariant shape of objects varying in slant. *Child Development, 1979, 50,* 716–721.

Cohen, L. B., & Caputo, N. *Instructing infants to respond to perceptual categories.* Paper presented at the Midwestern Psychological Association Convention, Chicago, May 1978.

Cohen, L. B., DeLoache, J., & Strauss, M. S. Infant visual perception. In J. Osofsky (Ed.), *Handbook of infant development.* New York: Wiley, 1979.

Cohen, L. B., & Gelber, E. R. Infant visual memory. In L. Cohen & P. Salapatek (Eds.), *Infant perception: From sensation to cognition* (Vol. 1). New York: Academic Press, 1975.

Cohen, L. B., & Strauss, M. S. Concept acquisition in the human infant. *Child Development,* 1979, *50,* 419–424.

Cornell, E. Infants' discrimination of photographs of faces following redundant presentations. *Journal of Experimental Child Psychology,* 1974, *18,* 98–106.

Flavell, J. H. Concept development. In P. H. Mussen (Ed)., *Carmichael's manual of child psychology.* New York: Wiley, 1970.

Goldman, D., & Homa, D. Integrative and metric properties of abstracted information as a function of category discriminability, instance variability, and experience. *Journal of Experimental Psychology: Human Learning and Memory,* 1977, *3,* 375–385.

Homa, D., & Chambliss, D. The relative contributions of common and distinctive information on the abstraction of ill-defined categories. *Journal of Experimental Psychology: Human Learning and Memory,* 1975, *1,* 351–359.

Husaim, J. S., & Cohen, L. B. Infant learning of ill-defined categories. *Merrill-Palmer Quarterly,* 1981, *27,* 443–456.

McDonough, S. *The use of habituation to investigate basic level and superordinate level categorization in cerebral palsied infants.* Unpublished doctoral dissertation, University of Illinois at Urbana-Champaign, 1981.

McGurk, H. Infant discrimination of orientation. *Journal of Experimental Child Psychology,* 1972, *14,* 151–164.

Medin, D. L., & Schaffer, M. M. Context theory of classification learning. *Psychological Review,* 1978, *85,* 207–238.

Neumann, P. G. Visual prototype formation with discontinuous representation of dimensions of variability. *Memory & Cognition,* 1977, *5,* 187–197.

Posner, M. I., & Keele, S. W. On the genesis of abstract ideas. *Journal of Experimental Psychology,* 1968, *77,* 353–363.

Posner, M. I., & Keele, S. W. Retention of abstract ideas. *Journal of Experimental Psychology*, 1970, *83*, 304–308.

Rosch, E. Principles of categorization. In E. Rosch & B. Lloyd (Eds.), *Cognition and categorization*. Hillsdale, N.J.: Lawrence Erlbaum Associates, 1978.

Rosch, E., & Mervis, C. B. Family resemblances: Studies in the internal structure of categories. *Cognitive Psychology*, 1975, *7*, 573–605.

Rosch, E., Mervis, C. B., Gray, W., Johnson, D., & Boyes-Braem, P. Basic objects in natural categories. *Cognitive Psychology*, 1976, *8*, 439–483.

Strauss, M. S. Abstraction of prototypical information by adults and 10-month-old infants. *Journal of Experimental Psychology: Human Learning and Memory*, 1979, *5*, 618–635.

Strauss, M. S. *Infant memory of prototypical information*. Paper presented at the meeting of the Society for Research in Child Development, Boston, April, 1981.

Strauss, M. S., & Cohen, L. B. *Infant immediate and delayed memory for perceptual dimensions*. Paper presented at the International Conference on Infant Studies, New Haven, Conn., April 1980.

Wittgenstein, L. *Philosophical investigations*. New York: Macmillan, 1953.

Younger, B. A., & Cohen, L. B. *Infant perception of correlated attributes*. Paper presented at the International Conference on Infant Studies, Austin, March, 1982.

11

Perceptual Categorization and Sensorimotor Intelligence During Infancy: A Comparison of Theoretical Perspectives

Richard De Lisi
Rutgers, The State University
of New Jersey

INTRODUCTION

Cohen (1979; Cohen & Younger, this volume) makes the point that there has been a lack of communication between those working in the fields of infant perception and later cognitive development. Cohen and Younger's lucid review of research on perceptual categorization in infancy suggests that this line of investigation may shed as much light on cognition in older subjects as does the explicit study of children and adults. By working from the "bottom-up" Cohen and his colleagues have made strides in closing the gap between two areas that were becoming increasingly distinct.

In this chapter I seek to contribute to the dialogue envisioned and initiated by Cohen. Toward this end, I discuss some of the theoretical underpinnings of his research program on categorization in infancy. This aspect of the program was ignored by Cohen and Younger who chose instead to communicate their methods and results. A discussion of theory is in order for two reasons. First of all, research methods and interpretation of results rarely exist apart from theoretical perspectives, and this work on perceptual categorization is not an exception in my view. Moreover, scientific progress is not a mere accumulation of facts but, instead, has been described as a shift in paradigms that serve to govern "fact" gathering and interpretation (Feldman, 1981; Kuhn, 1970). Thus, Cohen is correct to call for a dialogue, but he needs to communicate his theoretical perspectives on perception, categorization, and so on, along with methods and results if he hopes to have a meaningful exchange with those working in related fields.

In order to infer the theoretical perspectives underlying this work on perceptual categorization it is necessary to review and consider the rationale for experiments along with methods and procedures. Such a review reveals an interesting mixture, as the rationale for the design of experiments stems from modern cognitive psychology (e.g., the work of Rosch, Posner, etc.), whereas the methods are derived from behavioristic psychology (e.g., habituation and operant conditioning techniques). If this characterization is correct, then it seems that this research program has not incorporated *developmental* perspectives on categorization in infancy, except perhaps to test for age differences.

Many who work in the fields of infant and childhood cognition are guided by issues in developmental psychology, in particular, issues raised by Piagetian theory and research. Piaget hypothesized that there exists a fundamental continuity between the practical intelligence of infancy and the theoretical intelligence of childhood and adolescence, such that the latter is built upon the former. As early as 1927 Piaget (in Gruber & Voneche, 1977) noted:

> If only we could know what was going on in a baby's mind while observing him in action, we could certainly understand everything there is to psychology. Unfortunately, this knowledge will always be denied us. Certain authors scorn the primitive mind as a subject unfit for study, limiting themselves to the study of observable gestures. But it cannot be denied that adults do think, and that children of all ages think, and very differently from us. This leads to the unavoidable even if exceptionally difficult question of how thought originates, and particularly of how thought begins in babies [p. 199].

This insight, coupled with the era in which he began his research (an era in which developmental psychology had not yet differentiated from experimental psychology, let alone form specialties such as infant cognition or adolescent cognition) led Piaget to investigate the intelligent conduct of both infants and children. Based on this work Piaget formulated an account of cognitive development which is unusual by today's standards for its comprehensiveness.

But does the accuracy of Piaget's theory of cognitive development match its comprehensive scope? One consequence of the recent focus on specific periods of the life space is a growing sense that Piaget may have underestimated the cognitive competencies of young children (Gelman, 1978). In this same vein, the work of Cohen and others has been cited as evidence that Piaget may have also underestimated the cognitive abilities of infants (Flavell, 1979; Mervis & Rosch, 1981). For example, Flavell (1979) proposes that by focusing on motor skills, Piaget may have missed many neonatal cognitive competencies. That is, according to Flavell (1979) recent evidence suggests that: "the infant has more going for him cognitively than his initially poor and very slow developing motor abilities would lead us to suspect [p. 25]."

Although recent assertions that Piaget underestimated children's cognitive competencies may be ironic (Beilin, this volume), it is true that Piaget and Inhelder (1969) recently admitted:

It would be appropriate to begin our analysis [of perception] with a study of the perceptions of the newborn child and to follow them throughout the sensorimotor period. Unfortunately, however, nothing is more difficult to study than the perceptions of the young infant, since we are unable to subject the baby to precise laboratory experiments [p. 29].

So is it the case that now that the precise laboratory experiments have been done, Piaget's description of infant intelligence has been shown to be inadequate? The rising tide of opinion, which would answer in the affirmative, provides the second rationale for a discussion of the theoretical underpinnings of Cohen's program of research. For once the theory behind this research is clear we will be in a better position to judge its relation to Piagetian theory and research. This is important because if the field is abandoning Piaget's account of infant intelligence, it should be clear as to what is filling the void. Such a discussion should therefore be of interest to those who study cognition in infancy as well as "later" periods of cognitive development.

PERCEPTUAL CATEGORIZATION: DEFINITION AND MEASUREMENT TECHNIQUES

Cohen and Younger (this volume) define a category as a recognized equivalence among stimuli, objects, or events that are discriminably different. The experiments they review used three techniques to measure perceptual categorization in infants: (1) habituation–dishabituation paradigms; (2) novelty or visual preference paradigms; (3) operant conditioning paradigms. There is an elegant match between the definition of categorization and the techniques used to measure it. For example, when infants habituate to repeated presentations of different stimuli they are satisfying the equivalence aspect of the definition. Dishabituation to subsequent presentations of different stimuli is taken as evidence of discriminability.

In their review of infancy research through 1969, Kessen, Haith, and Salapatek (1970) noted that habituation is an important paradigm because it can be used to: (1) study infant memory; (2) provide evidence for (perceptual) discrimination; (3) tell us something about early learning because it does not require the occurrence of new responses, which may be confounded with age. As Cohen (1979) noted, for a long time investigators focused on item 2 and thereby remained distinct from cognitive-developmental research. However, when researchers took item 1 seriously, they began to expand the use of habituation (and other) paradigms to study not only memory abilities but also concept or category formation. The latter line of research, which became popular in the 1970s, stands as a fourth use of habituation. Based on this work, those who study infant categorization are now in a position to communicate not only with other infant researchers but also with those who focus on later periods of cognitive development (Cohen, 1979).

The study of visual memory or perceptual categorization via habituation or novelty-preference paradigms hinges upon an important theoretical assumption, namely, that an internal representation or code is responsible for observed patterns of fixation or looking. This assumption, which is borrowed from the literature on adult cognition, is discussed later on in this chapter. For now we first critique the definition and techniques used to investigate perceptual categorization in infancy.

Definitional Pitfalls

Although Cohen and Younger's definition of categorization as recognized equivalence among discriminably different stimuli is reasonable in terms of its face validity, as a heuristic tool, and in terms of prior work, it is not without problems. As Flavell (1970) and Neimark (this volume) indicate, when categorization or concept formation is defined in terms of response equivalence, we may be forced to attribute concepts or categories to subhuman or even nonorganic entities (see Neimark's car-gasoline example). Such attributions may not make those who feel categorization is a basic cognitive process uncomfortable (Mervis & Rosch, 1981), but according to Flavell (1970), it has caused some such as Hunt (1962) to arbitrarily exclude "all infrahuman equivalence responses from his definition . . . [p. 985]."

Note that even Cohen and Younger seem to have had some difficulty in applying their definition consistently. In this volume they refer to an attempted replication of the Cohen and Caputo study using 5-month-olds rather than 7-month-olds. They report that the infants assigned to the "same" group performed just like their 7-month-old counterparts, that is, having habituated to a picture of a single stuffed animal they dishabituated to a picture of a novel stuffed animal and to a picture of a rattle. The 5-month-olds in the "change" group, however, did not perform like their older counterparts. Having habituated to pictures of different stuffed animals, they did not dishabituate to either the novel stuffed animal or to the rattle. In other words, they treated the latter two stimuli as if they were members of the original habituation stimulus set ("stuffed animals").

Cohen and Younger conclude that the 5-month-olds in the "change" group had not formed the category of stuffed animals as had 7-month-olds exposed to the same treatment. The authors later refer to these age differences as evidence for developmental changes in categorization ability, with the age of 7 months being an important period for categorization onset. If we assume that the study in question used random assignment of infants to treatment groups ("same" vs. "change"), then Cohen and Younger's conclusion concerning 5-month-old infants' categorization abilities is inconsistent with their own definition of categorization. That is, if we assume that 5-month-olds in the "change" group could discriminate among pictures of the original group of stuffed animals, the novel stuffed animal, and the rattle, then we are left with the fact that *these infants evidenced a recognized equivalence among the three sets of stimuli* (i.e., they placed them all in the same category). Note that we can assume discriminability because 5-month-olds in the "same" group evidenced the expected pattern of dishabituation as well as habituation.

Rather than conclude that 5-month-olds in the "change" group had not, or could not, form a category, it would be more in accordance with the operational definition of categorization to conclude that they had formed a category, albeit not the one intended or expected by the experimenter. Thus, rather than forming a stuffed-animal category, the infants apparently formed a superordinate category such as "toys" or maybe even "pictures of toys."

In point of fact, we have no way of knowing what category was formed, but given the working definition and measurement techniques, we must conclude that one was formed. I think this points to a potential weakness in the categorization-as-recognized-equivalence approach. With subhuman and infant subjects there will always be some uncertainty as to the basis of an equivalence response. This is not to argue that infants cannot categorize visual inputs and instead respond on the basis of some other mechanism. Indeed, my argument is predicated on the acceptance of Cohen and Younger's definition and their reported findings. The point is that situations in which infants respond in accordance with intended experimental manipulations do not conclusively demonstrate that the categories of the experimenter and those of the infant are identical. (At least in one part of their chapter in this volume, Cohen & Younger would seem to agree.)

At the very least the foregoing discussion underscores Nelson's remarks (this volume) concerning the difficulties in precisely defining concepts and categories. The discussion also exemplifies Flavell's (1970) point as to how an equivalence-response definition may force investigators to infer categories when they do not want to. The main point, though, is not to discount Cohen and Younger's definition of categorization but to highlight its *adevelopmental flavor*. Defining categorization in terms of recognized equivalence among discriminably different stimuli without further specification of the mechanism(s) responsible for the recognized equivalence, or the nature of the category itself, avoids issues of change over ontogenetic time or change across species.

Although categories across species or across the life span may share commonalities, cognitive-developmental findings have also identified differences even in perceptual recognition. For example, Piaget and Inhelder's (1956) study of shape recognition via haptic perception identified developmental changes in tactile exploration of objects (perceptual activity) as the mechanism responsible for a sequence in shape recognition (topological then projective and Euclidean shapes). This raises again the need to consider the developmental origins of the internal representation or code presumed to underlie habituation–dishabituation or visual preference responses. But before doing so, some further comments on research methodology are offered.

Methodological Considerations

Kessen et al. (1970) indicates that effector fatigue and maintenance of arousal or alertness rival habituation as alternative explanations of experimentally induced response decrements. Thus, infants may stop looking at simuli not because they have habituated but because they tire or fail to attend. The research conducted by Cohen and his colleagues cannot be faulted on these grounds because proper methodological controls were employed in the various studies. For example, use of the dishabituation paradigm in which the original stimulus is represented to see if habituation reoccurs rules out fatigue as an explanation of the original habituation. Similarly, in another study (Cohen & Strauss, 1979), a checkerboard was presented both prior and subsequent to presentation of test stimuli. Inasmuch as significant differences in checkerboard fixation times were not obtained, arousal or alertness is an unlikely candidate to account for habituation to test stimuli.

Another methodological strength in Cohen's research is the use of a 50% decrement in mean fixation time to the first three trials as a criterion for the occurrence of habituation on subsequent trials. This approach, rather than presentation of a fixed number of trials, provides a more powerful assurance that infants who participate do in fact habituate during the course of the experiment. Cohen and Younger were somewhat modest in that they did not highlight these aspects of the research program. Readers should be aware that this research is solid in that checks which guarantee the occurrence of habituation during testing were built into each of the experiments.

GENERALIZABILITY OF RESULTS

Having considered several aspects of the internal validity of Cohen's experiments on infant perceptual categorization, let us now consider its external validity. Following Campbell and Stanley (1966), I consider four dimensions of generalizability: (1) organisms or experimental units; (2) settings; (3) treatment variables; (4) measurement variables.

Almost all psychological research can be faulted for its lack of generalizability across subjects. In infancy research there is a seemingly unavoidable problem with selectivity. Many subjects, especially younger ones, drop out due to crying, fussiness, sleeping, and so on during testing. The experiments on perceptual categorization are not immune to these problems. For example, in the Cohen and Strauss (1979) study 108 infants constituted the final sample, but an additional 88 infants had to be dropped from the experiment. Can results be generalized to those infants who do not finish the procedures and to those infants whose mothers choose not to volunteer for the experiment? Clearly, the results of perceptual categorization research may be limited to a select pool of subjects.

This point is somewhat "textbookish" in that there is very little that can be done to overcome the difficulties. There is a related problem though, which can be easily corrected. In reading many of the original publications cited by Cohen and Younger, I was surprised to find that more often than not mean fixation times were reported without the accompanying standard deviations. That is, there was very little information given about within-subject differences in category formation. Given the wide variability that is known to exist in later cognitive development, one might expect considerable variability in perceptual categorization. Without knowledge of the magnitude of within-subject variability, it is difficult to assess whether selectivity is indeed a threat to the generalizability of perceptual categorization findings. Moreover, age-group variability comparisons are necessary to get a complete picture on developmental patterns.

As for settings, all of this research was conducted in laboratories. Infants were brought into a laboratory room and shown pictures of objects on a screen while seated on their mothers' laps. There is no reason to assume that testing infants in a more naturalistic setting (e.g., on their backs in a playpen with real toys) would significantly alter obtained results. However, very little is said about the instructions to mothers and their role, if any, during testing. What do the mothers do while slides are flashing on the screen? We will assume that mothers do not guide the gazes of their babies, but replication of results without mothers would make a stronger case for the generalizability of results across settings.

The extent to which findings are generalizable across treatment and measurement variables can be considered together. Inferences about categorization are made on the basis of differences in visual fixation times to experimenter-generated stimulus sets. The various procedures have a passive quality to them, especially the habituation paradigm, as there is more to visual perception than fixation. One wonders about the role of eye movements (perceptual activity) in fixation patterns. Are infants looking at selective, distinctive features or at the whole figure? Are there age differences in visual scanning (which may or may not coincide with differences in categorization)? Moreover, results are based on statistical analysis of log fixation times. Many significant differences are actually less than 2 and even 1 second in duration. Are such differences psychologically significant? That is, is there a model of infant visual perception which demonstrates that such differences are a reflection of higher rather than lower levels of processing?

Although the phenomenon of perceptual categorization was robust in that it was identified across three types of laboratory treatments, findings of categorization with completely different procedures would provide additional important evidence of generalizability across treatments and measures. Such findings may be forthcoming. Starkey (1981) measured concept formation in 6-, 9-, and 12-

month olds using an object sorting paradigm. Younger infants evidenced less facility in "concept formation" than their older counterparts on two indices, sequential touching and object grouping. Starkey notes that these age differences coincide with Cohen's findings even though the two studies used very different measures of concept formation. If findings such as these can be replicated, it will provide additional evidence that the period of 6 to 9 months marks the beginnings of object categorization.

THEORETICAL ASSUMPTIONS

Thus far our discussion has indicated that: (1) the internal validity of the laboratory experiments used to assess perceptual categorization is strong; (2) the operational definition of categorization is rather broad so that, even if one assumes that categorization underlies obtained patterns of fixation and head turns, the exact nature of the categories is ambiguous; (3) the generalizability of the results of the various experiments is at least adequate and may prove to be quite robust.

A key point, of course, is the assumption that categorization of stimuli is responsible for obtained patterns of fixations times, directed gazes, or head turns. It is doubtful, for example, that Pavlov (1927) would have appealed to categorization as a cognitive concept to account for the orienting reflex. Indeed, the "what-is-it reflex" was described as a tendency to orient toward any novel stimulus without regard to its significance. Similarly, the founders of operant conditioning techniques would probably account for patterns of head turns without appealing to "mentalistic" concepts such as categorization (viz., Lipsitt, 1981). In short, although many of the findings in recent infancy research are new and exciting, psychologists have known for some time now that organisms habituate and can be conditioned.

In my view, what makes this line of research particularly exciting is the manner in which such findings are discussed and interpreted. Changes in psychology during the past 20 years have provided a language and a metaphor that allow investigators to describe and interpret results in cognitive rather than stimulus–response terminology. Neuronal models of memory (e.g., Hebb, 1949; Sokolov, 1960) might be considered accounts of habituation that are midway between strict behavioristic and modern cognitive theories. If this characterization is correct, it provides a nice illustration of a point made at the outset of this paper concerning the role of theory and paradigm shifts in scientific progress. Be that as it may, the view that categorization (as a cognitive process) underlies fixation patterns and head turns constitutes one theoretical assumption in the program of research summarized by Cohen and Younger.

A second assumption concerns the nature of these perceptual categories. Although Cohen and Younger were not explicit on this point, I believe it is their position that some sort of internal representation or code, such as a mental image, constitutes perceptual categories. I think Cohen and Younger were not explicit on this point because they feel it is obvious that categorization requires some sort of mental encoding of stimuli. Certainly, such a view would be in line with recent work in cognitive psychology dealing with adults or children (e.g., Shepard's, 1978, discussion of perceptual and mental images; Kosslyn's, 1978, 1981, computer model of imagery).

Given these two assumptions, much of the research reviewed by Cohen and Younger was addressed to explication of the processes by which infants form categories. That is, experiments were designed to determine what types of invariant features an infant is capable of abstracting, whether these features are integrated into prototypes via averaging or modal summaries, whether infants can note correlations among features of visually presented stimuli, and so on. The logic and design of these recent experiments are based, at least in part, on the adult categorization literature. Questions such as what develops in perceptual categorization and how does development occur have not been addressed in this program of research to date. Thus, Cohen and his colleagues have borrowed terms and procedures from the adult literature in order to study categorization in infants. Rather than work from the bottom-up, this approach is really top-down. Such a research strategy is not theoretically neutral. Instead there is an implicit assumption that the processes and mechanisms that underlie adult categorization also underlie categorization in infants.

In sum, there are three theoretical assumpts implicit in Cohen and Younger's discussion of perceptual categorization in infancy:

1. Categorization underlies habituation/dishabituation fixation patterns, visual preferences, and head turns.

2. An internal representation constitutes the categories.

3. The processes or mechanisms that determine perceptual category formation in infancy are similar to those that determine conceptual category formation in adulthood, that is, categorization is a basic cognitive process which undergoes little if any development once it enters the individual's cognitive repertoire (Mervis & Rosch, 1981).

Each of these assumptions are discussed with explicit reference to Piagetian theory in the following sections.

RELATION TO PIAGETIAN THEORY

1. *Categorization of Stimuli Occurs During Experimental Testing.*   The idea that infants form perceptual categories seems to me to be perfectly consistent with Piaget's (1952) account of infant intelligence. Consider Piaget's definition

and discussion of sensorimotor schemes—internal coordinations of adaptive, overt actions that function via the processes of assimilation and accommodation. Assimilation is an incorporative process that moves in the direction of object → scheme. With assimilation, an object is "taken into" a scheme and thereby has meaning conferred on it vis-à-vis the scheme. Accommodation is an outwardly directed process that moves in the direction of scheme → object. With accommodation, schemes are adapted to the specific features or nature of the object. This may or may not result in a new scheme being formed, but in either case, there is accommodation to the object.

Assimilation and accommodation are simultaneous (not sequential) processes that occur in every act of knowing ranging from perceptual recognition to logical inferences. Of course, schemes, like perceptual categories as discussed by Cohen, are hypothetical constructs, which cannot be measured directly but are inferred from regularities in behavior. For example, when we see infants take several objects into their hands and grasp (suck, shake, etc.) them, we can infer a scheme for grasping (sucking, shaking). Thus, a child might grasp (what we adults know to be) a rattle. In Piaget's terms the rattle is incorporated into a grasping scheme and thereby becomes known as a "graspable." However, it is only during the act of grasping that the rattle is known as a graspable, for sensorimotor schemes coordinate *overt conduct*. Each time the rattle is grasped, and especially when other objects such as stuffed animals or blankets are grasped, we observe accommodation as the acts of grasping compensate for the particular configurations of the objects.

The parallels between Piaget's description of sensorimotor schemes and Cohen's description of perceptual categories seem clear. When an infant assimilates a rattle, a stuffed animal, and a blanket to a grasping scheme and thereby knows them as "graspables," the infant has treated different objects equivalently. Due to accommodation, no two objects are grasped in exactly the same fashion, thus, the infant is responsive to and can discriminate differences among objects. In short, sensorimotor schemes allow infants to categorize in the sense intended by Cohen and Younger. Objects that are discriminably different are treated equivalently.

Although Piaget may have had difficulty accepting the notion of experimentally induced categories, the assumption that infants use some sort of internal psychological mechanism to interact with and process environmental objects and events is consistent with Piaget's constructivist (antiempiricist) orientation (e.g., see the quote from Piaget, 1927, earlier in this chapter). The fact that such categories are being described at the level of perception rather than motor behavior in no way contradicts Piaget's account of sensorimotor intelligence, in which references are made to perceptual as well as motor schemes.

2. Perceptual Categories Consist of Some Sort of Internal Representation. It is on this point that Piaget's description of sensorimotor intelligence and Cohen and Younger's account of infants' perceptual categories begin to part company. This is not surprising, for it is on this point that Piaget's theory is in a clear minority among current cognitive theories.

Piaget maintained that sensorimotor intelligence was a pre-representational, practical "know-how" (Furth, 1981). Such an intelligence is capable of discovering properties of objects, reading cues from the environment, and mastering one's own movements in the environment without using a mental representation as a basis. Such an intelligence describes perfectly well the intelligent behavior of subhuman organisms (e.g., Koehler's apes or the locomotion of cats and dogs through their neighborhoods) without attribution of symbolic representation. In this connection, note that a sensorimotor scheme is not an internal *representation* of action, but rather an internal *coordination* of action. As such, a scheme does not rely on a specific representational modality such as mental imagery or language. Recognition of previously experienced objects and generalization of schemes to new objects were "built into" schemes by Piaget rather than being derived from a symbolic representation.

Piaget argued that in the case of the human infant representation was a cognitive derivative of sensorimotor intelligence. That is, increasing levels of sensorimotor development were said to culminate in the first "theoretical" knowledge—object permanence, which is knowledge that an object exists independently of action on it. As a consequence of this cognitive construction, representation was said to make its appearance in the cognitive repertoire only after object permanence appears, during the end of the first year of life. This view was a key point of difference between Piaget and Chomsky in their accounts of linguistic structures (Piattelli–Palmarini, 1980).

In contrast to Piaget, modern cognitive psychology attributes an internal representation whenever evidence for memory (e.g., recognition memory) occurs. Note that this position is not a passive empiricist one in which visual experience is said to be the origin and cause of knowledge in the form of perceptual or mental imagery representations via internalization. Instead, perception, mental imagery, and so forth are described as active processes in which the organism's cognitive machinery is very much at work.

The key difference, then, between these two views of infant intelligence concerns the attribution of a representation of reality to the child during the first year of life. Piaget's unwillingness to do so and modern cognitive psychology's willingness to do so no doubt stem from a difference in perspective on the nature of the subject-object relation. Piaget maintained that infants and objects are inextricably bound as far as the infant is concerned in early life. If babies do not know that objects exist, how could they form representations of specific objects? Modern cognitive psychology is willing to begin with the environment and the baby as two distinct entities. This position asks: How could current information be recognized without prior encoding of previous information?

Having highlighted a difference between categorization and sensorimotor accounts of infant intelligence, I would like to make two further comments. First, whether or not one attributes an internal representation to account for infants' intelligent behaviors is a matter of theoretical preference and assumptions. Time will tell which approach is more efficacious in terms of generating research, asking interesting questions about infancy, and placing this period in evolutionary as well as ontogenetic perspective. Classical behaviorism was loath to attribute mental processes and structures to any organisms, including adults, let alone infants (Lipsitt, 1981). Other more recent investigators of sensorimotor intelligence feel that the usual tests of object permanence are not sufficient to insure that infants have represented the hidden object (Corrigan, 1981a, 1981b; Fischer & Jennings, 1981). Thus, some recent work suggests that representation "enters the picture" even later than Piaget suggested. What is puzzling and somewhat troublesome are statements to the effect that recent findings on perceptual categorization are evidence that Piaget underestimated the cognitive capacity of infants (Mervis & Rosch, 1981). As I have suggested, Piaget's theory could account for these findings but would do so with different theoretical constructs. Sensorimotor intelligence is an important *form of knowing,* not an underestimation.

The second point I wish to make is that the theoretical difference in attribution of representational competence to infants might be more apparent than real. That is, much of the evidence for categorization comes from (self-selected) infants aged 7 months or older. In Piaget's account of sensorimotor intelligence, object permanence, like all cognitive constructions, is not an all-or-none acquisition. The period of 7 to 9 months is one in which an initial, stable form of object permanence has been identified. Babies aged 9 months or so will search for a hidden object in the place where they last retrieved it. This early form of subject-object separation may underlie an early form of representation in the sense intended by Cohen and Younger. When perception alone, rather than perception plus retrieval, is required (e.g., in perceptual categorization studies), this early form of object permanence may be present in some 7-month-old infants and provide the bases for perceptual categorization.

One way to check my assertions would be to screen infants aged 7 to 9 months for this early form of object permanence, which is usually called the Stage IV or AB̄ error (Gratch, 1977). Two groups that differ in their level of object permanence development could then be compared in perceptual categorization studies. It would be interesting to see if the more advanced group habituated more quickly, evidenced a greater memory capacity, categorized more readily, and showed smaller within-group variability. Such an experiment would examine perceptual categorization development using Piagetian operative level, rather than age, as an index of developmental level.

3. *The Processes by which Perceptual Categories Are Formed in Infancy Resemble Those of Adult Conceptual Categories.*   The last set of experiments

reviewed by Cohen and Younger was designed to uncover the processes and mechanisms responsible for infant perceptual categorization. From this review they conclude that the ability to abstract invariant features from a set of stimuli is necessary but not sufficient to account for category acquisition. For example, the principle of invariance cannot explain the fact that infants were found to respond to prototypes they had never seen before as more familiar than exemplars they had seen before. Thus, perceptual category formation is not a passive process of picking up information from the environment; instead, it involves active cognitive processes, which turn out to be similar to those of adults when forming conceptual categories (e.g., averaging stimulus dimensions to form a prototype).

This is as far as Cohen and Younger go in terms of using their data to communicate with those interested in later cognitive development. However, others such as Mervis and Rosch (1981) refer to these findings to make two points: (1) basic level categorization is a basic cognitive process (i.e., a process that does not change during ontogenesis once it appears in the cognitive repertoire during infancy); (2) the process of categorization is prototypic in a Roschian sense (core and peripheral members of categories) rather than logical and classificatory in a Piagetian sense. Inasmuch as the second point is discussed elsewhere in this volume (papers by Rosch and Neimark), I need only address the first.

The view of basic level categorization as a process that undergoes little, if any, change during ontogenesis presents a challenge not only to Piagetian theory but to any developmental approach to cognition. Just as developmentalists such as Vygotsky and Piaget objected to the notion of cognitive structures (e.g., perceptual Gestalten) being innate and unchangeable over time, I think today's developmental theorists will object to the notion of (apparently innate) unchangeable cognitive processes, such as averaging stimuli to form a prototype.

This is not to deny that there are aspects of cognition which are innately given or that there is a fundamental continuity to cognition which links perceptual categorization and later conceptual categorization. For example, although Bruner and Vygotsky assumed that infants were born with competencies for representation and speech, respectively, they each argued that the nature of this representation and the use of speech changed during ontogenesis (from enactive to iconic to symbolic for Bruner; from social to egocentric to inner speech for Vygotsky). Similarly, although Piaget assumed that the cognitive processes of assimilation/accommodation were lifelong, the structures from which they emanate were said to be qualitatively different as a consequence of cognitive construction, which occurs during ontogenesis.

This difference in theoretical and perhaps philosophical views of cognition goes beyond the issue of categorization per se. Cognitive psychologists and cognitive-developmental psychologists unite in their critiques of behavioristic accounts of cognitive phenomena as each feels comfortable positing mental structures and processes (e.g., Chomsky's and Piaget's respective critiques of

Skinner's approach). The two disagree, however, in their explanation of the origins of these structures and processes (e.g., the Chomsky–Piaget debate in Piattelli-Palmarini, 1980). Many cognitive psychologists see developmental accounts as gratuitous; they maintain that the human cognitive system must be formally constrained in order to account for phenomena such as rapid and universal language acquisition (see Keil, 1981, for a more complete discussion of this point). The recent work on perceptual categorization in infancy fits in nicely with this view and provides further evidence for its efficacy. For their part, developmentalists counter that appeals to innatism merely push the search for origins from ontogenesis to phylogenesis (Piaget, 1971) and overlook the fact that human cognition does not exist in a vacuum but is a function of historical and sociocultural contexts (Baltes, Reese, & Lipsitt, 1980; Vygotsky, 1978).

A detailed discussion of the foregoing points is way beyond the scope of this paper. However, we can return to a few of the points raised at the outset of this chapter. A dialogue between those who work in the fields of infant perceptual categorization and later cognitive development is probably not soon in coming. For it appears that the two sides are deeply divided in their theoretical views of human cognition, which result in markedly different interpretations of phenomena such as early categorization. The issue of whether or not perceptual categorization turns out to be a basic (i.e., nondevelopmental) cognitive process or one that undergoes transformations during the life span may perhaps be settled in future research.

For now it appears that rather than leading to a dialogue across disciplines research on perceptual categorization is serving to polarize views further. This is not surprising, however. Researchers on each side no doubt realize how critical this "turf" is and will compete to offer a satisfactory account of cognitive phenomena during the early months of life. As Piaget noted some 50 years ago, the position that can explain what occurs in the minds of babies while observing them in action will no doubt have captured everything there is to psychology.

REFERENCES

Baltes, P. B., Reese, H. W., & Lipsitt, L. P. Life-span developmental psychology. *Annual Review of Psychology*, 1980, *31*, 65–110.

Campbell, D. T., & Stanley, J. C. *Experimental and quasi-experimental designs for research.* Chicago: Rand McNally, 1966.

Cohen, L. B. Our developing knowledge of infant perception and cognition. *American Psychologist*, 1979, *34*, 894–899.

Cohen, L. B., & Strauss, M. S. Concept acquisition in the human infant. *Child Development*, 1979, *50*, 419–424.

Corrigan, R. Defining mental representation: Comments on Fischer and Jennings. *Developmental Review*, 1981, *1*, 31–33. (a)

Corrigan, R. The effects of task and practice on search for invisibly displaced objects. *Developmental Review*, 1981, *1*, 1–17. (b)

Feldman, D. H. The role of theory in cognitive developmental research: A reply to Brainerd. *Developmental Review*, 1981, *1*, 82–89.

Fischer, K. W., & Jennings, S. The emergence of representation in search: Understanding the hider as an independent agent. *Developmental Review*, 1981, *1*, 18–30.

Flavell, J. H. Concept development. In P. H. Mussen (Ed.), *Carmichael's manual of child psychology* (Vol. 1) (3rd ed.). New York: Wiley, 1970.

Flavell, J. H. *Cognitive development*. Englewood Cliffs, N.J.: Prentice-Hall, 1979.

Furth, H. G. Piaget and knowledge. *Theoretical foundations* (2nd ed.). Chicago: University of Chicago Press, 1981.

Gelman, R. Cognitive development. *Annual Review of Psychology*, 1978, *29*, 297–332.

Gratch, G. Review of Piagetian infancy research. In W. F. Overton & J. Gallagher (Eds.), *Knowledge and development* (Vol. 1). New York, Plenum Press, 1977.

Gruber, H. E., & Voneche, J. J. *The essential Piaget: An interpretative guide and reference*. New York: Basic Books, 1977.

Hebb, D. O. *The organization of behavior*. New York: Wiley, 1949.

Hunt, E. B. *Concept learning: An information processing problem*. New York: Wiley, 1962.

Keil, F. C. Constraints on knowledge and cognitive development. *Psychological Review*, 1981, *88*, 197–227.

Kessen, W., Haith, M. W., & Salapatek, P. H. Human infancy: A bibliography and guide. In P. H. Mussen (Ed.), *Carmichael's manual of child psychology* (Vol. 1) (3rd ed.). New York: Wiley, 1970.

Kosslyn, S. M. Imagery and cognitive development: A teleological approach. In R. S. Siegler (Ed.), *Children's thinking: What develops?* Hillsdale, N.J.: Lawrence Erlbaum Associates, 1978.

Kosslyn, S. M. The medium and the message in mental imagery: A theory. *Psychological Review*, 1981, *88*, 46–66.

Kuhn, T. S. *The structure of scientific revolutions* (2nd ed.). Chicago: University of Chicago Press, 1970.

Lipsitt, L. P. Sensorimotor development: What infants do and how we think about what they do. In I. E. Sigel, D. M. Brodzinsky, & R. M. Golinkoff (Eds.), *New directions in Piagetian theory and research*. Hillsdale, N.J.: Lawrence Erlbaum Associates, 1981.

Mervis, C. B., & Rosch, E. Categorization of natural objects. *Annual Review of Psychology*, 1981, *32*, 89–115.

Pavlov, I. P. *Conditioned reflexes*. London: Oxford University Press, 1927.

Piaget, J. The first year of life of the child. *British Journal of Psychology*, 1927, *18*, 97–120.

Piaget, J. *The origins of intelligence in children*. New York: International Universities Press, 1952.

Piaget, J. *Biology and knowledge. An essay on the relations between organic regulations and cognitive processes*. Chicago: University of Chicago Press, 1971.

Piaget, J., & Inhelder, B. *The child's conception of space*. London: Routledge & Kegan Paul, 1956.

Piaget, J., & Inhelder, B. *The psychology of the child*. New York: Basic Books, 1969.

Piattelli-Palmarini, M. *Language and learning: The debate between Jean Piaget and Noam Chomsky*. Cambridge, Mass.: Harvard University Press, 1980.

Shepard, R. N. The mental image. *American Psychologist*, 1978, *33*, 125–137.

Sokolov, E. N. *Perception and the conditioned reflex*. New York: Macmillan, 1960.

Starkey, D. The origins of concept formation: Object sorting and object preference in early infancy. *Child Development*, 1981, *52*, 489–497.

Vygotsky, L. S. *Mind in society: The development of higher psychological processes*. Cambridge, Mass.: Harvard University Press, 1978.

FINALE

12 Is the Concept of the *Concept* Still Elusive or What Do We Know About Concept Development?

Irving E. Sigel
Educational Testing Service

One of the most perplexing and indeed vexing issues facing cognitive psychologists is that of *concept attainment*. In spite of a long history of research with children and adults, the problem of how humans develop an understanding of and a construction of classes, categories, or concepts is still baffling. This is the case in spite of the well worked out theories and research strategies (e.g., Bruner, 1966; Inhelder & Piaget, 1969; Miller & Johnson-Laird, 1976; Werner, 1948; Werner & Kaplan, 1963).

The commonality among these investigators is limited to their fundamental interest in identifying the what and the how individuals come to organize and integrate the vast array of experiences so that they can function with some degree of efficiency. There is little doubt about the fact that individuals arrive at a developmental level that enables them to think in terms of logical and nonlogical classes, to assimilate and accommodate new experiences into groups, and to employ linguistic and nonlinguistic forms to label arrays of objects, people, and events. At one level there is also agreement as to *what* classification behaviors are, which in a sense is the end of commonality. This overarching commonality persists in spite of the diversity in concept and method of the investigators. There are those who accept a particular paradigmatic approach and claim that it does answer all the important questions. Investigators, however, differ in their descriptions and explanations of how individuals come to organize, to classify, and to reason logically. At issue, then, is what theoretical model has the most explanatory power.

Gleitman (this volume) reviews three main theoretical and paradigmatic approaches to the study of concepts and rejects each of them as insufficient or not empirically supportable. She identifies a *word meaning* model, which she contends is of two main types—the feature and the holistic: "All of these hold that a word is not semantically simple, but rather is the lexical label for a bundle of semantic elements." The primitive feature aspect of the approach is not a tenable perspective. The primitive features have yet to be identified. Gleitman is not alone in her rejection of word feature analysis for defining concepts. Sokal (1977) gives an excellent example that undermines the primitive feature approach as the sole organizing way of dealing with concepts. Four-legged creatures that give milk are cows. Is a three-legged cow that does not give milk still a cow? What is "cowness"?

The second type of componential theory Gleitman rejects is the theory of *prototypes*, most eloquently presented by Rosch (1977) and her colleagues. Rosch's position is the central antagonist in Gleitman's paper, thus her position is presented in some detail here. Rosch (1977) and her co-workers believe: "that the world does, in a sense, contain 'intrinsically separate things' " [p. 213]." Three principles undergird her position (Rosch, 1977):

> In the first place, real world attributes, unlike the sets often presented laboratory subjects, do not occur independently of one another. Creatures with feathers are more likely also to have wings than creatures with fur. . . .
>
> In the second place, the objects of the world are determinately structured because levels of abstraction in class-inclusion hierarchies are themselves not random but are highly structured. . . .
>
> In the third place . . . categories are maintained as discrete by being coded in cognition in terms of *prototypes* of the most characteristic members of the category [p. 213].

The issue is joined when Gleitman rejects Rosch's position on conceptual as well as empirical grounds. It is difficult to define clear, unambiguous boundaries or generalizable features for concepts. Gleitman (this volume) states: "We should begin to wonder whether there is a general psychological domain encompassing 'all concepts' parallel to, say, a general psychological domain of 'all sensory experiences,' 'all emotions,' and so forth".

Let us take Gleitman's wonder as a question and ponder whether we face an all-or-none argument regarding general or specific domains in concept definition, whether there is some way to integrate these, or whether we, as developmental psychologists, are addressing a relevant issue. Our aim as psychologists is to try to understand the ontogenesis of concepts and to understand the course of that development.

Gleitman concludes her chapter with the suggestion that the direction we take to reduce the confusion in identifying real concepts is: "by examination of the richly structured domains, singly and in great detail". My argument is that this suggestion is not a solution because the assumption that richly structured domains exist engenders the same problem identified by all students of concepts, that is, whether one uses space, time, language, or any other domain, one is constructing concepts. Space, time, and language do not exist in nature. Humans generate these concepts and define their boundaries. To be sure, there is some confirmation in reality about space and time, but we also know that the definition of those domains vary. For example, Piaget & Inhelder, (1963) write: "Philosophers and psychologists have argued about the nature of space for centuries. They have debated whether it is an empirical concept derived from perception or from images, whether it is innate to thought and consciousness, or whether it is operational in character, and so on [p. vii]." Thus, the solution proposed by Gleitman is no solution. Definitions of concepts and delineation of their parameters are inherently problematic.

In this essay I do not intend to venture a solution because in a sense the problem is an everchanging one: Concepts, though functional in our own experience, have an ephemeral quality if we seek ostensive, pointable properties. My interest is not to argue the existence of concepts, but rather to describe how individuals come to organize into concepts the array of objects, events, and individuals encountered in the course of day-to-day existence, and to label these arrays with some symbol.

I plan to deal with three broad areas and in so doing provide a developmental perspective. These areas include: (1) a discussion of definitional issues, focusing on concept, classification, and categorization; (2) a review of some of the developmental views to demonstrate their congruence relative to the developmental issues; (3) a discussion of the relationship of language to concepts.

CONCEPT OF A CONCEPT

To begin at the beginning is to ask: What is a concept? It would take us far afield to review the various theories addressing this question, and it would require immersion into complex and hairsplitting problems of definition posed by philosophers since the time of Socrates and Plato (e.g., Abelson, 1967). However, philosophical analysis does help clarify some of the issues because it highlights the problem of establishing a definition by demonstrating that variation in types of definitions presumes different perspectives. It is therefore difficult to realize consensus. This is even more the case from a psychological perspective because proponents of particular perspectives may not be aware of their own underlying biases.

The psychologist cannot totally eschew the philosopher's concerns because psychologists have the same requirement to clarify what a concept is and to conceptualize the ontogenesis of concepts. According to Heath (1967):

To have a concept 'x' is, we may say (with some exceptions), (a) to know the meaning of the word "x"; (b) to be able to pick out or recognize a presented x

(distinguish non-x's, etc.), or again to be able to think of (have images or ideas of) x (or x's) when they are not present; (c) to know the nature of x, to have grasped or apprehended the properties (universals, essences, etc.) which characterize x's and make them what they are. These descriptions of conceptual use are neither exclusive nor exhaustive, nor even particularly clear. In a sense, however, they are indisputable. No one denies that we can do such things as identifying specimens of a kind or learning the meanings of words [pp. 177–178].

Philosophers have differed as to which of these definitions is primary. It seems that the answer is reduced to the choice of a model of concept as construed by the theoretical bias of the investigator. Heath (1967) suggests: "The term 'concept' is thus essentially a dummy expression or variable, whose meaning is assignable only in the context of a theory, and cannot be independently ascertained [p. 178]."

The foregoing quotation demonstrates that differences of opinion and of definition are not unique to psychologists. The resolution of the definitional issue is not simple, perhaps as Gleitman (this volume) writes in her conclusion:

A host of thinkers from Aristotle to Wittgenstein, from Katz to Fodor, from Rosch to Osherson and Smith have shown us that there is enormous difficulty in explicating so simple and concrete a concept as 'bird'. They have shown that the difficulty becomes greater by orders of magnitude when our theories are confronted with the requirement to describe an abstract functional concept like 'game.' We believe psychologists are more than a little overexuberant to suppose it will be easier to explicate the concept 'concept.'

In view of the history of disagreements among philosophers and psychologists, can there be anything new to add to the apparent confusion?

Many psychologists have struggled, and no doubt will continue to struggle, not with the issue of what not only a *concept* is, but also with how humans come to order the world in such a way as to be able to act and to react to events (also a concept) and to communicate with a high degree of precision? As Heath (1967) has indicated, we seem to know that a person "has a concept."

The investigator has a choice in how to pose the question and pursue the answer. Aristotle did it by inventing the term *category* and then proceeding to set the rules. Later, Kant offered his own perspective, the notion of a priori intuitions, which had considerable influence. We have had many forebears in the search to understand this fundamental activity. Thus, the definition of concept that I propose here is not intended as unique, but rather as I have distilled it from these many views.

Let me turn now to presenting my idea of concept. The term concept refers to an abstract label that encompasses an array of diverse instances deemed to be related. The word "fruit" instantiates a concept; the word "vehicle" instantiates a concept; the word "animal" instantiates a concept. Essentially, a concept is an organizer of instances, and therein lies its structure. Concepts provide an efficient way of organizing diversity under a single rubric.

This definition refers to *verbal* labels and to structural and functional properties as referents for more labels. As we argue later, concepts can be nonverbal as evident in the organizing behavior of preverbal children (Nelson, 1977; Ricciuti, 1965). If a verbal label is removed as a requirement for a concept, what can we substitute? I suggest any symbol or action or set of actions that implies that the array in question has coherence. The verbal label facilitates the notion of coherence, but it is not a necessary requirement. What is necessary is that any array has a coherence or a family resemblance. For example, in a study done some years ago using sorting tasks with children from low-income families, it was found that a number of children grouped items together but could not or would not articulate a reason for their organization (Sigel & McBane, 1967). Yet when analyzed in terms of probabilities the groupings they made indicated that these were not chance arrangements, but systematic organizations. I contend the children had a concept or some equivalence criterion, which formed a basis for organizing the array. In essence, they had a functional concept.

In sum, then, a *concept* generally refers to a verbal label or to a set of actions that organizes an array of diverse items into a coherent whole.

A second characteristic of a concept is the *content*. Every concept refers to a body of substantive instances. There is a need to establish criteria for delineating the content boundaries of a concept. What are the boundaries of the concept animal? As simple as this may appear, the boundaries are fuzzy (e.g., should one-celled creatures be considered part of the animal concept as cows or monkeys might be?). The content is influenced by social, cultural, and historical factors. Such definitions of animals, families, numbers, space, and time are in part defined substantively by sociocultural factors. What is an animal? Who is a family member? What is edible? What is sacred or profane? The contents in each of these concepts are culturally defined.

It is by virtue of these factors that the same items are not always in the same category. For example, a Moslem would exclude ham from the concept *edibles,* whereas a vegetarian would exclude all meats. Thus, the concept *edibles* is common to both Moslems and vegetarians, but the content of the concept differs. Does this perspective argue for content to be a priori, or does it argue for an interaction between the existence of events (objects) and the individual's competence to conjoin these instances within a common, culturally accepted rubric, eventually ending in a verbal label? Thus, for me, content includes substantive information delineating domains of experience. Inasmuch as arrays of items organized are so arranged *because* of sociocultural criteria, I can say that all concepts are organized on the bases of explicable criteria through experiences, as articulated by John Dewey (in Ratner, 1939):

> Concepts are formed by comparing particular objects, already perceived, with one another, and then eliminating the elements in which they disagree and retaining that

which they have in common. Concepts are thus simply memoranda of identical features in objects already perceived: They are conveniences bunching together a variety of things scattered about in concrete experience. But they have to be *proved* by agreement with the material of particular antecedent experiences; their value and function are necessarily retrospective [p. 883].

Implicit is the idea of an abstraction ladder in which increasingly more items are subsumed in a category; therefore, the concept is increasingly extended. This brings us to the idea that concepts are comprised of two additional characteristics: extension and intension. Though these terms are used by Inhelder and Piaget (1969) in reference to classes, I apply them to our discussion of concepts. (In a latter section I elaborate on the class-concept relations.) According to Inhelder and Piaget (1969): "The 'intension' of a class is the set of properties common to the members of that class, together with the set of differences which distinguish them from another class. . . . The 'extension' of a class is the set of members (or individuals) comprising that class (as defined by its intension) [pp. 7–8]." Intension and extension are formal characteristics having essentially no substance. The content selected as the "common" elements of the concept are products of sociocultural and even personality characteristics (Kagan, Moss, & Sigel, 1963; Sigel & Brodzinsky, 1977). Irrespective of the content selected, a concept does involve these structural properties of intension and extension.

In sum, a concept can be characterized as a rubric (expressed in verbal or action terms) possessing the following properties: level, content, intension, and extension. Given the structure-content definition of concept, how do we proceed to identify or generate concepts? In effect, this is a problem of taxonomy.

Biologists, botanists, and zoologists, in particular, have dealt with taxonomies for many years and have had to organize the observed diversity of living instances. Animals or plants, for example, have been organized in a hierarchical arrangement after first defining the attributes that are shared by the members of the same group, thereby creating distinctive and definable groups. Hierarchies are generated by identifying commonly shared attributes. To be sure, not all concepts are classes (e.g., the concept mind, love, or hate). These are abstractions that refer to nonhierarchically defined labels, which are but one type of concept. These abstract concepts, I think, are acquired through a different route than the taxonomic classes of the zoologists.

If these taxonomies are conceptualized as concepts, then how do concepts differ from classes? After all, the zoologist generating a taxonomy defines his organization as one of classification. Is there a difference between the two? Implicit in these comments is the notion that concepts subsume classes. Hence, classes are concepts, but not all concepts are classes. The type of concepts Gleitman uses are classes or families of instances. For this reason, I interpret her paper as involving classification, where the process is classifying and the product is a class or a concept.

Of course, the reader might ask whether the use of concepts and classes, as suggested, is an idiosyncratic perspective and hence not to be taken seriously, or if there is some coherent logic to the argument that the terms concept and class overlap. The point of this paper is to argue that the terms are overlapping, and hence the research literature on the ontogenesis of classification can also be interpreted as the study of the ontogenesis of concepts or, in common language, concept formation. Specifically, then, I address the literature on concepts or classification as a coherent body of knowledge, and a process necessary and sufficient to generate classes or concepts is basically *classifying*.

Before proceeding, however, I should also address the definition of the term *category,* which is another synonym for class or concept. Concept, class, and category as nouns share a common meaning, namely, each refers to assertions that objects, events, notions, and so forth can be defined as to *their* similarity, expressed by a particular label. The verbs to classify, to categorize, and to conceptualize also have a shared referent, namely, a mental process by which ideas, events, and objects are divided and placed in groups, and each of these groups can be given a particular label, which identifies the collection subsumed under that label. Thus, those who know the identifying features of "vehicle" will usually understand what instances will be identified under the rubric vehicle. For example, trucks, cars, airplanes, and wagons will be recognized as belonging to this class (concept, category). They will also know what is not an appropriate referent. For example, pencil and desk are not *generally* accepted in this category. A category is defined in terms of positive and negative instances. However, the boundaries between categories can be blurred. For example, is a baby carriage a vehicle? Is a horse a vehicle? It depends on the definition of the category. Webster's dictionary definition is no help because a vehicle is, on the one hand, defined as: "any device on wheels or runners for conveying persons, or objects"; thus, a horse is not a vehicle, but a baby carriage is. However, a vehicle is also identified as: "any means of carrying, conveying, or communicating." From this definition a horse is a vehicle as is a television set, a book, or a newspaper. The latter do not physically carry and do not have four wheels, but they *do* convey ideas, not objects. Thus, what a vehicle is is a moot point.

It would appear from this discussion that given the multidimensional nature of *all* instances, any criterion could or would be selected as a basis for categorization. Although this is possible, it is important to note there is more order than disorder in the identification of classes. In general there is agreement as to class membership. If this were not the case, we would have insurmountable problems of communication—in fact, the whole field of intelligence testing would be in chaos.

What is the case is that in spite of the polydimensionality of instances, conventional taxonomies have developed and are expressed in our language and thought. (I do not want to get into the thought/language issue here.) Formal logic describes the particular way of organizing instances, but the content of such organizations derives from implicit taxonomic categories. For example, Berger and Luckmann (1966) state: "I apprehend the reality of everyday life as an ordered reality. . . . The language used in everyday life continuously provides me with the necessary objectifications and posits the order within which these make sense and within which everyday life has meaning for me [pp. 35–36]."

It is within that social reality that the child develops the appropriate operational schemata to deal logically with classes and relations. Lunzer (1969) writes: "Classification only becomes logical when it carries with it an explicit recognition of its criteria [p. xv]." *But* we see later that this statement is inadequate because the definition of what the criteria are that define a class as logical versus nonlogical is moot.

In sum, the study of the ontogenesis of concepts necessitates the study of classification behaviors. I make the bold assertion that this declaration holds for *all* concepts. The only qualification, which I discuss later, is that the type and quality of classification behaviors are functions of the developmental level of the individual.

A DEVELOPMENTAL PERSPECTIVE

Let's start out with the argument that the basic developmental task for humans, irrespective of culture, is to be able to move efficiently and effectively in their environments, a necessary requirement if individuals are to adapt to a multidimensional environment. Objects, events, and people (hereafter referred to as instances or items) are multidimensionally defined—physically, socially, and idiosyncratically. For example, the bird has many observable features such as legs and feathers (physical attributes); it also has socially defined functions (e.g., source of food, sacred object, etc.). The child may come to know birds in many ways (e.g., picture books or observations). Two levels of definition may occur— the physical and the social. As we see later, as knowledge about birds increases, this knowledge will be organized and reorganized as the child comes to evolve the concept *bird*. The universal requirement is to come to know and understand something about the nature of birdness as a basis for classification.

Intrinsic to the human is a biological system that enables the individual to carry out all the cognitive and motoric routines needed to come to know, to understand, and to represent experience. Piaget speaks of the child's action on objects, which can be viewed as manipulation involving feeling, touching, and so on. Through this engagement the child comes to know something about that object and its relation to other objects. However, there are objects that are not manipulable in their totality; they are seen as a Gestalt, but can only be interacted with partially. For example, the child only interacts with some elements of the automobile, not the total. This may result in only a partial understanding or partial definition of the concept *automobile*. There are also items such as the moon, the stars, and airplanes that are only perceptually evident, and the engagement can be only at the perceptual level (or with representation of the item).

The construction of knowledge and its consequent organization are embedded in a cultural context, which contributes to the definition of what is equivalent to what and on what basis. Although cultures may contribute to homogenization of experience, idiosyncratic experience is also inevitable. Thus, individual differences in organization are expected because of these individual differences in experience. Such variations not only involve cognitive aspects of objects, but also affective experiences with the objects as well. Thus, joy or sorrow, pleasure or displeasure, calmness or anxiety accompany the individual's journey in organizing the environment. No category is constructed neutrally; affect is an intrinsic component of *all* categories.

From the perspective of the individual, category boundaries are permeable, that is, the individual can extend or retract a category boundary, depending on the defining attributes, his or her knowledge, and the permeability of the category boundary. Permeability involves not only cognitive processing, but also personality factors that enable the individual to accept new information. Essentially, I am describing an individual's flexibility or rigidity in dealing with information.

In the course of such engagements, direct and indirect, the developing child begins to operate on the equivalence principle (i.e., noting that items share some common features, functions, or meanings). Equivalence is necessary to construct classes (e.g., a dog and a cat are judged as equivalent relative to the concept *animal*). This is the case in spite of differences between them. Further, the word dog, the picture of a dog, and the three-dimensional dog are judged as equivalent instances of *dog,* although each instance is expressed in a different representational medium (Sigel, 1953, 1978). Individuals come to organize instances on some type of equivalence principle. The criteria selected as the bases of equivalence are determined by cultural, social, emotional, and cognitive factors. For example, take the concept *edible*. Rabbits and cows can be culturally defined as edible in the United States. Jews and Moslems, however, do not define rabbits as edible, but cows are edible, and particular individuals may have a personal aversion to the edibility of a cow but not a rabbit. This example illustrates the way an array of factors might influence when and under what conditions cows and rabbits are judged as equivalent in the category edible.

Another way of conceptualizing equivalence is in terms of meaning. This brings us to two levels of analysis: *conventional meaning* and *personal meaning*. Conventional meaning refers to that which is shared by members of a society, where in spite of idiosyncratic experience there is an overarching social definition. Personal meaning, on the other hand, refers to idiosyncratic groupings of instances where meaning may not be shared. An example of conventional meaning is that attributed to an automobile as a vehicle by which individuals can transport themselves from place to place; or there is shared meaning that a gun is a weapon that can kill. An example of a personal meaning is one in which a phobic person may attribute danger to the class feline, a meaning not conventional or shared. Meanings, shared or not, are acquired by children as a consequence of their experience with objects, events, or people as well as attributions and labels proposed by others.

Meaning is also conserved. As children engage with objects, events, and people they come to internalize these experiences. The meaning of the experiences begins to transcend the three-dimensional physical interaction and comes to be attributed to other modes of presentation of experience (e.g., pictures, stories, etc.) (Sigel, 1978). In this sense the meaning is conserved. But, it is only conserved because the child is now evolving representations of objects, events, and people—in effect, of experience. These representations are analogous to Piaget's notion of schema, the mental organization of experience. Representations can be considered as internalized constructions. Why representations? I use the term *representation* because the internalized, organized experiences are not isomorphic to the reality, but rather are abstractions of that reality as construed by the individual. These representations change in organization with increasing development (i.e., age and experience). (See Sigel & Cocking, 1977, for further discussion of this issue.)

One type of experience that contributes significantly to the development of representational thought and to the facility to conserve meaning among various representations of objects and events is the distancing behavior used by significant others interacting with the child. Distancing behaviors are defined as those experiences that serve to "force" the individual cognitively to separate self from the here and now. Once the demand is made by some socio-environmental event (e.g., parental queries), the individual has to re-present experience prior to actions. It is this fundamental social process that enhances the development of representational thought (Sigel, 1979, 1981; Sigel & Cocking, 1977; Sigel, McGillicuddy-DeLisi, & Johnson, 1980).

Accompanying these developmental changes are concomitant shifts in understanding because as Piaget (1978) notes: "Understanding brings out the reason of things [p. 222]," these understandings enable the child to attribute meaning to events. Meaning and understanding are overlapping cognitive functions that are intrinsic to the representational process. Knowledge (experience) is internally organized into classes, which are essentially representations. We discuss the role of representation in categorization later in the context of Bruner's work.

The child comes to understand and share meaning at the phenotypic level. Each of us develops a manifest agreement on how to define, evaluate, and act on everyday objects. We have established common behaviors for tools, vehicles, and so on. In this sense we share the meanings of actions toward a wide array of instances. But, in spite of the behavioral commonalities, we may differ in our feelings, attitudes, beliefs, and expectations toward the same object. These are what I would call *personal meaning*.

We have different types of attributed meaning: conventional and idiosyncratic. These meanings may contribute to the development of family resemblances, which bring us back full circle to the notion of equivalence because resemblances are also virtually synonymous with meaning. This descriptive presentation becomes the framework within which to examine the question developmentally, and that means to seek to understand cognitive structural changes in the child's understanding of the environment.

DEVELOPMENTAL THEORIES
OF CLASSIFICATION

My major thesis is that classification processes underlie concept development. Therefore, one of the major sources for understanding the ontogenesis of concept development is the development of classification. Defining the task this way does not make it any easier. Certainly there is much confusion and disagreement regarding what classification is and how it develops. It begins, of course, with the process or processes that are involved, the materials being considered, the domain of knowledge, and the levels of symbolization.

I have selected a number of theories of cognitive development that have something particular to say about the development of classification. They are presented to demonstrate that there is a basic agreement regarding the transition from early sensorimotor concrete organization of experience to a more autonomous categorical-inferential mode. The overall agreement regarding the developmental progression might provide a framework within which to integrate the details—a major task, which perhaps might be possible contrary to Gleitman's assertion that such an overall theory is not practical. To help in this comparative effort, I have constructed Table 12.1, which lays out each of the approaches and enables the reader to compare visually each of the theoretical positions.

In the past 50 years there have been a number of theoretical perspectives devoted to the problem. I reach back in history to bring up some of these with the hope that they provide the basis for explicating classes of variables that must be considered and that contribute to helping deal with the task at hand.

Vygotsky's Theory

From Vygotsky's (1962) perspective, a concept is acquired when: "the child's mental development itself has reached the requisite level . . . [of] deliberate attention, logical memory, abstraction, the ability to compare and to differentiate [pp. 82–83]." To study children's concept development, Vygotsky adopted a procedure from Ach (1921) in which children are asked to sort an array of blocks varying in color, shape, and size. Langer (1969) writes: "The situation is such that all objects belonging to the same class have the same volume and the same, artificially constructed, name printed on their underside [p. 80]." Using these

TABLE 12.1
Schemes Used for Developmental Analysis of Children's
Categorization Behavior

Vygotsky (1962)	Goldstein & Scheerer (1941)	Werner (1948)[a]
Phase I: Unorganized congeries (heaps) "... disparate objects grouped together without any basis. ..."	The concrete attitude is one which does not imply conscious activity in the sense of reasoning, awareness, or a self-account of one's doing. We surrender to experience of an unreflective character; we are confined to the immediate apprehension of the given thing or situation in its particular uniqueness. This apprehension may be by sense or percept, but it is never mediated by discursive reasoning. Our thinking and acting are directed by the immediate claims which one particular aspect of the object or outer-world situation makes.	*Sensori-motor:* "The striking characteristics of [sensorimotor level] are *immediacy, limited motivation* and *lack of planning* [p. 191]." Action is "set in motion by vital drives on the one hand, and by the concrete signals of the milieu on the other [p. 194]."
Stage 1: Trial and error stage.		
Stage 2: Syncretic organization of visual field.		
Stage 3: "... *elements taken from different groups or heaps that have already been formed.* ..."		*Perceptual:* "This perceptual grouping is dependent on a basic tendency in perceptual organization to bring elements together which exhibit any kind of perceptual similarities. For example, our desk is in great disorder. Papers lie scattered round, strewn amid books, inkwell, pencils, pens and knife. Observe how, when we cast a critical eye over the surface of the desk, the white papers unite in a sort of group. Other objects also tend to come together. Hard objects such as the penwiper, ash tray and inkwell seem to attract each other. ... And so, of a sudden, a harmonious organization arises out of disorder. It is characteristic of this grouping that it may be completed in the purely perceptual sphere with hardly any conceptual-abstract support. It operates according to the laws of configuration [p. 223]."
Phase II: Thinking in complexes. "... a concrete grouping of objects connected by factual bonds."		
Type 1: *associative* type—based on any bond.	The abstract attitude is the basis for the following *conscious* and *volitional* modes of behavior:	
Type 2: *collection*—"... is a *grouping of objects on the basis of their participation in the same practical operation*—of their functional cooperation [p. 63]."	1. To detach our ego from the outer world or from inner experiences.	
	2. To assume a mental set.	
Type 3: *chain complex*—"... relations between single elements, but nothing more [p. 64]."	3. To account for acts to oneself; to verbalize the account.	
Type 4: *diffuse complex*—"... is marked by the fluidity of the very attribute that unites its single elements [p. 65]."	4. To shift reflectively from one aspect of the situation to another.	
	5. To hold in mind simultaneously various aspects.	*Conceptual:* "He is able consciously to perceive that objects have different qualities,
Type 5: *pseudo-concept*—"... generalization formed in the child's mind, although phenotypically resembling the adult concept, is psy-	6. To grasp the essential of a given whole; to break up a given whole into parts; to isolate and synthesize them.	

(continued)

TABLE 12.1
(*Continued*)

Vygotsky (1962)	Goldstein & Scheerer (1941)	Werner (1948)[a]
chologically very different from the concept proper; in its essence, it is still a complex [p. 66]." *Phase III:* Thinking in concepts, where a concept ". . . is a complex and genuine act of thought . . . [where] a concept embodied in a word represents an act of generalization [pp. 82–83]." Stage 1: classifying objects on basis of maximally similar (adding not isolating attributes). Stage 2: Potential concepts ". . . isolating single attributes (precursors of true concepts) [pp. ■]."	7. To abstract common properties reflectively; to form hierarchic concepts. 8. To plan ahead ideationally; to assume an attitude towards the "mere possible" and to think or perform symbolically.	any one of which may be taken as the point of departure for an ordering process. In other words, the development indicates an immensely important step away from abstraction closely allied to sensory organization and toward an abstraction guided by deliberately selected categories such as color, shape, number, size, etc. The behavior involved in this higher form of abstraction has been called *categorical behavior* [p. 240]."

Sigel (1953)	Bruner (1966)	Piaget (1977)
A. *Perceptual* 1. *Affective*—grouping based on feeling. 2. *Identity*—grouping based on identify of structure or function. 3. *Partial Identity*—grouping based on identity of certain aspects of structure or function. 4. *Centroid*—grouping based on belongingness in a geographical area. 5. *Functional*—grouping based on use.	Representational Systems *Enactive*—Representation of past events through appropriate motor response. *Iconic*—Summarizes events by selective organization of percepts and images by spatial, temporal, and qualitative structures of the perceptual field. *Symbolic*—Represents things by design features that include remoteness and arbitrariness.	*Level I:* The irregularity in classification "indicates that there is no overall plan" in creating a class. "Such a configuration is called a *figural collection*" [Gallagher & Reid, 1981, p. 98]. *Level II:* "This transition level is not well defined but marks the beginning of what will be stage III. (Here are nonfigural and hierarchized collections which correspond to the complete but empirical seriation. . . . The organization at this level corresponds to the

(*continued*)

TABLE 12.1
(Continued)

Sigel (1953)	Bruner (1966)	Piaget (1977)

B. *Conceptual*—grouping in which the objects were treated as members of a class even though gross structural differences were apparent. Designation by a class name was required for a grouping to be scored conceptual.
 	
C. *Miscellaneous*
  1. *Mixed-1*—grouping in which conceptual and perceptual classifications are combined and treated as perceptual.
  2. *Mixed-2*—grouping in which two or more perceptual groupings are combined into a third perceptual category.
  3. *Thematic*—grouping based on a story.
  4. *Pseudo*—grouping that appeared incorrect in interpretation or information of reality.
  5. *Nongroupings*—objects that were not found to belong to any grouping and that were isolated intentionally.
 	
Sigel, Jarman, & Hanesian (1967)
___
Descriptive
  Part–Whole
  Global
 	
Relational-Contextual—where items are related to each other in terms of function. No
	Bruner & Olver (1963)
	___
	Grouping Strategies
	
	Superordinate concept formation—"Items are grouped on the basis of one or more attributes common to them all [p. 356]."
	
	Complex formation—"the subject uses selected attributes of the array without subordinating the entire array to any one attribute or to any set of attributes [p. 357]."
	  (1) *Association Complex*—associations made between first two elements.
	
	  (2) *Key-Ring Complex*—"taking an element and ringing all of the others on it by choosing attributes that form relations between one item in the list and each of the others [p. 357]."
	
	  (3) *Edge-Matching Complex*—finding complementary, contrasting, or other selected properties but not tying together.
	
	  (4) *Collection Complex*—"consists essentially in finding complementary, contrasting, or otherwise related
		uncoordinated pairs and trios which characterize the second seriation level; there is no serial structure for the whole, so there is only juxtaposition of small elementary series. The lower forms belonging to this level consist of figural collections but later they show superimposed alignments (or obliques and parallels, etc.), each of which includes analogous elements that are distinct from those of other subcollections. The superior forms are small, nonfigural, but juxtaposed collections without unique criterion, and there may or may not be a heterogeneous residue. An intermediaty form between levels II and III achieves the use of a unique criterion for classification (color, form, etc.) but still without hierarchies [p. 126]."
		
		Level III: The child is now able to construct nonfigural collections, generalizing on the basis of extension and intention and provides nascent hierarchies. ". . . as the type III seriations are not yet accompanied by transitivity, so the subjects at this same stage do not succeed in quantifying the inclusions. And, for a category B such that B = A ⏐ A′, they do not succeed in realizing that there are necessarily more individual elements in B than in A; in fact, if B is subdivided into A

(continued)

TABLE 12.1
(*Continued*)

Sigel (1953)	Bruner (1966)	Piaget (1977)
generalization, but chaining possible. *Thematic*—items related with a plot nucleus.	properties that all things have but not quite tying them together. . . . [p. 358]."	and A', the subcategory A is compared by them only to A' and no longer to any unattached B [p. 127]."
Categorical-Inferential— where each item represents the class that relationships are to core idea, not to each other.	(5) Multiple-Grouping Complex—"where several sub-groupings are formed [p. 359]."	*Level IV:* Classification henceforth involves the employment of logical categories subdivided into subcategories. Quantification of inclusion is possible as is a conscious shifting of criteria to construct multiple classification problems. In a sense, this is in Piaget's terms *logical reasoning* or the stage of formal operations.
	(6) Thematic Grouping— organizing items around a connecting theme.	
	Language Frames Perceptible—observable Functional—purpose Affective—value Linguistic Convention— class norms	

*a*According to Langer (1970), the overarching principle governing the described progression is called orthogenesis which asserts that: "development is a process of increasing differentiation and specification of the organism's relatively global organization, coupled with a process of progressive centralization and hierarchic integration of the more individuated systems so that progressive equilibrium is achieved [p. 734]."

blocks, Vygotsky identified three stages of concept development: Stage 1 is where blocks are heaped together, linked by chance, not by reason; Stage 2 is where the blocks are put together on the basis of physical similarity (thinking in complexes); Stage 3 is characterized by synthesis and analysis. These three stages are in a sense summative. Vygotsky describes the steps or stages in considerable detail (see Table 12.1). Suffice it for now to summarize Vygotsky's (1962) position as follows: "The child unites diverse objects in groups under a common 'family name' [shades of Wittgenstein]; this process passes through various stages. The second line of development is the formation of 'potential concepts,' based on singling out certain common attributes [p. 81]." For Vygotsky (1962), however, in contrast to other theorists: "The use of the word is an integral part of the developing processes, and the word maintains a guiding function in the formation of genuine concepts, to which these processes lead [p.

81].'' Words or language, then, are integral to the classification process. We have more to say on this in a subsequent section.

These descriptions of block arrangements are congruent with an unpublished study by Sigel and Brodzinsky, (1971), which indicated that grouping occurs with little evidence of language involvement. Working with children about 24–26 months of age and following them up to 4 years, these investigators were able to identify nonoverlapping stages in classifying an array of wooden blocks of various sizes and colors. At first the children selected two blocks at random. In the second stage blocks were organized into a tower, but with some indication of deliberate judgment. The children would select a block, bring it close to the block selected as the base of the tower, and decide by visual comparison whether it matched. If it seemed to match, the child would place the block in place; if not, the child would scan the array for one that would fit and then repeat the procedure. This stage was superseded by alignments, wherein blocks would be arranged by color or shape and stretched out on the table. The final stage observed was for children to organize the blocks in separate groups. This sequence of nonoverlapping stages indicates the evolution of classification behavior. Labeling of productions did occur as the child became more adept in language.

Although Vygotsky's perspective focuses primarily on classification behaviors as intrinsically involved in concept formation, a position akin to my major thesis, Goldstein and Scheerer (1941) not only provide considerable support for developmental differences, but also provide a more comprehensive view of *how* the individual approaches the environment.

Goldstein's Theory

Much of Goldstein's theory grew out of his work with brain-injured adults. He was led to conclude that the main difference between the seriously brain-injured and the normal, or between very immature and mature individuals, is the proportion of adjustments made on a concrete as opposed to an abstract basis, as well as the degree of shifting that is possible between these two bases. Because they can abstract readily and respond abstractly, intelligent, normal adults may be said to have an abstract attitude or capacity level. The designates *abstract attitude* and *concrete attitude* are applied by Goldstein (Goldstein & Scheerer, 1941): "to a behavioral range which involves a number of performances and responses [p. 1]." According to Goldstein and Scheerer (1941), the concrete attitude is one that:

> does not imply conscious activity in the sense of reasoning, awareness or a self-account of one's doing. We surrender to experience of an unreflective character; we are confined to the immediate apprehension of the given thing or situation in its particular uniqueness. This apprehension may be by sense or percept, but it is never *mediated by discursive reasoning*. Our thinking and acting are directed by the immediate claims which one particular aspect of the object or of the outer world situation makes [pp. 2–3].

The abstract attitude, on the other hand, say Goldstein and Scheerer (1941) implies "conscious activity in the sense of reasoning, awareness, and self-accounting of one's doing [p. 3]." Furthermore:

> The abstract attitude is the basis for the following *conscious* and *volitional* modes of behavior:
> 1. To detach our ego from the outerworld or from inner experiences.
> 2. To assume a mental set.
> 3. To account for acts to oneself; to verbalize the account.
> 4. To shift reflectively from one aspect of the situation to another.
> 5. To hold in mind simultaneously various aspects.
> 6. To grasp the essential of a given whole; to break up a given whole into parts, to isolate and to synthesize them.
> 7. To abstract common properties reflectively; to form hierarchic concepts.
> 8. To plan ahead ideationally; to assume an attitude towards the "mere possible" and to think or perform symbolically [p. 4].

Of paramount importance, then, in achieving the abstract attitude, according to Goldstein is "conscious will" (Goldstein & Scheerer, 1941). In fact, without the involvement of conscious will one cannot have abstraction in Goldstein's (Goldstein & Scheerer, 1941) sense:

> The abstract level is not simply a combination of existing lower functions in a next higher synthesis. And it seems also insufficient to characterize this level as the more complex capacity of synthesizing, or as the ability to shift and to perform a greater number of shifts. For, there is a decisive difference between active synthesis, active shifting, and a passive global reaction to stimulus constellations or a passively induced change in reactions which only overtly coincides with the true characteristics of synthesizing activity and shifting [p. 23].

Abstraction, as it requires conscious will, can only occur in those organisms mature enough to have this type of consciousness directing their activities. Hence, in Goldstein's view, abstraction does not occur in very young children. The young child, he believes, perceives objects as Gestalten with but one functional property, the figure. The response to these objects, says Goldstein, is a function of phenomenal groupings in that the impressions are sensorially organized. Only when the child can rise above the sensorial configuration, and aspects achieve some sort of independence so they can be reacted to voluntarily, does Goldstein believe abstraction has occurred.

Werner's Theory

Werner, in contrast to Goldstein, implies that the analogues of the abstract attitude are to be found in sensory-perceptual and conceptual organization. Using as an analytic and conceptual construct the notion of analogous processes,

Werner provides us with an interesting and valuable perspective by which to conceptualize the development of classification behavior. The construct "analogous process" was adopted from comparative anatomy. For psychology, Werner (1948) defines analogous mental processes: "as processes at different genetic levels directed toward the same achievement but involving different function patterns [that] can easily be demonstrated to exist in almost any field of mental activity [p. 214]." The achievement in question is that of organization of arrays of items. Identification of similarity among diverse arrays is assumed to be a fundamental necessity (not necessarily logical) for efficient and effective functioning in a world filled with diverse instances.

Werner (1948) rejects an absolute genetic approach to origins of mental activity; rather he writes: "It would seem to be more constructive to analyze mental development in terms of genetically related, analogous processes. We must not frame the question to ask: 'At what age level does concept formation first come into existence?' Rather, we must ask: 'What are the different function patterns underlying the concept formation which appears at different age levels?' [p. 216]."

From this perspective he identifies the three levels and/or identifications of relations mentioned earlier: (1) sensorimotor, such as comprehension of size relations between hollow blocks that fit into each other or construct a pine cone from wooden rings; (2) perceptual levels, where the organization is determined by the proximity of other concrete similarity (here Werner refers to some of the classical Gestalt principles of configuration and of perceptual wholes); (3) these relationships form a true generalization where the quality (e.g., color) common to all elements is deliberately detailed—mentally isolated, as it were—and the elements themselves appear only as a visible exemplification of the common quality. Werner (1948) writes: "The generic concept 'leaf' is formed when a multiplicity of leaves is ordered in a group or class [p. 243]."

Werner believes that the perceptual level is considered to be the more primitive. Although it makes its appearance early ontogenetically, it must be remembered that it is present at all ages. According to Werner (1948), perceptual abstraction is an expression of certain laws of perception, such as the law of grouping according to similarity:

> This perceptual grouping is dependent on a basic tendency in perceptual organization to bring elements together which exhibit any kind of perceptual similarities. For example, our desk is in great disorder. Papers lie scattered round, strewn amid books, inkwell, pencils, pens and knife. Observe how, when we cast a critical eye over the surface of the desk, the white papers unite in a sort of group. Other objects also tend to come together. Hard objects such as the penwiper, ash tray, and inkwell seem to attract each other. . . . And so, of a sudden, a harmonious organization arises out of disorder. It is characteristic of this grouping that it may be completed in the purely perceptual sphere with hardly any conceptual-abstract support. It operates according to the laws of configuration [p. 223].

The conceptual type of abstraction, in contrast to the perceptual, is characterized according to Werner (1948) by the ability of the individual to shift his point of view in purposeful grouping activity:

> He is able consciously to perceive that objects have different qualities, any one of which may be taken as the point of departure from an ordering process. In other words, the development indicates an immensely important step away from abstraction closely allied to sensory organization and toward an abstraction guided by deliberately selected categories such as color, shape, number, size, etc. The behavior involved in this higher form of abstraction has been called *categorical behavior* [p. 240].

This categorical behavior involves the ability of the individual to generalize from one set of stimuli to others. The generalizations are not sensorially determined in the sense discussed under perceptual abstraction, but rather the individual is able to treat objects as members of a class. When operating on the conceptual level, a person is able to extend the use of generalizations developed in one set of situations to new situations. For example, the child may learn the concept of roundness and be able to use it in a variety of situations having a perceptual organization quite different from the original situation in which the concept was learned. To Werner the change from perceptual to conceptual abstraction is one of kind as well as of degree. When the change is one of kind, he can offer no adequate description of the transition process. However, Werner (1948) presents a conjecture as to some types of process intermediate between perceptual and conceptual abstraction:

> There are . . . peculiar conceptual forms which are concrete forerunners of the subsumptive class concepts. I should like to call them "quasi class concepts." They are concrete modes of generalization such as are frequently used by people on an advanced mental level when non-scientific thought is to be communicated. Verbally they are expressed by the common suffix "-like" or "-ish," or by the expression "something like . . ." When we speak of pot-like hats, we do not mean that these hats belong to the class of pots, but that the impression made by such hats is approximately equivalent to that made by a pot [p. 245].

Whether an individual who makes a classification such as this may be said to do so because of a deficiency or because of the inability to make more abstract classification is not made clear by Werner. Nor is it clear whether these transitional cases should be thought of as representing differences in degree or kind.

Sigel's Theory

Building on these previous theorists, I set out to examine how children of different ages actually sorted familiar items using a free sort approach with representations of real objects such as vehicles, animals, furniture, and humans (Sigel, 1953). Elementary school children, aged 7, 9, and 11, participated in five tasks involving different levels of symbolization (e.g., three-dimensional representational objects, pictures, and words). Children sorted the items into any number of groups they wished. In each of the classes one object was discrepant in a major way from other members of the class. For example, among the vehicles with wheels and motor, a sailboat (no motor or wheels) or a baby carriage (no motor, but wheels) was used; in the animal category, a snake was used (no legs). This procedure allowed for grouping a core set of items, and then the "odd" one could be added. This is just what happened. The groups were scored on the basis of verbal rationales the children gave for their productions. The results revealed that children selected similar items across age groups (e.g., the most typical vehicles were chosen by 7-, 9-, and 11-year-olds). This would suggest prototypicality. However, when queried as to the basis for their grouping, individual differences in rationales were evident. The responses varied from selection of a critical feature (e.g., vehicles were grouped because they had wheels) to more general characteristics (e.g., function—things you can ride in). Thus, although similar objects were selected, the reasons varied. Children aged 9 and 11 tended to produce class labels (e.g., human, furniture, animals, etc.) and provided rationales that were generalizable. These results are consistent with those of Werner in spite of the fact that the content of the task differed. Further, the level of symbolization did not significantly influence the ways of grouping, suggesting that the children could transcend one representational level of the material. It is as though by age 7 they must have had the "concepts" in mind and could ignore discrepancies between the appearance of objects. This led to a second analysis (Sigel, 1954), which set out to demonstrate that the "meaning" of the object was more important than its form. This is discussed in a subsequent section.

Piaget's Theory

The studies and perspectives discussed to this point address issues of the development of categorization, but they are not concerned with the development of logical thought in particular. The only system that sets out to study classification as an aspect of logical thinking is that of Piaget and his colleagues (Inhelder & Piaget, 1969). There is no need here to review Piaget's total system, except to highlight what distinguishes Piaget and his colleagues from the investigators described to this point in terms of conceptual development. Although it is generally recognized that children do vary with maturity level, how they categorize, and what labels they employ, for Piaget classification becomes logical when it carries an explicit recognition of the criteria. Piaget (see Lunzer, 1969) refers to this process as "abstraction," by which he means: "Abstracting the criteria of a classification involves a different kind of abstraction. It is a 'turning round' on the actions of grouping and re-grouping, and the logical inferences which it generates depend on abstraction from the activity of the subject [p. xv].'' Lunzer (1969) argues that Piaget's analysis is an advance on the thinking of previous investigators studying classification behavior because: ''[I]t is this co-ordination of actions which, for Piaget, confers the element of necessity on the inferences which we draw. Logic itself, he argues, is not an innate characteristic of thinking, nor is it simply a mode of organization forced on us by the world as experienced. It is one that we construct by co-ordinating our own actions and abstracting the relations between them [pp. xv–xvi].''

Piaget's studies of categorization or classification, then, are in the service of investigating the origins and development of logical thought. First, let it be said that Piaget approaches the problem of classification as an instance of operational thought, as in seriation. Classification is an operation, an instance of logical thought. Concepts for Piaget are the content of intelligence. Concepts are developed, according to Piaget (Piaget & Inhelder, 1969), through ''structuration'', which is ''always present and stems from actions or from operations [p. 44].'' This is not to say that Piaget denies the significance of perception in the development of concepts. Rather, it is to say (Piaget & Inhelder, 1969) that although perceptual data are necessary for conceptual development of physical concepts, ''these concepts cannot be elaborated without a logico-mathematical structuration which goes beyond perception [p. 49].'' Thus, Piaget's position differs from abstraction and generalization of the ''critical features'' approach. The construct structuration is of critical conceptual importance. Piaget does not deny the significance of perception in the development of concepts.

The logical operations involve the understanding of classes and relations. The classes are defined in terms of some perceived criterial attributes and the relations defined in logical and hierarchical terms. It is in this context that the class-inclusion paradigm comes to the fore. Class inclusion involves hierarchical relations between parts or subclasses and the whole class. For example, the basic question posed to the child when presented with an array of ten animals, six of which are rabbits, is: Are there more rabbits than animals? Solution to the problem requires understanding of the relations between the subset (rabbits) and the class (animals). Not only does the child have to understand the nature of classes and all that it entails (e.g., extension and intension), but also quantitative concepts of more and less, affirmation (i.e., the identification of positive instances), and negation (e.g., in our example, the nonrabbit aspects of other animals). In a sense, a category is defined by what it is as well as by what it is not. In this way category boundaries can be established (Gallagher & Reid, 1981).

Piaget's contribution to concept development was not addressed by Gleitman, and by failing to do so she excluded an important dimension to the understanding of concept development. Piaget's uniqueness rests on his contribution to tracing the development of the processes (operations) involved in the construction of concepts. To be sure, many of the processes described are appropriate for the understanding of physical concepts. Further, Piaget and his co-workers have described the stage sequences involved in the development of moral concepts (Piaget, 1948). However, concepts of this type do not encompass *all* the ideas conventionally called concepts (e.g., love, hate, goodness, evil, etc.). These concepts do not necessarily have objective bases, either in the actions of the individuals or in observations. How does the child come to understand the concept "good," "love," or "hate" (i.e., social concepts)? Piaget (1970) argues that some of these are learned by rote. Morality also forms a different class of events because it is embedded in the child's interpersonal experiences (Piaget, 1981).

Interestingly enough, Piaget did a number of studies using real-life representational objects (e.g., animals, furniture, vehicles) as well as geometric two- and three-dimensional forms (Inhelder & Piaget, 1969). In addition to the concern with materials and varied instruction, Inhelder and Piaget (1969) report that children's classification behaviors vary as a function of these two factors. For example, asking children to sort items on the basis of *similarity* produces different responses than asking children to group items on the basis of *belongingness*.

Inhelder and Piaget (1969), though reporting differences in contents and types of classifications that result from the use of different materials and instructions, are able to integrate these arrays of results to produce a coherent set of explanations regarding the ontogenesis of classification behavior. Children at the preschool age: "[A]re perfectly well able to discover relations of similarity and difference by a process of successive assimilation. Nevertheless they are unable to avoid occasional lapses in the course of which other forms of association are substituted for the relation of similarity. In particular they are constantly misled by considerations of pattern or by the situational and descriptive properties of the material [p. 45]." This interpretation is similar to Werner's notion of perceptual-based behaviors and Goldstein and Scheerer's concrete attitude. Inhelder and Piaget add one other interpretation, which reflects a sensitivity to the cognitive processing involved in these tasks. For in addition to the perceptual or stimulus boundedness aspects of the situation, they (Inhelder & Piaget, 1969) argue that in spite of the discovery of relations of similarity and difference the children "cannot unite 'all' the elements having a common property (similarity) to form a simultaneous whole (still less can they focus on 'some' as a sub-class) [p 45]." The children are unable to coordinate the extensive and intensive properties of objects; rather they oscillate between these two features. This lack of coordination is in part a function of the child's life experience in handling and acting on objects.

In view of frequent misinterpretations of Piaget, let me quote extensively his explanations regarding development of classificatory behaviors. It can be recalled that among the many studies Piaget and his colleagues conducted they employed varieties of stimuli and instructions. Each of their experiments contributed to an in-depth understanding of the developmental processes. Of particular interest are the insights Piaget (Inhelder & Piaget, 1969) reported with the use of representational materials:

> Both extension and intension exist in embryo, but they are neither fully differentiated nor completely co-ordinated with one another. However, there is a second lack of differentiation which is partly independent of the first, but which constantly interferes with it: lack of differentiation of the logical (or pre-logical) structures characteristic of discontinuous sets from the sub-logical (or pre-sub-logical) structures characterizing the subdivision of a continuous whole. It is partly independent because from the sensori-motor level onwards, children can be expected to be as familiar with the handling of discrete collections (piles, etc.) as they are with objects whose parts can be dissociated and reassembled. So it is that under the influence of perceptual configurations, they attribute shapes to discontinuous collections just as they do to continuous objects. Herein lies an initial reason for the lack of differentiation which continues through the present stage. For there can only be one way of clearly differentiating a collection of discrete objects from continuous wholes, and this is to impose some kind of stable structure on it which is quite independent of its disposition in space. In order to achieve such a structure the subject must first arrive at a clear differentiation between extension and intension, and second, he must co-ordinate the two. Thus lack of differentiation between extension and intension is itself partly caused by a similar confusion between what is logical and what is sub-logical, but, at the same time, it helps to maintain that confusion. In other words the two failures in differentiation tend to sustain one another, yet they are not identical [p. 46].

The level described in this quotation defines the stage of graphic collections. Two subsequent stages are defined as nongraphic collections. Inhelder and Piaget use the word *collection* in this context because collection carries no implication of hierarchical structure in contrast to *class,* which for Inhelder and Piaget does have a logical hierarchical implication. Nongraphic collections, then, are additive in nature, and children have to coordinate intension and extension because they are now able to differentiate the two. This level and level II characterize the preschool child (Inhelder & Piaget; 1969; Piaget, 1977).

Piaget describes level II as still lacking hierarchization. Inhelder and Piaget describe this level as quasi-categorization, whereas level I is paraclassificatory. The context for interpretating the terms quasi-categorization and paraclassification is the narrow definition Inhelder and Piaget have for "class" in contrast to "collection where class is." So at level II children are constructing nongraphic collections. Inhelder and Piaget provide 10 criteria as discriminations for level II as compared to levels I and III. The following selection provides a description of level II classificatory performance.

Level II. Piaget (1977) writes:

> This transition level is not well defined but marks the beginning of what will be stage III. (Here are nonfigural and hierarchized collections which correspond to the complete but empirical seriation. . . .) The organization at this level corresponds to the uncoordinated pairs and trios which characterize the second seriation level; there is no serial structure for the whole, so there is only juxtaposition of small elementary series. The lower forms belonging to this level consist of figural collections but later they show superimposed alignments (or obliques and parallels, etc.), each of which includes analogous elements that are distinct from those of other subcollections. The superior forms are small, nonfigural, but juxtaposed collections without unique criterion, and there may or may not be a heterogeneous residue. An intermediary form between levels II and III achieves the use of a unique criterion for classification (color, form, etc.) but still without hierarchies [p. 126].

Level III. The child is now able to construct nonfigural collections, to generalize on the basis of extension and intension, and to provide ascending hierarchies (Piaget, 1977):

> As the type III seriations are not yet accompanied by transitivity, so the subjects at this same stage do not succeed in quantifying the inclusions. And, for a category B such that $B = A + A'$, they do not succeed in realizing that there are necessarily more individual elements in B than in A; in fact, if B is subdivided into A and A', the subcategory A is compared by them only to A' and no longer to any unattached B [p. 127].

Level IV. Classification is from now on to employ logical categories divided into subcategories. Quantification of inclusion is possible as is a conscious shifting of criteria to construct multiple classification problems. In a sense, this is in Piaget's terms *logical reasoning* or the stage of formal operations.

Bruner on Representation and Categorization

Bruner's developmental approach provides us with two important perspectives germane to our discussion. The first has to do with the course of cognitive growth in the context of representational processes; the second has to do with his work on the equivalence issue, as discussed in an earlier section of this chapter.

Bruner (1973) argues that a useful way of conceptualizing the growth of the intellect is by employing the concept of *representation:* "Representation or a system of representation is a set of rules in terms of which one conserves one's encounters with events [p. 316]." The implications of this statement are that children have to develop a rule system by which events are organized and understood because otherwise they could not conserve their encounters with the environment.

Bruner contends that representations must be in some medium because events are presented by media such as pictures, actions, words, or other symbols. Further, representation of an event is selective, consistent with the constructivist position of Piaget, for example, or Werner. Thus, according to Bruner (1973) the child does not assimilate everything but only that part of the environment that serves: "to amplify our motor acts, our perceptions and our ratiocinative activities [p. 327]." Only by representing these encounters can such experiences be of value as needed. For Bruner (1973) the representation finally becomes "a system of coding and processing [p. 327]." Bruner (1973) identifies three modes of representation—enactive, iconic, and symbolic: "Their appearance in the life of the child is in that order, each depending upon the previous one for its development, yet all of them remaining more or less intact throughout life . . . [pp. 327–328]." Bruner (1973) defines each of these three modes as follows:

> By enactive representation I mean a mode of representing past events through appropriate motor response. . . . Iconic representation summarizes events by the selective organization of percepts and of images, by the spatial, temporal, and qualitative structures of the perceptual field and their transformed images. . . . Finally, a symbol system represents things by design features that include remoteness and arbitrariness [p. 328].

The growth and development of representational processes can be summarized as follows: Initially the child is primarily enactive, and responses can be organized on a motoric basis (e.g., grasping objects, mouthing objects, etc.). Similarly for iconic representation. Later, symbolic representation brings into play verbal labels by which particular attributes are identified as a basis for classification. According to Bruner (1973), language not only enables the child to label classes, but also functions: "as a cognitive instrument, it becomes possible for him to represent and systematically transform the regularities of experience with far greater flexibility and power than before [p. 330]."

It may appear that focusing on these stages of representation is remote from our concern in dealing with classification. But on reflection, all classifications are in essence organized representations because classification is mental organization of diversity. Thus classification, from my perspective, involves identification of equivalence—a necessary requisite for classification and the generating of a concept—a mental representation of that array. Interestingly enough, development of representational processes and classification or grouping strategies can be tied together from Bruner's own work. Although Bruner has not done this himself, I am taking the liberty of showing how representational processes and classification are in fact interdependent.

Bruner's article (1973) raises the question: "How shall we now most fruit-fully conceive of the growth of cognitive powers—of intellect, most broadly viewed as man's capacity to achieve, retain, and transform knowledge to his own uses? [p. 313]." Though Bruner answers the question sketchily in the aforemen-tioned article, he could have integrated the data he had acquired in his work with Olver (Bruner & Olver, 1963) on the development of children's equivalence transformations. These data add considerably to our understanding of concept development, a critical element in achieving, retaining, and transferring knowl-edge. Specifically, the Bruner and Olver study adds the type of specific informa-tion needed to articulate the relationship between the development of representa-tional processes and understanding of equivalence. Both of these functions provide the critical covariates for concept attainment. Instances of experiences are assimilated into organized wholes, which are esentially concepts because the individual constructs divergent instances into the organized units, which are in fact mental representations. The rules of organization children use depend in part on their developmental level. The decision regarding whether an instance is equivalent to other instances already organized into wholes or concepts will depend on the criteria the child uses to define equivalence. For example, if a child has established a category, *transportation,* and it includes "cars," "trucks," "airplanes," and "boats," will it include "horses"? Does the child construe "horse" as equivalent to cars, trucks, and so on? It will depend on the rules the child uses.

Bruner and Olver (1963) did address the question of what people do when faced with the particular task of relating any type of instance—objects, events, or people (see Table 12.1). Their point of departure is that classification is an example of rule-governed behavior. Disparate instances, these writers argue, are grouped by some rule (which is analogous to my concept of class). The grouping rule is simpler than the elements in the array that is being grouped. This produces a load reduction, and thereby it becomes more efficient. To group items on the basis of a common attribute (e.g., referring to apples, oranges, and grapes as fruits) requires a host of attributes such as colors, textures, and so forth. A second grouping rule is generalizability. As Bruner and Olver (1963) describe it: "The second feature of grouping . . . is that the grouping rule usually relates to previous rules of grouping that the organism has used. . . . We place things in a context that has been established [p. 354]."

The rules Bruner and Olver identify are at two levels: a strategic level and a content level (see Table 12.1). Reviewing the strategies, one is immediately struck with the similarity between the Bruner and Olver strategies and those of Inhelder and Piaget, Sigel and Werner. To identify the similarities one must ignore the names and look at the rules and the examples. Both the strategies and the content are, in my estimation, exemplars of mapping representation onto the material. Bruner and Olver describe how children of different grade levels em-ploy some organization with different degrees of sophistication. For example

(Bruner & Olver, 1963) at grade I a bell and a horn make noise; at grade IV these same items are grouped because "you can get information from all of them [p. 356]"; and at grade VI they communicate ideas. Note how the organization is similar but the quality of the content changes. But the same items can be grouped in a number of ways, for example, superordinate concept, association complex, and so on (see Table 12.1). I am convinced that the mapping of relationships among objects is a function of representational processes (applying a mental construction to the item) and an equivalence principle—bell and horn can be construed as equivalent (i.e., belong to the same organization).

In sum, Bruner's work on representation and equivalence can form a coherent description of concept attainment, describing some of the cognitive processes involved in individuals' ways of adapting to an environment containing a host of diverse objects, events, or people.

Sigel on Categorization Styles

Another approach to the understanding of principles of organization can be conceptualized under the rubric of categorization styles. Sigel and Brodzinsky (1977) write: "Categorization styles refer to the differences in approach individuals use to organize arrays of stimuli [p. 309]."

Because every item irrespective of its mode of representation is polydimensional, individuals are given a free choice to organize materials as they wish. For example, a child is given an array of objects (e.g., an apple, an orange, a banana, and a pineapple) and asked to organize the objects on the basis of similarity; the child may organize them on the basis of size, shape, apply a class label (e.g., fruits), or any other attribute. Each of these responses is valid and accurate, but not necessarily conventional. The question arises as to whether the criteria selected have any general psychological significance.

In a series of studies, Sigel and his colleagues report that styles of categorization do seem to relate to personal-social characteristics of children. A threefold classification system was developed to code the responses: (1) descriptive, which refers to the selection of items on the basis of some observable characteristic, e.g., "auto and wagon alike because they have wheels." There are two types of descriptive categories: (a) part–whole, in which an element is selected as a criterion for grouping; (b) global, in which a manifest characteristic of the item is used as a basis of organization; (2) relational-contextual, which links items on some theme or function; (3) categorical-inferential, which includes objects in a common class. These types of responses are, of course, classifications of an individual's grouping response. However, they are not to be viewed as hierarchical but rather as different approaches to organization of instances. Descriptive and relational-contextual would not be considered as logical in the formal sense, as would the categorical-inferential approach, which involves the application of a class label to an array. The use of a class label, however, does not necessarily mean that the child will include *all* items that can be so classified. For example, in a free sorting task, children around the age of 7 tended to include only four-legged creatures in the class "animal", omitting a snake, a chicken, and a duck (Sigel, 1953). The use of the label, then, is not a necessary indication that the child is actually using a logical system. However, there is some indication that ways of organizing arrays of material at the preschool and kindergarten levels differ for boys and for girls in relation to personal-social characteristics. The results are based on highly reliable teacher judgments. Boys who employ the descriptive part–whole approach tend to be relaxed and to control their emotionality; girls, however, tend to daydream, to be inattentive and impulsive. Boys who use descriptive global labels tend to be independent and are judged as good retainers of material; girls using such approaches tend to be nonanxious, uncontrolled emotionally, noncautious, relaxed, unambitious, and inattentive. The personality correlates of the categorization styles are similar for descriptive part–whole global responses for girls but not for boys. Relational-contextual labels were negatively related to emotional control in boys but not so for girls.

Sigel, Jarman, and Hanesian (1967) write: "Categorical-inferential labels yielded the greatest consistency between boys and girls. Most of the correlations were in a similar direction, with the notable exception of anxiety and emotional control; the girls using the categorical-inferential mode tended to be anxious, while the boys did not; boys also showed greater emotional control than girls [p. 12]." The results of this study demonstrate that the way children organize arrays of familiar material reflects or at least relates to how children function on a personal-social level.

Role of Language in Development of Classification

To this point, I have minimized the tremendous body of research seeking to answer the question of how classification and subsequent concept formation are related to language development. For some, language is a system whose ontogenesis can be described as separate from but related to concept formation; for others, concept development and language development are so intimately related as to be inseparable. The issue is pointed when classes of objects or events are labeled, thereby involving a language system. Yet, there are those who hold that classification precedes language. There are data that describe preverbal children as being able to group or organize arrays of objects, not solely in terms of action characteristics as Inhelder and Piaget (1964) argue, but rather in terms of attributes of objects (Ricciuti, 1965). For Werner (1948), such organizations by the infant in fact involve processes analogous to abstraction or, in Gestalt terms, figure–ground relationships (i.e., where one part of the whole stands out from the surround). It seems the data from many sources suggest that the preverbal infant is differentiating or partitioning objects or events, but the breadth of the partition is initially undifferentiated and proceeds to increased differentiation (Langer, 1980; Ling-Bing-Chung, 1941; Ricciuti, 1965; Werner, 1948). Preverbal infants may differentiate objects in terms of their actions, their functions, or their "thing" quality, later increasingly identifying and differentiating object characteristics (e.g., size, shape, function, etc.). Objects and events possess many dimensions that can be employed in part or in whole as bases of classification depending on what is needed or asked for at the time. This brings us back to the basis of salience of the dimension issue discussed previously.

Does this suggest that the preverbal child is not classifying or grouping? It seems to me that the preverbal child is grouping objects and events on some nonverbal basis. That these behaviors are purely functions of the perceptual demands of the stimuli seems unlikely because close observations of children's engagement with objects, for example, will reveal that there is some evidence of deliberate choices (it would be presumptuous to call them logical matchings). Watching a 15–18-month-old build a pine cone is revealing because the child often makes a move, and then may retract it and make another move in a seriation-type task of building the cone. If the children are classifying objects on a criterion during the preverbal period, then such organization is not dependent on language.

With the onset of language major changes become evident. The question now is the attribution of labels to objects and their constituent elements as well as to events. The child is faced with two sets of events: the objects and the language. We have seen how Goldstein and Scheerer, Piaget, Werner, and Bruner deal with this issue. Children tend to employ global terms, in fact overgeneralized labels for objects. For example, Werner cites examples of the child applying the term bow-wow to four-legged creatures. On the other hand, I found that even 7-year-old children attribute the word animal correctly to a limited group of items because animals have four legs. Defining animals in this way excluded nonfour-legged animals from being classed under the animal rubric. The chicken, duck, and snake were rarely if ever placed in the animal category (Sigel, 1953). Why not? If language guided the classification and if the child used the word correctly, why only part of the time? My argument is the child does not yet have the concept of the whole of *animal,* but only a limited part in contrast to the young infant who does just the reverse—attributes the word to a wide, undifferentiated array of items. If these observations are accurately interpreted, then it seems children start out with groupings of objects to which they attribute one word. With increasing age, they are more differentiating with words attributed to objects, which are ostensively similar.

Vygotsky's (1962) explanation of this phenomenon should not be overlooked: "[The adult] merely supplies the ready-made meaning of the word, around which the child forms a complex—with all the structural, functional, and genetic peculiarities of thinking in complexes, even if the product of his thinking is in part identified in its content with a generalization that could have been formed by conceptual thinking [p. 68]." The child learns a lot of words that only in part mean the same thing to each.

From this point of view it seems that language does fulfill certain functions in classification. By mapping on the competence for organizing and grouping items, language provides an opportunity to label the grouping. Words also facilitate extending the grouping as children extend their understanding of labels. Children's understanding of the concept animal, I am convinced, is based in part on the frequency with which it is used by adults, usually to refer to common farm animals. Perhaps this is one type of prototypic thinking about objects. The operational definition adults use for animal is probably restricted if ever explicitly used. They do not provide a conceptual definition of animal. Interestingly enough, the term animal is a superordinate concept used as a low-level concept in daily parlance.

Thus, I argue that the child selects attributes (whole or part) of objects, and labels are attached to these drawn from the child's linguistic environment. If language becomes more sophisticated, involving more precise and/or elaborated terminology, the child's repertoire for labeling attributes will be extended to that degree. Further, as Bruner (1973) has stated, language provides the child with a means of representing experience with greater versatility than previously. Further, the child can communicate this information. The limited types of classification labels and groupings made by children with parents of limited education support this line of reasoning (Sigel & McBane, 1967).

What has been de-emphasized in this analysis is that objects and events are multidimensional, possessing a number of salient and prepossessing cues. For example, a horse can be classified in terms of its structure, its function, or its class membership. Each of these components can be expressed in language terms, and each term is not overlapping in definition with the other.

This brings us into two lines of nonoverlapping research, each derived from a different frame of reference. One comes from the word meaning research, which has its roots in a language tradition—particularly the word-association literature (Nelson, 1977). The other line of research deals with categorization styles, arguing that individuals, by virtue of their own personality and experience interacting with their cognitive level, influence the characteristics of objects that are selected as bases of categorization. Related to this are those studies which contend that the content abstracted from objects is dependent on level of development.

Gleitman makes a strong case rejecting the word-meaning approach. Her position is in part supported by Nelson (1977). The problem with some of this research may be the methodology that stems from the word-association prototype. Yet, in spite of this disappointment with that body of work, there is no question that the "meaning" of an object is a viable factor in determining how the object will be classified. I gave children groups of objects identical in color, but representing diverse classes of instances (e.g., a red horse, a red table, a red ladder). Children as old as 11 failed to provide a label for this array. Yet when asked: "What was the most difficult thing you had to do today?" almost every child said: "I do not know why you put all those things together." Redness was not a salient cue, but the *meaning* of the items was (Sigel, 1954).

Objects are multidimensional in physical terms and multidimensional in attributed meanings. This natural state of affairs contributes to the complexity of the problem of understanding how order is generated in the face of such complexity. The outer and inner worlds of individuals intersect as they organize what is understood to be "out there" as guided by internal structurization of the idea and the word. We do know that knowledge of object characteristics and function, language (vocabulary level), and personality conjoin in an organized way to yield the congruence needed to adapt to the environment.

CONCLUSIONS

In approaching the question of concept attainment, I argued that the issue reduces itself to how the environment is classified (i.e., organized). The criteria selected, the domains identified, and the labels employed (if at all) evolve through a series of changes (qualitative transformations as well as accumulated quantities of knowledge).

I have also attempted to demonstrate that the search to identify the nature of the *concept* is an age-old issue. Although there is general agreement that all of us have concepts, it has been difficult to identify what the *it* is. It may well be an unsolvable problem when posed as: What is a concept?

I have striven to offer another perspective. There is general agreement that we do live and function in a polydimensional world. To function in such an environment it is necessary to organize it somehow or other. This capability is intrinsic to the human condition. The evidence that virtually all organisms do categorize events is, I believe, incontrovertible. Even the simplest creature discriminates between noxious and nonnoxious substances, dangerous and safe environments. For the human, at least, the task for such organization is intentional. The human nervous system allows for employing a virtually infinite set of arrangements. Constraints, of course, do exist but vary in quality and quantity. Two types of constraints can be identified: One involves the environment, broadly conceived; the other involves the nature of the organism. In the latter case, the constraint of particular interest is the developmental level of the individual.

The student of human behavior is interested in how the individual, given the constraints, comes to organize reality. Thus, rather than being preoccupied with philosophical problems (e.g., Is there a reality? Is there a concept? etc.), the question we pose is: How does the individual go about the business of organizing social and physical reality? The central reference is the developing person. To be sure, subsequent categorization of reality needs to be done in order to define just what the individual is dealing with.

The literature review demonstrated that there is consistent agreement (Anglin, (1970) that: "There does appear to be a concrete progression, whether the progression is defined intuitively or empirically [p. 99]." Of course, the names for the concrete–abstract performance vary. For example, Smiley and Brown (1979) use the terms thematic and taxonomic to describe the concrete–abstract progression; *thematic* refers to functional relationships akin to Sigel's functional or relational-contextual; and *taxonomic* is a class label similar to Sigel's categorical-inferential. Inspection of Table 12.1 reveals a high degree of agreement as to the developmental trends. Nelson (1977), in reviewing the categorization literature, concludes that functional and perceptual properties of objects and events serve as complementary aspects of concept definition. The pictorial aspects of objects are fundamental as criteria for categorization.

Although there is considerable agreement that this is the case (Bruner & Olver, 1963), there is an interesting paradox. If young children tend to be global, are these global concepts functional early on, yielding to more perceptually based categories with the advent of language, and then becoming increasingly functional as children consolidate their previous knowledge? This process may well be a U-shaped function, not only over the long haul but over the short one, namely, this functional-perceptual–functional-categorical process may well be the paradigm that describes concept acquisition.

The developing of prototypes may reflect a central concept, which may have shared meaning. But because both cultural and individual differences in experience combine to define the core, variations in the content of a prototype may exist. Related to this is the fact that we use concepts to define different domains of our existence. Some involve logical progressions (e.g., artificial zoological taxonomies), whereas others do not seem to allow for such hierarchization. Essentially, in *all* cases, the versatile human mind has been able to map systems onto the world. The task is to identify the development of this *mapping* process.

I do not want to conclude with a closed statement, which would be erroneous—the field is wide open, and the questions are fascinating because of their intriguing complexity. But, I feel a reflective assessment of what we know and where we are coming from is in order. We have a rich tradition, and some of the major thinkers were discussed. Other perspectives can be assimilated into an integrated systems approach, such as those stemming from information processing (Klahr & Wallace, 1976; Siegler, 1978; Simon, 1969) and associationist theories of children's logical reasoning (Welch, 1940), to name but some. To overlook this body of theory and empirical findings is to deny the significance of the past. Regrettably, the fractionation of psychology and the need for each of us to be his or her own theorist limits the incorporating of and building onto our rich tradition.

I would argue that the research questions for the future must move toward various levels of integration. Perhaps we are ready to take Simon's (1969) notion of hierarchy seriously because concept formation is in Simon's notion a complex system: "The path to the construction of a nontrivial theory of complex systems [concept formation] is by way of a theory of hierarchy. Empirically a large proportion of the complex systems [including thinking] we observe in nature exhibit hierarchical structure. On theoretical grounds, we could expect complex systems to be hierarchies in a world in which complexity had to evolve from simplicity [p. 117].'' Implicit in any development theory is a theory of hierarchization, hence Simon's suggestion may serve as a theoretical principle underlying systematization.

I disagree with Gleitman's assertion that an overarching theory of categorization is not feasible. The evidence to date does not appear to be on her side. On the contrary, Denney (1974) writes: ''In reviewing many of the seemingly unrelated cognitive changes that occur in childhood, it becomes apparent that a number of these developmental trends reflected the same underlying change—a change from a tendency to categorize according to complementary criteria, to a tendency to categorize according to similarity criteria [p. 41].'' Denney (1974) goes on to say that interpretations are based on ''studies of free classification, conceptual style, word association, word definition and memory clustering [p. 45].'' So, now the task is to get on with putting our house in order and moving up the hierarchy to investigate the increasing complexities observed in development, which include engaging superordinate types of variables (e.g., culture, personality, cognition, etc.) in the search for understanding group performance and individual differences. For in the end, the concept is in the head of the cognizer. The question is: How does this achievement (a concept) come about?

REFERENCES

Abelson, R. Definition. In P. Edwards (Ed.), *The encyclopedia of philosophy* (Vol. 2). New York: Macmillan, 1967.

Ach, N. *Ueber die Begriffsbildung.* Bamberg: Buchner, 1921.

Anglin, J. M. *The growth of word meaning* (Research Monograph No. 63). Cambridge, Mass.: MIT Press, 1970.

Berger, P. L., & Luckmann, T. *The social construction of reality.* Baltimore, Md.: Penguin Books, 1966.

Bruner, J. S., & Olver, R. R. Development of equivalence transformations in children. In J. C. Wright & J. Kagan (Eds.), Basic cognitive processes in children. *Monographs of the Society for Research in Child Development,* 1963, *28*(No. 2, Serial No. 86).

Bruner, J. S. On cognitive growth. In J. S. Bruner, R. R. Olver, & P. M. Greenfield (Eds.). *Studies in cognitive growth.* New York: Wiley, 1966.

Bruner, J. S. The course of cognitive growth. In J. M. Anglin (Ed.), *Beyond the information given: Studies in the psychology of knowing.* New York: Norton, 1973.

Denney, N. W. Evidence for developmental changes in categorization criteria for children and adults. *Human Development,* 1974, *17,* 41–53.

Gallagher, J. M., & Reid, D. K. *The learning theory of Piaget and Inhelder.* Monterey, Cal.: Brooks/Cole, 1981.

Goldstein, K., & Scheerer, M. Abstract and concrete behavior, An experimental study with special tests. *Psychological Monographs,* 1941, *53* (2, Whole No. 239).

Heath, P. L. Concept. In P. Edwards (Ed.), *The encyclopedia of philosophy* (Vol. 2). New York: Macmillan, 1967.

Inhelder, B., & Piaget, J. *The early growth of logic in the child.* New York: Norton, 1969.

Kagan, J., Moss, H. A., & Sigel, I. E. Psychological significance of styles of conceptualization. *Monographs of the Society for Research in Child Development*, 1963, *28*(2, Serial No. 86), 73–112.

Klahr, E., & Wallace, J. G. *Cognitive development: An information-processing view*. Hillsdale, N.J.: Lawrence Erlbaum Associates, 1976.

Langer, J. *Theories of development*. New York: Holt, Rinehart & Winston, 1969.

Langer, J. Werner's comparative organismic theory. In P. H. Mussen (Ed.), *Carnichael's manual of child psychology* (Vol. 1). New York: Wiley, 1970.

Langer, J. *The origins of logic: Six to twelve months*. New York: Academic Press, 1980.

Ling, Bing-Chung. Form discrimination as a learning cue in infants. *Comparative Psychology Monographs*, 1941, *17*(2).

Lunzer, E. A. Translater's introduction. In B. Inhelder & J. Piaget, *The early growth of logic in the child* (E. A. Lunzer & D. Papert, trans.). New York: Norton, 1969.

Miller, G. A., & Johnson-Laird, P. N. *Language and perception*. New York: Cambridge University Press, 1976.

Nelson, K. Some evidence for the cognitive primacy of categorization and its functional basis. In P. N. Johnson-Laird & P. C. Wason (Eds.), *Thinking: Readings in cognitive science*. New York: Cambridge University Press, 1977.

Piaget, J. *The moral judgment of the child*. Glencoe, Ill.: The Free Press, 1948.

Piaget, J. *Science of education and the psychology of the child*. New York: Orion Press, 1970.

Piaget, J. *The development of thought*. New York: Viking Press, 1977.

Piaget, J. *Success and understanding*. Cambridge, Mass.: Harvard University Press, 1978.

Piaget, J. *Intelligence and affectivity: Their relationship during child development*. (T. A. Brown & C. E. Kaegi, Eds. and trans.) Palo Alto, Cal.: Annual Reviews, 1981.

Piaget, J., & Inhelder, B. *The child's conception of space*. London: Routledge & Kegan Paul, 1963.

Piaget, J., & Inhelder, B. *The psychology of the child*. New York: Basic Books, 1969.

Polanyi, M. *Personal knowledge*. Chicago: University of Chicago Press, 1958.

Ratner, J. *Introduction to John Dewey's philosophy*. New York: Random House, 1939.

Ricciuti, H. Object grouping and selective ordering behavior in infants 12–24 months old. *Merrill-Palmer Quarterly*, 1965, *11*, 129–148.

Rosch, E. Classification of real-world objects: Origins and representations in cognition. In P. N. Johnson-Laird & P. C. Wason (Eds.), *Thinking: Readings in cognitive science*. New York: Cambridge University Press, 1977.

Siegler, R. S. The origins of scientific reasoning. In R. S. Siegler (Ed.), *Children's thinking: What develops?* Hillsdale, N.J.: Lawrence Erlbaum Associates, 1978.

Sigel, I. E. Developmental trends in the abstraction ability of children. *Child Development*, 1953, *24*, 131–144.

Sigel, I. E. The dominance of meaning. *Journal of Genetic Psychology*, 1954, *85*, 201–207.

Sigel, I. E. The development of pictorial comprehension. In B. S. Randhawa & W. E. Coffman (Eds), *Visual learning, thinking, and communication*. New York: Academic Press, 1978.

Sigel, I. E. On becoming a thinker: A psychoeducational model. *Educational Psychologist*, 1979, *14*, 70–78.

Sigel, I. E. Social experience in the development of representational thought: Distancing theory. In I. E. Sigel, D. Brodzinsky, & R. Golinkoff (Eds.), *New directions in Piagetian theory and practice*. Hillsdale, N.J.: Lawrence Erlbaum Associates, 1981.

Sigel, I. E. & Brodzinsky, D. M. Categorization behavior in two-year-olds. Unpublished manuscript, State University of New York at Buffalo, 1971.

Sigel, I. E., & Brodzinsky, D. M. Individual differences: A perspective for understanding intellectual development. In H. L. Hom, Jr., & P. A. Robinson (Eds.), *Psychological processes in early childhood*. New York: Academic Press, 1977.

Sigel, I. E., & Cocking, R. R. Cognition and communication: A dialectic paradigm for development. In M. Lewis & L. A. Rosenblum (Eds.), *Interaction, conversation, and the development of language: The origins of behavior* (Vol. 5). New York: Wiley, 1977.

Sigel, I., Jarman, P., & Hanesian, H. Styles of categorization and their intellectual and personality correlates in young children. *Human Development,* 1967, *10,* 1–17.

Sigel, I. E., & McBane, B. Cognitive competence and level of symbolization among five-year-old children. In J. Hellmuth (Ed.), *The disadvantaged child* (Vol. 1). Seattle, Wash.: Special Child Publications of the Seattle Sequin School, 1967.

Sigel, I. W., McGillicuddy-DeLisi, A. V., & Johnson, J. E. *Parental distancing, beliefs and children's representational competence within the family context* (ETS RR 80-21). Princeton, N.J.: Educational Testing Service, 1980.

Simon, H. A. *The sciences of the artificial.* Cambridge, Mass.: MIT Press, 1969.

Smiley, S. S., & Brown, A. L. Conceptual preference for thematic or taxonomic relations: A nonmonotic trend from preschool to old age. *Journal of Experimental Child Psychology,* 1979, *28,* 249–257.

Sokal, R. R. Classification: Purposes, principles, progress, prospects. In P. N. Johnson-Laird & P. C. Wason (Eds.), *Thinking: Readings in cognitive science.* New York: Cambridge University Press, 1977.

Vygotsky, L. S. *Thought and language* (E. Hanfmann & G. Vakar, Eds. and trans.). Cambridge, Mass.: MIT Press, 1962.

Welch, L. The genetic development of the associational structures of abstract thinking. *Journal of Genetic Psychology,* 1940, *56,* 175–206.

Werner, H. *Comparative psychology of mental development* (rev. ed.). Chicago: Follett, 1948.

Werner, H., & Kaplan, B. *Symbol formation: An organismic developmental approach to language and the expression of thought.* New York: Wiley, 1963.

Author Index

Numbers in *italics* denote pages with complete bibliographic information.

Subject Index